Familiar Unto Me:

Witches, Sorcerers and Their Spirit Companions

Also by BJ Swain

Living Spirits: A Guide to Magic in a World of Spirits
Luminarium: A Grimoire of Cunning Conjuration
Heaven and Hell 2018: The Grimoire Issue (Contributor)

Familiar Unto Me:
Witches, Sorcerers and Their Spirit Companions

BJ Swain

Familiar Unto Me
Edited by Suzanne Hill Thackston
Typeset by Brian Swayne

ISBN- 9798375903224

This book is affectionately dedicated to all familiar spirits with whom I have worked and with whom I will work, to my ancestors who watch over my family and me, and to AAE.

Spirits of the forest,
I pronounce my intentions to thee.
Come forth and seek me,
and equal we will be.
Not master and servant,
but familiar to familiar,
to share our knowledge,
our spirit, and our traits.
And now, spirits,
we will wait.

- Sabrina Spellman
Chilling Adventures of Sabrina

Anne Bishop and Other Witches Sticking Pins in Poppets with The
Devil
From The Wellcome Collection, Morton, Hall, Hale et al, W.P. 1720

Acknowledgements

First and foremost, I should thank Stephanie Olmstead-Dean. Stephanie was an excellent lodge master at a very successful OTO body. When controversy arose due to our work with the familiar spirit we kept in the lodge, everyone who was present at the ritual in question stood up in defense of us. Not only that, but comments and letters of support poured in not just from local members and guests but from people worldwide who had heard about the work we had been doing. I believe this is because Stephanie helped build a beacon of inclusiveness, diversity, and openness to magical experimentation with real, deep, traditional magic. I firmly believe this is something many people are now seeking. My thanks to Stephanie isn't just for her being a great leader or even for being a supportive friend; Stephanie asked me to organize the capstone ritual for the 25th Anniversary celebration of William Blake Lodge. That request became the foundation for our adventures with Tobias, the Demon of Baltimore, which became the materials and inspiration for part three of this book.

I would also like to thank Rebecca Doll, James Gordon, and Jeren Hope, not just for their friendship and encouragement but also for their participation in rituals involving and working with and caring for Tobias. They also helped me with a panel discussion which inspired me to write this book.

Thank you also to all those who stood up for William Blake Lodge, Stephanie, and me. It was heartwarming. Thank you to those who have attended rituals and magical experiments with me at William Blake and Azul Nox.

I would like to thank Wade Long, whose tutelage in my youth helped prepare me for the Abramelin working. I would like to thank my fellow brodepti, Sarah Clark, Jared Praniewicz, and Suzanne Thackston. Our discussions on magic are always enlightening, and in particular, their achievements with their tutelary spirits have made them valuable friends for having discussions about familiar spirits. I additionally thank Suzanne for her efforts as an editor. Any mistakes or errors are my own or result from me adding material after her thorough editing. I would also like to thank Octavian Graves of the Strange Dominions Podcast; our discussions around the time he interviewed me, during which time I was working on this book, gave me things to think about. Further, he kindly read some sample chapters to give me feedback.

I would like to thank Cat Heath for providing me with several resources for researching the concept of the fylgja and resources linking to other projects I'm currently working on.

I would also like to thank Rufus Opus, Alison Chicosky, Jason Miller, and Jake Stratton-Kent for their ongoing friendship, support, and insights. These thanks and appreciation are also owed to a host of magical people I have the pleasure of interacting with online. Thank you to the podcasters, interviewers, and friends who have hosted me on their shows, promoted my work, shared links, photos, and reviews of my work, and otherwise helped people find me. There are too many people to note, but I always appreciate the kind words and seeing my work recommended. I will take a moment to point people to the wonderful podcasts, Barbarous Words with Aequus Nox, Glitch Bottle, Esoteric Scholar, Saroth the Magus Experiment, Inside the Magical Circle, Applied Hermetics, ThelemaNOW!, The Blackthorn Grove Podcast, and Stange Dominions.

I deeply regret that Jake passed away weeks before I finished this book. The original familiar spirit conjuration at William Blake Lodge was partially inspired by Jake's book <u>Goetic Liturgy</u>. As you will see in part three of this text, the ideas related to the connection between liturgical and initiatic frameworks and those of conjuration and practical magic form a central component. Jake's <u>Goetic Liturgy</u>, and the work of Dr. Francis Young, both influenced my thinking in this regard. A Glitch Bottle interview with Jake once inspired me to write about clerical realities as they relate to conjuration, and I enjoyed discussing that subject and many others with Jake. He will be missed, and I regret that I am unable to mail him a copy of this book which was influenced by one of his smaller works which, despite its size, impressed me greatly.

Friends outside of the magical community deserve thanks as well. Aidan Evans, nearly daily, reminding me to write and asking about progress is always helpful. He frequently looked at or listened to sentences or paragraphs I was particularly excited by. He would listen to me talk about research or struggles and would curiously ask questions despite his lack of involvement with any sort of magic. Eric Sieling, my long-time friend, has as always continued to encourage me and ask about progress and remind me to set time-lines and goals for myself. The support of each is immensely appreciated.

Several Facebook forums provided questions and discussions around familiar spirits which helped me realize how useful this text would be. As always, thank you to the community in Living Spirits, both for cover design feedback, and in general for being a great community for discussing spirit work. Thank you to Morgan Daimler and the Fairy Witchcraft Facebook community for interesting and informative threads which sometimes gave hints of things to look at and consider regarding the fair folk. Thank you to PASP for fighting the good fight regarding magical feral cats.

Thank you to authors who have previously written about familiars, particularly academic authors whose ideas regarding and publication of witch trial accounts have been invaluable. Thank you to magical writers like Mat Auryn, Storm Faerywolf, Christopher Penczak and others who have provided informative thoughts in their work which has lead others to work with familiars and which gave me new ideas to consider in this work.

Less personally, I would like to thank Susanna Clarke, the author of Jonathan Strange and Mr. Norrell, and the writers of "Chilling Adventures of Sabrina" for depicting magic and spirit relationships in a useful way for the general populace. This provided better cultural touchpoints to reference than were available in the past and provided things to think about concerning magic, familiars, and spirits in general.

Finally, I thank you, the reader. There is a wide world of spirits and magic out there. I hope this book helps you in your journey to experience it.

Introduction

We reside in a living world teeming with spirits of multitudinous variety and kind. Some of those spirits are embodied, like humans and animals, then there are those who are no longer embodied - the dead. Others are attached to natural formations or special places. Many spirits have more conceptual physical associations. Spirits might arrive from a particular direction, or reside in a certain altitude. Some spirits might connect to a particular nature or power tied to a physical referent but without so firmly being attached to an actual location - like those attached to things such as storms, a group of animals or particular times. While others have no real relationship to specifics of the physical world, at least not so clearly as to indicate how or where they manifest.

With all these spirits connected to different things, it makes sense that there would also be spirits who have special relationships and connections with people. When we look at our normal lives we have a multitude of life around us in the form of animals, plants and people - all manners of embodied life. Our relationships and interactions with those lives are not all the same. Some people are outside of our direct experience, and while they impact our lives we have limited ways of impacting them. Others might be people we can contact, maybe with some difficulty or through an intermediary. There are people we can call upon directly with whom we can easily initiate interactions. Some, we can reach quickly through more personal means, and others are virtually always with us. Likewise, there are plants and animals remote in the wild, others near to us that we encounter routinely, and those we keep domesticated in our spaces.

This variety of connections is also the case in the spirit world. As we explore these we can understand how we have different types of personal connections with spirits. In the NeoPagan community the idea of patron, or patron and matron, gods and goddesses has become common. Some living spirit traditions have similar relationships between an individual and particular spirits. Some of these traditions have spirits who attach to the initiate specially. In Catholicism, we see the Guardian Angel as a spirit specifically attached to a person to teach and guide them. In earlier Platonic tradition, we saw the daimon as a being who came into existence with the individual and became their guide and intermediary. Magic and initiated religion have a host of specific individual close relationships between people and their

I

guides and spirits appointed to teach them and coordinate their movement through this spirit filled world.

Our ancestors allow us to have a family within the spirit world. The overall "spirit court," or the collection of spirits with whom you work regularly and who have become a special spirit world community of which you are a part, can be like a family. Your ancestors are a family with whom you have natural ties by blood, by affiliation or a relationship in life. Those other spirits are like friends and professional contacts with whom you have developed a close and bond, sometimes tied together through routine work, devotion, or initiation.

Generally, those spirits we consider in our spirit court, or to be our spirit allies or spirit guides, will be the ones to whom we give routine offerings and devotions. Maybe we have a household shrine, or maybe we go outside and make offerings. This could be a daily, weekly or monthly thing that we do as part of our general spiritual upkeep. We may include something like "and to any spirits to whom I owe a debt," or "to any spirits who bring benefit to my life," but we may also name the spirits who form our particular spirit court or group of spirit allies.

We might also develop ongoing relationships with spirits we call upon or encounter routinely, but have not brought into the cycle of offerings, devotions, or routine work which we do as our baseline spiritual activity. Other spirits like specific angels or demons we conjure sometimes, or local spirits or nature spirits we might go to for particular needs likely receive offerings when we interact with them for something specific. These are our broader network of spirits. We might have a relationship with them, but its less close or personal. It might be like a teacher, colleague or professional associate with whom we work sometimes but who isn't part of our day-to-day lives. We can call them, they know us, and they'll provide help when we request it correctly.

We have all these relationships, some very close, intimate and individual. Some are personal and like our extended family, while others are like broader professional relationships. Do we have a spirit who is a companion and friend rather than a teacher and guide appointed over us? Maybe. It's possible. But the specifics of this relationship will vary based on the type and nature of the spirit and the needs and personality of the individual magician. Magicians historically keep spirit companions. Sometimes they are friends, sometimes servants, sometimes co-conspirators. The relationship may

II

have multiple elements and may vary over time or based on situations. Magicians might have more than one spirit in this kind of role and each relationship might have a different specific character.

This type of spirit relationship is called a "familiar spirit." Familiar spirits are one of the most well attested elements of European Traditional Magic. We see them described in folk stories and stories about famous magicians. They appear in witch trial accounts. Spirit lists and grimoires talk about how various spirits give good familiars and some even provide instructions specifically for receiving one. The concept seems fairly consistent throughout these materials. Despite its ubiquity, it seems to have fallen away from common magical practice within the "occult revival" of the 19th and early 20th centuries. A lot of this was probably because that revival largely abandoned the role of spirits in magic. Instead of spirits, revivalists attempted to explain spirits as psychological phenomena, and attempted to compress and combine myths stories and spirits from across a myriad of sources and cultures into neat little boxes in which everything was all the same. The need for this revival to be modern and scientific has also led to a lot of attempts to make magic about feelings and image rather than a real and miraculous experience of those things we would routinely deem supernatural. A personal spirit companion doesn't really fit into such a modern world, but may be necessary for making the modern world a magical one.

As we reach the late 20th century and early 21st century some people have explored the concept of familiars and worked them into their practice. Some have realized it should probably be present in magic but have felt the need to work it into a more physical and materialist framework. With the revival of a focus on spirit magic, the materialist box is breaking. We can see how traditional elements of magic - work with the dead, initiated spirit contact, positive possession, divination gifted by spirits, and work with familiars; are necessary for revitalizing our connection to the world's magic and exploding out of the toil of reconstructing a tradition into the experience of a new and living tradition.

Familiar spirits create a relationship in which we have an ongoing contact with a spirit who helps us, protects us, assists in magic, does magic and teaches magic. It's a spirit with whom we can talk about the spirit world and magic in a way that does not have to be so consistently tutelary as the relationship with some other spirit guides might be. This ability to gain insight and experience as well as creating

III

a model that allows for more involved spirit cultus is part of how familiar spirits might aid us in moving magic forward.

With all this potential for such a great relationship, what is a familiar spirit and what do they do?

The first thing which should be understood is that a familiar is not a particular kind of spirit. A familiar is a role which is described based on the nature of the relationship. Anyone or anything can be familiar to you. You have people and animals in your life with whom you are familiar. In a certain sense, it just means you know who they are; you have an awareness of them. In another sense, familiar can refer to things which have a connection such as we have with family. The primary definition of familiar is that one has a long close, perhaps intimate association with the thing being described. This is what we mean by familiar spirit.

Since familiar refers to the role which is defined by this relationship of familiarity it can refer to just about any sort of spirit. A familiar spirit may be a faery, a ghost, a demon, an angel, or any number of other types of spirit. We will talk about the way in which some contemporary practitioners conflate familiars with animals with whom they have a special bond. It is important to note that those animals with whom they are bonded are familiar animals; they are animals with whom they have a long and close personal association. The familiar in magic, however, is a familiar spirit specifically. The adjective familiar is a substantive which implies the word spirit because of the context. All examples of familiars in magic historically are spirits, and this is important when we explore what a familiar does and why you have one.

We have talked a little bit about how the familiar spirit provides a different sort of spirit relationship. Through that relationship we can learn about magic directly from a spirit in a different way than some other contexts. It is also a spirit who can work magic with us and guide us in what magic to do, as well as a spirit that can directly perform magical tasks for us. Familiars protect their familiar humans. They provide information and service. We'll talk more about all these things as we move into more detailed sections on working with them.

Insofar as their ability to give us a model for spirit cultus, familiars present a type of spirit whom we might house in some physical object. We might provide a shrine, or offerings. We work with them more closely and directly than with other spirits. This kind of relationship can illustrate how covens, lodges, or other magical groups can receive spirits around whom their group may be built or spirits who can guide and facilitate the work of that group. It can also illustrate and guide us towards spirit work in which a god or spirit imparts some intermediary to reside with a person or group as their local contact with that spirit or god.

Magicians and witches can receive familiars in many ways, and we will look at several of them. Most typically they are received by initiating contact with some spirit who appoints a spirit under its authority to serve the witch or magician as a familiar. Sometimes they can be gifted or received from another magician who had a familiar spirit. In some instances, the magician may encounter a spirit directly who enters into this familiar relationship with them.

The idea of receiving the familiar from another bigger spirit also addresses some element of how the relationship works. When we conjure spirits, part of the goal should be to gain names, signs and agreements which allow us to call upon those spirits more simply and more quickly. A familiar spirit might be another thing we receive which allows us to contact the higher spirit more easily. If, for instance, we call upon Aratron, the Olympic Spirit of the sphere of Saturn, and Aratron gives us a familiar, we might use that familiar to call upon Aratron in addition to the various tasks and powers within the familiar's purview. Aratron might also give us a special sign or name which allows us to call upon him directly without ritual. The familiar he gives will reside with us. We won't usually have to call upon him because he will already be near. This is how the relationship differs from other relationships with other conjured spirits and why it is closer, or, more familiar. Familiars are still, ultimately, conjured spirits, because they are bound by oath, even if they are not called upon through ceremonial evocation in the magician's routine interactions therewith.

This book is divided into three parts, each addressing different elements of our exploration of familiars. Part one introduces concepts general to witches and sorcerers working with familiars. In this section, we will explore all of the above mentioned elements in more detail. We will explore how to maintain the familiar relationship and what the relationship looks like. We will address some misconceptions. We will provide some examples for approaches one might take in acquiring one.

Part two explores a familiars in Pagan and folklore contexts and how that informs the historical presence of familiars amongst witches and cunning folk. We will look in depth at mythology, faery stories, and traditional folklore to explore the history of ideas that could have impacted how familiar spirits were understood. We will explore early modern ideas about spirits and how they impact our understanding of the familiars possessed by early modern witches and cunning folk. We will look at traditional methods of magic and how they can inform our attempts to acquire familiars. We will also look at certain ideas from folklore and traditional Pagan spirituality which have been conflated with the concept of the familiar. We will explore some ways those terms are used in contemporary traditional witchcraft, the ideas associated with these terms in that movement, and how those ideas compare and contrast with the traditional uses of these terms and the idea of the familiar spirit.

Part three explores working with a familiar and the implications for that work in exploring European Traditional Magic in a contemporary context. In this section, we will look in detail at a particular adventure in which a group of magicians bound a familiar spirit. The work with this spirit created noted positive impact for this group, but it shook up their broader fraternal community as they deepened their interaction with the familiar. This case study will explore elements of how to establish the relationship, and be a jumping-off point for exploring how familiar spirits can push magical work forward. We will look at how work with familiar spirits can be a basis for exploring positive possession and where that fits into contemporary magic. We will look at where familiar spirits fit into modern magic and in doing so see that even with the reductionist tendencies of the 19th century revival, familiar spirits were still present in modern magic. We will also consider the tension and difficulty that navigating traditional magic in the context of modern groups can bring, why it's important, and the ways in which blending these modalities becomes possible.

Each section is almost like its own book and will have different levels of appeal for different readers. Altogether, these sections provide a very complete picture of work with familiars. Taken together they present numerous opportunities for exploring different modes and approaches to magic. The reader will, hopefully, find elucidation, information, and direction towards new opportunities for magic throughout. The themes and content of each section inform what is presented in the rest. While each has its own focus, we hope that the broad focus will give you, the reader, the most thorough exploration we can.

Part One:

Familiar Spirits

The Love Potion by Evelyn De Morgan 1903

The Kingdom of Darkness
Nathaniel Crouch, 1688

I
Care and Feeding of your Familiar

The discussion of work with familiar spirits often focuses on what they are and how to acquire them. There may be some questions about what they do, but rarely do we see people thoroughly talking about how to work with them. As a result I've seen people ask what ritual methods are used to call them, when the whole point is that you no longer need those methods once you have that familiar relationship.

Certain special circumstances may involve more ritualized methods, but the familiar is more like a friend and companion, or an attached aid who accompanies you and is at hand to assist you. With that being the relationship, an important consideration beyond how you receive aid and communicate your desires to them is how you facilitate and provide for their needs.

As we consider caring for the needs of your familiar you will see how this directly ties to working with your familiar and empowering it to fulfill your goals. Spirit work is not just about you demanding that God place a spirit before you and tie its hands in favor of fulfilling your requests. We are able to communicate with spirits, frequently, because we create a sort of nexus point in which our nature and awareness, the nature and awareness of the spirit and the spiritual power of the time, the place, and the God under whose authority the spirit is called create a blended or negotiated space in which reality and awareness behave differently.

The mechanics of this can adjust with different systems and approaches. Sometimes it's a matter of blending our space and perceptions with those of the spirit and the various factors of the ritual moment. Sometimes it's a matter of bending and breaking boundaries and barriers to perception and interaction. The precise means of our facilitation of interaction will vary. In all cases, a spirit working to impact the physical world may need assistance by providing things which aid in allowing the spirit to interact with the world. Maintaining the ability to routinely interact without formal ritual components removes the moments of ritual where we provide those things to bridge and strengthen their interaction with the world. To facilitate and strengthen that ability to affect the world might also require that we routinely provide things which empower the spirit. Like muscles, we should regularly exercise our connections with our spirits to strengthen communication and the link that we provide them with the world.

In short, providing for our familiars' needs and routinely interacting with them not only gives them sustenance, but it also maintains our relationship and deepens their ability to be effective in the material world.

Historically, in accounts of witches' familiars, the familiar spirit is paid with blood. A lot of people assume this means there is a large blood sacrifice of an animal, or the witch allows the spirit to consume blood in vampire-like proportions which would drain and weaken the witch. In detailed accounts, and in some contemporary examples, it is often just a couple of drops. In those cases where this is the routine interaction, it is often the case that the spirit needs this offering in order to operate. The blood might be viewed as an exchange for what the witch is requesting much like any other offering. The blood may be viewed as a means of aiding the spirit in acting in the physical world. There are several ways to think about the exchange of blood for assistance, but these two will be the ones which serve us most.

When working with a familiar spirit, the spirit will communicate to the magician things which it likes or desires. Specific expectations may be, and likely should be, set when the magician initially contracts the familiar spirit. A place for the spirit to reside is one of the most basic things to offer and should likely be established in the ritual for acquiring the familiar. Candles, liquor, incense, and particular services rendered by the magician might be the sorts of things outlined in the initial contract. Things to decorate the spirit's space, particular foods or specific liquors or scents might be the sorts of things the spirit reveals it desires over time. Some might want blood, but some might be offended by blood offerings. Many contemporary magicians assume most spirits want blood or sexual fluids but this is not so standard as some people would like it to be. The best thing to do is look at what is traditional for the type of spirit and to do divination to receive clear instruction from the spirit on what it wants.

These basic offering elements can be viewed as payment for ongoing service or for a particular service. In most cases, you want to give an offering in exchange for something, not as an act of worship. The exchange might just be the spirit's attention and the ongoing assistance it provides in your life. It does not always have to be for a specific discreet incident of the spirit doing something. If you're working with spirits like this routinely and effectively, they should be bringing things into your life and protecting you from things within their capabilities. Some offerings can be in thanks for maintaining the relationship of ongoing mutual aid. Others might be for specific requests.

If you're asking your familiar to help you with some special need or task, it makes sense to pay them for that service. If you ask for help acquiring a job or finding a relationship, it is routine to give some offering in thanks for the assistance the spirit has provided. This could be viewed as appreciation, or as paying for what was received. Some might view it as an exchange of energy, the spiritual power of the offering in exchange for the spiritual power involved in manifesting the magician's desire. Most would say that some payment should be made once the spirit has done what you request regardless of how you interpret it. There may be some who would consider the general maintenance and upkeep of the relationship as covering this, and would not feel the need for some offering as a specific response to the spirit's successful completion of your request. In the experience of many spirit magicians and the lore of many traditions which work with spirits, these kinds of offerings are often seen as motivators to the spirit. Letting a spirit know that you have what it wants and will give it to them if they do what you ask works much as when we do the same thing with people.

While most magicians are on board with providing a payment or offering to a spirit after work is done, some will highlight that giving something before work is done is a mistake. After all, if you have already given the spirit their slice of pound cake, why should they do what you're asking? They already have what they want. There is some logic to this and it tracks when we think about interacting with people. It's a well known scam for people to pose as contractors or home repair workers, take a large up-front payment and then disappear with no work done. The unscrupulous are unscrupulous regardless of whether or not they have bodies.

That doesn't mean we should never give spirits an offering before they do work. There are times when it makes sense, and times when it is necessary. To follow the pattern of human interactions, some transactions require a good faith deposit to show that the customer is serious about doing business. In other circumstances, you might pay a portion of the cost upfront to fund materials or to pay subcontractors needed to do the work. Some kind of offering made upfront with a spirit might fall into similar circumstances. If we're working with a spirit with whom we don't have a relationship, some offering upfront might show that we intend to make good on our promises and are willing to give something for their help. When we're working with a familiar, this won't be an issue. The whole idea of a familiar spirit is that it is one with whom you have a close relationship. Rather than a good faith offering, an offering made to a familiar prior to service rendered might be an offering made to facilitate the work.

In several forms of spirit work, offerings are made because they facilitate spirit contact or empower the spirit. If you're attempting to communicate or to receive the aid of the spirit, these sorts of offerings will be useful before the spirit begins to work. Offerings such as prayers made on their behalf, certain types of foods, libations, some incenses, will serve to strengthen the spirit. This might be viewed as feeding, or it might be viewed as energizing. However you conceptualize it, the spirit's ability to work in certain capacities is strengthened by these offerings. Other offerings like fire, alcohol, powders and dusts, certain scents, some foods, and water, can help with the process of moving between spirit spaces and physical spaces. Spirits are not always understood as directly inhabiting material space so their ability to interact with and impact material reality is less direct than ours. Ritual actions, gifts, and certain substances can help bridge their substantial state of being with our own so that they can more fully act in the world.

You may have a familiar request that some offering be made before it begins the work in addition to whatever is being given once the work is done. You can, of course, ask the familiar to explain to you why it needs or wants it done that way. In my experience and understanding, it will often either be because it helps empower them to do the work or connects them with the sphere in which the work is manifesting.

Attention is another component of maintaining your relationship with your familiars. We have noted how some offerings help bridge the gap between our phase of material existence and the space in which spirits reside and operate. Attention and interaction can help with that bridge. Beyond that, attention also shows that you have a desire to maintain the relationship and appreciate the relationship. That alone may be important to some types of spirits. For others, recognition can be important. It is unlikely that a familiar will need routine public recognition and be concerned with spreading fame, because it will be working just with you. For some spirits this is important. Depending upon the type of spirit your familiar is, or how it operates, it may need some public acknowledgement. More likely, it will want your acknowledgement. It will want you to keep it an active part of your life with attention to maintaining open lines of communication and interaction. "Stay with me," is an oft repeated request of devils to their witches. The implication is that the devil is requesting sex with the witch, but it could also be a matter of requesting time and attention. Just as with people, your time and attention can be valuable to spirits.

To summarize, your relationship with your familiar isn't just a matter of you binding a spirit so you can rub a lamp and get whatever you want. You have to maintain that relationship and be familiar towards your spirit just as you want it to be familiar to you. This will involve providing it a space in which it will reside, and giving it things it desires and enjoys for that space. You'll need to make routine offerings and give it routine time and acknowledgement. You'll also need to make offerings for special requests, sometimes as payment after, sometimes as part of helping to get the work going. You'll need to pay attention to the relationship and maintain your part of it.

Flemish Painting of an elderly woman spoon feeding a cat.

II
Working With your Familiar

When the clock ticks three minutes towards midnight, under the waxing Gibbous Moon, before the dawning Thursday, with the moon moving swiftly, and adjacent no malefic, preferably in Cancer, Gemini or Taurus, and, most powerfully when she is square to Aldebaran, the true source of all familiars' powers, you may begin your ritual. Retire to a secluded space, knocking thrice as you enter, taking only a stalwart assistant or a dog, but not going alone. Each carrying a sword and wearing a lamen made of virgin lambskin and painted with French hyssop, rue, and ochre, enter the abandoned space of your rite and begin tracing the circle, while reciting the full songs of David the Psalmist.

With this preparation in place, repeat the Vinculum Salamonis thirteen times while lighting a new candle and adding incense to the brazier each time. The brazier must be made of wrought iron and the fire must be royal oak soaked in the urine of a hind or a jaguar which has not known another of its kind.

Only then will you be able to access the help of the spirit which has already been bound to help you and follow you around and be your magic buddy.

Clearly, these instructions are written with tongue firmly in cheek.

Sometimes when people ask "how to work with a familiar" and if it follows the normal processes of "Solomonic" magic, I have to wonder if they expect that it is something so complicated as this. It isn't. That is the whole point, or at least, a significant portion of it.

A familiar spirit is one that you have on a special sort of speed dial. It's not like an angel or devil that you have licensed to depart after getting special seals and names to use to call it without doing all the fancy rituals of introduction which we find in those magical primers we call grimoires. Rather, the familiar spirit is set to work with you, and often to remain either with you or near you. It is set to cultivate a working relationship with you and be on call as you need. It may be that it is routinely with you. It may be that it routinely has a touch point in your home or temple or working space. It may be that it is in close proximity ready to come when needed. Whatever the particular arrangement and nature of the relationship, it is one in which it is familiar to you. This familiarity is not just in the sense that it is known, but in the sense that it is close and contact is routine.

The particulars of the relationship will determine how you work with them. Maybe they move around somewhat attached to you, and simply thinking of them, or calling their name, is sufficient. Maybe they have a special place in your temple and you go there to speak with them. Maybe you have a piece of magical jewelry connected to them or in which they reside and you simply touch it and speak to them. There are many ways this can work. The nature of the arrangement will depend upon the type of spirit, the agreement set with them and the nature of the spirit who bound them to you. In none of these arrangements will it be so complicated as I laid out above, or even so complicated as is laid out in the average grimoire.

Let's presume your familiar resides in some artifact which is kept in your temple, or in a magic ring which you might wear or that you might set upon your altar when you have need of the familiar. In such a case, you might prepare yourself as you would for any ritual work, or the relationship with the familiar might allow you to approach it and interact without having to go through cleansings or getting yourself into the right head space. Whatever preparation or lack thereof that is needed, once it is done, you enter your temple. You go to the altar set up for your familiar, or your move the artifact or the ring onto your altar. At this point you probably make some basic offering as part of making contact. Perhaps you pour a bit of whiskey, light the spirit's favorite incense, and light a candle. You might knock on the altar or you might just begin speaking to the spirit. If it gave you a particular call to use or name or series of names to say, this is likely where you would use them. Once that is done, you're ready to begin working with the spirit.

It may even be simpler than that. If you've given your familiar a permanent altar, you can simply go to the altar and begin talking with it. You give it routine attention and service at the altar, you provide its routine offerings and clean up after doing so; because that is maintained, you simply need to enter the space and speak with it. If it resides in your ring, put the ring on and say the name it has given you, or perform the agreed upon sign used to call it, such as turning the ring three times or tapping the ring.

If it is a spirit which simply accompanies you, like Agrippa's famed black dog or the cats and toads of witches, then it is with you waiting to speak with you. It may even initiate conversation with you from time to time. It might observe your needs and act as it thinks you would like or as you have previously instructed it to. Then when you need something specific, it is already attending to you, waiting for you to simply say its name and begin talking with it.

I'm sure some readers are frustrated. Why would I open with a silly mocking description of a ritual? I did so to clearly illustrate that it's silly to expect that sort of method because the whole point is to bind a spirit so you don't need to do all that. Some might wish that I would just give a simple set of clear instructions to use for working with the familiar once you have acquired it. Some might wonder why I'm not just giving you a ritual script here. The reason is that these relationships are individual and personal. You have to define and navigate the relationship with the spirit itself. Me giving a single instruction for all such interactions would be like me telling you how to go on a date, or make love to your partner, or how to talk with your bartender or your therapist. Those things will be organic. You might have some ideas of how it works because you've seen TV and movies, read books, talked to friends, but in the end, you know how to do them because you feel it out as it's happening. You build the relationship and the interaction. Your interaction with your familiar spirit is the same. I can give you some ideas of what the relationship may look like, and how to responsibly maintain it. I have to acknowledge that it may look a lot of different ways. I can't tell you it will always be exactly this. I can show you how to get there to have the conversation, and tell you what conversations might be like in different contexts. In the end, you'll set the context and figure out how to have the conversation.

Looking at how we work with a familiar doesn't just address the specific ritual actions or lack thereof, it also addresses why we do it and what things we do it for. These will also have some individual and personal specifics to them, but there are still some things we can broadly consider. Some of the whys and wherefores are things that should be obvious, and some are things people often seem to miss.

One of the elements of work with a familiar which seems exceedingly important, but which is often overlooked, is the ability of the familiar spirit to teach the magician. Throughout grimoires and spirit catalogues, almost as ubiquitous as the description "gives good familiars" is the description "teaches." I've seen several times in forums where people ask about calling on spirits to make them better at magic or to teach them magic. Almost all the answers given are either to scoff and claim that the person needs to read and work like everyone else and that there are no short cuts, or that such an idea is exceedingly dangerous. For those less familiar with magical forums these are common answers to most questions, often by people who don't know very much.

The reality of European Traditional Magic is that a great deal of it is taught by and empowered by spirits. The spirit catalogues all include the spirits teaching various disciplines of the liberal arts, of alchemy, astronomy, and various sciences. Some teach the speech of animals. Some reveal secrets. Some teach elements of magic. The Ars Notoria texts and the related Flowers of Heavenly Teaching texts provide means of learning through work with angels. The Excellent Booke of the Art of Magic involves the magicians conjuring dead magicians to teach them and to reveal magic books to them. The mythology of magic books involves angels writing books on pages of sapphire and other fantastic stories of how they revealed magic to mankind. Even the Bible presents witchcraft as stemming from angels coming and teaching it to humans.

Not just in the story of the Nefilim, but through the Middle Ages and the early modern era, witches historically learned their craft from spirits. I often hold back in recommending witchcraft books or particular practices for witches because witchcraft is a power, not a particular art. This is why many people have trouble describing the specifics of what differentiates practicing witchcraft from other magical practices, because they're trying to describe it as an art rather than a peculiar power and relationship to the spirit world which arises from possessing that power. The first lesson my witchcraft teacher gave me was to simply sit in nature. Next steps involve encountering and listening to spirits. The specific acts and magic performed by a witch are often individual and are taught by a combination of intuition and by interaction with spirits, and are then supplemented by formal magical study. Almost all historical accounts of witchcraft involve the Devil or the Faery Queen or familiar spirits not just facilitating magic but teaching magic to the witch.

A significant component of the familiar spirit is therefore to instruct the magician in magic. This can take on various forms. If you communicate very clearly, they may directly explain things or give you visions. The spirit might bring books, people, objects or experiences into your life which help to instruct you or answer the questions you ask of it.

Gaining information from a familiar is not limited to learning magic. Your familiar can be the spirit to guide your divination. Your familiar might warn you of dangers or problems. Your familiar might answer questions about issues in your life or how to resolve them. People sometimes forget that as a spirit your familiar will have a different vantage point than you and can provide information from its bird's-eye view. Your familiar may have special areas of expertise and be able to provide information on those. These will likely be related to the areas of expertise held by the spirit who provided it, but that spirit and the familiar itself will be able to clarify for you what special areas the familiar excels in.

Protection is another common task for the familiar. The relationship with the familiar should benefit it as well as the magician. If this is the case, it is in the spirit's interest to protect that relationship. Your familiar may be aware of dangers or difficulties or the movements of various forces and influences in your life before they become evident to you. Your familiar should be charged to help protect you and conduct the development of events around you as best as it is able to lean them towards your benefit.

Your familiar is a spirit which may be with you through your day-to-day life. It is positioned better than many other spirits to be a magical first response to typical trials, tribulations, needs and occurrences which arise. You might decide you want to call on a well known spirit for some big task when a major issue faces you. There is no reason not to turn to your familiar spirit for the small issues. If you can't find something, or you think you might be getting sick, or some problem might be developing in your home or with your car, your familiar is a good first ally to turn to for magical remediation of such issues. This doesn't mean your familiar can't help with big issues too. You'll need to look at the familiar's skills and capabilities, and the nature of the issue. If its something your familiar can't do or it isn't the best choice for help on this particular issue, if you have open communication, it may be able to direct you to the appropriate spirit or magical method to pursue.

Your interaction with your familiar will be individual to your particular relationship. This will be reflected in how you call upon it, communicate with it, feed it and ask it for help. The nature of the individual relationship will also determine what sorts of goals you work together to accomplish. Learn to be comfortable exploring. Ask the spirit who provided the familiar what it can do, or ask for a familiar that other spirits can help with particular needs. Once you establish the relationship with the familiar, reach in deeply and explore that relationship. Exploring it will help strengthen and maintain it. As you explore it, it will also help you understand how to work with that relationship. As you ask it to give you guidance and as you continue working together, you will grow to understand better how to communicate, what to offer, and how it can best help you.

III
How Much is that Feral Cat in the Window?

While working on this, I saw a post in a witchcraft forum about how someone had yet to encounter their familiar. They were concerned over their lack of a familiar until a feral cat appeared in their yard and they wondered if it was the awaited familiar finally presenting itself. I feel like we shouldn't just gloss over the fact that having a familiar isn't something which automatically occurs because you get into witchcraft. There isn't a board of spirits or witches handing them out or directing them to you. Deciding to get into magic or witchcraft doesn't convert you from Joe Schmoe to the Chosen One, with gods and spirits lining up to enter your life and select you. You have to go out and make the connections you want. If you want to work with a spirit, research how to work with it and take steps. If you want to be devoted to a god, read mythology, select one which excites you, learn how to give it offerings and devotion. If you want a familiar, contact a spirit who can give you one and ask for one.

Having touched on the fact that it isn't automatic, the real point I want to explore is the idea that this random feral cat might be this person's familiar. The chances of that are slim to none. Pointing that out can get a bit hairy. Some people got really upset when people explained that familiars are spirits and are rarely physical animals. It's become common in similar forums for people to start threads asking to see people's "fur babies and familiars." This latter sort of post could just be a cutesy thing, but many people really think of their pets as familiars.

It's understandable that if you've been attached to this idea and worked it into your practice, or if you feel it defines the special bond with your pet, that it might feel hurtful or confusing when someone says it isn't real. So, let's try to unpack a few things here for readers who are thinking of pets or physical animals as familiars.

The first thing I want to address is the difference between explaining to someone what a concept or item is versus telling people how they can and can't practice. I think this is one of the areas where people get really agitated. Not just in the case of familiars, but in a lot of areas of witchcraft and magic, people get some muddled ideas because - honestly - some publishing companies don't vet authors or review content for accuracy. A lot of authors think it's reasonable to make things up or guess when they don't know what something is, or they've made things up in their own practice and eventually write about it. Over time some of these ideas and misinterpretations get repeated frequently. Even if the wrong words are being used, or the history or ideas attached to a thing are wrong or don't make sense, some element of the practice might be effective and create some meaningful experience for people. If that's the case, it's not really anyone's business to dismiss that meaningful experience.

When we talk about something being incorrect, we should be mindful of what we're saying. In some cases, someone might be practicing something that just won't work or which could be dangerous or counter-productive in the way they're doing it. The idea that magic is about intention only means that magical acts are usually intentional acts. A group of otherwise mundane acts becomes magic when the magician engages them in a magical context with the intention to work magic. I can light a green candle because I want a warm candlelit ambience, or I can intentionally light it to do money magic. It doesn't mean that regardless of what you do your intentions will make things work. So it's possible to do things that are just incorrect.

More frequently, the mistake is a misconception related to what a word or idea or concept actually is. When this is the case, people say they're doing something, or that they're part of some tradition or have some status, but that claim isn't valid. For instance, if I read a book on Wicca which draws on Haitian practices to flesh out the system, I could be practicing something meaningful for me, but I wouldn't be a Houngan and my practice wouldn't be Vodou. In an instance like that, it would be appropriate for someone to tell me I'm wrong if I made those claims. It's ok for eclectic Wicca or NeoPaganism to be flexible. It's good to recognize that magic can be amorphous. Being open to flexibility and personalization still don't validate claims about status, tradition or practices that would otherwise be incorrect.

Similarly, people may say that some practice comes from some place that it doesn't, or the reason we do a particular ritual a particular way is because of some piece of lore that is either modern and made up or doesn't relate to the actual practice.

None of these ways of being incorrect invalidate what the person is actually doing, or make it ineffective or wrong to do. What the person is saying about the history, or context, or provenance is incorrect, and should be corrected, but that doesn't mean their practice has to change.

A person can do something which is powerful, meaningful, and effective and call it the wrong thing or think it comes from some place it has no relationship to at all. Correcting that can allow them to deepen their practice, either by exploring it for what it is or pointing them to more authentic material.

When we're looking at these kinds of misconceptions, it's helpful to look at where the misconception comes from. It's important to look at what justifies the correct understanding. We should be careful to look at how the words used can be fixed without trying to fixate on the idea that what the person is doing is wrong, because it might not be wrong at all, it might simply be something different from what they're calling it. Some people might say it's pointless to fix these misconceptions or worry about material providing accurate information. In reality, it's very important. For one part, we can't communicate clearly if people are using terms incorrectly. More importantly, allowing misconceptions won't allow us to collectively explore magic as deeply as we could if we clear up these misconceptions. Maybe the thing someone who has studied some bad info is doing is really great...but how much greater could it be if they deepened it by looking at the context it comes from and details and elements which could surround it and expand it? If they learn about the actual concept, maybe that introduces some other deep and meaningful practice to their lives.

That's why we're going to unpack some of the common confusion about familiars. We want to give people a chance to deepen what they're already doing, and learn about something else they could be doing. We want to clarify communication. We want people to have a clear idea of what we mean when we talk about familiars.

As far as I can understand, the idea that familiars are pets is influenced by two things. In the media, for decades, witches were depicted with animals as familiars. These animals, to the casual onlooker, would seem like pets. The familiars contributed to establishing the image of the witch, but weren't important to the story being depicted in books or films, so the nature of the familiar didn't need to be explored. Familiars in witch folklore were spirits pretending to be animals. In TV and movies it didn't matter if it was an animal or a spirit pretending to be an animal. Writers and directors could depict a witch with an animal and leave it to the audience to determine if it was a real animal or a spirit pretending to be one.

For a lot of people today, their image of witchcraft is shaped and influenced by witches on TV and in movies. It's reasonable that people would see an element like a familiar depicted in a way which seems like the witch's pet, and have no context or reason to assume that it isn't a real animal. Then, when exploring witchcraft, people see that real witches did indeed have familiars, and having seen familiars as pets in movies, it would be natural to assume that their pet might be their familiar. TV and movies are starting to get clearer in some of their depictions of familiars. Shows like <u>The Chilling Adventures of Sabrina</u>, and a few other movies and TV shows have shown familiars who are spirits masquerading as animals in very clear ways. So, maybe in a few years we'll get witches influenced by TV who understand familiars in a more traditional way.

I believe the second element which has helped shape the idea that familiars are pets is Raven Grimassi's book <u>The Witch's Familiar</u>. When the book came out, the familiar was not a well explored concept. Most people did not have them, did not seek to have them, and did not talk much about them. Some people might have considered pets their familiars, but it wasn't common. The revival of traditional spirit magic had not begun to flourish yet, and modern NeoPagan witchcraft didn't spend much time on familiars. As a result, there weren't many entrenched views, because familiars weren't a commonly engaged concept. Grimassi's book came out and incorporated the idea that familiars could be pets and animals involved in the witch's life, and the idea has spread dramatically. There may have been earlier books addressing the concept. Grimassi might have also treated familiars more broadly than readers understood them, as some reviews complain that Grimassi focuses on astral familiars, but the descriptions from the publisher lead with the idea of familiars as "beloved pets" and physical animals. He clearly did not create this interpretation, but was part of popularizing it.

TV and pop books on witchcraft don't need to be the basis of our understanding of familiars. The familiar spirit is one of the most well attested ideas in European Traditional Magic. There are a lot of things we have to piece together, guess at, or work out about routine magical practice because not everything is spelled out in grimoires. A lot of modern magic looks the way it does because its framers had incomplete sources. Modern witchcraft largely draws on modern ceremonial magic because there wasn't a clear continuation of witchcraft knowledge passed along into the public sphere. We have to interpret clues and make comparisons with other systems for some things. Familiar spirits aren't one of those things that needs a comparative reconstruction.

In many cases, we have to question what we see in witch trial accounts. Some regions and periods have accounts which may be more reliable. Other accounts seem to be wholly fabricated. Between these poles, there is a full range of accounts mixing truth, legends, and lies. One element we can look to them for with some surety is descriptions of witches' familiars. The reason we can look at accounts of familiars as somewhat reliable is that they match up with what we see in folklore and stories about magicians and witches. These folk stories also match up to what we see about familiars in magic books and grimoires. So, the three main forms of documentary evidence of magic in an historical European context all treat familiars as a common, if not ubiquitous, concept and they all treat them more or less the same way.

Consistently in historical sources, familiars are spirits who are given to the magician or witch by another spirit. In most cases, this spirit has also given the magician power or knowledge, or has performed some task for them. In stories of magicians the task is usually revealing treasure or providing wealth or fame; for witches it is often harming someone who slighted them. Conferring a familiar adds to and enhances this gift. The familiar spirit remains with the witch or magician generally until the end of their life. In some cases, the spirit may depart if the witch or magician recants magic and in a few instances it may be given to another witch or magician.

These spirits tend to do the things we've discussed elsewhere in the text. They teach the witch or magician. Familiars fetch things and perform tasks. They aid the witch or magician in magic, not simply by sitting in a circle or on an altar with them, but by guiding them in the act or accomplishing elements of it for them. They provide protection, they give information and insights, and overall provide service.

Familiar spirits are described as doting on their familiar humans. They will dance with them, sit by them, ask that they stay with them. In some stories, witches are known to have sex with their familiars or take meals with them, in others they feed their familiars their blood. Familiars speak and coax and encourage the witch or magician in magic. They proactively offer service in most accounts. In animal forms, they talk and walk on their hind legs. They're often colored in strange ways which indicate otheredness or faery origins; this occurs in animal form or when they appear as small humans or faery-like creatures.

Familiars change shape. This is significant to understanding the animal appearance. In folklore, a familiar was understood to be a spirit that might appear as an animal, just as a witch or magician might change into an animal, so that it could travel with its human without arising suspicion. In some accounts, these animals change shape into other animal forms when needed, indicating that at no point were they understood as a physical animal.

Considering these elements of the familiar in folklore and history can help us understand what familiars are and how to work with them. It also illustrates how much being a physical animal would limit the capability of a familiar to do any of the things a magician needs it to do. When we consider the common forms of familiars, we might further determine that viewing them as common animals is inappropriate.

Familiars taking the forms of animals are often seen as cats, black dogs, and toads. Sometimes we see other animals, but these three are common. The reason for this is not because they were creepy animals, or because witches were outside of society and had to associate with these particular animals. Each of these animals has an association with magic. Black cats have bones which have been used in spells going back to antiquity and into the modern age. Additionally, there are ancient spells involving the boiling and drowning of cats because of their magical faculties. Toads likewise have a magic bone which was known in the ancient world and has continued to be sought after for use in rituals to become a witch or a horse-whisperer. These bones appear in spells for procuring love and power in ancient and modern sources. In the medieval period, toads were believed to possess a magical stone which was able to cure poison and epilepsy, and could be made into magical amulets. People believed the stones existed in the heads of toads. In magic and folklore, black dogs were seldom a physical animal with magical attributes. Black dogs appeared as an element of folklore related to faeries and the dead. Different regions had different stories about black dogs, why they appeared, what they did, and what their appearance might portend.

When we consider the common animal forms spirits would choose to take, we may consider that we don't want to associate our pets with the way these animals have historically been used in magic. That is, of course, assuming we don't want to boil our pets or feed them to ants in order to obtain magical powers.

Another common explanation often provided for why we wouldn't want to view our pets as familiars is the idea that familiars take "magical hits" for the witch or magician, and forcing a pet to do that would be abuse. I'm not sure where this idea comes from. I've asked a few people who repeat it commonly and they are only aware of having seen it online. Someone recently informed me it comes from a fictional story, but could not remember the story. Either way, it seems a little off base to me. It seems to suggest that people are beaming aggressive and damaging rays of force at each other like some kind of comic book. Usually, magic doesn't work that way. So there isn't a "hit" for the familiar to intercept. Protective magic of this type tends to be proxy magic, like witch bottles and simulacrums. In those cases, the spirit sent to harass someone is distracted, bound up, or fixed upon a decoy.

A lot of curse work involves moving things into someone's life to cause chaos or decay, to take away things they want, to stifle their efforts, or to cause sickness or some particular bad occurrence. A familiar wouldn't jump in front of the magician and take on the bad experience for them. More likely, the familiar would observe the magical currents involved or the vexing spirits involved and redirect or dispatch them as best as they are able. This should not be so violent or rudimentary as the familiar "taking hits," for their human. Still, it is something the average pet could not do, otherwise, pets of all stripes would constantly be doing this for their beloved humans. If pets had the capacity to perceive and redirect ill-fated moments from their humans, what pet would not do so? There wouldn't be some special status as a familiar involved in this. Pets generally can't do this though; this is a role for which we need disembodied spirits.

We've looked at the evidence describing what familiars are. We've looked at things associated with the animals which appear as familiars, and how we wouldn't want that for our pets. We've looked at what familiars do and how witches and magicians work with them, and that clearly doesn't fit what our beloved household animals do or how we treat them. It should be clear, having explored these things, that familiars in the context of magic and witchcraft aren't pets. But, could a familiar spirit possess a physical animal and live as your pet?

I've only ever seen about three people suggest this. It feels like a sort of desperate reach to make pets familiars, but it has elements worth discussing. The first time I saw it suggested was by a professional magician who responded to the dismissal of the idea with "do you even magic?" While I think in 98% of cases this is not what's going on and most people suggesting it wouldn't be able to facilitate or work with that situation, I do think it's possible. I also think it's not just improbable, but also impractical, and is morally questionable.

There is very little additive reason for a familiar spirit to possess Fluffy the Cat and remain in her permanently as your familiar fur baby. We often give spirits a living residence. In some traditions, spirits inhabit statues or images. We might make spirit houses for them. We might have rings or other talismans in which spirits reside. These give us a locus on which to focus attention and offerings, but they are not necessarily the permanent or full presence of the spirit. We also see traditions in which people, and possibly animals, are possessed for temporary interaction with spirits. A spirit possessing a person can talk through that person, touch people, and more clearly deliver communication and contact. When possessing either a person or animal, a spirit can physically consume and enjoy things being offered to it. There are additive benefits to those occurrences of possession. We will be talking about temporary possession a lot more later.

Most of what a familiar spirit does can be done without hanging out full-time in Fluffy the Cat. However, there may be moments when it is useful for the familiar to possess a person or animal. Maybe it needs to deal with something in your immediate vicinity, and physical contact with the thing is the most effective way to address it. Maybe it wants to eat an offering, or tell you something directly. None of these things needs an ongoing state of possession, and there isn't much gained by doing so. If anything, the spirit is likely limiting itself from being able to fully work for you by attempting to maintain a full and constant possession of some other creature.

The fact that this is unlikely isn't just illustrated by how it wouldn't be especially helpful, but also by how people talk about familiars. No one thinks their human bestie is their familiar. Your spouse, or lover, or best friend might even have a relationship that involves a deeper bond and might have more committed wide ranging service, or the ability to teach you things. It is as possible for a person you know to be possessed by your familiar spirit as it is for your familiar to possess your cat. Both are possible, but incredibly unlikely. No one ever gets attached to thinking some other human is their familiar spirit possessing a person and bringing them into their life to be their familiar. The fact that we don't have people assuming that this happens illustrates that we don't really expect it to be common for pets to be possessed on an ongoing basis by familiar spirits. It also illustrates the moral difficulty with this idea.

People talk about pets as familiars being immoral because they don't like the idea of pets being your proxy to absorb magical attacks. If we consider possession though, is it really for us to decide that our pet should be a vessel for a spirit? Maybe it's fine to do that. Or maybe it's fine in particular contexts. I'm not someone who fixes on debating the details of the morality of magic. This does stand out to me, though. I think it's easier to think of with a person. Would it be ok to tell your familiar to possess your neighbor full-time and live out their relationship with you in your neighbor's body? You'd erasing your neighbor and telling them to take a backseat in their own life. For a lot of people, this wouldn't be an issue with an animal, because they wouldn't see the animal as having consciousness or self-awareness and self-direction the way humans do. For people who think of their animals as their fur babies or as pets they have a special close bond with, it's unlikely that they think of animals as soulless automatons with no awareness.

Reviewing the full range of issues, familiars as pets seems like a pretty untenable position. We can see how the idea likely grew out of a lack of thorough exploration of the concept. We can see how the historical idea of a familiar doesn't fit with viewing familiars as pets. We can see how familiars do a multitude of things which our pets simply do not do and other random animals in our lives could not do either. We can see how there might be moral issues in the magical associations of certain animals commonly viewed as familiars or in the idea of familiar spirits possessing animals. Replacing the familiar spirit with your pet is a non-starter. When we consider the fact that "familiar" refers to the relationship rather than the type of being though we can understand how people can see similarly close relationships with animals. We have similarly close relationships with family and friends too. We don't call them familiars because they don't do what familiar spirits do. It can still be meaningful to have close spiritual bonds with your pets or other animals. There are other spiritual and magical benefits you can explore through relationships with actual animals. But that is a subject for another time.

A witch receiving a familiar from the Devil in the Green Meadow of
Blockula

From the Wellcome Collections's The History of Witches and
Wizards: Giving a True Account of All Their Tryals in England,
Scotland, Swedeland, France, and New England; with Their
Confession and Condemnation / Collected from Bishop Hall, Bishop
Morton, Sir Matthew Hale, etc. By W.P., 1720

IV
A Witch's Familiar

In modern thinking, it is common that people associate the familiar primarily with the witch. Familiar spirits have also attached to magicians, not just witches, throughout European magical history. We see depictions of magicians with attached spirits, or the expectation of attached spirits in modern stories too, but we don't always see them referred to as familiars. Frequently, they are not depicted as animals or pets the way they are for witches.

The differences in depiction of familiar spirits in popular media depicting witches and sorcerers does not really indicate a difference in the nature of the spirits, or the relationships which occur in real life magic. Most likely, they are distinctions based upon the artists' assumptions about what sort of person would be a witch rather than a sorcerer or a magician and how that changes what they do and what they would have.

If we wanted to break down the actual differences between familiars for witches and familiars for sorcerers or magicians, it would primarily be in how they are acquired.

When we consider the witch, we encounter two main modes of becoming a witch. One receives witchcraft, the power held by witches, either through conditions of their birth or through a transformative encounter with a spirit. If a witch is a witch because of conditions of birth - which could include either heredity or particular signs, occurrences or elements of timing that indicate the presence of witchcraft; they have one foot a little closer to the spirit world already, and will likely have some awareness of unseen phenomena. In cases like this, the witch might be approached directly by a spirit and they might come to some arrangement. We see some cases of this historically. More commonly, we see witches obtaining a familiar either from the Devil or the Faery Queen. This is not dissimilar from instructions for magicians and sorcerers to conjure spirits to obtain a familiar. In both cases, a spirit with authority over the familiar provides it. The means by which the magician operates and the spirit giving the familiar are what changes.

When we say "The Devil" we might mean several different things. In some cultures and in some European folklore, the Devil is a spirit who has some rulership amongst the spirits of the physical world. He often appears more like a trickster or dealmaker than as the nemesis of God or someone stealing souls to torment. Lucifer, Satan and the Devil were not always viewed as different names for the same being. So, in magic and witchcraft, "the Devil" may be a particular trickster spirit of nature who makes deals, teaches skills, and causes mischief who folk tales use to teach lessons.

Some people look at the Devil as the Faery King to go along with the Faery Queen. The Faery King figures, like Weyland the Smith, are often used when describing who the Devil is. People make assertions that the Devil is a Pagan God who has been demonized by Christians. The problem with this is that the folklore devil isn't fully demonized. We see plenty of instances of Pagan Gods becoming saints and positive figures, so it's not a given that all Pagan Gods get demonized. More to the point, while some Gods haven't been maligned, the Devil is not clearly one particular God.

The Devil very possibly draws on elements of several Pagan Gods and is a figure representing the particular type of divine energy or force which connects to these various Gods rather than a specific God itself. The Devil, therefore, might be the wild living force of nature and the generative force of magic that stirs growth and kindles inspiration.

In all these variants, the Devil has some power over the world and is able to teach magic, grant requests, and give familiar spirits.

The Faery Queen is not so much a faery as we might see in faery tales, or even old mythology, but rather something akin to the magical women we see in the various chansons de geste. There are grimoires which present various faery queens and provide names and sometimes signs or methods for contacting them. The Queen of Elphame referred to in witch trial accounts does not typically receive one of these names that appear in spirit catalogues, at least not in British accounts. In Italian witch trial accounts dealing with a particular group of faery witches, there is a possibility that the faery queen they serve is some combination of Diana, the moon goddess, and Sibyllia, who is tied to one of the Arthurian Faery Queens and appears frequently in grimoire literature. Sibyllia's origin can be traced further to the Mediterranean in the form of the Sibyls.

Both the Devil and the Faery Queen are described as taking witches as lovers. This act is the transformative act which conveys power or the "craft" of the witch to the individual who, up to that point, had not been gifted with such spiritous awareness. This liminalizing act changes the person and situates them in a space between the civilized and the wild, the human world and the spirit world, and creates the queerness of being which characterizes witch power. We see this in other cultures as well, in which gods, dragons, and other spirits take on lovers and give them power, or magically change them in fundamental ways which imparts upon them witch power.

In accounts of witchcraft, it is this relationship with these faeries or the Devil that grants a witch their familiar. Rather than working with "the Devil" himself, the familiar, which often has elements that could indicate a holdover from faery beliefs, is referred to as that individual witch's devil. In some such cases the witch initiates their witchcraft by means of keeping their particular devil rather than recourse to The Devil. It is often through the agency of the familiar that the witch works their magical will.

We are going to sketch out ideas of how a witch might contact these powers, the Witches' Devil, the Faery Queen, and the Faery King to receive a familiar spirit. Operations for receiving a familiar by way of necromancy are a possibility as well, and we have presented one such option in <u>Living Spirits: A Guide to Magic in a World of Spirits</u>, drawn on Hekatean magic as depicted in ancient texts.

Let's begin with the Witches' Devil. I, myself, once coordinated and helped lead a ritual in which over 20 individuals signed pacts to receive teaching, power, and familiar spirits through encountering the Witches' Devil. Because of some elements of how that ritual was constructed aesthetically, I won't present it here, nor will it be the basis for our proposal of how one might begin that process.

To start, identify a crossroads which will serve as a locus point for parts of your working. This should be a particularly liminal crossroads space. All crossroads are liminal, but that liminality can be highlighted by certain elements. Is it a road leading out of town? Is it at the border of town, or the border of two particular types of spaces? Are there other strange elements or phenomena which lead to a particular supernatural character? You could use the crossroads at the end of your street, or even where your walkway intersects the street, as a crossroads for a lot of magical purposes, possibly even this one. Finding a crossroads which truly embodies that liminality is the best option.

Decide when you want to go there. Midnight and 3am are times which are typically associated with spirit activity. Some people brush off 3am as a modern idea stemming from a movie, but some traditions teach that the sun begins to set in the spirit world around this time, so this is when the day winds down and the time to party and celebrate begins for citizens of the world of the dead. Thursday is a day frequently associated with meeting the Devil at the Crossroads.

I would recommend going at this time and making a prayer or petition and leaving an offering. You might also take some dirt from the place especially if you're going to use dirt in making the spirit house for the familiar. You might charge and add to the liminality of the space by exchanging dirt from the space with graveyard dirt from your altar. You could make a cross on the ground with that dirt and leave your offerings on top of it.

After preparing the spirit house and the pact for your familiar, return with the spirit house a week later on the same day at the same time. Make your prayer and petition for the Devil to come. Explain your desire for a familiar and to receive magical teaching and power. You can continue calling upon him there in that space until you see or experience something which provides you with the name and seal for your familiar. After that, complete whatever elements you have selected to bind it to your spirit house. If you are more comfortable communicating in dreams, you would still go to the place, do everything described, but then take home some token and ask that it be given the power to make you dream and receive communications. Then return home, repeat the prayers and petitions and go to bed. When you wake, complete binding the familiar with whatever names and signs are revealed in the dream.

This could be what our ritual would look like.

Ritual for Acquiring a Familiar from the Witches' Devil

Take a small urn and place graveyard dirt, herbs, and blood of an animal within. Leave the urn at home and go to a crossroads at midnight on a Thursday. Carry with you a bay leaf to be undisturbed and a bit of the graveyard dirt mixture which was used in the urn. Make a cross with the dirt near the crossroads, asking the powers inherent in the dirt to open the way.

When you have done this, pray the following:

Our Father, whose Light is Darkness
Power be thy name
Thy pleasure come
Thy race be run
Through my body
As were it heaven.
Give us this day your ecstasy
And awaken our power
That we may use power on those set against us.
Lead us far from fear
And strengthen us against weakness
For you are the Kingdom, and the Power and the Glory
Behind all things.

Knock on the ground three times, repeat the prayer and the knocking twice more then chant:

Eko, Eko Dendritos,
Eko Eko Bromios
Eko Eko Sabazios
Eko Eko Zagrios
Bagahi laca bachahé,
Lamac cahi achabahé,
Karrelyos.
Eko, Eko Dendritos,
Eko Eko Bromios
Eko Eko Sabazios
Eko Eko Zagrios
Lamac lamec bachalyos,
Cabahagi sabalyos,
Baryolas.

Lagozatha cabyolas,
Samahac et famyolas,
Harrahya.

Knock on the ground and repeat the chanting and knocking, pacing deosil through the space, until you experience the presence of the Devil.

If this is your first encounter, introduce yourself and petition him for power and that he may teach you magic. Ask him to come to you in dreams. Tell him you will take a stone and some dirt from this place so that it will return home with you, and that you will return in a week with a further offering to receive a familiar spirit.

Return home and add the dirt to your urn and place the stone by your bed. Invite the Devil the join you in your dreams. If inspired, engage in sexual activity, either partnered or alone; this is a common form of communion.

Record any dreams.

After a week, return with an additional offering and bring your urn. Write out three copies of a pact outlining what you offer in exchange for the familiar, what you expect of it, and what you will give it routinely. Repeat the ritual, but this time petition for a familiar. If provided with a name and seal, sign each pact with your name and with the familiar's name and seal. Roll one copy and bury it in the urn, roll another and bury it in the ground at the crossroads, retain the third as a talisman of the pact.

Make your offering in exchange for the familiar.

Return home, enshrine the urn and make the appropriate offerings.

If you do not receive a seal and name at the meeting place, ask for it to come in a dream. Return home, dream, and then complete the portion of the ritual with the pacts and offerings.

End.

Next we will consider the Faery Queen. Some historians of Scottish witch trials have noted that early on she appears more routinely than the Devil, but as the Reformation raised concerns about correct religiosity, the Devil began to take center stage. The function of the Devil, for the most part, was the same as that of the Faery Queen. It is possible that he became a mask for maligning things that had already been occurring with a less diabolical tone. Like the Devil, the Faery Queen was frequently the object of a sexual encounter which would initiate the individual's use of witchcraft. She would instruct in magic and, presumably, provide familiar spirits.

For those curious about the Queen of Elphame, looking up the case of Andro Mann is a good starting point. The trial of Andro Mann also presents an alternate look at the Devil. For Mann, the Faery Queen was married to Christsonday. Christsonday was an angel, clad in white, who held divine power from God. He was understood by Mann to be God's son-in-law. While Mann described Christsonday as once taking the form of a stag and appearing amid a troop of elves, the prosecutors believed the spirit to be the Devil rather than a faery or an angel. Mann's relationship with the Queen of Elphame includes most of the standard elements. He knew her from childhood. In his thirties he began a sexual relationship with her and was granted magical power and knowledge. He was killed for it in his seventies.

While figures like Andro Mann and Marion Grant met Christsonday through their relationships with the Faery Queen, others met her through their relationship with the Devil. In cases like that of Isobel Gowdie and Janet Broadhead, she appears in conjunction with the Devil. In these confessions, the witches were gathered by the Devil and taken into the earth to the faery spaces to dine with the Queen of Elphame in her supernatural abodes.

Several faery spells in the grimoire period continue this theme of meeting and dining with a faery queen and her sisters. Often sexual congress was part of this experience. Frequently, the magician set the meal and engaged in his conjuration, then retired to bed to encounter the faeries in his dreams. This type of faery contact accords with what we see in some older faery myths. These dream spaces seem to be an in between space in which humans can encounter faeries and the dead without either the human or the spirit fully having to leave their appropriate space. The tenuous nature of sleep, with the body in a state of different functioning, vulnerability and apparent weakness, matches certain elements of allowing a shift towards awareness of the spirit world.

In some instructions for encountering the Faery Queen, the magician engages in necromancy to compel a shade to fetch her for him. Again, in traditional mythology, the fair folk and the dead often occupy related spaces. Sometimes it isn't fully clear if there is a separation between the dead and some faeries. They occupy similar spaces. The activities of some faeries portend death, and days and times associated with faery activity are also often associated with the dead. Some faerylore includes faeries collecting human souls as a tithe to hell, while other faeries imprison the dead as servants.

So, the components we might consider when assembling an approach to meeting the Faery Queen involve offering a meal and possible sexual congress, meeting in a dream, and perhaps enlisting the aid of the dead. As such, there are a few simple common ritual elements we can combine to facilitate this meeting. Alcohol offered to the dead is a common offering and may be pleasing to the Faery Queen as well. The magician may wish to select a beverage they can drink, along with a tea which will help put them in a state to be appropriately aware of the spirits they are calling. Consuming alcohol and infusions is common in some traditions which encourage such direct spirit contact.

Ritual for Acquiring a Familiar from the Queen of Elphame

Take a long bath steeped in herbs to calm yourself and awaken your awareness. Clean yourself thoroughly. Wear cologne or oil, adorn and dress yourself well, focus on being relaxed but also as clean, well groomed, and nicely dressed as you can manage.

In your room, not far from your bed, set a table with three chairs. Burn appropriate incenses for your work; place them near the table and near the bed. Set three places with a candle at each place. Each place setting should have a glass for water and a glass for whiskey or whatever alcohol you choose to offer. The setting across from you should have four small dishes for libations.

Prepare food, and add an apple at each place setting.

Knock three times on the table. Light the candle for the place setting across from you. Pour water in the glass for that setting.

"I call upon mighty Charon, ferryman of the dead, bring forth my ancestors to dine with me. May Hades and Persephone give them leave to enter for this visit. I offer light to light their way, and heat to burn through the barrier between worlds, I offer water to cool and soothe them. May this candlelight be the light of their presence here."

Place two matching coins before their place setting.

"I call on my ancestors to join me for this meal and ask that the gods who grant their passage might also partake in these offerings."

Pour honey, wine, milk, and olive oil for the dead into the libation dishes.

Serve food to your place and your ancestors' place, and spend time telling your ancestors about what is happening in your life and the lives of your family. After that, say:

"I have need to meet with the Lady Sibylia, Queen of the Faeries. Since the dead have access to the fair folk, I ask that you will kindly seek and retrieve her, bring her here to dine with us so that as I serve her plate and light her candle she might arrive."

Knock on the table three times. Serve food to Sibylia's place, pour water for her, and say:

"Lady Sibylia, Queen of the Faeries, come swiftly with my kin, enjoy this meal, let this water give you cool comfort, arrive here with my ancestors as I light this candle and give its gift of light and warmth."

Light the candle. If Sibylia has arrived with your ancestors continue; if not, repeat the call to her.

"Welcome fair Sibylia, most beautiful of women, most regal of faeries, most kind and pleasant of all guests. I am honored and brought joy by your presence. Dine with me and my family that we may be friends, and accept this apple as a sign of our friendship."

Place the apple for Sibylia at her place. Eat and talk with Sibylia, complimenting and honoring her with your words.

Then say:

"I give this gift of whiskey to my ancestors to thank them for bringing the most gracious Sibylia. I give this gift of whiskey to our Lady Sibylia as a sign of our friendship and in appreciation for aiding me with this request that I now ask. Kind Lady Sibylia, as a sign of our friendship, grant me a familiar spirit from your court that I may learn from it and it may help me in all endeavors and that it may be a link to maintain our friendship. I will give this whiskey, and should you desire, my company for the night in payment for this gift from your faery court. I will tend to the well-being of this spirit and will give to him (list what you will provide as offerings to this familiar). Tell me what name and sign to use in speaking with him."

Once you receive the name and sign mark them on the pacts you have prepared. One should be placed in the house for the spirit, one should be retained by you, and one should be burned for the faery queen.

Pour the whiskey that you have offered.

"My ancestors, I appreciate this gesture and your friendship and will speak with you again soon."

Blow out their candle.

"Fair lady, should you so choose, join me this night either wakefully or in dreams."

Let her candle continue to burn, undress and retreat to bed. Either continue as you are moved by the spirit or retire to sleep if the spirit does not inspire you to enjoy congress.

End.

* * * * * *

Should you choose to pursue some faery king such as Weyland or Oberion to receive a familiar you can easily modify our ritual to Sibylia for that same end.

A Sorcerer and his spirits
From The Wellcome Collection, Morton, Hall, Hale et al, W.P. 1720

V
A Sorcerer's Familiar

In the previous chapter we discussed witches and their familiars. In common awareness, the familiar spirit is more associated with the witch than with other types of sorcerers and magicians. Historically, grimoire magicians also had familiars, and it is likely other sorts of magicians may have had them as well given their ubiquity in witchcraft and learned magic. In contemporary media, we still see reference to familiars for other types of magicians, although they are not always named as such. In Jonathan Strange and Mr. Norrell, Mr. Lascelles asks Gilbert Norrell where his "faery servants" are in one of their early encounters. In the early aughties film "The Order," Heath Ledger's character finds that his late mentor had two spirit children attached in service to him. We see learned magicians in popular folklore alleged to have familiar spirits. It was often claimed that Agrippa had a black dog in his service, and there have been claims that Crowley had one as well.

While we are noting that both witches and other sorts of magicians have familiars, we have elected to separate out witches and sorcerers. Why? Are the familiar spirits different? Is the process different? Are the types of magicians involved fundamentally different in a way that changes the relationships with the familiars?

I think answering that might involve determining what we mean by sorcerer, witch, magician, or any other terms we might apply. In the previous chapter we talked about what constitutes a witch, and when one considers that, it becomes clear that witches aren't the same as other magicians. Witches possess inherent power which comes from being changed by spirit interaction or particular birth conditions. Witches are fundamentally othered, and are characterized by a queerness connected to their liminality and otheredness which allows them to apprehend the spiritual and the mundane simultaneously. Witches are a crossroads for the various possibilities that could manifest, and witchcraft is rooted in a sort of moving dynamism of potentials and juxtapositions that creates witch-power. We often use terms for magic and magicians interchangeably and in doing so lose nuance and understanding by not using them more definitively.

"Magician" clearly refers to anyone who practices magic, and all magicians could elect to have familiars whether it is associated with their particular sort of magic or not. "Sorcerer" often gets tossed out to refer to any sort of magician, but frequently carries a connotation of working with spirits and having a mode of working that can partake of both folk magic and learned magic. In works by Nicolaj Mattos Frisvold, in which he discusses modes of traditional sorcery, I am struck by how certain elements of it feel like witchcraft. Frisvold gives the explanation that while witches are born and have an inherent power based on an innate nature, sorcerers receive power. Both concepts involve a power that can be transmitted, and that power seems to relate to the ability to work with and command spirits. In fact, sorcerers in many traditions receive access to certain spirits, or connections to them, or special modes of communication with them. The liminality, otheredness and queerness of witchcraft are not necessarily as tied to the nature of the sorcerer or the ways in which they approach and cause magic.

For our purposes, sorcerer will refer to magicians who utilize and draw from both folk magic and learned magic. They might directly work magic through their own efficacy or through direct interaction with spirits outside of spells and rituals. Even in traditional modes of sorcery, sorcerers seem to be practical and open to being innovative. Sorcerers are not born, although they may be astrologically predisposed.

I like the idea of a transmission of power, and, with it, special access to select spirits, or bonds forged with spirits, through initiation. However, I don't think we can argue that that is a standard enough set of elements, among those who use the word sorcerer, to say it's part of what constitutes one. It is, however, an element of sorcerous practice which might be considered as people try to revive European modes of sorcery and create living traditions from them.

Insofar as the kind of familiar is concerned, sorcerers and witches might have almost any type of spirit as a familiar. While witch trial accounts tend to allege that witches had demons and devils as familiars, most of the details make it look like faeries, and the dead were more common sources of familiar spirits for witches. In the context of grimoire magic, we find the dead, and demons or devils might be the most common source of familiar spirits for sorcerers. Within grimoire tradition we do also see angels and faeries providing familiars. The number of "fallen spirits" associated with providing familiars seems to be far greater, though.

The process for obtaining a familiar, and the point in one's career in which it happens, seems to be another point of variance for the witch and the sorcerer. For a sorcerer it seems like they are engaged in the work of magic and learn to conjure spirits and then contract a familiar. The sorcerer has their books or their teacher and learns elements of preparation and timing. Then they begin experiments of conjuration, and possibly other magical operations. Eventually, they are able to bind a spirit to provide a familiar. Conversely, the witch, might begin their magical journey with the process that provides a familiar. If a person is being made a witch, it is through some intimate and fundamentally transformative interaction with a spirit. It is in the process of these interactions that the spirit provides the familiar. A witch who is born with witchcraft may encounter a spirit directly, begin a relationship, and learn magic from that spirit. The acquisition of the familiar might then be seen as an element of beginning the process and practice of magic for the witch, while it is a step along the way, achieved by an experienced magician, from the perspective of a sorcerer.

With this in mind, sorcerers often obtain familiars by means of ritual conjuration. The grimoires abound with spirits who are described as giving good familiars. Even those who are not noted as giving good familiars are described as having legions and hosts of spirits at their command, so they could still provide familiars from amongst their subordinates. The grimoires provide the means of formal contact with these spirits. While they don't dictate or discuss the acquisition of familiars from the spirits conjured, typically, we can presume one would utilize the ritual means provided and request a familiar during the portion in which the magician questions the spirit and requests what they desire.

Later in this text we will explore in detail a ritual in which a demon is conjured to provide a familiar spirit. Since we will be going in depth with an example in the second part of the book, we don't need to provide a conventional conjuration example here. Essentially, the magician would select the appropriate conjuration approach for the spirit in question. He might draw from any of the grimoires which provide methods for dealing with that sort of spirit. When the spirit appears, the magician would request a familiar spirit and ask for its name and seal. The magician should have some sort of object or spirit house to which to bind the spirit. We will present a method of this from Reginald Scot's Discouerie of Witchcraft later; The Cambridge Book of Magic also presents an alternate example of binding a spirit to a crystal sphere. In the process of attaching the spirit to its house, the magician should have a pact prepared to outline what he expects

A conjurer summons a demon to procure the love of a woman for his young male patron. The young man leaves the circle with the demon unconstrained and pays with his life.

From The Wellcome Collection, Morton, Hall, Hale et al, W.P. 1720

from the spirit and what he will provide to the spirit. I recommend a copy of the pact be retained by the magician, a copy given to the spirit providing the familiar, and a copy encased within whatever houses the familiar. Magical paints or inks are a good choice for signing the pact, which should be signed by the magician, and the magician should mark it with the name and seal of the spirit once those are provided.

We have summarized the typical grimoire based approach and will provide a detailed explanation of a version of that approach later. While most grimoires do not present specific instructions for familiars, and simply note that the spirits will provide them, there are some examples of specific grimoire rituals for obtaining familiars. To help illustrate other approaches, we will present a specific grimoire approach to acquiring a familiar in this chapter. In certain "Key of Solomon" texts the Olympic spirits are referred to as the familiar spirits of the planets. While some magicians who have not yet worked with these spirits have suggested that they are equivalent to, and their names are mispronunciations of, the standard planetary archangels, there is no real basis to this assertion. Most magicians who work with them do not hold this view. Further, in some instances, like in The Keys of Rabbi Solomon, they appear alongside the traditional archangels as separate spirits. In one point in The Keys of Rabbi Solomon they are referred to as the familiar spirits of the planets. I believe the reason for this is that the Olympic spirits readily provide means of calling upon themselves directly and simply without aid of ritual. In fact, the method of The Arbatel is simple and relatively without ritual. The Arbatel notes that the Olympic spirits rule over a host of angels and they provide familiars. In The Keys of Rabbi Solomon it provides instructions for obtaining a familiar from the Olympic spirits and binding it to a ring.

It is interesting to note that the text conveys that the spirit is attached to the ring permanently and therefore the ring, along with the spirit, may be gifted to another magician. While many grimoires note that spirits will provide familiars and how to obtain a familiar, it is less common to see express instructions for conjuring a familiar to attach to an object. The ritual also provides a separate depiction of how to construct a circle from the one more generally presented in the text. I have always found the idea that the ritual comes with a specialized circle to be of particular interest. So, while we have suggested that generally the approach of using grimoire methods to conjure an angel or demon and obtain a familiar can, in most cases, follow along closely with standard grimoire rituals, or with standard ritual methods typically applied by the magician, it seems worthwhile to present this approach. This will serve as an example of conjuring a more angelic spirit for a familiar, as well as a traditional conjuration method for that purpose.

* * * * * * *

Ritual to Bind a Planetary Familiar to a Ring

Instructions and Commentary

The instructions for this ritual describe the ring being presented to the spirit so that the familiar spirit of the planet can imbue it with the desired virtues. In <u>Angel Magic: The Ancient Art of Summoning and Communicating with Angelic Beings</u>, Geoffrey James describes the mechanism for this. The angel makes contact with the material of the ring, talisman, or pentacle and converts the underlying spiritual substance to match the essential qualities of the angel or spirit. The physical object remains the same physical material, while the object's spiritual essence becomes identical to the angel's. The spiritual power matching the nature of the angel can radiate out force akin to the presence of the angel, it can act as a tincture to impart virtue to things with which it comes into contact, or it can be drawn from in magical rituals. This is the concept Saint Thomas Aquinas describes in <u>Ente et Essentia</u> as the basis for the transubstantiation of the Eucharist. The description Aquinas provides reflects essential alchemical concepts and is an expression of Aristotelian conceptions of Platonism.

Almost all modern magicians working with astrological talismans, planetary pentacles, and tools of grimoire magic explain this phenomenon differently. Rather than an alchemical change, the process reflects the ongoing presence of spirits. Contemporary magicians believe a subservient spirit, under the authority of the conjured spirit, is placed in the object by the conjured spirit. This spirit, from the conjured spirit's legion, serves the owner of the object and fulfills the magical purposes of the object.

After a fashion, both ideas are the same. Whether a spirit resides in the object or the object's essence becomes identical to the conjured spirit's essence, the spiritual nature of the object is converted to the living nature of the magical power that has been conjured. Either the material has an essence that is a smaller copy of the conjured spirit, or it houses a smaller or lesser spirit of the same nature as the conjured spirit. The concepts are overlapping, though not identical.

For our purposes, it may make more sense to conceptualize the interaction as the spirit commanding one of the spirits under its authority into the ring.

The ritual text says to call the familiar spirit of the planet. In The Keys of Rabbi Solomon, the familiar spirit of the planet is the Olympic Spirit. This does not mean that the Olympic spirit is your familiar; rather, this is a more approachable spirit within the planetary sphere. The Arbatel describes the Olympic spirits as providing good familiars. When you tell the spirit what virtue you want in your ring, you would tell it to place a familiar there and can specify a particular area of magic under that planetary correspondence, or leave it more general. For instance, the magician might request a spirit provided by Hagith for general facilitation of Venus-related tasks, or it might be requested to assist with legal cases or love interests specifically.

The timing of the ritual is not specified, but it says to perform the same preparations and ceremonies as you would to make a pentacle. Thus, the ring is engraved during the day and hour of the planet. It notes the good fortune of preparing the ring under a good constellation. This means that while an astrological election is not necessary, the creation of the ring can be improved by electing the time of its creation. Like an astrological talisman, the ring should be censed with perfumes and incense. The instructions specify that this is done in honor of the spirit which rules it.

The Ritual

Tools

Chalk or salt to make the circle
A ring made from the metal of the planet with a stone appropriate to the planet
An engraving tool
Incense appropriate to the planet
A small new censer
A candle of virgin wax
A wooden wand consecrated to the planet
A clean new small box or a silk bag of the color appropriate to the planet

Preparation

In the day and hour of the planet, engrave the name of the familiar spirit ruling the ring inside the ring.

Prepare the circle with the design provided.

The Ritual Itself

Burn incense.

Hold a lit candle of virgin wax and respectfully recite the conjuration:

I conjure you, [Spirit] by the Great Living God, Sovereign Creator of all things, that you come here under any visible form that you wish, without noise and without fright, to imprint on this ring which carries your name the glorious qualities of which you are the minister and dispenser. I make this conjuration to you by the sacred names of the Great Living God, who you must obey. Hear, therefore, with respect and with swift submission these names which are terrible and fearful to all created beings. Adonai, AGLA, YHVH, Gaha, Agari, Thetron, He Elhi, Cotlyis, Ygaha, Emmanuel, Vau, Ory, Elohim, Goth, Geni.

When the spirit arrives, hold the ring at the end of the wand to present it. Explain what virtues and powers you desire for the spirit placed in the ring to possess.

When this is complete say:

Faithful minister, go in peace in the name of the Great God, your Master, who has sent you to be sympathetic towards me.

Put the ring on your finger and light additional incense. Cense the ring in the incense.

Brush away the circle and exit.

The original description of this ritual may be found in <u>The Veritable Key of Solomon</u>, by Stephen Skinner and David Rankine.

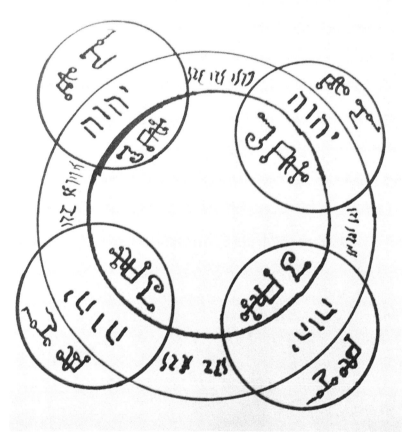

Magical circle for attaching an Olympic Familiar to a ring. Based on the circle presented by Skinner and Rankine in <u>The Veritable Key of Solomon</u>.

VI
The Abramelin Familiars and The Use of the Abramelin Squares

We have mentioned the Abramelin as an example of acquiring familiar spirits in the grimoire tradition. It falls a bit outside what we might consider sorcery and is definitely outside the range of witchcraft. Discussing details of the Abramelin method is outside of the scope of this text. However, it is still worth noting a little about it regarding familiar spirits.

The essential Abramelin procedure is simple. First, a person acquires a space and fits it out as an oratory for ongoing prayer. The individual working the method then spends months praying multiple times a day and putting more and more focus and attention into connecting with an angel sent to them by God. As you get deeper and deeper into the spiritual retreat, the amount of prayer increases. You begin cutting more and more distractions out of your life until you are essentially cloistered in prayer. In the end, your angel appears and begins to teach you. A special ongoing relationship with this angel is established.

The angel provides the magician with means of working with demons and spirits without using magical circles, long strings of divine names, or magical seals and pentacles. My experience and understanding of this is that the angel works as an intermediary and retrieves spirits for the magician. The magician goes through an initial process of binding the spirits to perform tasks based on a series of magical symbols in the form of letter squares, which are presented in the text. The magician begins by calling upon the kings or chiefs of the demons. He then calls upon the princes underneath them and their dukes and the spirits which serve them.

The spirits are bound to come when the magician calls them or when the magician uses the squares they have sworn to fulfill. The different squares are assigned to various demons. Several collections of squares can also be managed or performed by the familiar spirits serving the magician.

When the magician has conjured all the demons and obtained their oath of service, he is able to request four familiar spirits. The familiar spirits serve the magician, each for a quarter of the day. There are squares to use in conjunction with those spirits and the quarters of the day. As we have mentioned, there are also several squares that the text says can be administered not only by the demons to which they are assigned but also by the familiar spirits. It notes that they can be fulfilled by them "to a great extent," so it may be that the familiars are not as expert or powerful in these tasks as the appropriate demons.

This book is on familiar spirits and not the Abramelin working. We aren't recommending an alternative form of Abramelin to create a relationship with familiar spirits similar to what is presented there. However, exploring the list of powers assigned to the familiar spirits in the Abramelin might give magicians working with demons as familiar spirits further ideas of the powers such a demon might possess. You will likely want to ask your familiars if and how they can assist you with these goals should you decide to explore working with your familiar to that end.

Each chapter containing magic squares in the Abramelin presents a general purpose for which the squares of that chapter may be used. Then it shows individual squares for specific goals under that more general heading. We will give the chapter numbers and topics from the French Abramelin as translated by S. L. MacGregor Mathers. If you wish to explore these particular powers with your familiar, you might also consider looking at the specific squares given and asking about the specific goals of the specific squares, or asking if your familiars can operate through the application of the squares as well.

Some magicians assume that the squares can only be used in the context of The Sacred Magic by someone who has completed the retreat. Anyone familiar with magic through history knows that signs, symbols, words of power, and incantations get borrowed and recopied endlessly. The seals and images of ritual and grimoire magic traditions eventually make their way into folk magic traditions and forms of popular magic. The letter squares are simply symbols. If you were to complete the rite and bind the demons and not include the oath to fulfill the tasks of the squares, there is no reason to assume they would work. The binding to fulfill the tasks of the squares fits traditional work with demons in which they are bound to obey the rituals, calls, and seals included in the magician's magical book. The magical book is frequently a living being that serves as a contract between the magician and the spirits. It is consecrated and is the basis of the pact for their interaction. The magician creating a book of squares and binding the demons to fulfill the tasks described is the same process.

With that in mind, it is entirely possible to bind any demons who are effectively conjured to work based on the application of the squares. As we said, you can explore the squares for inspiration as to possible things a demon familiar can do, or you could consider making a book of squares and binding your familiar to operate the squares in the book. In theory, you could create a whole new set of symbols or have the demon who is giving you the familiar also give you a set of seals by which to work with the familiar.

Here are the chapters and descriptions of magical categories from The Sacred Magic of Abramelin the Mage:

"The Operations of the following Chapters can also (to a great extent) be administered by the Familiar Spirits, namely:--

Chapter II. (Scientific Information.)
Chapter IV. (Visions.)
Chapter XII. (Secrets of other persons.)
Chapter XVIII. (Healing of Maladies.)
Chapter XIX. (Affection and Love.)
Chapter XXIII. (Demolishing Buildings.)
Chapter XXIV. (Discovery of Theft.)
Chapter XXVII. (Causing Visions to appear.)
Chapter XXVIII. (Obtaining Money.)
Chapter XXX. (Visions of Operas, Comedies, etc.)"

Alchemists Laboratory from Amphitheatrum sapientiae aeternae
written by Heinrich Khunrath
1595

VII
Are All Familiars the Same?

As we have mentioned, when we talk about familiars, we're talking about a spirit with whom we have a particular sort of relationship. This does not mean it is a specific sort of spirit; instead, it is a spirit we can readily contact, work with, and maintain an ongoing interaction with. It is a spirit that is familiar to us, and we are familiar to them. Are all familiar relationships the same?

No. Some authors will refer to a familiar spirit relationship very broadly. For example, in discussing historical witchcraft, the encounter with the Devil or the Faery Queen is sometimes presented as contact with the familiar. The witch might have been familiar with the Devil and the Faery Queen. They might have been carnally familiar with them. But the Devil and the Faery Queen were not the witch's familiar spirits. Chrisonday, for example, was a tutelary spirit for Andro Mann. Chrisonday taught him and likely offered some guidance and protection, but he was not bound to Mann's service. When we read accounts of historical witchcraft, we want to keep in mind that the familiar refers to the spirits given to serve the witch or magician, and not the spirits who the witch serves. Nor are they the spirits who give the witch their initial power and spirit servants.

Some spirits will develop familiarity with us without having the formal relationship we generally mean when we say familiar. The Olympic spirits, for instance, are described as giving the magician a unique name by which to call them. They also provide methods for calling them easily. This is a common thing magicians should seek with spirits in general, but it's spelled out in the case of the Olympic spirits, and they seem particularly keen to develop this familiarity and friendly access. I believe this is why they're called the familiar spirits of the planets in some texts. The Olympic spirits also provide familiar spirits, so while we might develop familiarity and comfort in calling on Bethor or Aratron, that isn't the same as having them as a familiar.

Familiar and familiarity refer to how well we know someone or something and how comfortable we are with it. But in context, familiar refers to that specific bond in which the spirit performs certain services for us as magicians in exchange for the care we provide them or because of the agreement we make with the spirits set above them. Even with that relationship, there is still room for variance. The type of care we offer a familiar might be different from that provided by someone else. The frequency with which we work with the familiar might vary. The things the familiar does for us will be based on our needs and possibly on the type of spirit it is. Our relationship with our familiars might look different from the relationship another magician has with theirs. If we have more than one familiar, and they come from different sources or are different types of spirits, our relationships with our individual familiars will also look different.

This brings us to two big questions. Are different types of spirits going to give us different experiences of the familiar spirit relationship? And, how do we decide what kind of familiar we need?

This wasn't something I initially thought to address. My editor mentioned this question in a note. It is a question I've thought about before and discussed with other magicians. These questions can hold people up in deciding which way to go because they can be significant questions.

For some people, the driving factor in deciding what type of familiar to seek will be what type of magic they tend to do. Someone who avoids work with demons probably won't try to make a pact with a demon for a familiar. If you only work with faeries, then you'll probably look for a faery familiar. Your comfort and your familiarity might be driving factors.

In other cases, it might be determined by the method you're using to obtain one. For example, if you're working with the Sacred Magic, you'll bind the demons and receive four demon familiars after you achieve Knowledge and Conversation. If you're meeting the Devil or the Faery Queen at the crossroads, you'll obtain whatever familiar they choose to give you. If you're working with <u>The Keys of Rabbi Solomon</u>, you might look for a familiar from the Olympic spirits.

The general approach to magic you pursue is also a factor. "Elite magic," which has often been called learned magic, or the magic practiced by clergy, court sorcerers, and aristocrats, is rooted in grimoires, alchemy, and formal magical practices. When we think of those magicians, we tend to think of demon familiars because we assume they're conjuring devils from grimoires and binding them. However, those books also provide access to the Olympic spirits, angels, faeries, and the dead, so the range of spirits to choose from is there, even if infernal spirits are the assumption. "Popular magic," often referred to as low magic or folk magic, might be more commonly associated with faeries as familiars. But, popular magic encompassed a broad range and included "learned" magic sources like grimoires alongside traditional folk wisdom. So, a cunning man could just as easily have had a devil from a grimoire for a familiar as they could a faery.

Prevailingly, your comfort, nature, and goals, in comparison with the nature of the spirit, its talents, and the system by which you would connect with it, should be the factors that play into that decision.

Some spirits might not have the nature and character to be a familiar spirit. A nature spirit might be less comfortable being housed in your home and going along with you. It might also have a limited range of things it would be as inclined to accomplish. Familiars often take the appearance of animals, but when we talk about the spirit of the ravens, or the toads, or some sort of broad animal spirit, we're usually talking about the overarching spirit which rules and protects that class of animals. So, an "animal spirit," in the sense that one might go journeying to connect with an animal nature is not likely to be appropriate as a familiar. The spirit of an individual dead animal could be conjured as a familiar, but it might also be limited in its range of functions. Certain folk spirits considered domestic or household spirits might be great spirits to build a relationship with, but as we will see in part two, they might not be the right spirits to seek as familiars.

So, what spirits make good familiars? Again, when we consider popular magic, as we will see in part two, there is a fair chance that most familiars were either faeries or the dead. We can't be certain because many historical records still call them demons or devils, or just imps or familiars. A faery might be a good choice if you're inclined to use approaches that draw on natural magic rather than conjuration or if your goals tend to be well-suited to the things faeries do. Having children, basic prosperity, glamour, stealing resources, healing, blighting, travel through spirit flight, and quickly accomplishing labor and tasks are all things associated with faery magic in folklore and accounts of witches.

On the other hand, if you want a familiar to help you accomplish magical tasks and you want a formal, traditional ritual as your approach, a demon might be the best way to go. A demon can help with the standard magical goals of sex and money, but it can also bring honors and dignities; it can teach you about magic or about other areas of knowledge, it can help with transportation, it can help defeat enemies, it can do the broad array of things demons are described as doing in the grimoires. Demons are also practical and tend to focus on getting things done. An angel might be a good option if you want your familiar to help provide guidance or achieve "lofty" goals. It could be a good familiar if you're pursuing knowledge and wisdom, but it can also be good for protection, healing, blessing, and a host of other more down-to-earth needs. Angels are sometimes less to the point than demons as far as practical goals go, but for some people, their way of handling things might be more appropriate.

Think about the types of spirits you have worked with. Think about what your experiences have been. From there, you should be able to determine what kind of spirit with which you will work best in a close ongoing manner.

Part Two

Faeries, Fetches, and Fylgja:
Familiars in Pagan and Folklore Contexts

Image: The Ghost of Cathmor, King of Atha, visits the Young
Woman Sulmalla and a Druid, engraving by W. Angus 1803

Pythia Foretells the Oracle at Delphi
Heinrich Leuteman
1880

VIII
History and Comparative Concepts

In exploring the familiar spirit, we have noted that this phenomenon appears throughout much of what we would consider European Traditional Magic. The familiar spirit is a thread that unites witch folklore, witch trial accounts, magical books, and the records of working magicians. Looking further back, we see related concepts in late antique Mediterranean magic. When we consider the story of the Witch of Endor, we find that ancient Levantine magic also had some sort of familiar spirits. Is the thread of the familiar spirit one where if we keep tugging, we will also find links back into the Pagan magics of Northern Europe and Britain? Or do those regions draw the concept from Greco-Egyptian and Near Eastern magic?

It is hard to say with certainty. By the time we have recorded sources describing Northern European, British, and Irish folklore and magic, we are looking at sources with hundreds of years of outside influence potentially impacting them, as well as the beliefs and practices. We often consider this influence in terms of the impact of Christianity, but for Continental Europe and Britain, there was also a significant period of Roman influence. For example, one of the earliest histories of British monarchies gives "Brutus" as the folk etymology of British based on a claim that the British were descendants of a Trojan prince.

Aside from the question of sources and whether or not they reflect indigenous understandings or beliefs already syncretized with Christian or Roman influences, we also have to consider the imperfect nature of comparison. We might find things that have similarities to what we mean when we say "familiar spirit," but it may not be possible to say for certain that the ideas are the same. A similar concept might have influenced how the relationship with the familiar developed in European magic. Conversely, an idea that seems related might be similar because it developed from foreign influence. Concepts with some similarity might be entirely unrelated and may have differences that are not as immediately evident to us.

Despite the difficulty in nailing down a definitive assertion that the familiar spirit and some other local custom or idea are the same, and therefore it proves that the concept existed in native Pagan traditions, these comparisons are worth exploring. Some of the value rests in giving us more practices, beliefs, and ideas to explore. Some of it is found in the ability for these comparisons to further inform our concept of and relationships with our familiars. Finally, as we've noted, discussing and developing nuanced understandings requires clear terminology. Since some people assert a sameness between the familiar and other concepts from mythology and folklore, while others insist they are different, it's worth unpacking what these various spirit relationships are.

The story of the Witch of Endor, which appears in I Samuel, involves an act of necromancy. King Saul found that his diviners were unable to answer him suitably using their approved methods. Saul had driven out the magicians and necromancers, and so he traveled to Endor, where it was rumored that a woman possessed an "ob." The translation of "ob" is debated, and even the description of the woman and her skills varies depending upon the source and the period. Some have suggested that "ob" refers to a necromantic pit, like those seen in Greek necromancy. Others have suggested that the "ob" refers to a familiar spirit. If it refers to a pit, this fits the story, which depicts the Witch seeing spirits rise up from the ground. On the other hand, if the "ob" is a familiar spirit, we might consider the interaction in two ways.

The Witch conjures forth the prophet Samuel, who had anointed Saul as king and was his advisor. Some commentators have asserted that this isn't possible. Explanations have included dismissing the Witch's work as ventriloquism, while others have suggested that a demon or devil deceived Saul by posing as Samuel. If the Witch were party to such a deception, then it would be reasonable to understand her familiar spirit as the demon who posed as Samuel. Being more generous regarding the Witch's character and honesty might give us a more useful idea of what her familiar was capable of.

Let's presume the witch was being honest in her dealings with Saul. She was under threat of harm or death once she realized it was the King who had cast out people engaged in similar magical acts. Defrauding him could add to the danger. The story doesn't provide any reason to believe she was deceptive unless we presume that witches are deceptive. The spirit does not comfort Saul or tell him things he wants to hear, nor does it try to entrap him in some pact or bargain. Instead, the spirit berates Saul for failing to serve God properly. This doesn't seem likely if it's a devil pretending to be Samuel in order to trick Saul.

A demon posing as Samuel does not necessarily mean that a devil is tricking Saul. If the witch had a familiar spirit, it is the familiar which gives her the ability to see spirits rising and allows them to communicate with the living. The most straightforward way for this to work would be the spirit going into the underworld and raising the dead. The spirit might even provide some bridge to aid communication between the living and the dead. Alternatively, if, as some commentators assert, the witch was not capable of raising Samuel, the familiar might serve as a hotline. If the dead can't be retrieved, then the familiar could go to the dead, obtain the message, and then return to communicate the message. Both of these methods would be reasonable powers for a familiar spirit and are, therefore, ways we might interact with a familiar spirit.

Interpreting the "ob" as a necromantic pit through which the Witch raises the spirit of a dead individual provides greater parallels with Greek necromantic practices often associated with goeteia. Greek sorcerers are theorized to have used mourning and funerary practices, sleeping in places of the dead and traveling into underground spaces to connect with the spirits of the dead and sometimes raise them up to speak. Accounts in Greek literature depict the use of pits and offerings to draw the dead and give them the fortitude to move and speak in a manner perceivable by the living. This interpretation doesn't fit our exploration of familiar spirits, but that doesn't mean that Greek magic didn't also have elements that are reminiscent of the familiar spirit.

In Greek magic and religion, spirits, or daimones, exist throughout creation between the world of men and the world of the Gods. Often it was understood that offerings made at a temple or prayers of supplication were received by a spirit who worked in service of the God. The spirit might appear as the God, act on its behalf, and possess some measure of the God's power. When statues were imbued with life to provide oracles from and receive offerings for the Gods or to bestow their blessings and protections, it was these spirits who inhabited them. Humans were also understood to have spirits attached to them. The nature of these spirits and their attachment to humans varied between schools of thought. When we think of the spirits naturally attached to humans, they are more like a Guardian Angel or the divine guide appointed to us. The spirits protect us, reveal to us elements of our nature and character, and they inspire us. In some ways, they might be viewed as a part of us or an extension of us, while in other ways, they are something separate from us that is simultaneously unique to us but also eternal in nature.

In Greek magic, we find spirits attached to humans who are less theurgic in nature than this Platonic idea of the daimon. Exploring the Greek Magical Papyri, which spanned a range of places and were written over several hundred years, we find examples of rituals involving spirit assistants. These spirits might aid in producing visions, providing service, or working with other spirits. Contemporary magicians often associate these rituals for obtaining a spirit assistant with methods for developing a relationship with the Guardian Angel. In some instances, that comparison may make sense, but not always. Part of our association between the spirit assistant and the Guardian Angel may be because we associate the concept of the Platonic Good Spirit, or Agatha Daimon, with the Guardian Angel. "Good Spirit" can appear in various contexts and refer to various things. We have to consider the function of the spirit in the spell and what the results of obtaining the spirit are before we can say it is the same as the Guardian Angel or it is the same as the familiar.

A distinction between the Guardian Angel and the familiar is the acquisition. One does not acquire a Guardian Angel or their Platonic Daimon. Those spirits are present from birth and in some manner before your birth. Rituals to achieve those spirits are about achieving access and communication, not conjuring a spirit and binding it to you or binding it to service. A familiar spirit, like some spirit assistants, is a spirit that you acquire through some pact or agreement. The spirit is presented to you by some other spirit, or you encounter the spirit, and you negotiate a relationship that is mutually beneficial. The familiar spirit, like some forms of the spirit assistant, is in service to you. Your Guardian Angel is a guide who inspires and leads you, whereas the familiar is either a servant or a partner that provides service to you.

The Guardian Angel, or the Platonic Daimon, and the familiar spirit do have some similarities. Both are able to teach and can be called upon to teach magic. Both spirits can aid in spirit communication and networking. Both can provide protection. This gets into where similarities aren't identity. A lot of spirits, in a lot of cultures, do these things. "Tutelary spirits" is a large and encompassing category. We have to consider the nature of the relationship, the focus of the interaction, and how they accomplish what they do when we're evaluating whether or not spirits in different cultures and systems are the same. There are a lot of nuanced elements which express a diversity of spirit relationships. Exploring these gives us a richer world to engage.

When we look at some of the concepts which appear in the mythology and folklore of Northern Europe, Britain, and Ireland, we might see things that share some similarities with some of these concepts. If you asked me to answer off the cuff without thinking about it and without having explored it specifically whether or not Irish or Welsh mythology depicts familiar spirits, I would have said "no, probably not." Faerytales start to get into depictions that we might recognize as familiars, and folklore definitely provides us with both clear depictions of familiar spirits as well as concepts that could be parallel or related. The question is more complicated than a simple yes or no once we broaden our scope.

The concepts we should consider for comparison are household spirits and stories of human and faery interactions, particularly faery lovers and faery captives. Household spirits probably reflect older Pagan practices which survived as examples of faery faith. The relationships with these spirits have some clear parallels to a relationship with a familiar spirit despite not being limited to professional magicians or witches. However, we will also see some differences. Stories of human encounters with faeries are diverse, and we will find some which reveal elements similar to the relationship with familiars. Others might depict mechanisms and relationships which could be built upon to develop the familiar relationship.

We will also look at two other concepts which are often tied together. The fetch and the fylgja are viewed by some modern practitioners as either precursors to the idea of a familiar spirit or as the same concept. I believe these concepts are different from the familiar, but the comparisons can still be revealing. I think the relationship is worth considering, partially because I am open to understanding the other viewpoint, and partially because it is one that you, the reader, may encounter elsewhere. Exploring these concepts in contemporary witchcraft will also provide examples of a phenomenon we discussed earlier: new, interesting, and useful ideas conflated with older folklore concepts.

"Robin Goodfellow" from Fairy Gold by Ernest Rhys, published 1906
Image by Herbert Cole

IX
Faery Faith and Household Spirits

The faery faith is sometimes treated as if it results from more established Pagan religions with large epic or cosmic Gods surviving by becoming something easier to overlook. Rather than larger-than-life figures like Zeus or Odin or the Dagda, we find small gods in the forms of faery kings and queens and a host of spirits in their retinue, replacing the pantheons of old. Instead of large public rituals, folk memory of those rituals and practices shrinks into more easily preserved hearth spirituality focused around the home in the form of folkways. There is some accuracy to this concept, but there is also a serious misconception here. Personal religion, around the world, in a Pagan context, always had these home-based practices.

As we explore evidence about personal and household religion, most scholars understand it as a space of small gods. Ancestors and other spirits of the dead often form the preoccupation for local household religion. Along with the dead, we find house spirits, local spirits, and nature spirits, and then there may be some presence of the Gods. The Gods might be understood in a particularly local form or a more folk-oriented form, or they might reflect the larger community religion. What we can deduce about personal religious practice and what we can see in comparable living practices reflects personalization and adaptation along with a focus on those more immediate spiritual presences.

When we look at the folklore surrounding household spirits and everyday folk interactions with spirits, we may be looking at something close to a survival of household religious practice rather than a miniaturization of larger cultus. With this in mind, a link between house spirits and familiars would be a solid indication of a familiar spirit concept indigenous to Northern Europe, Britain, and Ireland. Whether the concepts share a link or not is the question we have to unpack.

There is a wide range of household spirits throughout Northern Europe, Britain, and Ireland. There are some specific elements associated with particular types, but the specifics may be regional trends and traditions, just as some of the names may be regional variations. As such, we will consider household spirits as a group while still highlighting some specific individual characteristics.

Before we look at what makes household spirits like or unlike familiars, we need to consider what they are. In contemporary parlance, we often take the view that they are faeries. When we think of a brownie, a pixie, Robin Goodfellow, or various other household spirits, we tend to think of them as faeries and look for them in faerytales. They are fairly distinct from the faeries we see in older mythology, in grimoires, in medieval epics, and in the writings of Robert Kirk, Reginald Scot, and other early modern writers. In the bulk of these sources, faeries are powerful magical human-like beings. Household spirits are frequently small and often ugly. They are frequently human-like but hairy; they are often brown or dark-skinned. Contemporary faery enthusiasts might say that elves look one way, but brownies look another way. Elf, however, was once a general term for faeries rather than a particular sort.

Historical views and categories of magical beings were often different from those we have now, but they weren't always consistent. Depending upon the time or place, and sometimes even the writer, we might find different ways of understanding these beings. In a significant portion of history, spirits were immaterial, while other magical or supernatural beings were viewed to have bodies. Paracelsus, in his text on elementals, <u>A Book on Nymphs, Sylphs, Pygmies, and Salamanders, and on the Other Spirits</u>, spends a significant amount of time explaining the nature of the bodies of these beings. We often think of these elementals as a particular class of spirits, but for Paracelsus, they were not spirits, and these names represented categories that contained a broad range of beings found in folklore. If we look at <u>The Isagoge</u>, we see that angels were spirits in that they were fully subtle in their nature, whereas fallen spirits took on bodies of denser air as they descended towards the earth and became demons. These beings were still spirits, but it illustrates the idea that a spirit is ephemeral while other magical beings might be bodily.

Faeries and ghosts were once viewed as material beings. Much European folklore around resolving issues with the dead focuses on revenant corpses and keeping the dead in their graves. Household spirits would largely fall within Paracelsus's class of gnomes or pygmies and would have been viewed as material beings, although today, we would generally view them as immaterial spirits. Several legends talk about the way their skin felt if they allowed humans to touch them, suggesting some corporeal nature. Having bodies doesn't necessarily separate them from faeries, though, as faeries were also sometimes viewed as bodily.

Some authors, including Walter Scott, did distinguish household spirits from faeries. However, the distinction isn't consistent. Authors who dismissed folk beliefs often lumped ghosts, household spirits, and faeries together as a single phenomenon. There are common features of household spirits that seem to separate them from other spirits we would consider faeries. Most obviously, household spirits live with humans, whereas most faeries live in separate or remote spaces or in faeryland. Many faeries exist in faery communities, but household spirits are solitary and will reside individually in a human home or in a nearby natural formation. Faeries are often understood as generally dangerous, whereas household spirits are generally beneficial and desirable as long as they are not offended.

There are also elements that household spirits have in common with the imps given to witches. These imps can be understood as faery creatures and are often received from the faeries, although we will discuss that comparison at length in another chapter. Both imps and household spirits can provide wealth, luck, and protection. Shape-shifting and invisibility are powers shared by both types of being. Imps and household spirits are both known to steal grain and wealth from neighbors, and both have the power to maim livestock and damage property. Either type of creature can do chores and assist with household work, or they can undo that work by doing things like spoiling milk or preventing butter from forming.

Most people today would consider brownies, hobs, and the host of household spirits as members of the fair folk. Names like "Hob" and "Robin Goodfellow" might even follow the convention of calling faeries something pleasant to avoid thinking of them as frightening or displeasing them with a less friendly appellation. Even if some early folklorists distinguished household spirits from faeries, it would be harder to determine whether the common people who dealt with them viewed them as distinct. For our purposes, it is interesting to consider the differences between material magical beings and spirits or between faeries and other supernatural spirits that reside alongside us. Despite the interesting exploration, the potential taxonomical differences don't change a lot for us in a practical sense. The real question, whether or not household spirits are an example of the familiar spirit relationship, is more dependent upon interactions than what the spirits are.

Kobolds, hobs, brownies, nisser, tontut, and Robin Goodfellows were amongst the types of domestic spirits we considered. These spirits share many of the same features. Evidence suggests many traditions and beliefs around them either stem from a single source or are informed by each other. From a perspective in which we believe in spirits, we could interpret that as meaning these spirits are similar or the same, and that is why the beliefs about them seem to be shared cross-culturally.

These domestic spirits work nocturnally. They do household chores, chase away pests, and complete work that wasn't done before the end of the day. Some of these spirits could provide warnings about future events, particularly kobolds. These spirits can provide gifts, including wealth and good luck, although some of these gifts may be stolen from neighbors. This is not unlike the mechanism for achieving wealth, a good harvest, or strong beer described in witchcraft trials. In the case of Scandinavian spirits like nisser and tontut, there were points where achieving unusual prosperity could cause accusations of witchcraft and consorting with these spirits.

Like familiar spirits, these services had a transactional element to them, but one which existed as an ongoing relationship. Household spirits were not called for a particular task. In fact, trying to command or force them to do things might cause problems. These spirits resided with the family or in the home or business and continually provided their aid so long as the humans provided hospitality. These spirits expected gifts of food and drink regularly. They were also concerned with good behavior and would punish humans for laziness or immorality. Giving clothes to brownies, hobs, and other spirits from Ireland and Britain could cause them to leave, as could behaviors that they felt were offensive or inhospitable. If the relationship dissolved because the spirit was angered or not cared for properly, it might simply leave. Problems could escalate, though. The spirit might take away the luck and good fortune it provided, or it might curse the home or members of the family or even kill them.

The autonomy of these spirits is one element that clearly distinguishes them from familiars. A familiar can't just come and go as it desires, whereas these spirits can. A possible explanation of the prohibition against giving these spirits human clothes could be that it would indicate subjugation to human mores and behaviors and therefore being a servant of the human household. If that is why clothes are problematic, it would clearly separate this spirit relationship from the one held by familiars.

It would also be unusual for a familiar to kill the magician. Familiars are often understood to depart when the magician passes away. Some stories include more sensational elements in which the familiar receives the magician's soul upon his death. The reality isn't so hair-raising. Stories of kobolds cutting people apart and eating or making soup from them are possibly also a bit sensational, but a spirit taking away your luck or causing sickness or even death is very possible. It is not, however, something one would expect if a relationship with a familiar spirit did not work out. Even the idea of punishing you or your family for laziness, not treating your animals or farm or human servants well enough, or for excessive swearing is outside the realm of behavior for a familiar spirit. A familiar spirit might help provide guidance or direction if some behavior is harming you. Still, it's not there to chastise you or reshape you into its idea of a model citizen.

Domestic spirits will leave on their own if offended, and certain types will leave and refuse to return if offered clothes, but some are hard to remove if you choose to do so. Familiar spirits can be released from the pact and exorcised and banished. However, this might not work as well with household spirits. There is a story of a kobold tearing up a priest's prayer book during an exorcism and engaging in further mischief. Removing these spirits through religious and magical rituals seems to be possible in some folklore but difficult and inconsistently successful.

Like familiars, these spirits are not limited to the home. Some such spirits may choose to move with a family. Others prefer to reside with humans in workspaces rather than in homes. In such cases, the spirits provide services related to those workspaces. Ships and mines are common places associated with these spirits, but restaurants, breweries, and other areas of employment have been known to have them as well. Unlike a familiar spirit, these spirits keep their interaction and service to humans confined to the business of these shared spaces. In contrast, a familiar may be able to help with a large variety of requests.

Familiars are obtained through acts the magician enters into. Folklore varies as to how relationships with domestic spirits begin. Some folk beliefs include the idea that all homes have one of these spirits. Some believe that the spirits are the human souls of the original owner of the place or a servant or child who was killed there. In other cases, the spirit might simply choose to enter and reside there. There are also instances in which humans have some choice in the matter. For example, Robin Goodfellows are described as coming when humans speak and can be called to with joyful songs, laughter, and gestures of merriment, along with special signs. A kobold might be discovered in animal form in the wilderness and take human shape in response to an incantation spoken by the human who encounters it. When this happens, if the kobold goes with the human, it will reside in the home so long as the human provides hospitality. Other stories include kobolds making a mess to announce their arrival, and if the human accepts the mess, the kobold will join the household, but if the human cleans it up, the kobold will leave.

Not necessarily a domestic spirit, but Edwin Sidney Hartland recounts a story in his English Fairy and Other Folk Tales, which describes catching a faery and receiving service from it. A man was outside harvesting gorse and found a small man stretched out asleep on the griglan, or heath. He quietly scooped the sleeping man into his cuff, took him home, and set him upon the hearth. The faery man was pleased with the warm hearth spot and felt at home. He played with the children who called him Bobby Griglans. Bobby agreed to show the man where the faeries had their gold buried in the hills. A few days later, horsemen came to haul away the gorse, and while they were at dinner, the man locked his children with Bobby in the barn to keep him out of sight and away from curious neighbors. Bobby and the children decided to sneak out to dance around the brush. When they did so, they saw a small faery man and woman crying and searching for their son, Skillywidden. Bobby asked the children to wait behind the barn and explained that it was his mother and father looking for him. They complied, and as soon as he called out to his mother, the three faeries disappeared.

The method of quietly catching a sleeping faery might also seem as if it would apply to these domestic spirits. They often make their home upon the hearth. Setting personal spaces for them and a warm spot at the hearth for them to receive their offerings is an important part of keeping these spirits happy. Capturing them in such a way could be disastrous. There was a story of a famous kobold who allowed a man to think he had captured him in an empty jug only so he could chastise the man. He explained that the man was too stupid to need real punishment, otherwise, he would leave him harmed in such a way he'd never forget. These spirits aren't inclined to have humans trap them, force them to be seen, or coerce favors from them, and thus may not even be appropriate spirits to pursue as familiars. The relationship with them as local spirits who can bring blessings to your home and family when given hospitality and good treatment may be a worthwhile relationship to pursue, but it is one that is firmly different from the relationship with a familiar spirit.

While these particular spirits probably don't make good familiars based on their behavior in folk stories, they clearly form part of the worldview in which familiars exist. As we will see when we discuss imps and puckrils, early modern authors sometimes associated the familiar with the hobgoblin and other spirits common to stories of household spirits. We can see relationship elements that are similar to the relationships with a familiar, even if the common relationship with these domestic spirits is not the same as the relationship a witch or sorcerer would have with their familiar.

Lamia and the Soldier
John William Waterhouse, 1905

X
Faery Lovers in Myths and Folklore

In 2002 Walter Stephens released an academic exploration of witchcraft and witch hysteria titled <u>Demon Lovers: Witchcraft Sex and the Crisis of Belief</u>, in which he explained the medieval conception of the witch. His explanation of the power of witches is rooted in the idea that the witch does not have power but can exercise the power of a demon bound to the witch. The demon remains with the witch and offers assistance because the witch provides blood to feed the demon and sex to please the demon. This is, of course, describing the relationship with a familiar spirit. In considering faeries in more Pagan and folklore-driven contexts, rather than in the context of magical grimoires, we might consider stories of faery lovers as a space for comparison. The exploration of faery lovers as a prototype for the demon lover is apt since many witchcraft accounts focus on faeries.

Tales of trysts, elopements, and obsessions with faery lovers seem to exist from the earliest faery stories up through the most recent. When I say faery story, I am speaking of something distinct from the "fairytale" or the more contemporary post-Victorian era children's stories of fairies. Faery stories might include tales of old gods treated as faeries and mythology, which sets the stage for such stories. Other faery stories might include accounts told amongst locals of faery adventures they or some member of their community had. Many are cautionary tales or supernatural tales that explain things that seem to happen in life or warn us about supernatural encounters. Each of these types of stories might share common elements with the other types, but there will also be differences. These differences might reflect the story's purpose, or they might reflect changes in attitudes or ideas of those originating the story.

As we explore these different types of stories, we want to consider features to look for in comparison to the concept of the familiar. The relationship between the magician and the familiar is contractual; both parties agree to it. The magician provides care or support through sustenance, sex, and possibly a place to reside. The spirit provides protection, magical assistance, and magical instruction and cultivates things for the benefit of the magician. The spirit is bound to the relationship and can not simply leave, and the spirit is not typically hostile towards the human or inclined to harm or kill the human.

Initially, we will explore stories that clearly fall within the realm of mythology. These are older stories and are told as epic tales of the past. Then we will move towards stories with more of an air of folklore. Some of these will incorporate characters of mythology but are told as stories from the memory of the people rather than tales recorded by medieval scribes. Other folklore accounts will seem contemporary to the writers, and some will even seem like stories told by people familiar with the people and places of the stories. I do not expect the reader to know all of the referenced stories, so this chapter will present several myths, legends, folk motifs, and folktales at length. After each story, a few paragraphs will summarize and analyze how they might indicate a cultural awareness that could indicate or build towards the concept of the familiar spirit.

The Birth of CuChulainn

Love affairs between gods and humans and the production of specially gifted children from such liaisons are not uncommon mythological motifs. Aeneas, who fled Troy and settled in Italy, his descendants eventually becoming Romans, was a son of Venus. Romulus and Remus, who built the city of Rome and established its initial laws and dynasties, were sons of Mars. Alexander the Great, one of the greatest conquerors of the ancient world, was a son of Zeus. Mediterranean history, folklore, and mythology are full of demigods. In later folklore, the Nereids, or river goddesses, became faeries and retained this connection to demigods like Alexander and Achilles. Elsewhere in Europe, we find kings tracing their lineage to Gods as a justification for their kingship. Heroes, giants, and witches are all born of divine and human couplings. This concept is not limited to Celtic faery lore or mythology, but it continues to thrive there, remaining a part of faery experiences reported even to the present day.

In Irish mythology, we find the hero CuChulainn, the Hound of Ulster. His mother was Deichtire, the sister of King Conchobar. She was pledged to wed Sualtim, but as often seems to be the case for newly or soon-to-be-wed noblewomen, she caught the eye of a man of the sidhe. Deichtire was drinking wine while preparing for the wedding. Lugh, one of the Tuatha De Danaan, or the pantheon of gods of Ireland who later became associated with the sidhe and the heroic faeries of medieval epics, took the form of a mayfly and was swallowed by Deichtire. She and her attendant ladies fell into a deep sleep, and Lugh approached her in her dream. He explained that he was the mayfly she had swallowed, and now she and the women must come with him. They became birds and flew away to the lands of the sidhe. Conchobar, Sualtim, and the men of the kingdom searched to no avail. After a year and a day, a flock of birds appeared and devoured everything. Conchobar offered a reward for anyone who could catch them. Fergus, the former king and Conchobar's stepfather, found them and discovered a beautiful hall with rich hospitality and beautiful women. He ran to tell Conchobar, who came straight away with his men. They enjoyed the hospitality of the hall and went to sleep, but in the night heard wailing. Conchobar and his men roused and found that it was the screaming of a woman in childbirth. In the morning, they discovered it was his sister Deichtire; she had given birth to Setanta, who would grow up to be CuChulainn.

This story has many typical features of mythology in which a heroic or divine faery figure takes a noble as a lover. Swallowing a mayfly, turning into birds to flee, a magical time period such as a year and a day, and a journey to faeryland are all common. In this case, we don't see any particular agreement between the parties or negotiation, and nothing is exchanged between them. The human isn't harmed but also doesn't receive special gifts, blessings, or favors from the encounter. Instead, her child becomes a great and powerful warrior and a famed hero. This story has several variants and feels more like the mythological stories we find explaining the origins of heroes than it does a story of faery lovers, but it still has many of the features we find in the faery lover stories. We will see the swallowing of a faery fly again. In one Scottish witch trial account, a spirit blows into a woman's mouth, and then a faery familiar emerges from her mouth. This story does not particularly describe a familiar relationship but presents a world where the mechanisms for these spirit interactions exist.

The Voyage of Bran

Another mythological story is the "Voyage of Bran." One night Bran MacFebal was walking along and heard the sweet strains of faery music. The music haunted him, coming from somewhere behind him as he walked, emanating from a source he was unable to perceive. It was so sweet that it eventually lulled him to sleep. Once he awoke, he found a silver branch with delicate white blossoms in his hand. He carried it back to his hall, where he and his men discovered a beautiful woman. They did not know where she came from, and she began to sing a poem to Bran and his men. Her poem described a magical land full of joy and without strife. When she finished, the branch leapt from Bran's hand and returned to hers, and then she vanished. The next day Bran formed a party of 27 men, including himself, and they boarded ships and sailed for two days and two nights. They encountered Manannan, who prophesied to them before they went on to the island of women. Each man had a bed and a woman, and they passed there in joy and happiness, wanting for nothing for a year. Eventually, homesickness struck one of them. The women warned them not to return to Ireland and, if they did, not to touch the land. So they sailed back, and the men on the shore said they knew of an ancient story of Bran MacFebal, but no man by that name was alive in Ireland. One of the company rushed from his boat, and as soon as he touched the shore, his age reached him, and he turned to dust. Bran and his company then set off to sail towards unknown adventures.

Again, this story presents us with many common features. The sleeping strain of music, a visitor of unknown provenance in strange clothes, and a magical branch. These are frequent elements of stories in which someone is called to the house of Manannan Mac Lir. Crossing the sea appears in stories of visiting Manannan and of tales of visiting the land of faery. The branch in the story was an apple branch, and apples appear in some stories as gifts to access the brughs of the sidhe. An idyllic life with one's faery lover, being unaware of time passing, and time behaving differently in faery and in the world of men are common to faery stories. The inability to return home as normal, or in this case, to return home at all, is a very common element. As we will see in later stories, humans who went away to faery return different and sometimes can't reacclimate to society. In this older story, the stakes are higher. So much time has passed that Bran and his men are an ancient story when they return home. The magic which allowed them to survive in faery is stripped away when returning home, and their bodies decay to the dust that they would have become had they not been away in the faery islands.

The Lay of Volund

The Poetic Edda contains the story of Volund, who appears throughout Northern European myths in the various forms of Weyland the Smith. In the Edda, he and his brothers build a home in

Ulfdalir, where one morning, they find three Valkyries who are described as swan maidens. They take the swan maidens as brides and live with them for seven years before the Valkyries fly off to find battles. Volund's two brothers pursue their wives while Volund remains in Ulfdalir. Volund made seven hundred rings in the form of a ring that had belonged to his wife and hung them in their home to wait for her return. He was famous for his skill as a smith. When King Nithuth realized Volund was alone and vulnerable, he had him kidnapped and hamstrung so he couldn't run away. Nithuth's men first took one of the rings, which Volund noticed was missing before he fell asleep. He hoped his wife had returned for it, but upon waking, he found himself in chains in Nithuth's custody. Nithuth accused Volund of taking Swedish treasure to Ulfdalir, took Volund's sword for himself, and gave his daughter Bothvild the ring that belonged to Volund's wife. Volund was sent to an island to work as Nithuth's smith, and everyone but Nithuth was afraid to approach him because they knew he was the greatest of the elves. Volund's anger grew seeing his sword on Nithuth's belt and knowing Bothvild had his wife's ring.

Eventually, Nithuth's two sons grew brave enough to sneak along and watch Volund work. He saw them greedily desiring the treasures he held. So, Volund told them to come back the next morning but to tell no one at all and that he would give them gold. Volund cut off their heads, made silver treasures from them, and made beautiful gems from their eyes. He sent these to Nithuth and his wife. He made Bothvild a broach from their teeth. Bothvild came to Volund and told him how she broke the gold ring. He promised to mend it, better than it was before. Volund then took Bothvild as a lover, and she fell fast asleep. Volund rejoiced that he had his vengeance in all manners, save the cutting of his sinews, and he flew off. Bothvild was frightened that Volund flew and that he left her to her father's wrath.

Volund returned to Nithuth's court, and Nithuth demanded to know what happened to his sons. Volund declared that he had a wife who would be known to all of them and a child who would be born in Nithuth's court and compelled an oath from Nithuth and all his men that his wife and child would come to no harm. After extracting the oath, Volund revealed how he had slain the boys and taken Bothvild as a lover. Nithuth admitted how deeply this hurt him and bemoaned that no one could attack Volund because he could fly so high. Volund laughed and flew away.

This story could easily have fallen in with stories of captives rather than stories of lovers. Most of the story is one of captivity. It has a lot of elements that relate to the faery lover motif. While Volund is an elf, initially, it is his bride and her sisters who are magical in nature. Volund and his brothers are the sons of the King of the Finns, and they discover swan maidens to take as brides, which itself is a common motif. We have a magical period of time, seven years, and then as in most swan maiden stories, the women leave, and the men are left to pine for them.

This pining leaves Volund alone and vulnerable. As a result, Nithuth steals his faery treasure and captures him. In later stories, we will see how pining for a faery lover plays into the tales of wasting away or being consumed until death. Obsession and wasting are variants of the idea of giving one's life or having it taken by the faery lover. In Volund's case, his freedom and treasure are taken because of his pining. The setup is somewhat different, possibly because it's an older story and because Volund is an elf, but it is within the space of that theme. In stories of familiars, the witch does not waste away but feeds their life, in the form of blood, to the familiar. An entire range of this concept exists through these stories. The lover pines until life is disrupted, the lover pines or is obsessed until sickness or death take hold, the lover is physically consumed, or the witch physically feeds their demon lover from themself. The relationship between the human and the spirit, creating a dynamic exchange of love and life, exists as a continuum, even going back through the oldest stories.

While captured, he is pressed into service for the king, who binds him from escaping. Finally, the breaking of a convention frees him; the princes and Bothvild venture to Volund's island when no one but Nithuth would go there. This access to them gives him his vengeance, and he can leave. While on the surface, their presence allows him to take revenge, we can also interpret this as Nithuth's hold on him being eliminated because a restriction was violated. In many stories, faeries prohibit others from watching them work. They control who can see them. Violating these proscriptions allows them to leave. It can also be a transgression that results in being maimed or killed. Killing the boys and impregnating Bothvild allows him to feel satisfied, but their encroachment on his space may have also unbound him.

Volund leaves Bothvild pregnant. A woman having a faery child abandoned by the faery man who impregnated her is also common. Volund trades knowledge to secure an oath of protection for his wife and child. Again, a trade or some agreement that either begins or ends the interaction is a common element of such stories. In this case, it is simply misery that Nithuth receives because he had acted so wrongly in the beginning.

Nithuth gained many treasurers from Volund's work but ultimately received tragedy. Bothvild is taken as a lover and is given a child. She receives the broach and possibly the ring that belonged to Volund's wife. She is left with the fear of being unwelcome in her family and in her court and of danger to her child, such that she claims that she was forced by Volund, although that does not seem clear from the account of her visit to him. This seems not dissimilar from the inability of a faery's lover to return to their human community or the tendency for people to believe they have lost their minds or made up their story. Here, Bothvild is believed, but she has to craft an explanation to mitigate how her affair with the elf would put her at risk and possibly ostracize her.

The Wooing of Etain

Before we look at stories that seem to bridge the space of myth and faery story, our final mythological story is "The Wooing of Etain." This is a famous story of Irish myth, which may date from as early as the 8th century. It may be the source of inspiration for a later medieval faery lover story, "Sir Orfeo," which recasts the story of Orpheus and Eurydice in a faery lover context. Like the story of Deichtire, it connects to the tales of the Ulster Cycle and the stories associated with kings who were believed to be historical kings while being firmly rooted in a mythological context.

There is a significant amount of material in the tale before the introduction of Etain. First, we see The Dagda use magic to keep Elcmar busy so that he could sleep with Elcmar's wife Boand, and she could give birth to Angus MacOc. We see Angus fostered by Midir and then introduced to his father, The Dagda. Finally, the story includes The Dagda counseling Angus on how to trick Elcmar out of his possession of Bru Na Boinne so that it can become Angus's palace and lands. This all sets up for Midir to visit Angus at Samain and become injured while intervening with arguing youths on Angus's behalf. As a result, Angus gets Dian Cecht, the doctor of the Tuatha de Danaan, to heal Midir and asks Midir to remain as his guest. Midir asks for three boons in exchange for staying with Angus, the last of which is the most beautiful woman in Ireland, Etain, the daughter of Aillil.

The MacOc goes to King Aillil, who refuses to give over Etain because Angus is so powerful, his family is so noble, and Angus's father is even more powerful, such that Aillil has no measure of recourse should Angus wrong him or Etain. This is a pretense for Aillil to ask Angus to perform challenges as boons for him to pay for Etain. First, Aillil asks for twelve fields to be cleared to be available for grazing cattle, games, and strongholds. Angus goes to his father, who, by magic, clears the fields overnight. Next, Angus goes to collect Etain, and Aillil demands further payment; twelve waterways must now be established. Angus again goes to The Dagda who accomplishes it for him. When Angus goes to claim Etain, Aillil again demands a further price, this time claiming that the previous tasks benefit the people of the land and Etain's kinsfolk but were not directly for Aillil. Finally, he demands that Angus give him Etain's weight in gold and silver, which he will retain as the portion of the price that profits him. Angus provides the payment and takes Etain.

After a year, Midir and Etain left Bru na Boinne and returned to Midir's lands. As he left, Angus warned him to be watchful of Fuamnach, Midir's wife. Fuamnach had been fostered with the Tuatha de Danaan wizard Bresal and had all the cunning and skill possessed by their people. When Midir and Etain arrived, Fuamnach took them on a circuit of Midir's lands, as was the custom, and welcomed them hospitably. When they came into the bedroom, Fuamnach offered her seat to Etain, and when she took it, Fuamnach struck Etain with a wand and turned her into a pool of water. Fuamnach returned to Bresal, and Midir was left alone and wifeless. He left his lands, leaving Etain as a pool of water in his house. Heat caused the pool of water to become a worm, which eventually grew into the most beautiful and sweet-smelling purple fly.

The sight of her would nourish men, and the dew of her wings cured all sickness. She found Midir and accompanied him in his travels. This brought him happiness, for he knew it was Etain, so he took no new wife. She would hum by him as he slept and warn him of danger. One day Fuamnach visited Midir, with The Dagda, Lugh, and Ogma accompanying her as her protection. Midir announced that were it not for them, he would slay her for what she had done. Fuamnach explained that she was only concerned with her own well-being and therefore was not sorry; she would continue to harm Etain in any form she took in any part of Ireland where she encountered her. With that pronouncement, Fuamnach cast a spell and raised a wind that drove Etain far from Midir. Fuamnach knew the fly was

Etain, and she knew that the fly alone brought Midir happiness. Midir would pine away without the fly, taking no joy in music, food, drinking, or women with Etain gone. The wind cast Etain out such that for seven years, she floated about Ireland, unable to find a place to settle.

After seven years, she landed upon the MacOc, and he recognized and welcomed her, taking her in and protecting her. From then on, he took her with him where ever he went. He would sleep beside her and comfort her until she returned to health and happiness. Hearing of this, Fuamnach called upon Midir to send word that she wanted peace and would submit herself as Etain's guest. She snuck through a circuitous route to Bru na Boinne and entered Angus's chambers, where she again cast her spell. Etain was flung forth on winds of misery and sorrow for seven years until she fell in a golden cup in Ulster and was drunk by the wife of Etar. Swallowed by Etar's wife, she became a child in her womb and was reborn again as Etain, now Etain, daughter of Etar, one thousand and twelve years after she had been conceived Etain, daughter of Aillil.

Etain was set above the other young girls, and fifty maidens were set to attend her. One day as the maidens were out, a man, seemingly of the faery or of the Tuatha de Danaan, approached. He was beautiful and on horseback. The horse's mane and tail were curly, and it pranced as it approached. The man had golden blond hair, restrained from his forehead, with a headband made of gold. His cloak was green, and his tunic was red and embroidered. He had a shield of silver, trimmed with gold, and its band, which held it to him, was silver trimmed with gold. His broach was gold and reached from one shoulder to the other. His spear had five heads and was gilded. As he approached, he pronounced a prophecy, first describing Etain's history and then describing what would happen to the king as a result of Etain's presence. The things he foretold included the destruction of elf mounds, but also, the king chasing birds and drowning his two steeds, and a great deal of war. Then the man disappeared, and the women did not know who he was or from where he had come.

While this happened, Angus went to Midir, and they determined that Fuamnach had tricked them and likely would continue to hurt Etain. Angus found her with Bresal and cut off her head, taking it back with him to Bru na Boinne. At that time, Eochaid became the High King of Ireland and needed a wife before the other kings would convene the festival at Tara for him. Eochaid declared that he must have a virgin bride, who was the most beautiful in

Ireland. He searched the kingdoms and eventually came upon Etain, daughter of Etar, who was well-suited in beauty and lineage. He married her, and the festival was convened. At the festival, Eochaid's brother Aillil fell in love with Etain and concealed it so he would not shame himself or Etain. Unfortunately, his love led him to pine away with a wasting sickness, and it was thought he would die. Eochaid went on his circuit of Ireland to receive tribute and left Aillil in Etain's care. Etain noticed that as she visited Aillil, he would gaze longingly at her, and it seemed to make him well. Finally, she asked what the cause of his sickness was, and he revealed it. Etain chided him for not telling her sooner. She continued to visit him and care for him, and after twenty-seven days, he was well. At this point, he asked when he would finally have her so that he would be fully healed, and she agreed to meet him the next day.

Three times Etain went to the place appointed to meet Aillil for their tryst, but each time a man who appeared like him arrived. Aillil fell asleep each time and was left in sorrow that he did not meet Etain. Finally, on the third time, Etain explained that she was not meeting Aillil for sin or desire but because he was an honorable man who needed to be saved. She demanded to know who it was that had met with her. The man reveals himself to be Midir and explains their history together. He tells Etain that he made Aillil love her and put the wasting sickness in him, and took away his passion so that he would fall asleep. He tells Etain it would be better if she returned with him, but she refuses, not knowing who he is or what people he hails from. He suggests that she might come with him if Eochaid grants permission, and she agrees she would do that. Etain returned and found Aillil well, and shortly thereafter, Eochaid returned from his circuit.

Sometime later in the summer, a rider approached. He was bedecked in the finery of the Tuatha de Danaan. Eochaid was alarmed and welcomed the rider but noted that he did not know who he was. The rider introduced himself as Midir and challenged Eochaid to play chess. Eochaid agreed, but only if there were stakes involved. First, Midir offered up fifty faery horses, which Eochaid won. The next day Midir returned, and they played again; this time, Midir offered wild boars, gilded swords, faery cows, and several other wondrous things. Eochaid won, and when his foster father questioned him over where he was getting this wealth, Eochaid explained. His foster father suggested that Eochaid be careful, for he was playing with a man of magic, but that he should require tasks of him. Eochaid set four tasks for Midir, clearing stones, making a causeway, placing rushes, and setting woods. Midir accomplished the tasks but asked Eochaid to keep everyone indoors.

Eochaid set a steward to watch Midir's work. The next day when it was complete, the steward was explaining to Eochaid what he had seen, and Midir approached angrily. Midir contested Eochaid setting such difficult tasks upon him, and Eochaid apologized and offered another chess game. Midir agreed, but this time said the stakes would be whatever either asked of the other. Having honored his previous losses and then done laborious wonders for Eochaid, Midir was in a position to compel Eochaid to honor their wager, and so he won this game and asked to hold Etain in his arms and have a kiss from her. Eochaid was troubled but had to agree. He asked for Midir to return in a month's time to collect. The delay was so Eochaid could gather all the fighting men of Ireland from the five kingdoms to defend against Midir. After a month, Midir approached gracefully and demanded what was due to him. He acknowledged he had been courting Etain for a year and that she agreed if Eochaid gave her to him, she would go with Midir. Eochaid insisted he would not but granted that Midir could put his arms around her as agreed in the middle of the court. Midir did, and the two of them flew up through the skylight, to everyone's astonishment. Then they became swans and flew off to the sidhe.

Eochaid took all the armies of Ireland and declared they would destroy every sidhe fort and brugh until Etain was returned. Eochaid attacked a sidhe mound. Eventually, one of its people came out and declared Etain was not there but that their king had her in his fortress. They went to another mound and dug into it for a year and three months, but each night their work was undone. Faery animals, white ravens, and white hounds came out from the mound, so the men returned to the previous mound to dig again. The men of the mound came out and warned him that this was unfit for a king since they had done nothing to him. He refused to leave until they explained how he could be successful. They told him to leave two blind dogs and two blind cats each day. Eochaid took their instructions and attacked Midir's fortress at Bri Leith.

As they laid siege to the faery mound, Midir came out to meet them. He again criticized Eochaid's treatment of him but then agreed to give over Etain on the condition that Eochaid would not bother him again if he was content with what he was given. The next day Midir brought forth fifty women from the faery mound, each appearing as Etain, and commanded that Eochaid either select her or select another woman from amongst them to be his. Eochaid set a table and had the women each take a turn serving a drink, as Etain had more skill in serving drinks than any other woman. It came down to the last two, and Etain had not been found when finally, one of them served him, and Eochaid declared that it was her, but yet, not her. He took her home, and the men of Ireland rejoiced.

Sometime later, Eochaid and Etain were conversing in the court, and Midir approached. Again, he confronted Eochaid as to how unfairly he had treated him and the hardships he had placed upon him. Eochaid insisted that he never sold Etain to Midir. However, he agreed that he was content with things. Eochaid, having confirmed his contentment, was therefore committed to offer no harm or hassle to Midir, so Midir revealed how he had tricked Eochaid. Etain was pregnant with Eochaid's child when Midir took her. The child grew up in faery and appeared as Etain amongst the fifty women Midir presented. Eochaid had been living with his own daughter, believing she was his wife, and she was now pregnant with Eochaid's child. Midir confirmed that Etain had remained with him the whole time, and Eochaid's agreement to take his own daughter released Etain to Midir.

Eochaid was grieved and disgusted, both that his wife had left him to wed Midir and that he was about to have a child with his own daughter. He ordered that the baby be sent away, and it was cast into a kennel of dogs to be eaten. The couple owning the dogs returned home and found the splendid baby, and raised her as their own. Having come from kingly stock, she excelled beyond other women. Eochaid was eventually killed by Sigmall, the grandson of Midir.

This story is immense. It has so many elements and so many little substories that all feed into the main story. The Tain is spoken of as the Irish Iliad, but this story involves the king of Ireland calling all the kings who are sworn to him to wage war to rescue the most beautiful woman of the generation, his wife, who has been stolen by another king. Its summary is essentially a summary of the story of Helen of Troy. It has many elements which seem to echo other mythological traditions, which will be more familiar to the average Anglophone reader. More importantly, for us, it has several elements which are echoed in faery stories.

Midir's consistent request for trades and games, often coupled with tricks, is very reminiscent of the common image of a faery figure. Midir claims to be wronged by people not keeping agreements they don't believe they made or by actions they didn't take. His reproach of Angus and of Eochaid for the harm he has suffered due to them feels familiar when one considers criticism levied by faeries in many stories. Angus is also guided by his father in using wordplay and trickery to obtain lands for himself.

We see magical trials set to obtain a woman who is kept away from her suitor. First, Angus is given a series of three things he must provide to Etain's father before he can take her. As is often the case in faery stories, the hero says he can perform the impossible tasks laid before him and then receives magical aid from some supporter to accomplish them. We later see Midir also given tasks to perform before he is positioned to even ask for Etain. There is some similarity in the tasks as well, but in this case, Midir, a magical king in his own right, is able to perform them. Midir also explains to the reborn Etain that he won her previously by performing such tasks as if he had performed the ones given to Angus.

Shape-shifting occurs in multiple instances. Etain becomes a fly. As we mentioned in the case of Lugh and Deichtire, becoming pregnant by swallowing a being who has become a fly is a common motif. Midir and Etain become swans. Like Volund, Midir flies off from the court, unable to be stopped by the gathered army of men. As we saw with Deichtire, and as we will see commonly in many stories, our lovers become birds. Swans, in particular, are common. The faery carrying off his lover in flight foreshadows stories of spirit flight, especially when we consider it in relation to stories of faeries taking the spirits of their lovers to faeryland instead of their bodies.

When Midir approaches Etain after her marriage to Eochaid, he does so in a form mimicking her brother-in-law Aillil. Etain's daughter is also presumably affected by some kind of shape-shifting or glamour in order to make her indistinguishable from Etain. When the daughter, who grew up in the sidhe, is traded to Eochaid without his knowledge that she is not his wife, we are reminded of changeling stories.

Magical time periods come into play several times here. Samain is itself a magical time and is the time at which Angus obtains Bru na Boinne. Angus passes a year at Bru na Boinne and seems not to leave it during that time. Midir and Etain pass a year at Bru na Boinne prior to heading to Sidhe Bri Leith. Etain travels as a fly lost on the wind for seven years before landing with Angus and then a second seven years before landing in the cup of the wife of Etar. These time periods are all ones that commonly occur for such magical and otherworldly interactions. Like many such interactions, time in the mortal world may have passed differently. 15 years are accounted for between the time Angus purchases Etain until she lands in the cup of the wife of Etar, but the tale tells us one thousand twelve years have passed. Later in the story, Etain has time to give birth to her child and for her child to grow up in the sidhe, while for Eochaid we might assume only two to three years have passed, if even that much time.

Interestingly, instead of Etain wasting away pining for Midir, he instead wastes away pining for her. In her form as a fly, her presence nourishes him, but when Fuamnach casts her away, Midir loses all enjoyment and benefit of things that would sustain him. We see the faery wasting sickness again with Aillil. He falls in love with Etain and, unable to have her, begins to waste away unto his death. At this point, arguably, Etain straddles the line between a faery and a human woman, but regardless, it is Midir's magic that causes this. As we discussed with the "Lay of Volund," such wasting away and dissatisfaction will come into play both in accounts of faery lovers and in the lore surrounding the danger they bring.

Fuamnach even seems like the prototype for the evil enchantress. She is almost the opposite of the evil stepmother, as she is the woman who is replaced, rather than the new and evil wife. She is jealous of Etain, and it is a jealousy that might have some merit. Still, Fuamnach seems committed to harming Etain until her own death and will use magic and trickery to do so. She does not even attempt to reclaim Midir or his lands for herself but returns to the foster father who taught her magic and then came back to further agitate the situation.

There is a prophecy, although Midir utters the prophecy and causes its events. Among those events is the war upon the faery mounds waged by Eochaid. This trend occurs elsewhere. Eochaid's conflict with Midir serves him poorly, as he is warned it will by the men of the sidhe. We might consider that Eochaid is the victim in the faery lover story here. Etain is a magical being - she was a person living in faery, shape-shifted by magic into a puddle which became a fly, and she was reborn by being swallowed. We have already noted that, although caused by Midir's magic, a man took to wasting sickness in her thrall. Eochaid's marriage to Etain binds him to business with Midir of the sidhe. Midir redresses Eochaid for poor treatment in their business with one another but never notes that Eochaid broke his agreement to have everyone remain indoors and away from Midir's work as he performed the tasks Eochaid set. In this instance, we see

Eochaid clearly breaking his agreement with the faery king, but whether he has met his agreements or not in other instances is also in question. He didn't offer anything in exchange for the tasks he requested of Midir. He tried to avoid fulfilling the debt of his wager with Midir. In the end, Eochaid loses his wife, and believes he is happy with her, only to discover he has been tricked into marrying and impregnating his own daughter. He gives up his child-grandchild and retires in grief, only to be murdered. Ruin and death come to Eochaid, and it seems to largely be because of his relationship with magical beings.

This story contains a lot of elements, and so we spent a fair amount of space recounting it. There is much there to chew on. Unfortunately, neither "The Wooing of Etain" nor our other mythological stories seem to present examples of familiars. That's ok, though, as the expectation was not that they would but that they might lay the groundwork for faery themes and interactions, which might eventually look more like a relationship with a familiar spirit. In all of these stories, we see beings who shape-shift and who cause their humans to shape-shift. We see magical beings enter into relationships with humans where sex, attraction, or marriage are part of the interaction. We see magical beings make deals with humans. We see precursors to spirit flight. We also find death and destruction for the humans, or at least their inability to return to normal life is present in three out of the four tales we explored. We see humans receive wealth and services from magical beings in two of these stories.

While we're not seeing familiars, we're seeing a world in which humans and magical beings interact in ways that are adjacent to elements of the familiar relationship. We are seeing the mythological backdrop that developed into the folk awareness of the peoples whose adventures with familiars we will later explore. This backdrop reveals a world where humans and spirits have sex, enter into relationships of trade and negotiation, shape-shift and fly together, and facilitate magical tasks.

Ethna and Finvarra

Moving on from what we might consider "mythology," we will look at examples that seem to be reports of faery experiences collected by folklorists. Reports of faery encounters may be urban legends; these are stories where a community knows the story as having happened to someone in their community, but no one directly involved remains. In many cases, reports of faery encounters are collected from the person claiming to have experienced it. Newspapers into the 20th and even the 21st century have stories of people explaining encounters with faeries. Sometimes whole communities are aware because it is the explanation for a person who went missing and then suddenly turned up again. Whereas these myths we have explored were recorded hundreds of years ago by historians and mythographers who were collecting stories that originated hundreds of years before they were recorded, there are living experiences of people which have been recorded as well.

Modern folklorists have also provided us with stories that are in between those two poles. Folklorists have recorded many faery stories that deal with characters from myths or in which the setting is remote, like in myths. These stories, however, were not recorded by monk-historians or monk-mythographers in the middle ages. Modern folklorists have been able to collect folk versions of myth and cultural remembrances of these characters from people who grew up with these stories. The storytellers understood these stories in the context of people who themselves may have experienced encounters with faeries, knew people who did or lived in communities with stories of recent people who had. We will look at two such myths. One could have a setting contemporary with its recording, despite slightly mythic events; the other pertains to characters from Irish myths but in a story preserved in folk memory rather than manuscripts.

Lady Jane Wilde, in her collection <u>Ancient Legends Mystic Charms and Superstitions of Ireland</u>, recounts the story of Ethna and Finvarra. Ethna is likely a variant of the name Ethniu. Ethniu was a daughter of Balor and the mother of Lugh, but her name is also connected to other figures and appears in variant myths. Many forms and variants of the name exist. It may be that this story connects to some earlier myth, or it may be a folktale on its own, and the character may simply have a name that has grown into myriad forms since its original use to describe a titanic figure.

Wilde's story is clearly written in the language of folk and faery stories. It could reasonably be believed to be set in a time contemporary with or not long before the life of Lady Wilde. It begins by describing Finvarra's love for beautiful mortal women. Despite having his own beautiful faery bride, Queen Una, Finvarra was known for his desire for human women and the frequency with which he took them as lovers. The faeries in his service would spirit away women with enchantments and bring them to Finvarra's palace. There they would be kept under faery spells which made them forget their human lives. Magical faery music played, which lulled them into a dreamlike state of pleasure and ecstatic trance.

Near to Finvarra's mound was a lord with whom Finvarra maintained a friendship. The lord left casks of fine Spanish wines out for the faeries to take in the night. One day, this lord took a young bride who was the most beautiful in all of Ireland; her name was Ethna. The lord was so happy with her that he held parties at his castle daily and devoted his life to feasting, merriment, hunting, and pleasure in celebration of his bride. Finvarra, however, heard of her beauty and wanted her for himself.

One evening at a party, Ethna was dancing in a gossamer gown bedecked with jewels such that she was more brilliant and beautiful than the moon and stars. As she danced, she stopped suddenly, her hand fell from her partner's, and she fainted. As she lay there on the floor, no one could rouse her or determine what had happened. She was taken to her room and awoke in the morning. Upon waking, she described how she had gone to a beautiful palace and how happy she was there. She declared that she wished she could return to sleep so that she could continue enjoying it. The next night everyone was watchful as evening came. Soft, faery music played outside her window, and a nurse was set to watch over her when she drifted to sleep. The nurse grew tired and fell asleep; when morning came, she and the household woke to find Ethna had disappeared.

The lord sent men to look everywhere, but there was no sign of her. Finally, the lord set out to find Finvarra and ask his advice, not having considered that his faery friend may have taken her. As he approached, he stopped his horse to rest, and he heard voices in the air. They spoke of how happy Finvarra was now that he had the bride and how she would never see her husband again because Finvarra was so powerful. They mentioned that it might be possible to recover her if the lord dug all the way to the center of the earth.

The next day the lord gathered his men, and they began to dig. They made good headway and went to rest for the night, but when they returned, they found all they had done had been undone. Finvarra had power over land, sea, and air and commanded the earth to reset itself. This happened for three days, and the lord almost lost hope until the voices whispered that he should salt the dirt to prevent it from being returned. The lord gathered salt and took precautions against Finvarra's magic. The next day he returned with his men and found their work preserved. They continued digging and came so close that they could hear the faery music. The voices began to describe how a single shovel breaking into the palace would cause it to crumble and vanish, but that Finvarra could save the faeries by giving up the bride. Finvarra conceded, called out for the men to stop, and promised to return the bride at sunset.

Sunset came, and Ethna appeared, walking up in her gossamer dress towards her husband. He scooped her up onto his horse and swiftly carried her away back home. Once home, they discovered that she could not speak or move and seemed entranced. Days passed with no improvement, and sorrow took the lord and his people as they were certain she was under some faery spell and was lost to them. Then, one day, the lord was out riding near the mound and heard the voices. They explained that it had been a year and a day since the lord had recovered his bride but that she was in a trance because her spirit was with the faeries. The voices further explained that the lord could free her by destroying the faery girdle and burying the enchanted pin which kept her spelled. The lord rushed home and did as he heard, and his bride recovered. She thought her time with Finvarra was just a night's dream and awoke from the spell as if no time had passed since she had disappeared.

This story lays things out a little more clearly because the presentation intends to be a faery story, and it is told from the perspective of someone immersed in faery stories. It was conceivably modern or contemporary for the time it was collected. To begin, it lays out who Finvarra is and how he operates. We see spelled out that the faery king lusts for mortal women and will take them. We see that he can take them in dreams, like witches who travel in spirit to the sabbat; his women might be enchanted to come to him in spirit. The use of faery music to bring sleep appears here. We see the time in which her spirit is held by faeries matches to the magical period of a year and a day. We see that the lord maintains his relationship with the faeries by giving them gifts of wine, but this does not prevent Finvarra from stealing his bride. The lord gets his ability to recover his bride by listening to the faeries, although we are not given insight into why the faeries seem willing to help him.

Ethna seems to be in the position of a faery lover rather than a captive. In our mythological stories, it's unclear how much women desire these encounters. In the case of Deichtire, Lugh simply flies into her mouth, and there is no real mention of her response to the situation. The women in the "Voyage of Bran" are the faeries, and they initiate contact with Bran, but Bothvild and Etain may be more ambiguous about what relationship they want with their faery lovers. In the case of Ethna, she is taken, but she desires to go back. The nature of the spell she is under and how it affects her while she is in faery, makes it pleasurable and desirable for her to be there. Even afterwards, it was all a pleasant dream for her. We don't see any particular consequence or issue at play for Ethna or her husband in the end. She recovers and is fine. She has lost a year of life, and he has lost time with her and expended the effort of his men in attacking a faery mound, but listlessness, wasting, and estrangement from normal life don't seem to be issues here.

This story doesn't provide any examples of an exchange or arrangement between parties. It simply presents the faery desire for human lovers. It also shows us how these human interactions with magical beings look in more contemporary stories, as compared to the earlier mythological stories. The main connection to the motifs related to familiars are spirit-flight, and through ecstatic trance, reaching a place with an otherworldly lover where people are engaged in merriment.

The Daughter of the King Under-Waves

A story that more clearly straddles the space between ancient myth and the modern folk story is the tale of "The Daughter of the King Under-Waves." This story appears in J. F. Campbell's <u>Popular Tales of the West Highlands</u>. The story involves Diarmaid of the Fianna, who is well known from the story "Diarmaid and Grainne." In "Diarmaid and Grainne," Diarmaid is pushed by Grainne, the bride of Finn MacCumhail, to run away with her such that they both betray Finn. Campbell collected several other folk stories involving Diarmaid.

In this story, the men of the Fianna are out on an adventure, and the rain is striking, violent, and cold upon them. They seek shelter. As they wait the night under their shelters, a woman approaches. Katherine Briggs believes this woman is Cailleach Bheur, the Veiled Hag, or perhaps Veiled Witch. This figure is possibly a goddess of winter, and Briggs believes this story indicates her role as both summer and winter. There are several Cailleach Bheur figures, and I do not believe Campbell's informant describes this woman as such a figure. Her role as the daughter of the king of the underwater fair folk might also separate her from Cailleach Bheur. Still, if this figure is an example of Cailleach Bheur, it may be possible to also link a figure from "Diarmaid and Grainne" to this character which could tie the stories further together.

The woman first approaches the portion of the shelter where Finn rests. She asks to be let in, and Finn rebukes her for her ugliness and refuses to let her in. She leaves with a shriek and then makes her way to the cover of Oisin, and the same thing happens. Finally, she makes her way to Diarmaid's shelter, and while he comments on her ugliness, he lets her in. She explained to Diarmaid that she had traveled over sea and ocean for seven years and had not rested a night until he had let her in. She asked to be let near the fire, and Diarmaid invited her, but her appearance frightened off the brave and mighty Fenian warriors. Shortly thereafter, she asked if she might come under the blanket with Diarmaid. He rebuked her boldness, but he allowed her to join him. Not long after she was under the blanket, she transformed into the most beautiful woman. Diarmaid called the men together, and they all agreed that she was the most beautiful woman men had ever cast eyes upon, and they took to covering her and watching over her as she slept.

She woke in the night and asked Diarmaid where he would like to have a castle, and he answered before going to sleep. The next morning she bid him to rise and go to his castle. He did not believe it was there but once confirmed, he agreed to go if she would go with him. She agreed on the condition that he could not speak three times of how they had met.

After three days together in the castle, Diarmaid seemed saddened and admitted to missing the Fianna. The woman suggested he go see them and put his concerns about leaving at ease, particularly over his greyhound and her three pups. Later in the day, Finn approached, and in exchange for his company, he requested one of the pups, which the woman gave to him. When Diarmaid returned home, the greyhound yelped once, and Diarmaid bemoaned that a pup was missing and commented that the woman should have taken more care, given the condition she was in when they first met. The woman questioned what he said, and he asked for forgiveness, which she granted. The same thing happened the next day, but this time with Oisin claiming a pup and the greyhound yelping twice when Diarmaid returned. He made the same mistake again, and she forgave him. On the third day, Diarmaid left again, and another man of the Fianna came and requested a pup. The woman gave it to him. Diarmaid returned home to the greyhound, yelping thrice. He commented again on how he met the woman and then asked for forgiveness. This time, instead of joining hands with him and enjoying supper and the night together as she had before, he was now alone. He awoke to find himself wifeless, his castle gone, and his greyhound dead.

Diarmaid committed to finding the woman and went in search of her, carrying the greyhound on his shoulders. He made his way down to the beach, hopped into a boat, and sailed across the water. He went to sleep upon a hill, and when he woke up, the boat he had ridden was gone. He was sure he was lost until he saw someone rowing a boat towards him. He brought the greyhound and climbed in. The boat took him beneath the water, but he soon found land underneath on which he could walk. As he walked along, he found three gulps of blood, which he gathered into a napkin.

Eventually, Diarmaid came upon a woman gathering rushes. She explained that he was in the Land Under Waves and that the daughter of the king had returned home. She had been under spells for seven years and was now ill with no cure, and the rushes were for her. She took Diarmaid to the woman by hiding him in the bundle of rushes. When he revealed himself, Diarmaid and the woman rejoiced to be together again. She explained that she had been ill but that she had recovered, except that whenever she thought of him, she lost a gulp of blood. He explained that he had collected them and would give them to her to drink. Then, the woman revealed that she would need a magic cup from the King of the Plain of Wonder in order to recover by drinking the blood, but that it was impossible to get. Nevertheless, Diarmaid committed to getting it, and she told him where to go.

Diarmaid reached a stream that he could not cross, and he was unsure of what to do. A man appeared and offered to lift Diarmaid by the foot across the stream to the place he needed to go. He did so, and Diarmaid stood outside the King's palace and demanded the cup. The king sent an army, which Diarmaid killed. The king sent a larger army which Diarmaid dispatched, and then another larger one which was also felled by him. Finally, the king came out and asked who had destroyed the men of the kingdom. Diarmaid introduced himself, and the king explained that this act had been written in a book seven years before Diarmaid's birth, so if he had begun by saying who he was, the king would not have sent the armies. He gave Diarmaid the cup.

As Diarmaid returned, he realized he had no way over the stream since he had not mentioned the man or brought him in with him. The man appeared and offered to help despite how Diarmaid had treated him. He explained that Diarmaid would need to get water from a special well, mix it with each drop of blood, and let the woman drink three times. After she drank, she would be healed, but Diarmaid would no longer love her; in fact, she would become the woman he liked least in the world. He explained that the King Underwaves and the woman would both know that Diarmaid had taken a dislike to her. He told Diarmaid he must admit it when asked and that the king would offer him gold and silver as a reward but that he must not take any and should ask only for a boat that will take him back to Ireland. The man explained that he was a messenger from the otherworld and was helping Diarmaid because he had such a good warm heart which led him to do good things for others.

All went as the messenger had said, the woman was healed, but Diarmaid took to disliking her. The king offered him silver and the woman's hand in marriage, but Diarmaid refused and asked only for a ship to take him home to the Fianna.

This story contains many parts that could link us to the idea of the familiar through the idea of the faery bride. The woman comes as a hair-covered hag and leaves, shrieking when rejected. This image suggests some sort of witch or frightful spirit, and even the brave Fenian warriors are afraid of her. Witches in folk stories and witch trials were often believed to curse people who were inhospitable to them or who did not meet their demands for aid or service. Diarmaid accepts her, not just into his shelter but into his bed. It does not seem that anything carnal was to pass between them when she was still in the form of a hag, but he takes her for his bride the next morning. For his kindness, he gains a faery castle, the faery woman as his bride, and food and drink provided at the castle.

Like many stories of faery brides, Diarmaid is forbidden from acknowledging how they met. In some stories, there are taboos against exhibiting surprise, looking at where the faery goes at night or during some private activity or speaking of their faery nature. Any transgression could lead to them leaving. Sometimes the faery leaving just ends the relationship, but there can be various degrees of sorrow or catastrophe beyond that. Diarmaid fails to obey this taboo, and she departs. Unlike many faery brides, she wants to be reunited with him.

There seems to be some link between the greyhound and the woman. There is no mention of where she came from or why Diarmaid is concerned for the well-being of her pups. There is no explanation of why the Fianna want the pups or why Diarmaid seems able to converse with her. The greyhound dies when the woman disappears along with all she has provided Diarmaid. Diarmaid carries the greyhound to find the woman and believes the blood belongs to the greyhound. There is no animal shape-shifting in the story, but it may be that the woman and the greyhound are connected.

When Diarmaid loses his faery lover, he commits to finding her. It seems at first as if he will take no rest or pleasure until he does so. He falls asleep upon a faery hill which allows him to ride the boat under the waves. Ultimately he discovers his faery lover had been sick without him as well. She had undergone a magical period, seven years of wandering and being under spells. Diarmaid's arrival at the Wonder Plain had been predicted seven years before his birth. The time the faery woman spent with Diarmaid was three days and nights. both of them experience magical timeframes and both become lost or sick without the other. While different from the typical experience of a familiar spirit, the faery woman becomes well again when Diarmaid feeds her blood.

Diarmaid goes through multiple challenges to heal her. Unlike other heroes, his challenges aren't varied and don't require magic - he single-handedly defeats three armies. However, he is still aided and advised by an otherworld figure, the man who lifts him over the stream and gives him instructions. The instructions not to take the payment and only to ask for the boat back matches some other faery stories in which humans are brought to provide care to people in faery.

The end of the story does not leave Diarmaid unable to rejoin the world or with any sort of faery problems or ruination. There is a possibility, however, of connecting this woman to Diarmaid's death. In the story of "Diarmaid and Grainne," Diarmaid dies because a bristle from a great giant boar strikes a vulnerable spot on his foot. In Diarmaid's attempt to hunt the boar, there is a witch figure. Some view that figure as Cailleach Bheur. If both the figure at his death and the daughter of the King Under Waves are forms of Cailleach Bheur, it could be interpreted that Diarmaid's death was connected to this faery encounter. I would not make that assertion because the connections seem speculative.

We can take from this story the idea of an exchange creating a relationship between a human and a faery. The faery asks for Diarmaid's aid and gives him a gift when he provides it. He asks to continue the relationship, and by taking her as a lover, he continues to receive her gifts and blessings. At this point, we have a relationship potentially sharing elements with the familiar spirit relationship;

however, it may be read more as a partnership than as a servant being given to someone. Diarmaid cares for her by feeding her blood. In this case, it is her own blood, but it is blood she shed in her love for Diarmaid. The relationship falls apart quickly because Diarmaid can't keep his end of it. We don't get to see how else it would have played out as a longer relationship. Diarmaid isn't given instructions or magic due to the relationship; she simply provides him with magical wealth.

It is not the same as a familiar spirit relationship, but it has more overlap than we've seen in most other faery or divine lover scenarios. The elements present are so close to what we would see in stories of a familiar that it is tempting to say that this is an example of one. It has enough pieces that we might think that these ideas were kicking around in how people related to spirits, so something more like a familiar could have existed in a more magical context with similar elements.

Thomas the Rhymer and the Hidden Folk

Our first example of a report of a faery encounter adds another element that we might consider similar to the relationship with a familiar or the tales of witch power we see historically. The story of Thomas the Rhymer is the account of an historical man who was believed to have lived for a time in the land of the faeries. Thomas Earlston lived in Berwickshire in the 13th century.

One day, while he was sitting by a tree, a beautiful woman in a green mantle on a white horse approached Thomas. He thought she was the Queen of Heaven, but she corrected him and explained that she was the Queen of Elphame. She offered him a kiss, and once he accepted, she was able to take him to faery with her. In some versions, the Queen warns him that he must stay with her for seven years if he goes with her, whereas others say she warned that it would be one year, but he stayed longer, either for three or seven years. In some versions, the Queen retains her beauty, but in others, she warns she will lose her beauty if they share any act of lust. Thomas is not put off by this, and she agrees to marry him so he can come with her. She takes him down a road that forks three ways, one branch going to Heaven, one to Hell, and the third to Elphame. The story says he slept with her seven times but that she would become hideous afterwards. Eventually, she tells him he must go. Thomas believes it has only been days but discovers it has been years. In some versions, she wishes him to leave so that he is not selected as part of the tithe of human souls, which faeries must give to Hell. As a gift, she offers him the gift of prophecy or talent as a harpist, and he chooses the gift of prophecy.

This story is an example in which an historical person was believed to have gone off to faery and returned with powers. Some stories include him returning to faery, as he may have simply disappeared later in life. His prophecies held significance in England and Scotland for centuries after his life.

This story ties back to witchcraft a little more in that we're specifically dealing with The Queen of Elphame. Her land is between Heaven and Hell. Her relationship with Thomas is based on taking him as a human lover, and he receives a magical power as a result. The relationship does not seem to be one that is ongoing, at least not once he leaves Elphame, but the power he received for prophecy seems to have remained. So here we have an example of the faery lover producing essentially the relationship we see in witch trial accounts. Thomas was held in esteem as a prophet, possibly because he lived about 130 years before the beginning of the European witch trials.

Ongoing gifts from faeries could also come from small interactions. Katherine Briggs describes the Hidden Folk of Scandanavia as enjoying interacting with humans. According to Briggs, they have cow tails, and that is the only defect that marks them as faeries. Otherwise, they are beautiful. So, the Hidden Folk hide their cow tails when they wish to consort with humans. Briggs tells a story of some women from the Hidden Folk attending a human dance. One of the girls begins to dance with a human man, and after a time, he notices her tail. Rather than reveal her identity, he privately told her she was losing her garter and complimented her. Appreciating his discretion, she blessed him with prosperity for the rest of his life.

In this account, we don't know that the interaction became anything more than dancing. It does not sound as if there was an ongoing interaction either. Nevertheless, it does seem to indicate that faeries who desire the attention of humans will reward human kindness and affection, sometimes powerfully. This basis of attention and interaction in exchange for aid and magical benefits is at the basis of the faery familiar relationship, as these familiars, in particular, seek sexual comfort and time and attention from their humans.

Faery Widowers

We will round out our accounts of faery lovers with the idea of the faery widower. In these accounts, it does not seem that the girls are taken as lovers. However, the faeries appear as beautiful to them, and the girls are smitten with them. There may even be the potential that they could become the faery's lover.

Two examples of the faery widower tales are the story of Jenny Permuen, presented in Robert Hunt's <u>Popular Romances of The West of England</u>, and the story of Cherry of Zennor also presented in Hunt. The version of the Cherry story that I recount here is based on the description by Katherine Briggs, which differs slightly from the record given in Hunt. The author of the blog "British Fairies" notes that Zennor is a rich area for faerylore and mentions a story of a mermaid from Zennor. The Skillywidden story presented in our chapter on household spirits also occurred there. Jenny's story even includes a mention of Zennor. The two girls meet their faery widowers at the same crossroads.

Both stories involve young girls who need to set out into the world. In each, they come to a crossroads and wait. In Jenny's case, she came to the crossroads of Lady Downs and was unsure of which road to take. She sat down and began to aimlessly break off fronds of ferns. Cherry, like Jenny, was sent from home to find employment. She intended to go to a local fair to look for work but became frightened and ran off. She came to the crossroads at Lady Downs and sat down crying.

Shortly after settling at the crossroads, each young girl was approached by a man who asked them what they were doing there. In both cases, the man seemed handsome and friendly and offered the girl a job caring for his son, as he was recently a widower. Jenny's faery procured an oath from her before taking her into faery. She had to kiss a fern and swear to stay for a year and a day. Both girls were led over long terrain. Finally, they crossed streams and went down into the earth. On Jenny's journey, she grew weary and began to cry. The faery took her to a mossy bank, comforted her, and dried her eyes with leaves. She was overwhelmed by his kindness and forgot her weariness. They made the rest of the journey to his home, but before entering, he dried her eyes with leaves again, explaining that no human tears could enter their homes. Then he changed his appearance into the most beautiful small man in a green silk coat and revealed himself to be the king. He showed Jenny his son, who was sleeping, and seemed to be the most precious-looking child, and explained that Jenny's only duty was to care for him and keep him happy.

Cherry's journey had no incident, but when they arrived, she discovered the boy's grandmother was there caring for him, and she was dissatisfied with Cherry. The grandmother revealed the faery's name to be Robin. Robin assured Cherry that it would be alright and that the grandmother would be leaving once Cherry was acclimated. The home had statues that struck Cherry as dead people, and there was a large coffin that Cherry was told to polish. When Cherry polished it, the coffin groaned, and she fainted, at which point Robin took her outside, kissed her, and comforted her.

In Jenny's case, she does not seem to be taken as a lover by the faery. The faery king wishes his son to know about humans and thus selects a human nanny for him. Jenny and the boy are very happy together, and like other stories of being in faery, Jenny has no thought of her mother, her home, or any of the things which it concerned her to leave behind. Jenny loses her sense of the passage of time, happy in the luxury of the faery king's home. Eventually, her year and a day ends, and she goes to sleep one night, happy in the king's home, and wakes up surprised to find herself back home in her own bed.

Cherry's experience differs a bit; she had a slightly broader range of duties. In addition to caring for the boy, she had to milk a cow that would appear mysteriously when called. She also spent time with the faery, helping him tend his garden. At the end of each garden row, he would kiss her. This was Cherry's favorite duty. There seems to have been some relationship between Cherry and the faery, not just based on these kisses, but also his absence. The faery would disappear for several hours each day, and this was the only source of unhappiness Cherry experienced there. She would ask the boy where his father went, and he would refuse to answer and threaten to tell his grandmother if she kept asking.

Each morning, Cherry had to rub a bit of faery ointment on the boy's eyes. One day, she decided to distract the boy and sneak a bit of the ointment to rub into her own. Now she could see little creatures swarming throughout the garden. She ran to the well to wash out her eyes, and when she looked below, she saw Robin, now small, with other small faery people playing in the bottom of the well. The story says that Robin and the other faeries, including the faery ladies, were on very familiar terms, and this infuriated Cherry. Presumably, she saw them kissing or engaging in some sexual play. After this,

Cherry saw Robin return to his normal size and enter a locked room that she was not permitted to enter. She peered through the keyhole and saw him open the coffin. A woman came out, and they played upon the coffin while the statues came to life and danced.

After witnessing her faery master's cavorting, she joined him in the garden to tend to the plants. As was their custom, he leaned in to give her a kiss as they finished the first row. She pushed him away and began to cry, insisting that he should go kiss the faeries he had been with in the well. Robin realizes what she has done and explains that she must leave. Cherry cried and begged, but Robin made her pack her things and led her home.

While Jenny does not seem to have been taken as the faery's lover, Cherry clearly was and felt scorned discovering that he also had faery lovers. Despite the feeling of scorn, she wished to remain. Robin explained that he would have to bring Grace, the grandmother, back to care for the boy. As it turns out, Grace was a mortal woman, a school teacher from Cherry's village, so like Cherry, Robin's last wife had been a mortal woman. This is why the boy needed the faery ointment, as humans do, to see the fair folk. Even though Jenny and Cherry had different relationships with their faeries, the results were similar.

When Jenny returned home, no one believed her. Before she left, she had a reputation for being a beautiful but vain and somewhat dim girl. When she returned, she seemed strange and disconnected from everything around her. People thought she had lost her mind. Many women came to see her, and she told her story, but they didn't believe her until one, a woman named Mary from Zennor, came and tested her. She confirmed that Jenny was telling the truth and that if she continued to tell the truth, she would come to be ok, and her faery lord would likely take care to see that she was well provided for. Jenny did not come out well, though. She married but was always unhappy, pining away for her faery. People thought she must have given the faery some slight, as she received no gold or treasure from him. In Jenny's case, he had offered her gold at the start of the relationship, as he offered her a position of employment. So it is all the more strange that Jenny received nothing but sorrow since her story doesn't indicate that she did anything wrong; she just ran out of time.

Like Jenny, Cherry did not return to the world well. As is common for those who have faery lovers, Cherry could not make anything of herself in the world. She would routinely return to the crossroads and wait for Robin to return and take her away, but he never did. Cherry was fortunate that he had not blinded her for using the ointment, which she had been instructed not to do. Like Jenny, Cherry provided the service requested and was pleasing to her faery master. Additionally, Cherry seems to have either been taken as a mortal bride or would have been taken as such. However, Cherry lost her place with Robin because she broke a rule and gained faery sight for herself.

These stories present a more personal impression of the experience of being taken by a faery. Like many accounts we see reported by people, each girl disappeared for a time and then simply reappeared. In many accounts of people being faery-led, everyone in the community looks for them, but no sign of them is found. One day they might simply appear, wandering out of the woods or back at home, sometimes naked, sometimes in the clothes they left in. In Cherry's case, Hunt describes Robin as leaving her on the granite stone at Lady Downs and telling her if she was good, he would return for her. Cherry waited there for a long time before returning home. Her family had heard nothing of her, although, like Jenny, they knew she was setting out to find work. Since they never heard any update from her, they thought she had died. Initially, they thought it was her ghost returning to them.

Cherry and Jenny both felt affection for the faeries with whom they interacted. Both wished to return to them. Some faerytales depict humans who are trapped and who hate the strange customs of the faeries. Some show captive humans who are treated as slaves. In these stories, the experiences were largely positive. The girls chose to go and wanted to stay. This shows us that the relationship can be a reciprocal one that people elect. The faeries are satisfied with the work the girls do, and all parties are pleased, at least initially. This is really the only element that links us to the familiar relationship, though. Cherry may have retained the faery sight, but since the boy needed the ointment each day, it is unlikely that she kept that power. Neither girl received wealth or protection from their faery lord. Both simply pined away, possibly touched by madness as a result.

All in all, our mythology and our folk accounts of faery relationships don't present examples of familiar spirits. We see a world of faery interactions in which many of the pieces are there. We can see beliefs about how spirits behave, what they can do, and what they want with humans. Ideas about familiars overlap with the folk beliefs these stories reveal. The interactions are different, though, so we don't see a depiction of this specific relationship occur. We see a lot of similar pieces, sometimes even in a single story. Still, we don't see a human acquiring a spirit assistant or servant, feeding them, and then receiving magical education, protection, and tasks performed at their request.

Some of the differences may be that these are not magical relationships. The problem with dismissing the differences because the humans involved are not magicians is that many accounts of witches involve people who are prone to seeing spirits; they encounter the faeries and then begin magic. They're not entering the relationship on some even footing because they possess magic, nor are they directing the relationship through the application of magical knowledge.

These stories show us that many faeries want relationships with humans and often on some sexual basis. These stories show that these relationships can be strange and magical. Sometimes these relationships are beneficial, but they can also often be dangerous. We see faeries exhibit powers like those we attribute to familiar spirits. We also see faeries demonstrate their ability to trick, beguile, and manipulate humans. Despite the fact that we don't see a familiar spirit relationship in the myths, legends, and folk accounts of faery lovers, we do see all the mechanics that allow one to exist. We see that faeries are willing to take human lovers, they are willing to give them gifts and use magic on their behalf, and in the case of Thomas the Rhymer, they are willing to give gifts that grant humans magical or supernatural capabilities. We see shape-shifting and spirit flight, but so far, we haven't seen spirits teach their humans magic or protect them, nor do they usually perform tasks upon request for their human lovers.

A magician adding a contractual component could redefine these relationships into one which gave rise to a relationship more like that with a familiar. Contractual relationships are also present in these stories. Jenny Permuen must swear an oath before being taken into faeryland. Midir repeatedly negotiates to create what he wants. Bargaining to obtain Etain could be viewed as an example of one powerful being exchanging another magical being to the person with whom they enter into a pact. Etain accompanies Midir, and then Angus, in animal form. So there are elements, there are pieces, just not the full image. We can see where the familiar spirit could arise in a world filled with these sorts of faery encounters and experiences. These are not, however, the only faery experiences that people had, even in regards to sexual congress with the Other Folk.

The Leannan Sidhe and Fatal Lovers

Our stories thus far have focused on the Daoine Sidhe, the noble faeries who were once gods and heroes of Irish myth. These faeries are like, and possibly inspired, the magical knights and witches of medieval romances who were themselves sometimes described as faeries and giants. The faeries depicted in such stories, and in the faerytales inspired by these epic, mythic figures, may be easier to relate to the faeries we see in the grimoires than some other faery figures. The domestic or household spirits, which are more often than not taken as faeries, clearly seem a different sort of creature than the Daoine Sidhe and similar faeries. These faeries are not the only sidhe, or the only creatures that we might readily think of as faeries. There are others who are significantly more monstrous or bizarre. Some are more dangerous, and others are simply less human. Some are associated with the dead and might be more human. Our final exploration of the faery lover will focus on people of the sidhe whose love for humans can be fatal.

The story of Ethna, and perhaps that of Jenny Permuen, would indicate that a soul can be whisked away from the body in dreams to go to faery. Like in the story of Ethna, an ongoing comatose paralysis could result from losing one's soul to faeryland. In modern mythmaking, the plight of Lady Pole in Jonathan Strange and Mr. Norrell illustrates how a faery might take a human soul through dreams to indulge the faery's pleasure in their far-off kingdom. The kidnapping of Arabella Strange depicts how a faery might trade a changeling for a human and capture the human's body, enchanting their mind to forget their home and family. Such stories still fascinate people today, and such adventures with the fair folk are still sometimes reported. A more dangerous air accompanies other stories, in which being led away by the faeries is being led to one's death. In some tales of being faery-led, there is an adventure to be had by the human, or the human's family learns how to see that the faeries have their missing loved one and how to reclaim them from the faery's court. In others, the human is simply never seen again, or the human stumbles off the path in a mist or strange place, perhaps having seen or heard something which enchanted them, and they are later found inexplicably dead. Other faery encounters may be ongoing, or they may be a one-time encounter, but the pining away and disconnect from life that we have seen in the stories above turns into a wasting sickness that leads to death.

Stories of faery interactions that result in death may not seem like they would give rise to tales of familiars or the supernatural knowledge to create such a relationship. These tales illustrate how the faery's carnal desire for humans might come with a desire for human blood or life force, which does relate to the relationship with the familiar spirit. In some such tales, humans also receive insights, benefits, or inspiration from these spectral powers. A few even present pretty compelling examples of relationships that look like familiar spirits.

Such spirits exist throughout the world, spirits whose beautiful voices or appearances can bewitch humans and lure them to their death. Often these spirits are associated with water and might reflect water's own tendency to offer us both beauty and danger. Merfolk, lamias, and sea-bound sirens are not the only such creatures. In British and Irish folklore, the leannan sidhe is the most well-known faery to prey upon human desire, but it is not the only one. It may be more accurate to say that leannan sidhe is not the only name for such faeries, as it simply means faery lover and could refer to any of the faeries in the stories we have described above, as well as other similarly frightening faeries. The leannan sidhe, however, has come to be associated with certain types of faery relationships, and so we will explore it from that viewpoint. We will round out our look at faery lovers with a look at these and related spirits.

The leannan sidhe can be difficult to get started with. On the one hand, we have a handful of names for faeries who pursue mortal lovers and feed on them, take their lives, or collect them at death. On the other hand, as we have noted, the name simply means "faery lover," and so any story of a faery and a mortal could be referred to as a leannan sidhe story. Many sources highlight mythological stories like Lady Gregory's "Dream of Angus" as leannan sidhe stories. In "Dream of Angus," the MacOc has a vision of a sidhe woman and falls in love but can't touch her or get her to remain with him after seeing her many times. He develops a wasting sickness, and the doctor diagnoses it as lovesickness. Angus's parents are Boand and The Dagda, so he has the aid of powerful divine rulers in finding and obtaining the object of his affection. He is able to learn where she is and get the help of the mortal king and queen of her region in obtaining her, and they fly off happily as swans to his home at Bru Na Boinne. It's not a story of a faery vampire or even the story of a human falling in love with a faery. It is just a story of someone taking a lover from amongst the sidhe. Even though he is haunted by her and pines for her, it ends happily, and he navigates it safely because he is a god who also resides in the sidhe.

Oxford Reference delineates between two sorts of Irish leannan sidhe stories. The first is the pattern we've outlined and what we've seen in our other faery-lover stories. A human and a faery fall in love, and they agree to be together, but with some taboo placed on the human. The human fails to maintain the taboo, and so they are separated. In some versions, the faery pines away for their human, and in others, the human pines away for the faery. According to Oxford Reference, the other sort involves powerful faery women who desire dominion over human lovers. They note that Manx lhiananshee differ from their Irish counter part. The Manx version generally lives near a well or a spring and selects a single human lover to whom they make themselves visible, but they remain invisible to everyone else. If the human lover accepts their affection, the lhiananshee will consume their life like a vampire or succubus.

The second sort of Irish leannan sidhe, along with elements that Oxford Reference associates with the Manx lhiananshee, occur in folklore and legends across the range of Gaelic and British regions. One story we will explore which fits this latter type is English. The idea that the difference is regional provides an easy explanation. Some folklorists have pointed to trends regarding the range of faery behavior from tame and friendly to outright hostile as reflecting qualities of the region from which the story comes. Regions with dangerous faeries also have tame ones, and vice versa. Another consideration is the possibility that a taxonomical use of leannan sidhe to refer to a particular type of faery creature is relatively modern and begins with Lady Wilde and W.B. Yeats. This is not to say that they invented this creature, but that the idea that the term refers to this particularly sinister sort of faery lover as opposed to all faery lovers may have become more common due to folklorists' use of the term.

Lady Wilde presents the leannan sidhe as a distinct type of faery being in <u>Ancient Legends Mystic Charms and Superstitions of Ireland</u>. For Lady Wilde, the leannan sidhe is not a monster but a spirit of life which stands in juxtaposition to the bean sidhe. Lady Wilde explains that both the Irish and the fair folk hold youth, beauty, generosity, splendor, music, song, feast, dance, and merriment in high esteem such that it characterizes the spirit of each. It is this shared spirit that leads the faeries to love Irish mortals in particular. For Lady Wilde, as the spirit of life, the leannan sidhe inspires the excitement of the soul to express itself in the form of poetry, and prophecy. She believed the leannan sidhe could also use poetry to stir men to valor in battle. This particular facet calls to mind Roman accounts of Celtic warriors galvanized by the women screaming and calling to them as they headed off to battle.

For Wilde, the bean sidhe wailed and heralded death, while the leannan sidhe inspired expressions of life and roused the spirit. Wilde does not present this characterization as one of good and evil but rather as different modes by which the depth of experience is expressed. Where the leannan sidhe creates poetry, the wail and lament of the bean sidhe are, for Wilde, the deepest expression of the mournful passion of Irish music.

Wilde says the leannan sidhe sometimes takes the form of a woman and gives the example of Eodain, the poetess. She tells the story of Eugene, king of Munster, who left for nine years to travel in Spain. After marrying the Spanish princess and returning with a Spanish retinue, he finds the kingdom he abandoned is in shambles. Raiders and drunkards have taken it, and the people no longer respect him. Eodain tells him to rule with strength and justice, and her powers of poetry and prophecy inspire him. He becomes a good and successful king from that point.

The story of Eodain, as told by Wilde, doesn't make the leannan sidhe seem supernatural at all, let alone frightening. Similarly, the story of Birog, who helped Dian Cecht conceive and rescue Lugh, departs from the frightening image. Birog is sometimes referred to as a druidess, and other times as a leannan sidhe, but her role, like Eodain's, is one of support, not consumption.

Yeats was amongst the next generation of authors exploring Irish folklore. He also wrote about the leannan sidhe, and his life may have had connections with this supernatural source of inspiration. For Yeats, the more sinister elements of the leannan sidhe are evident, though they do not seem to have been as present in his own life. To Yeats, the leannan sidhe was the Gaelic muse; it would inspire poets and artists but lead them to an early death. According to Yeats, if the leannan sidhe comes to you and you reject her, she will serve you, but if you accept her affection, you become hers. She will inspire you, but as she does so, she will consume your life, causing you to waste away and die. This description of the leannan sidhe fits the more succubus-like role which has come to be associated with the term. The relationship exceeds stories of men ridden by night hags. The consumption by the leannan sidhe is ongoing, and even death does not free her beloved from her grasp.

The Irish Times noted in "In Search of the Banshee and the Elusive Leannan Sidhe," that Yeats's own life seems to have been touched by the leannan sidhe. Yeats had an obsession for the English actress, suffragette, and supporter of Irish independence, Maud Gonne. Over the course of ten years, Yeats proposed marriage to her at least four times. She inspired much of his work. Eventually, years after Gonne married another, Yeats married a much younger woman. The article's author suggests that early in his marriage, his work still reflects an obsession for Gonne. Being inspired by an obsession for an untenable woman reflects the nature of the relationship with the leannan sidhe. Fortunately, Yeats didn't waste away into an early grave.

His marriage possibly involved a more supernatural connection with the leannan sidhe. His young wife, Georgie Hyde-Lees began to experiment with automatic writing one evening. Yeats, a leading member of the Hermetic Order of the Golden Dawn, was thrilled and encouraged her to spend some time each day on this endeavor. Her received messages coaxed Yeats to be a better husband and lover but also produced significant literary output, which inspired Yeats. Yeats was directly inspired by a supernatural presence speaking through his young lover in what the author of the Times article suggests is his most significant work.

Yeats's life does not seem to reflect the persecution by the leannan sidhe that Yeats describes. The contemporary Irish website, Emerald Isle, retells various Irish myths and describes elements of Irish folk and faery tales. The website gives a modern view of the Irish understanding of the leannan sidhe. It clearly incorporates the elements Yeats ascribes to this particular sort of faery.

According to Emerald Isle, the leannan sidhe, like other daoine sidhe, was once one of the Tuatha de Danaan. Her desire to consume the life of the descendants of the Mileasian Gaels is her vengeance for humans, having driven the Tuatha de Danaan underground. She does not have a face of her own but takes on the appearance of the most beautiful woman the man looking upon her has ever seen. The lust and obsession she inspires cause them to seek her in every waking moment. It is this pining for her that inspires poetry, literature, art, and music. While the longing is torturous, it draws them into a deeper obsession with her. Then, when her apparition appears to them, it inspires them further, but their longing causes madness and death. The lover of the leannan sidhe either takes their own life or wastes away and then in death, they join her in her realm and sing for her for eternity.

In <u>Folktales of England</u>, Katherine Briggs presents Ruth Tongue's account of "The Fairy Follower." This story is particularly interesting because it presents the magical ritual by which a young man conjures a faery to assist him in acquiring the love of a young woman. The story focuses on the man bungling the ritual repeatedly at each step along the way. This might be an explanation for why his faery encounter goes so poorly, but more likely it is either intended to communicate the danger of attempting to turn to faery magic or to obscure the way to do so. The story begins by saying it was foolish for him to attempt this.

Essentially, the young man cleans the hearth and sets out a pail of spring water on the night of the new moon after several months of incorrect attempts. The next morning he finds a golden oil has formed on the water's surface. Faery ointments made of this oil, said to be the result of faeries bathing in the water, are used in several spell books to acquire faery sight. The young man in the story collected the oil and used it with meal to make a cake and offered it in the night to a faery woman. First came a dark-colored faery, and the man said, "not for you." Then he did the same with a fair-colored faery. Finally, a beautiful faery woman in green came and said, "for me," and took the cake.

The faery attached herself to the man, always at his side, whispering to him and guiding his choices. She brought him a wife and, through his wife, wealth. Unfortunately, the wife was not the young woman of his desire but a cruel old woman. The wealth did him no good because a plague began to kill off the people of his village, starting with the woman he loved. Nevertheless, he was a strong man who survived the faery torments for a while, but eventually he died. At his funeral, the faery descended upon his body in a dark cloud and said, "for me."

Here we see the faery taking the man after death. She stays with him through his life, ever at his side, like a familiar. She provides for his various desires, but he established the relationship poorly, so she provides for him poorly. While not spelled out, he enters into an agreement with her for the relationship through a magical ritual. We don't see him pining for her or wasting away. We don't even know if she became his lover while in life. The overall relationship, though, runs parallel to the relationship between a magician and a familiar spirit. The character of the interaction differs somewhat when we consider her taking him in death and rendering torment under the guise of service.

In his blog "British Fairies," John Kruse shares several summaries of stories Dora Broome included in her, sadly out-of-print, book <u>Fairy Tales from the Isle of Mann</u>. As we mentioned, the Manx lhiananshee is thought of as being more consistently vampiric. Kruse presents stories that show the persistence of the lhiananshee.

In one example, the faery becomes besotted with a human and leaves him a chest of gold and a strand of golden mermaid hair. In his poem "The Mermaid, " John Leyden" says, "her ringlets waved in living gold," when describing the hair of a mermaid temptress off the coast of Scotland. His descriptions of her leave the reader with the impression that mermaids are not simply blonde but that their hair is like a living version of precious metal and, thus, a treasure in itself. In the story of the lhiananshee, the man recognizes the danger and tries to ignore his faery suitor. He marries a woman and hopes this will put her off, but she continues to pursue him. One day he chances to see her and falls in love. The man leaves his wife for seven years to join his faery lover. When he returns, his wife has moved on, and he is left a ragged wretch.

This story illustrates the ongoing relationship with the faery and the ability of the faery to provide gifts. However, in considering the leannan sidhe specifically, it illustrates the destructive nature of the relationship. Kruse relates another story in which the faery lures a man with gold.

In "The Fisherman and the Ben-Varrey," a mermaid seeks to lure away a man. The Ben-Varrey, or mermaid, sings to the man in such a lovely voice that he is drawn to follow her into the sea where he would drown. The fisherman's wife saves him from diving in after the enchanting voice. To further entice him, the ben-varrey gives him a chest of gold coins. The people of the village assume he has stolen the gold, and because he believes he has wealth because of the gold, he stops fishing. His family becomes poor, but eventually, the gold is lost, lifting the faery's spell. With the loss of the gold, the fisherman is saved from being taken by the lhiananshee.

This story is like "The Fairy Follower" in that the faery's presence comes with gifts that are destructive in nature. It is also interesting in that it presents the gift as an element of the faery's agency in influencing the life of their chosen mortal. The gift also represents a bond that allows the relationship to occur. In some magic involving spirits, particularly familiars, it is useful for some gift to be given to allow them to work. The exchange of gifts and services builds and maintains the relationship between the magician and the familiar.

Here we see a similar mechanism but contextualized towards a different purpose.

Two other Manx stories of the ben-varrey illustrate this exchange of gifts. These two stories don't fit our life-devouring faery lover focus. Still, mermaids frequently consume the men they attract, and the Manx lhiananshee is closely related to these mermaid and siren figures. These two stories present such creatures more congenially but show a relationship in which they provide benefits in exchange for friendship and an offering. The benefits they provide are not unrelated to the benefits that the mermaids of the Isle of Mann offer when luring a man to their thrall.

The first story is from Manx Fairy Tales by Sophia Morrison. In "The Mermaid of Gob-Ny-Ooyl," Morrison recounts the story of the Sayle family. The Sayle family was befriended by one of the ben-varrey, and she blessed them with what seemed to be endless luck and good fortune. Mr. Sayle was known to be very fond of apples and made his living as a fisherman. He would carry apples out with him onto his boat every day and work the sea. As he grew older, he could no longer make his way out to sea, and his sons took on more of the work. As his age wore on, the family's luck wore out. His sons, at times, had to take to hunting for food as their ability to make a living grew less reliable. Eventually, most of them left to find other work, while one, Evan, stayed behind. One night, as Evan was finishing his work, he heard a pleasant voice call out and ask him how his father was. He looked and saw a beautiful woman sitting on the rocks. At first, he was frightened, but she seemed pleasant, so he gathered his courage and told her of his family. When he returned home, he told his father of the woman, and his father grew excited, exclaiming that their family's luck might return. He told Evan to bring apples with him in the boat when he next went out.

Evan went out in the boat the next day with a bundle of apples. He pulled the boat around near the rocks where he'd seen the mermaid and looked for her. Suddenly she swam up, reached over the edge of the boat, and took an apple. She began to eat it and to sing a little chant:

> The luck of the sea be with you,
> but don't forgetful be,
> of bringing some sweet land eggs,
> for the children of the sea.

The family's luck returned. Evan, taken with the mermaid and her with him, began to spend all his time at sea. It got to the point where people became concerned, so he decided to look for work in foreign lands. The mermaid was upset with this prospect, but Evan planted an apple tree by the sea to calm her. He explained that the "land eggs" would become sweet and ripe, and she could collect them as they fell into the water. This pleased her for a time, and the family's luck continued even with Evan gone. Eventually, the mermaid's longing for him grew, and she left the shore to find him, and neither was ever seen again.

This story depicts the family trading a gift to the faery for prosperity and success. They establish an ongoing relationship in which they continue to provide for the faery, and she provides for them. This comes closer to the familiar spirit relationship and remains in the realm of being beneficial. It is limited to prosperity, success, and luck rather than a broad range of magical activity, but again, the people in the story aren't magicians. There is a faery lover component, as Evan and the faery clearly become preoccupied with one another. As is common in leannan sidhe stories, Evan attempts to escape his obsession by moving away. In his case, it seems that he did not see himself as being destroyed by the faery. He planted a tree to please her. This may have been out of love for the faery or concern for his family's well-being. It could possibly have been both.

There is a similar Manx story about a ben-varrey, a fisherman, and an apple tree. A fisherman by the last name of Caine had a beautiful house by the edge of the sea. When he wasn't at sea, he had a cow to tend and a beautiful garden. He grew grain, flowers, and apples. The scent of the apple blossoms in the spring and the ripe sweet red apples in the autumn dominated the garden's aroma. The man was successful and happy, and he would sing whenever he was at home working. He had a beautiful and joyful singing voice.

One summer, his luck ran out as he couldn't find any herring to catch. This problem continued the whole summer and disrupted his livelihood and, with it, his happiness. With no joy to stir him, he no longer sang in his garden. One night, he went out to smoke in his garden beneath his trees so that the sounds of nature might tell him what weather to expect when fishing the next day. Suddenly, he heard a voice asking if it was him there in the garden. He answered but protested that he could not see anyone. He questioned if it was the ben-varrey. The voice ignored his probing and wanted to know why she never heard his beautiful voice anymore. He explained his situation, and she promised she would show him where to find the herring if he would sing.

The next day, he followed her advice and brought home a boat full of fish. He was so happy; not only did he sing, but he offered her roses. She asked if she might try an apple and explained she had always wondered about their taste since they smelled so sweet and looked like jewels. So, he gave her one, and from time to time, she would return and ask for an apple as she listened to him sing. From then on, he always had good luck and a full haul. Eventually, he planted for her a tree of her own so that she could enjoy the blossoms falling in the water in the spring and reach up and harvest apples for herself in the autumn.

Again, we find a story where the mermaid is like a familiar spirit. They visit each other and spend time together. There may be affection, as he initially offers her roses and grows her a tree of her own. She enjoys listening to him sing more than anything else. Ultimately, we see an example of an exchange of good fortune and faery blessings for the attention and gifts that the mortal gives. This keeps with the view A.W. Moore gave in The Folk-lore of the Isle of Man. He explains that the leannan sidhe is the "spirit friend" and serves as a familiar spirit. He explains that the leannan sidhe and the dooiney-oie, or "night man," are two faery spirits, separate from the faeries proper, who serve as friends and familiars. Moore compares the dooiney-oie to the bean sidhe in a manner reminiscent of Lady Wilde's link between the two. Moore provides two stories of the leannan sidhe. One is in keeping with his idea that the spirit is a faery guardian, whereas the other presents a spirit of madness.

The first tale of the leannan sidhe presented by Moore accords with his view that they are guardian spirits that befriend families. He explains that the Fletcher family of the Ballafletcher Estate had a special crystal cup. The cup was dedicated to the leannan sidhe, who resided at the estate. Each year at Christmas, the lord of the manor would drink from the cup in the faery's honor. To not observe this annual ritual would bring misfortune, but presumably, the intention was to keep the leannan sidhe pleased with the family so she would bring blessings of peace to the household. The guardian spirit seems connected to the house since the ritual continued to be observed by the next family to possess the estate. The elements included don't seem to be similar to other leannan sidhe stories, and Katherine Briggs notes this story in particular as if it is a unique example. However, it does illustrate the idea of an established relationship involving exchange for the benefit of the mortals involved. Still, other elements may be missing concerning how the relationship was established or what it is like.

The other story provided by Moore will seem more familiar to those expecting a story of the leannan sidhe to involve pining, madness, and faery romance. Moore describes an otherwise normal man who had a faery sweetheart. Problems occurred when the man noticed the faery, who did not wish to be seen. As a result, the man was struck mad. He became quiet and started to sleep in the barn. He would talk with the faery but then quiet down if he heard anyone around.

We can assume that when the man is described as having a faery sweetheart, initially, it was the faery in love with the man, and the man did not know. However, the story seems incomplete, and Moore's recounting is used as an example of how people might interpret something like a person going mad through the lens of folk beliefs. Kruse presents a similar Manx story. In this one, the man is a strong man who takes up with a faery woman. No one could see her but him. He began to share his food and drink with her and would move his cup to offer it to her. The man would laugh and talk with her but was guarded about other people hearing what he was saying. He became paranoid that people were watching him and believed that the faery was warning him about people spying on him.

This example depicts a familiar spirit in the sense that the faery and the man have a familiar relationship. We don't see any benefit the man receives from it. The faery gets offerings of food and drink consistently in this relationship. We might assume that the man wastes away because he stops taking his fill of food and drink. Most clearly, this story reflects how a deep spirit relationship can force a person into the space of the liminal. In both of these stories, humans become so involved with their faery courtships that they can't properly operate in human spaces. They are living in a space between the human and the faery worlds, not physically, but in so far as the vector of their efforts and attentions. We see this alluded to in other stories, like those of Cherry of Zennor and Jenny Permuen. They couldn't operate in the human world and were fixed upon pining for their lost faeries.

Kruse also discusses the persistence of faeries in these love affairs. Stories include faeries traveling across the sea to follow their human lovers. Kruse notes that the leannan sidhe is often described as haunting their human lover because of how consistently they are present. This element of ongoing proximity and presence is again reflected in the relationship with the familiar. I have described the tutelary spirit relationship with the Guardian Angel after one undergoes the process to establish "knowledge and conversation" as a possessing spirit relationship. As we have noted earlier, the relationship with the familiar is not quite that of a possessing spirit, at least not one which is seated as in the case of knowledge and conversation and certain types of spirit-priest relationships. We might consider that the familiar relationship could involve a form of the first phase of possession, in which there is close contact, and there is some blurring of boundaries between the human's awareness and the spirit's communication reflecting an intimate closeness. However, a familiar relationship doesn't always have that kind of interwoven nature. Routinely, the familiar is simply present with the magician most of the time or "near" enough to easily be called upon. As the magician moves through life, including moving from one place to another, the familiar goes along with them.

As we said at the on set of our discussion of the leannan sidhe, the term simply means "faery lover" or "faery sweetheart" and can refer to many types of faeries and faery relationships. The contemporary use of the term is often taxonomical and seems to refer in particular to a sort of faery that seeks out human lovers and is nourished by their life. Some of the stories we've seen don't necessarily depict a vampire-like relationship, but causing obsession, taking the lover in the afterlife, or consuming their food and leaving them unable to function in life do seem to occur commonly. Some faery lovers are more clearly vampiric in nature.

Katherine Briggs describes the Baobh Sith as a Highland Scottish variant of the bean sidhe. The behavior of these spirits overlaps with what one might expect of the leannan sidhe. In her Encyclopedia, she tells the story of four young men who took shelter one night while hunting. They began to make music and dance to pass the time. One of the men wished they had partners with whom to dance. Almost as soon as he said it, four women entered the shelter. Three took to dancing with the men, while one sat with the young man making music. As he hummed his tune, he saw blood dripping from his friends, so he ran from the shelter. His partner ran after him, and he hid among the horses. Their iron shoes may have kept the woman at bay because she spent the night circling him, unable to approach. At daybreak, she vanished, and the man returned to the shelter to find his friends dead and drained of blood.

Amongst stories associated with the leannan sidhe, we see stories of merfolk like the ben-varrey. They are often presented as women, but male merfolk are also frequently known to take human lovers. The leannan sidhe in most places refers specifically to female faeries, but in Ireland, we also find the gean canach, or love talker, which might be thought of as a male corollary to the leannan sidhe.

Briggs presents the poem "The Love Talker" by Ethna Carbery to describe the gean canach or ganconer. In the poem, the faery has black but fiery eyes, cold lips, and the breath of death. He has a sweet voice with words that ensnare. When he clings to the woman, it is like a mist takes her and shuts out the world. Eventually, the woman in the song banishes him with the sign of the cross, and he vanishes as a cloud that dissipates. Once he was gone, she recalled a rhyme that warned that the lover of the gean canach would soon need a death shroud. So the woman went home and was met with the tearful eyes of her mother and was saddened by the loving eyes of her father as she set to make her own shroud. She described the hour she spent with the faery as a bitter one that drained her life.

The gean canach is known to smoke a pipe. They appear as handsome faeries and play hurling like other faeries amongst the daoine sidhe. In some stories, they live in caves and kidnap women from crossroads. If the woman has a sweetheart, he might come and win her back from the faery at Halloween. The faery taking a woman from a crossroads is a motif we also saw in our faery widower stories.

Kim McNamara-Wilson offers a description of the gean canach, which sounds more like the leannan sidhe and has elements that might remind us of familiar spirits and bewitched women in her article "Irish Faerie Folk of Yore and Yesterday – The Gancanagh." According to McNamara-Wilson, the gean canach would appear, smoking his pipe and waiting for a woman to chance upon him. He would appear to her as whatever her ideal man looked like. If she touched him at all, she would become obsessed with him and unable to resist him. Each subsequent contact deepened her obsession and further removed any will or resolve she might have to resist him. She would become a slave to him, giving into his desire whenever and where ever it struck. The desires of the faery man would strike often, and even in places and times that might be inconvenient or embarrassing for the woman, but she would no longer care. Other people could see him, but he would just appear like an ordinary stranger. The woman's obsession with him and her willingness to succumb to him would be confusing for her friends and distressing for her family.

McNamara-Wilson also suggests that the gean canach delights in bawdy gossip. So he shares his exploits with his bewitched lover with the local men and entices them to share their own sexual stories. It would not take long for the gean canach to get bored with his conquest and desire to move to the next. When that happened, he would disappear. As is frequently the case with a faery lover, the woman would pine and search obsessively. The obsession might drive her to madness or fits of rage over the loss of him. She would lose interest in food, drink, and sleep and would search and pine. It wouldn't take much time for this situation to lead to her death.

Unlike the leannan sidhe, the gean canach doesn't seem to provide anything of substance to its victims. Men might also be the victim of a gean canach; if they have wasted time and money pursuing a woman fruitlessly, it's said that they have met a gean canach. In addition to the threat of death, encountering them could bring bad luck. These spirits seem to provide flattery and the fulfillment of fantasy more than anything else. When we consider what a relationship with one would look like, there are elements that might remind us of witch folklore.

Let's imagine a scenario. A young woman who has generally been well-behaved and pious and proper goes about running errands through town. She takes a detour to walk by the fields and pick flowers, and at a crossroads, she sees a striking young man leaning against the rough wooden fence post. He has a pipe in his mouth, beautiful golden hair, and dark smoldering eyes. His voice is sweet, and he says the kindest, most flattering things. As he speaks to her, it's like the rest of the world is gone. He is more beautiful than any man in the village and is like something out of her own dreams and fantasies. She gives herself to him there at the crossroads. From then on, she thinks of him constantly. He appears randomly, and she is always ready to rush off to be with him. Perhaps at times, she is taken in fits of passion, quivering as if some invisible lover has taken her in moments or places not fit for such things.

In the right century, this would be the beginning of an accusation of witchcraft. The victim would be seen as having taken the devil as a lover. Fits of passion and ecstasy with some invisible lover would be the ecstatic seizures that frequently pop up in bewitchment stories. The gean canach doesn't give us a tale of a spirit providing help or favors. The gean canach doesn't remain with his lover throughout a long life. Instead, the gean canach desires attention and for his victim to stay with him whenever he asks, much as familiars do in trial accounts. The gean canach bewitches his lover, as witches were often thought to be bewitched by the spirits they were accused of giving themselves to. The sensational element of succumbing to the carnal whims of devils is mirrored here but with a much less fortunate outcome.

The risks of the leannan sidhe and related spirits may point us away from them as far as spirits we might seek as familiars. If such a relationship could be managed to avoid fatal obsession or being taken as their entertainment after death, many of these spirits do seem keen to provide favors and blessings to their lovers. Some of these spirits even seem to provide luck and prosperity with only attention, affection, and small gifts given to them rather than taking the life of the mortal.

Conclusion

Mostly, these stories of faery lovers are not stories of the familiar spirits of witches and sorcerers. When we explored the various mythological stories, mechanisms for relationships between the human and faery worlds were present that could be the basis for building relationships like the relationship with a familiar spirit. But, for the most part, those stories didn't present examples which looked like familiar spirits or a prototype for the idea. Instead, we saw powers, behaviors, and means of interaction that presented a worldview in which familiars could exist, but we didn't see that relationship. In most stories, we saw gods rather than spirits who would function as familiars.

As we moved into the various folk stories, we began to see more elements that could relate to familiar spirits. Generally, those elements were isolated points of comparison. Still, we could see across a host of stories a collection of elements that could be brought together to build an idea like that of the classic familiar. Again, we confirmed that the world inhabited by the people telling these stories and having these encounters is one in which the familiar spirit could occur. By the time most of these folklore stories are being recorded, we are two hundred years after the peak of the witch trials. The stories don't pre-exist the presence of familiars. The stories likely reflect the folk beliefs that reach back to times contemporary with witch trials, cunning folk, and aristocratic magicians. They may draw on beliefs and practices that reach back before that point, as we see in the case of Thomas the Rhymer. In general, taken with the mythology and the continuation of these sorts of folk encounters, they indicate some continuity.

The leannan sidhe stories all but depict the relationship with a familiar spirit in some cases. The stories depart from the type of relationship we'd see with a familiar because they're not magical contracts, and often the faery is in charge of the relationship. In the best cases, we see an ongoing relationship, with an exchange of gifts and services, close and consistent proximity, and possibly some affectionate or sexual element. In the worst cases, we see a human victim driven to madness and death. Some of these stories look so close to the familiar spirit relationship that it is easy to see a connection.

In many of these stories, the point is not to illustrate faery relationships as a road map to building them. The stories are sometimes entertainment and sometimes warnings. Sometimes they're explanations of bizarre things that happened around bizarre people. Just like trial accounts will focus on the criminal activity of witches, these stories will present the dangers of people encountering these powers because that's what the average person needs. Stories of skilled magicians or empowered witches accessing these powers present the other side of the tale. The side not often told.

The connection we can see does not necessarily indicate that the familiar spirit was present in the magic of Britain and Ireland before more southern influences. It does show that the progression of ideas from medieval mythology into early modern folklore could have resulted in a concept that looked like the familiar spirit. It also suggests that those looking to work in a more Pagan or folklore-derived context rather than a grimoire magic or historical witchcraft context can turn to faery lore as a basis for developing a relationship with a familiar spirit. The fact that we can't indicate with certainty by looking at myths and folktales that familiar spirits existed natively without southern influence doesn't mean that it isn't the case. The spirit world depicted in these stories can easily contain familiars, going back to the 9th century. Elements of this view of the spirit world are consistently present and endure. The witches described in English and Scottish accounts, even while understanding themselves to be Catholics, lived in the spirit world described in these stories.

XI
The Faery Familiar

In his blog "British Fairies," John Kruse discusses overlaps between the witches' imp, or familiar, and faeries in the August 2022 article "Witches' imps, faery familiars." He begins by noting that some folklorists have suggested that the imp or familiar spirit doesn't seem to show up before British witch trials in 1560. He then quotes an unnamed author who suggests that it is unlikely that the imp was a previously unknown species of creature but rather naturally developed out of existing faery folklore. This has been a core element of this section of this book. We're looking at relationships between faery lore and familiar spirits to explore the possibility of these tutelary relationships existing in Northern Europe, Britain, and Ireland and giving rise to the use of familiars by magicians. Connecting faery lore to the common experience of the familiar spirit helps us explore options for Pagan and faery-familiar relationships. In addition, exploring faery lore and myths allows us to look at threads in magical concepts and spirit experiences to gain a more complete picture of how to explore the nature of familiar spirits and our options for working with them.

I don't believe many contemporary people think faeries are outside the realm of the familiar spirit. It's pretty clear that witches' imps behave very similarly to faeries. Anyone familiar with the history of witch trials will be aware that certain regions have consistent faery activity tied in with their witch trial accounts. Faeries as familiars are noted in some historical explorations of magic. There isn't much debate as to whether or not there were faery familiars. The questions we can explore are whether or not the imps treated as demons by magistrates were, in fact, faeries and whether or not familiar spirit relationships existed with faeries outside of accounts in witch trials.

Regarding the existence of faery familiar relationships outside of witch trial accounts, we have explored several examples of myths and faery stories that give us an idea of whether or not those themes and elements are present in folk belief. We can see elements similar to the relationship with familiar spirits, at least in certain folklore relationships with faeries. Exploring accounts of witch trials, the spirits the witches claimed to know, and the behaviors of their familiars and imps will answer whether we should view them as faeries or follow the footsteps of the witch hunters and assume they are devils. Some researchers have pointed out that earlier accounts tend to depict faeries and elves, whereas later accounts, likely influenced by fears and social destabilization related to the Reformation, shift to more frequent references to devils and demons.

While some very notable Scottish witch trial cases, like Isobel Gowdie and the North Berwick Witches, seem to involve the presence of The Devil, there are many notable witch trial cases involving faeries and elves. Even in cases involving the Devil, the Faery Queen is often present. Marion Grant, Andro Mann, Bessie Dunlop, Margaret Alexander, Alison Pearson, Katherine Jonesdochter, and Stein Maltman are all examples of witches whose trials reflect relationships with the faeries. Outside of Scotland, we find faery witches as well. The idea that witches might encounter faery nobility, make pacts and enter into love affairs with them, and then receive magical powers, knowledge, gifts of prophecy, and familiar spirits, is not at all uncommon in history.

A major difficulty in ascertaining the nature of the familiar spirits in trial accounts is that there is often no agreement as to what the spirits are. The accused might describe their familiar as a ghost, a faery, and a devil at various points. It seems likely that acknowledgment of the familiar as a devil results from torture or convincing by prosecutors rather than a belief that the concepts are interchangeable. At least, this seems likely in instances where the accused thinks their interactions with the fair folk are not at odds with their status as a Christian member of the community. For example, Elspeth Reoch of Orkney believed her familiar, John Stewart, was a deceased relative but also a faery. She confessed to lying with him and eventually confessed he was a devil. In this case, one would expect that she was convinced to change her view. Still, the idea that it was simultaneously a ghost and a faery, a relative and a lover, seems to add a layer of possible confusion. We might assume that this is an example of faeries and ghosts being viewed as the same, but this is not always the case. Bessie Dunlop viewed her familiar, Tom Reid, as a ghost, but he was commanded by the Faery Queen and took her to encounter the faeries. He had connections to faeries, but Dunlop understood him to be a human ghost.

There are complicated overlaps in the accounts and competing contemporary views. While the average person, especially those still sympathetic to a Catholic worldview, lived in a world adjacent to the lives and activities of the fair folk, the new religious standard did not have room for faeries. Bishop John Hooper published a pamphlet in 1579. In it, he described familiars as "devilish imps" and denounced the wisdom of the wise women who consort with them because they do not realize that they consort with the Devil. Hooper's dismissal of the wisdom of witches and cunning folk reveals that the people engaging these spirits did not themselves view them as devils. In The Meanings of Elf and Elves in Medieval England, Alaric Hall quotes the 13th-century Dutch poem, "Das Natuurkunde van het Geheelal," which describes night-riding hags. Hall demonstrates throughout his thesis, particularly in chapter eight, that these hags are witches who overlap the space of elves, valkyries, human women, and a host of supernatural functions. The poem describes the night wandering women as devils and connects them with maeres, cobalds, good protective spirits, elves, and water monsters, naming them all as devils. It is an excellent example of how clear taxonomical distinctions don't always exist, not only for these spirits but even for humans who consort with them in an historical context. The witch herself might be a devil, just as the prosecutor of the witch might define her faery associates as devils.

In "Fairies and The Devil in Modern England," Darren Oldridge discusses a poem from 1593 by Thomas Churchyard. The poem involves a dreamer who encounters the Faery Queen, who leads him to a group of beautiful faery maidens dancing. The maidens fade away into shadow and are replaced by dark loathsome bug creatures. Oldridge discusses this as an example of the Protestant effort to reorient the landscape of spirit beliefs. He notes that in Discouerie of Witchcraft, the bugbears and imps of faery stories were dismissed as part of folk superstitions belonging to Catholics. He quotes a Protestant minister from 1590, Henry Holland, who described faeries, goblins, and hags (witches) coming into the church in "a rotten mist of popery." Popery, of course, like "popish," referred to Catholicism. He goes on to quote Samuel Harsnett, the Archibishop of York, as saying in 1603 that fairies and imps were part of a popish mist that had befogged the English people. Oldridge explains that in early modern England, Protestants were left with either denouncing faeries as delusions or stories, or explaining that they were demons misleading people. He notes that these options were not mutually exclusive. While denouncing faeries as demons seems to have been the preferred choice, the delusion of a faery story could also be denounced as the Devil spreading lies through idle thoughts and stories.

The Protestant influence in the recharacterization of the view of magic and spirits is fairly evident. King James greatly expanded the purview of England's anti-witchcraft laws and made it easier to prosecute witches. Stuart McHardy comments in his notes on Isobel Gowdie's trial transcript that before the North Berwick trials and the relatively contemporary publication of King James' Daemonologie, witch hunters sought out cases of consorting with faeries. After these events around the 1590s, the focus began to shift towards the diabolical in Scottish witch trial cases. The height of European witch-hunting ran from 1560 - 1630, and thus the bulk of English and Scottish accounts come after the Reformation took hold. This further complicates looking at spirits and folk beliefs in trial accounts, as Protestantism espoused a worldview that left no space for such beliefs and required that they be understood through the language of diabolism. The instability of the social structure provided by Christianity and the suspicion of secret Catholics and secret Protestants through the power struggle between Reformers and Catholics also led to a perception of increased diabolical activity and a belief in clandestine organized Satanic cults fomenting division and instability in Christianity. This became the backdrop against which folk beliefs would be viewed throughout Europe, causing them to be seen as demonic and dangerous. While the good citizens of England and Scotland may have been befogged by Catholic superstitions of spirits, our efforts to untangle early modern spirit beliefs are befogged by Protestant fears.

It's also difficult to consider the nature of these familiars when one considers available historical writing on the subject. Emma Wilby notes in her book Cunning Folk and Familiar Spirits that very little has been produced on the witches' familiar, and even less on the familiar spirits used by cunning folk. She notes that "learned" magicians were understood to have familiars, and so were witches but that many writers on the subject assume familiars were either rare amongst cunning folk or at least that there is a lack of evidence to attest to the use of familiars. Wilby asserts that there is strong evidence that the use of familiars by cunning folk was common. Whether cunning folk routinely had familiars or not doesn't answer issues of the presence and nature of faery familiars for us. The lack of material on the subject presents part of the problem in exploring it.

Wilby's text is a popular standard, but it is not without its problems. In exploring the faery familiar in particular, one would expect to turn to Wilby. Unfortunately, the mechanism Wilby uses for addressing the nature of the familiar makes this a little harder. Rather than distinguish between witches and cunning folk based on folk understandings of the two or some difference in method or vocation, Wilby denotes cunning folk as magicians who seemed to predominately do beneficent magic and witches as those who predominantly did malefica. Wilby notes that cunning folk also commonly used malefica, so the distinction is blurry. As a result, Wilby recharacterizes many people who were convicted of witchcraft as cunning folk. This isn't much of a problem for our purposes, except that Wilby denotes cunning folk familiars as "fairy familiars," while noting that they are a wide range of spirits, and witch familiars as "demon familiars," while also noting that they are a wide range of spirits. So the denotation of a familiar as a faery or a demon only tells us Wilby's assessment of whether the trial account describing them is primarily describing positive or negative magic. It also doesn't leave room for exploring actual distinctions between the types of familiar.

After giving this delineation, Wilby goes on to explain that cunning folk and witches have very similar experiences with their familiars. Their familiars are received in similar ways. Their familiars appear to them in similar ways. They describe their familiars with similar attributes. Whether the familiar is a ghost, a faery, or a devil does not seem to create a consistent adjustment in how they are received or how they appear.

While this is frustrating in terms of turning to a source to find information on a particular sort of spirit encounter, it fits our general position. Many types of spirits can become familiars. The method by which they are acquired will vary largely based on the practitioner. Someone born with witchblood will likely encounter a spirit, perceive the spirit, and then begin to work with it, or they might receive it from a family member. A person acquiring witch power will likely engage a powerful spirit and, through bargain or intercourse, receive power and receive a familiar. A sorcerer will likely conjure a series of spirits and, at some point, ask one to appoint a familiar. Any of these types of magicians might receive a devil, a ghost, a faery, an angel, or perhaps something else altogether dependent upon the source of their familiar.

Another way to consider this similarity in accounts that Wilby describes is that most early modern English magicians encountered similar types of spirits. Regardless of whether we consider these individuals to be witches or cunning folk, it seems like many of them have spirits with similar powers, behaviors, and appearances. Magicians employing grimoire techniques, whether we are thinking of clergy, wealthy people and those under their patronage, or cunning folk, would likely have conjured demons and angels to receive familiars, but some may have called upon faeries as well. These aren't typically the people we read about in witch trial accounts. Local villagers who had magical skills and helped or hurt their communities are the people who described their familiars to prosecutors, and these are the people whose accounts share common elements. These people also lived lives not only tied to folk beliefs and customs but lives that were defined by them and in which they survived based on them.

When we think of a witch and her imps, our first thought is probably of Isobel Gowdie. Gowdie names all the spirits who wait upon the witches of her coven. Reading her confession, one is left with the impression that the coven gatherings are a feast followed by dancing and sex with the Devil and these spirits. The first time I read the confession, I confused the nicknames the Devil gives the witches with the spirits' names, leaving me with the idea that they were silly impish faery creatures. The reality is that the familiars are named and associated with the witches, but we aren't given a ton of specific information on the familiars. Accounts like those of the Pendle witches give us a lot more to look at regarding familiars.

Gowdie's confessions are often looked at as important because there are four of them, and they are detailed and vivid. Some criticize the fascination with Gowdie based on the belief that she was possibly delusional or simply telling the prosecutors what they wanted to hear. Gowdie's confessions have plenty of interesting material to sink into, particularly regarding how the witches did their magic. They aren't confessions that focus a lot on familiars. Whereas many insular confessions with interesting or useful material depict a familiar doing magic for the witch and the witch interacting with faeries and the dead, Gowdie's are focused on the Devil. Does this mean that Gowdie's account is purely diabolical and her covens familiars are, in fact, devils and demons? No, I don't think so.

The most diabolical component of Gowdie's confession is the baptism ceremony by which Gowdie becomes a witch. Without that, her confession would start to feel more criminal than diabolical. The witches described by Gowdie do their magic "in the Devil's name," but Gowdie professes a draw towards Catholicism and a desire for its return. Witches working with faeries, as we mentioned, seem in many cases not to see this as being at odds with Catholicism or their understanding of local folk Christianity. Gowdie's Devil provides elf-shot to the witches. This Devil takes them to dine in faeryland; although the Devil is not described as being at the table with the Faery Queen, the Faery King is. If Gowdie encountered the Faery Queen through the Devil or the Devil through the Faery Queen, we would likely see that pairing at the dinner rather than the Faery King, unless the Devil is the Faery King. Gowdie's Devil shapeshifts into a host of animals, and his main preoccupation seems to be sex with as many humans as possible. The animals listed aren't the goat we see in sensational continental Devil orgy stories. The Devil Gowdie experiences shows up as a deer or a crow, forms which we are more likely to see in tales of faery encounters. Gowdie's Devil helps his witches steal crops from fields, color from dyes, and strength from ale. Everything here fits with faery magic and faery stories. The Devil even employs "elf boys" in the production of elf-shot. One of the familiars is named "Thomas a Faerie." Now, we might consider that the other spirits aren't faeries since Thomas is specifically designated as such, but we can assume at least Thomas, if not all the rest, is a faery familiar. Some of the familiars are described as being dressed in various greens, a color popular for faeries and which often indicates faeries in folklore.

We can't say for certain what the nature of the familiars of the Aulderne coven was. Were they devils in service to a larger devil, as Gowdie describes? Or were they faeries that Gowdie described as devils due to her plight? It could be that the stenographer simply recorded them as devils regardless of how they were described, though they seem to have omitted recording details regarding her faery experiences. As rich and interesting as Gowdie's account is, there really isn't enough to dig deep between the lines and assert that the Devil is a faery, and so are the familiars. At least, not with real certainty. We can say there is room to consider the possibility that Gowdie's familiar and those of her coven mates were faery familiars. We can look at similar examples of familiars who were called devils and then take all those comparisons in light of the prominence of faery accounts.

Hall notes that, like Gowdie, Katherine Ross in 1590 described receiving elf-shot. Similarly to Gowdie, Ross's confession does not focus on elves. Instead, it mentions elves specifically in relation to elf-shot. Ross describes going into faery hills to speak with elf folk who gave her darts that she could use by shooting them at images of people she intended to harm. The presence of elf-smiths of witching weapons in Gowdie and Hall could indicate a distinction between faery and diabolical experiences. The women describe these specific interactions with the elves but otherwise speak of devils. Alternatively, it could be that elf belief, and faery faith were a common backdrop that influenced these witches. With that backdrop, they may have experienced spirits similar to those expected within their folk belief, but like the author of Natuurkunde, they may see no distinction between an elf and a devil.

Hall makes an additional interesting point about the prominence of elf-shot in these witch trial cases. Women riding in the night in spirit with supernatural elven power to cause harm is a common motif spanning centuries before the witch trials. Mythological women of power are also often shown as armed. The overlapping traditions linking armed elf-women, faeries, hags, valkyries, furies, and witches indicate a supernatural nature possessed by witches despite their human existence. Witches exist in a space that is foreign; they are othered in a way that links them to faeries, spirits, divine figures, and devils. Early fay women, or women connected to the powers of the fates, who were witches, queens, and the initial source from which we take the word faery, were part of a series of overlapping functions of power exhibited by groups and individuals who partook of both natural and supernatural stature. The fact that the witches we encounter in trials also rode out at night upon spirits, stole food, and shot pain and death from their fingers with elven weapons places them within the continuity of the witches of literature, who were themselves either powerful faeries, or the children of giants, faeries, gods, and other supernatural beings. While the witches recorded in history gained their supernatural stature from carnal intercourse with spirits rather than being born of such unions, the essential concept was still part of the backdrop of awareness that informed both the accusers and the accused.

The use of the familiar to cause harm is more prominent within the confessions of the Pendle witches. We do not see elf-shot as a recurring motif in the Pendle confessions. Instead, the familiars, in several instances, make contact with the objects of the witches' malice. The riding motif is also generally absent. But, the historical association of elves as a cause of unseen pains, and faeries as a cause of stroke are echoed in the use of the familiar to bring lameness, madness, and death.

One of the two main Pendle witches, Demdike, had a familiar named Tibb; he essentially shares his name with the faery Tib, from "The Life of Robin Goodfellow." Tibb is initially described as a spirit or devil. He appears as a young boy in a black and brown coat. Gowdie also described the Faery Queen as wearing a combination of brown and white. If these dual-colored clothes are checkered, that is a common motif for faery clothing. Neither source describes more than the dual coloring, though. While we initially see Tibb in human form, he appears other times as several animals, including a brown dog, a black cat, and a hare. Tibb routinely appeared at dawn during the first several years of his relationship with Demdike. Some faeries are known to disappear in daylight, often those who are hunting or intending to harm humans, but sometimes those who are simply avoiding human attention. Others interact with humans in daylight. In Tibb's case, appearing just before dawn, he arrives at a "betwixt and between" time, a time that is not quite day and not quite night. These twilight times are often associated with faeries because of their liminality. A familiar would tend to be a spirit that could be around at any time, but this behavior seems to have been common of Tibb before Demdike employed him for any purpose.

The other of the two most notorious Pendle witches was Chattox. Her familiar was named Fancy. Fancy initially appeared as a man but also as a bear and spotted dog at other times. Faery animals are also sometimes described as spotted, but another time Fancy appeared as a brown dog, so there may not be a particular otherworld indication in the appearance. Fancy is mostly described in the confession as killing people and animals or driving them mad. He is also described as taking Chattox's sight and causing weariness over time. If the spirit is draining her health rather than just living on a few drops of her blood and whatever food she provides him, that could be a malign faery. All in all, the description of Fancy doesn't give us much to go on, but there is an incident involving Fancy and Tibb together. They provide a banquet for Chattox and Demdike with meat, butter, bread, and cheese. The meal would be the common things desired by people of the time, but it also includes the sorts of things a faery might request. The food is illuminated by light with no source, and the women eat it but do not become full and receive no benefit from eating it. Food that isn't providing sustenance and seems illusory is a common motif of faery stories.

Demdike's daughter, Alison Device, briefly had a familiar in the form of a black dog. Black dogs are often associated with faeries, particularly as death omens. Agrippa, however, was also believed to have a black dog as a familiar, and it is unlikely that people believed his familiar was a faery. Alison Device's confession does not primarily concern her own dealings with her familiar, which seem limited. Instead they focus on accusing Demdike. In one story, Device acquires a quantity of milk and brings it to Demdike's home. It would seem that she left and returned in a short time, and upon her return, a significant quantity of butter was found in the milk, with the quantity of milk undiminished and the elderly Demdike still asleep in bed. The implication here is that Tibb produced the butter while Demdike slept, which would be well suited to the sort of tasks done by faeries and household spirits.

Alison's brother James Device had a familiar named Dandy. Dandy first appeared to him as a brown dog and later as a black dog. In another instance, it came and insisted that James had touched John Duckworth, a man who had failed to give James a shirt that was promised to him. Dandy explained that since James had touched John, this meant that Dandy now had power over John. James and Dandy then joined together and killed John. A faery's touch leading to death or the power to manipulate occurs in some of our faery lover stories, particularly those of the gean canagh. James's confession does not address a great deal of interaction with Dandy. Some other spirits appear to him in the form of animals, but it is not clear if they are other familiars or his own.

In general, there isn't anything conclusive in most of these stories. None of them have a ton of detail, and because the point of the confessions was to justify killing the witches, they are predominantly murder confessions. The same is true in Gowdie's case, the confession has a lot of vibrant descriptions of magical activity, but it's mostly a confession of murder and theft because that's what the prosecutors needed. What we can see here are the types of activities the spirits engage in. In the case of Gowdie, the spirits want sex, and they teach the witches magic and help facilitate it. The Pendle familiars want the witches to "stay" with them, which one can presume is a request for sex, and they want to suckle upon them. In some instances, the Pendle familiars teach magic, but they're mostly just killing people and animals. In the instances where we don't have murder, we have a man who is made lame, butter magically being churned, and faery food being provided.

For the Pendle witches, the initial encounter is another element that distances them from diabolical witchcraft. The Pendle witches have very little to indicate conspiratorial diabolical witchcraft within their confessions. They are not initiated into a coven and rebaptised to the Devil. There are no Devil orgies. Most importantly, they are not receiving their familiars from the Devil. Their familiars approach them while they are out and about. In the cases of Alison and James, there is an hereditary element. Their grandmother encourages a connection with the familiars, and their mother seems to have one as well. Encountering a familiar in a natural setting, directly, without an intermediary or another spirit gifting the familiar seems more common when the familiar is a ghost or a faery than an infernal spirit.

Oldridge and Wilby both point to the names of familiars as a connection with faeries. While Wilby seems to treat this as more indicative that there is a link or similarity between faery and demon familiars, Oldridge seems less certain. We have noted already that one of the Aulderne familiars is specifically noted in his name as being a faery. We have also seen that one of the Pendle familiars shares its name with a faery from a tale about Puck. Oldridge notes that in 1593 a character in George Gifford's <u>Dialogues Concerning Witches and Witchcraftes</u> provides puckril as a synonym for the witch's imp. Gifford also used the term in another work in 1587. Oldridge believes the term puckril relates the imps or witches' familiars to Puck or Robin Goodfellow and, therefore, with hobgoblins. Oldridge also notes the Ben Johnson play, <u>The Sad Shepherd</u>, which contained a familiar named Puck Hairy, who admits to being a devil but dances in the woods like a goblin. The names being shared in accounts of witches describing their familiars may indicate a folk awareness of faeries and household spirits being echoed in the expression of the witches' familiar. The fact that words used to describe familiars, both in trial accounts and in the literature of the time, evolved from words for faeries seems to indicate a widespread awareness of a connection between the imp and the goblin or the faery.

Oldridge seems to view this connection with some uncertainty. He notes that the words "imp" and "puckril" become common in trial accounts around 1645 but are fairly uncommon prior to that. Kruse, elsewhere, noted that the novel word would seem more likely to indicate a new word for an existing concept or type of spirit rather than some new spirit belief suddenly appearing. The similarity of descriptions of familiars before the prominence of the word imp would also indicate a continuity. Oldridge, however, points out that the imp has tendencies different from the faery or the goblin. For Oldridge, familiars appearing as small animals, drinking blood from the witch's body, being commanded by the witch, and being consistently wicked distinguish them from faeries. This distinction is, however, a weak one. Faeries appear in the form of animals and change their shapes. Faeries drink blood and drain the life of humans in many types of faery stories. While obeying a human is unusual, a faery who is trapped might obey a human, and leannan sidhe who are rejected by their human targets obey them in some descriptions of the leannan sidhe. Familiars may not be wholly wicked and may appear as such primarily because of the nature of trial accounts. Still, some trial accounts also depict familiars doing good things as well.

Wilby points out that both "fairy familiars" and "demon familiars" tend to be modest in their provision of wealth. Again, both categories could refer to faeries, dead people, or demons; the distinction in Wilby is simply beneficial magic versus harmful magic as a predominant activity. My own thinking regarding the Aulderne witches and the Pendle witches also turned to this. Wilby describes familiars teaching healing and magic and allowing the cunning man or woman to establish a career as a healer or a magician, and in some cases, this is true for the witch as well. This career can lift them out of poverty, or at least out of extreme poverty, which often catalyzed their willingness to accept aid from spirits. The familiars, in these cases, don't bring honors and dignities or the favor of kings and magistrates. They don't remove the spirits guarding treasure and show the magician where to find it. They don't facilitate alchemical transformations of metals or teach astronomy. They don't do the things ascribed to demons.

There is a degree to which one should consider the sort of magic they will likely focus on and what goals they need to bring to fruition when determining what sort of familiar spirit to seek out. There is also some space to say that spirits have a wide range of capabilities and aren't limited to a single area. Spirits of all types also perform variably as far as accomplishing any particular task. Even considering that, certain types of spirits will be better for some things than others. Some kinds of spirits will tend to produce results in particular ways. Stories of receiving large amounts of wealth from faeries often involve wealth that ends up being illusory. There are sometimes promises of wealth that don't manifest, like Skillywidden delivering his captor to the location of the faery gold. In stories of beneficial faery relationships, luck, prosperity, success in endeavors to make money, and ongoing basic support seem to be what humans receive when a good relationship is maintained. Stories of leaving faeryland and making deals with faeries often include the instruction not to take more than is owed even if more is offered.

Wilby notes that for both the practitioners she perceives as cunning folk and those she perceives as witches, their familiars may or may not promise treasure. Whether they promised treasure or simply a better life, what the magician receives is usually the means to make a living and success in doing so, or very small sums of money when needed.

This could reflect the nature of the familiars, or it could reflect the circumstances of the magicians. I don't know if there are stories of courtly wizards finding treasure using the aid of demon familiars. It seems unlikely that there is a lot of magical history depicting that. There are examples of such magicians in favored positions leading successful lives, but that could be their circumstance rather than their magic.

Looking at the nature of the acts performed by a witch's imps, devils, or familiars would be a great way to consider their nature. Unfortunately, the court documents focus on acts that paint the magicians as criminals, so we don't have a broad picture of their day-to-day magical experiences with their familiars. Non-trial and more modern cunning folk accounts may shed light. For example, George Pickingill is credited with claiming that his imps could perform a day's farm work in an hour. He was a cunning man who, in this instance, described his familiars doing something faeries or house spirits might do.

We do have many examples of accused witches describing their familiars as faeries. I think that, even if we can't say with certainty, many of those familiars who were described as devils were actually faery familiars. It is my assumption that amongst the average village magicians who either acquired the ability to contact spirits or naturally could perceive them, the fair folk and the dead were likely the most commonly accessible. The existing folk beliefs would have made encountering and working with the faeries an expected possibility, while the prevailing religion would have made selling oneself to Satan an untenable proposition.

Oberyon and the Seals of his Ministers
Folger Manuscript V.B.26

XII
The Faery Kings and Queens in Surviving Books of Magic

It's easy to look at the diversity of folk and faery stories, medieval romances, magic books, and the contemporary treatment of faeries and be left wondering if faery describes one type of being or many different ones. This question can get complicated. Contemporary people debate whether faery refers to something culturally specific or a broad cross-cultural phenomenon. Even in Britain and Ireland, faery is used for a narrow range of magical beings sometimes and a wide range other times. Within the narrow range of human-like creatures, the powerful women of medieval romances, the natural men of Robert Kirk, and the small people of folklore dressed in green and gold finery seem far afield from one another. Sometimes, the old gods live amongst the faeries, sometimes they are the faeries, and sometimes they're distinct, but a faery might have the name of a god or hero. There isn't a simple answer. Faery taxonomies often become problematic and inconsistent due to overlaps and inconsistent distinctions.

Adding household spirits and nature spirits might give us easier taxonomies. But, when we dig into them, boggarts, brownies, kobolds, and hobs overlap significantly. They allow us to create a category of less human-like creatures versus more human-like creatures. But, sometimes, they haven't been viewed as faeries. Further, categorizing them as two broad faery types doesn't add real distinctions within those two categories.

Looking at contemporary and pop-culture fairies adds complication. They don't seem like any of the historical conceptions. Yet, some people encounter faery creatures who exhibit some of these modern elements. Looking through modern history, we see advents of new thinking about faeries outside of folklore begin to bleed back into folk beliefs.

All of this shows us that beliefs and experiences develop over time. The reasons why experiences develop and change are open for debate. Because of this, we can recognize that not all descriptions will be the same. Even with this diversity, we do not have to look for strict taxonomies. We can recognize that certain types of sources describe beings who are often similar to one another but which might have some distinctions. Other sources might describe things that are more different but still recognizably related. Whether or not these beings are the same may not be answerable. Instead, we can consider how we interact with and what to expect when engaging beings described in a particular type of source or approached based on the customs or instructions of a particular context.

The faeries we see in medieval myth and in court romances share a relationship. The daoine sidhe, or the people of the hills, were viewed as the continuation of the Tuatha de Danaan after they lost control of Ireland when the Milasians came. Their stories interweave gods and faeries as the same people or neighboring people in the medieval period. Later, as the stories are retold in folklore and the characters reappear, they are more frequently depicted as faeries than gods living amongst the faeries. The medieval romances echo these beings in their depictions of faery witches and magical queens, magical knights, and giants. Daoine sidhe is an Irish name for these noble faeries, but we see this same process throughout the islands and in some of the courtly epics from the continent.

The faeries of the grimoires seem most closely related to these noble faeries. They are often described as kings and queens and sometimes have courts of ministers beneath them. Some of the grimoire faeries share their names with kings and queens in faery folklore and literature.

Since the faeries in the grimoires and the noble faeries in mythology are similar, sometimes overlapping, we can experiment with approaching the grimoire faeries for help with things the mythological faeries can accomplish. Likewise, we can pursue the powers of the grimoire faeries amongst the mythological faeries. The methods we consider for contacting each group might also be usable with the other group.

For our purpose, obtaining a familiar, it is safe to assume that calling upon and gaining the friendship of a faery king or queen is the first step. Then, that king or queen can assign a faery from their court or amongst those faeries subject to them. This kind of interaction would be within the realm of the social interactions we'd expect to find in mythology and epic romances. Sending someone from one court to another to maintain peace or build a connection was a normal activity of royal courts.

If your goal is to obtain a relationship with a particular type of faery-creature other than one of the small human-like faeries we see in folklore, or the noble human-like faeries we see in myths, these kings and queens could possibly facilitate that. A spirit like a brownie might chafe at being a familiar. More social faeries, and those known to pursue human interactions, may have connections to the kings and queens of the faeries even if these creatures are not daoine sidhe themselves. For example, the Robin Goodfellows, while more like the household spirits, sometimes appear in association with the faery kings and queens in literature.

With this in mind, we will provide information on the names of the faery kings and queens who appear in magical literature. We have already encountered several kings and queens in mythology, folklore, and courtly literature. Others from those sources are well known. Midir and Finvarra have shown up in our stories. Still, consider The Dagda, Angus, Lugh, Boann, Bodb, and other powerful members of the Tuatha de Danaan to have sway over the faeries and sometimes be counted amongst the daoine sidhe. Aine appears as a goddess and as a faery, as do some of the figures we've just mentioned. Outside of an Irish context, we also looked at the story of Volund, or Weyland. He is named as a chief amongst the elves. Nicnevin, Mab, and Titania are well known, along with Oberon, who will feature prominently in the magical texts as well as in courtly literature.

We should pause for special consideration of Aine. As we mentioned, like several other figures, she shows up both as a goddess and a faery. She is one of the Tuatha de Danaan. Some scholars, according to Briggs, have suggested she may be the same as Anu, one of the patronesses of Ireland. If that is the case, she would be a significant divine figure, but also one who continues to appear in faery stories. She is the mother of Earl Fitzgerald. Fitzgerald was a great warrior with powerful magic and the Irish hero against the Normans. He and his host of warriors disappeared to sleep under a mound until, one day, they would return, much like Arthur and his knights.

Aine is possibly connected with the Cailleach Bheur, and it has been suggested that she might be the queen of the leanan sidhe. Briggs notes that Donald Mackenzie believes that Black Annis, the monstrous hag, and Gentle Annis, the fair wind, are both derived from Aine and that she herself is derived from Anu. Briggs also notes that Eleanor Hull disputes the association with Annis but acknowledges the possible association with Anu. If Aine is the source of Black Annis - a monster who leaps from a cave and eats stray children; it might fit the assertion that the leanan sidhe are punishing those who forced them into the mounds. This assumes the belief that

Aine rules the leanan sidhe is correct. Annis's two-fold monstrous and gentle forms could relate to the summer maiden and winter hag associations of the Cailleach Bheur. Aine herself might be paired with Grian, one as the bright summer sun and one as the pale winter sun. She might also appear as a powerful Ulster faery named Aynia. She shows up with a high frequency that makes her an interesting figure for those looking to dig through myths and folktales to deeply explore a being that they might want to contact.

Turning to the grimoires, the first figures we will consider are Sybilia and Kale of the Mountains. There is an assumption that faeries occur solely in British magical texts. While Sybilia does appear in several examples of British magic and also in Arthurian courtly romance, she and Kale appear in the Hygromanteia texts known as The Magical Treatise of Solomon. We are starting here because these texts are older, possibly significantly older, than the British examples of faeries in grimoires.

Sybilia is derived from the tradition of the Sybils in Greece and Rome. The Sybils were demigoddesses who offered prophecy. Their prophecies were collected in a book which sometimes influenced the major decisions of powerful people in the Mediterranean. In the medieval era, we see the Sybils reduced to a single woman who appears as one of the sisters or compatriots of Morgan LeFay. She is one of the faery queens, or powerful witch queens, encountered by the knights. Her role in The Magical Treatise of Solomon is small, but she becomes a routine figure in later magical literature. Frequently, she is the primary faery contacted among the seven sisters of the faeries. While she is not included in the section of the Folger Manuscript listing the faeries, she does appear in a spell in the manuscript. In the next chapter, you will find a conjuration for Sybilia from The Cambridge Book of Magic. In it, she is listed with the following spirits, which may be her faery sisters, Coa, Rocoa, Trenda, Norma, Ristilao, Catica, and Cauca. In Reginald Scot's Discouerie of Witches, she appears in an invisibility spell along with her sisters, Milia and Achilia. Sibylia connects to invisibility, finding thieves, faery banquets, and faery lovers in the examples where she occurs.

Kale of the Mountain is primarily known to Anglosphere magicians through The Magical Treatise of Solomon. She appears as a bizarre-looking faery queen who lives in the mountains. She has been used as an example the depiction of demons in Greek demonology, but this does not seem to be a consistent element. In his edition of The Magical Treatise of Solomon, Ioannis Marathakis links her to Sybilia and Lamia. Kale of the Mountains, however, is traditionally the daughter of Alexander of Macedon. In Macedonian folklore, she drinks the waters of immortality, and in anger, Alexander curses her. As a result, she is sent away and becomes an immortal faery. She is the leader of the Nereids, a group of faeries who share their name with a group of Nymphs. They may have developed out of earlier Pagan beliefs regarding these Nymphs. Like the Pagan Nereids, the faery Nereids connect to water and, as such, to storms and rain. They are also a threat to newborn infants. This figure also features in Orthodox passion plays as a relative who insults and then is cursed by The Blessed Virgin Mary.

In The Magical Treatise of Solomon, the magician may appeal to Kale by presenting her with a gift of food. The food is left on a dish in the mountains where she resides. Then the magician hides until she comes out and finds it. When she asks who has done this kindness for her, the magician reveals that they have done this deed, and Kale grants them a wish in gratitude.

Separate from the well-known V.B.26 manuscript, currently published as The Book of Oberon, the Folger Library also contains a text with a spell for conjuring the seven sisters of the faery. The commonality of the seven sisters may harken back to the myths of the seven sisters, which seem to relate to the Pleiades. The sisters in this example are Lilia, Hestilia, Fata, Sola, Afrya, Africa, Julia, and Venulla. In this spell, the seven sisters are called upon to provide the magician with a faery lover.

The Grimoire of Arthur Gauntlet includes a conjuration of Oberion, which calls upon several angels. The way the angels are named suggests that they may be faeries. They are, Carmelion, the angel of the Moon; Scorax, the angel of the Sun; Raberion, the counselor of Mars; Kaberion, for whom no association is given; and Seberion, the counselor of Venus. This text potentially provides us with an incomplete set of faeries related to planetary powers. If these figures are faeries, it provides an additional example in which a faery is conjured with the faery host as part of the process or means of conjuring the primary faery.

While there are several examples of faery conjurations in grimoires, we will complete our set of examples with one of the more thorough presentations in popular modern awareness. The Folger Manuscript V.B.26, more popularly known by its modern name, The Book of Oberon. This extensive magical text began to be collected in the late 16th century. It incorporates pieces from several other texts and material that seems to survive primarily in this collection. It influenced several prominent 18th and 19th-century British occultists, including members of the Society of the Mercurii and Frederick Hockley.

Oberon, the King of the Faeries who appears early on in Huon of Bordeaux and more famously in Shakespeare's Midsummer Night's Dream, is listed as Oberion or Oberyon in this text. He was a popular spirit for magical texts, appearing in a handful of surviving examples of cunningmen's notebooks that have been published. While Huon of Bordeaux is often cited as his first appearance, his name is linked to the Norse dwarf Alberich, whose name means Elf King. As Alberich, he appears in the Niebelunglied and the Ortnit, both from the 13th century. He also appears as Alfrikr in the 13th-century Thidreks Saga. Each of these appearances is either contemporary with or slightly earlier than Huon of Bordeaux but may reflect the collection of older material.

In the Folger Manuscript, Oberyon initially appears at the end of the primary spirit list containing the demons which eventually made their way into the Ars Goetia. Here he is described as a king, specifically as the king of the faeries. He is governed by the Sun and the Moon. He teaches medicine and the nature of stones, herbs, trees, and metals. He reveals hidden treasures and obtains them, and if bound, will carry treasurers from the sea. He can also make people invisible.

The text goes on to name Mycob as the faery queen. She appears in green, wearing a crown, and shares Oberyon's office, in other words, his role and stature. She provides a ring of invisibility and reveals the nature of stones, herbs, and trees. Under her are seven faery sisters, who do essentially the same things as her. They are Lilia, Restillia, Fata, Falla, Afria or Africa, Julya, and Venalla. These are almost identical to those given in the other Folger text.

About two hundred pages later, the text begins providing specific conjurations, circles, and illustrations for a handful of spirits. Eventually, we reach Oberyon, who is presented as both Oberyon and Oberion. In one illustration, his advisors are Storax, Caberyon, Carmelyon, and Severion. Some of these names are similar to those in Gauntlet. Then he is presented with a list of spirits, Bentranas, Bethaca, Benedill, Pantagor, Petangor, Damadas, Penedill, Paentagoras, Ama-das, Oberyon, and Rex Lewsydisson. An additional illustration presents him and his four ministers again with a new set of characters for each.

Further information on these ministers is not provided, but an additional series of characters for Oberyon and his ministers is. While we do not have descriptions for these spirits, they provide us with a court of spirits who are called as part of calling Oberion. They might be approached as subservient spirits, called under the authority of Oberion and the Sun and Moon. Like the seven sisters, who mirror the capabilities of Mycob, it is likely that these ministers also mimic Oberion's capabilities. The ministers, however, are also described as connecting to the Sun, the Moon, Mars, and Venus in Gauntlet and may have powers reflecting those associations.

Should the magician choose to conjure a faery, there is a rich world of faery nobility to consider. Myths, folklore, and books of magic all provide us with names, descriptions, and in some cases, information on how they are contacted.

"The Faerie Queene" by Edmund Spenser
Image by Walter Crane 1895

XIII
Encountering a Faery

In part one, we talked about meeting the Faery Queen and the Witches' Devil to obtain a familiar. In those contexts, we might assume that the familiar would be an "imp" or the faery familiars we see in historical witchcraft. Many writers contemporary with the witch trials would have, like the witch hunters, assumed that those imps were devils rather than faeries. Some practicing witches and magicians today might also view them as such or may presume that familiars provided by these sources come from amongst the dead. There are definitely a few possible options, and while a faery familiar is a very reasonable possibility using those methods, it isn't the only possibility.

For those interested in working with a faery familiar in particular and those looking to work outside of a witchcraft context, it may be important to consider how to approach a faery.

The Book of Oberon, The Book of Treasure Spirits, The Cambridge Book of Magic, The Magical Treatise of Solomon, The Discouerie of Witchcraft, Grimorium Verum, and a host of other books of magic have spells for encountering Sybilia or Oberion or some other medieval noble faery. For those looking to work in a grimoire context, it would be worth exploring those texts and the spells they provide if a faery familiar in particular is your goal. However, even if you don't intend to work by that method, it may be worth exploring a few of these sources. These texts give us instructions for working with faeries that were written down one hundred to three hundred years before folklorists began recording folk practices.

Here is an example from The Cambridge Book of Magic, a grimoire from the middle of the 16th century. The text seems to be the working magic book of a clergy member from before the dissolution of the monasteries. It reflects the assemblage of pieces from various other occult texts. It is often overlooked as an example of a grimoire with a faery conjuration. In fact, I believe even the translator of the text said that it did not have one. There is a section containing a conjuration of Sybilla, a variation of the name of the sibylline Faery Queen who frequently appears in grimoires and medieval literature. This particular example involves a child scryer and, therefore, may be unappealing for many magicians. It reflects a ritual as presented in the text of a working magician, whereas many of the grimoires with faery conjurations represent more formalized grimoires. The Book of Oberon, which also seems to collect pieces from various sources into a magicians working book, contains faery conjurations, but they are longer and more complex.

A Ritual to Sibylla from the Cambridge Book of Magic

The magician should get a candle made of virgin wax, and a child no older than ten who was born within wedlock. The child should sit between the legs of the magician and hold the candle in his right hand. The magician should take the candle in his own right hand and say:

Have mercy upon me, O God, according to your loving kindness: according to the multitude of your tender mercies blot out my transgressions.

Wash me thoroughly from my iniquity, and cleanse me from my sin. For I acknowledge my transgressions: and my sin is ever before me. Against you, and you only, I have sinned, and done this evil in your sight: that you might be justified when you speak, and be clear when you judge.

Behold, I was shaped in iniquity; and in sin did my mother conceive me.

Behold, you desire truth in the inward parts: and in the hidden part you shall make me to know wisdom.

Purge me with hyssop, and I shall be clean: wash me, and I shall be whiter than snow. Make me to hear joy and gladness; that the bones which you have broken may rejoice. Hide your face from my sins, and blot out all my iniquities. Create in me a clean heart, O God; and renew a right spirit within me. Cast me not away from your presence; and take not your holy spirit from me. Restore unto me the joy of your salvation; and uphold me with your free spirit.

Then I will teach transgressors your ways; and sinners shall be converted unto you. Deliver me from blood guiltiness, O God, you God of my salvation: and my tongue shall sing aloud of your righteousness.

O Lord, open you my lips; and my mouth shall show forth your praise.

For you do not desire sacrifice; or else would I give it: you do not delight in burnt offerings. The sacrifices of God are a broken spirit: a broken and a contrite heart, O God, you will not despise.

Do good in your good pleasure unto Zion: build the walls of Jerusalem. Then you shall be pleased with the sacrifices of righteousness, with burnt offerings and whole burnt offerings: then shall they offer bullocks upon your altar.

I confess to Almighty God,
to blessed Mary ever Virgin,
to blessed Michael the Archangel
to blessed John the Baptist,
to the holy Apostles Peter and Paul,
to all the Saints, and to you, brethren,
that I have sinned exceedingly
in thought, word and deed:
through my fault, through my fault,
through my most grievous fault.
Therefore I beseech blessed Mary ever Virgin,
blessed Michael the Archangel,
blessed John the Baptist,
the holy Apostles Peter and Paul,
all the Saints, and you, brethren,
to pray for me to the Lord our God.

Return the candle to the child and lay your right hand on his head, and say:

Oh God, who sent your spirit upon the apostles, send your Holy Spirit upon this virgin boy and illuminate and clarify this intellect and soul for me, so that he can see truly all of your creatures and relate to me the truth regarding all things I ask, Oh God, who lives and reigns through all ages of ages.

I conjure you, Oh virgin boy, by the virginity of the Blessed Virgin Mary, and by Saint Margaret the virgin, and you will not have the power to move your mind, but, must reveal to me the truth of all things which I ask, through him who will come and judge the living and the dead and the world through fire.

I conjure you spirit called Sibylla, by the names Coa + Rocoa + Trenda + Norma + Ristilao +, by Sibella the helper of fate +, Catica +, Cauca +, by Mercury, by all infernal bodies and infernal tributes, Seunalfor Volgor, that you come to us immediately and without delay into this pure candle, with the form of a blessed and happy pearl statue strengthened by darkness; hold out diligently, sanctified against feminine lust and foul menstruations by the ambrosial blood of grace, all of you make haste towards the permanent and stable glories.

Repeat the conjuration until she appears in the candle in the form of a fair woman. Instruct the child to let you know if a woman appears, and when she does, the child should say *"Welcome, Lady,"* and then the child should say this conjuration:

I conjure you by the virtue by which you were called, and by the virtue of your sisters, and by the virtue of Christ's own blood, that was shed for us on the Cross, and by the virtue of St. John the Baptist's head, and by the wisdom of Solomon, by which he constrained you to be obedient to mankind +, and by the throne, and his diadem, by his ring and by his sceptre, that you come soon without any let, show me the thief who stole my things.

She will leave the candle, and so you must say:

Oh God, who sent your spirit.

And she will return with a gem in hand to show you the answer. She may be reluctant to answer more than one question, so the child may need to repeat his conjuration and say, *"Show me or tell me the things,"* and if she still will not answer the exorcist may need to repeat his conjuration. When you have finished use this license to depart:

Go to the place which God has ordained for you, and be ready to come without delay with others when I call upon you in the name of the Father, and the Son, and the Holy Spirit, Amen.

I have translated the Latin myself, and so it differs somewhat from Doctor Young's presentation. I have also summarized and modernized the English instructions. It should be noted that this is a spell to catch a thief or discover information about stolen goods, but instructions are given to add on other goals, questions, and requests once the Lady answers the original query. For our purposes, the magician would omit the line about the thief and modify it as instructed in order to amend it to their goal of acquiring a faery familiar.

An interesting component of this is the powers used in conjuring. The virgin child is conjured by two sacred virgins, The Blessed Virgin Mary and St. Margaret. In particular, by the virginity of the Blessed Virgin Mary. It would seem that the power inherent in the child's purity is ensured by means of binding the child through the sacredness of virgin powers.

Similarly, the Faery Queen Sibylla is conjured not by names of God but by names which we can presume are her faery sisters. There are seven of them, and the sisters are often listed as seven; however, adding Sibylla or Sibella makes eight altogether. Still, the idea that she is conjured by what could be names of faeries in her entourage is interesting and links to the idea of conjuring the child's purity by means of the names of sacred virgins.

Aside from the two prayers of purification at the beginning, it is a relatively short and simple ritual. Some of the grimoire faery rituals are simple and short like this. Some are faery table rituals, which we will consider in our examples of cunning folk approaches. We also presented a variation of such rituals earlier in discussing the Devil and the Faery Queen. Others are much longer; as we mentioned, The Book of Oberon presents a ritual much like one would expect in using grimoire methods to conjure demons.

This brings us to the problem some might see in this approach. The drawback of grimoire sources is that they essentially treat the faeries as demons. Even in the ritual above, Silbylla is described as having been bound by Solomon, which is a legend about demons. We have to remember that in a medieval or early modern context, demon does not necessarily mean devil, fallen angel, or evil spirit. In fact, devil was sometimes used specifically to refer to the infernal spirits, while demon was more encompassing. Still, this was not always the case. In some texts, we do see information on the faeries provided separately from information on the devils, even though both are classed as demons. Demon, in that context, simply meant a sub-lunar spirit, or a spirit that wasn't an angel from amongst the heavens. This could be taken as an indication of the spirit's character. It could also be taken as a description of where they reside, what powers they succumb to, and what their predilections are for the use of their own powers. It could also indicate the nature of their bodily substance. Exploring demon as a general term can lead to some useful considerations, but demon may not be the lens through which contemporary people are comfortable viewing faeries, and it may not be the lens through which they wish to be viewed themselves.

Another consideration is the language and method used. These texts are Catholic in nature, or universalist. Whereas Protestants dismissed folk beliefs, many Catholics recognized them as real; therefore, folk spirits and faeries existed within the bounds and structures of Christian cosmology. As such, if the world has one Supreme God and his host of angels and saints, and faeries exist in that world, the faeries operate within that same Christian hierarchy. So, the faeries are conjured using the names of God, the powers of the Saints, and other Catholic imagery. This is a reasonable and workable approach if one believes the faeries converted to Christianity, as occurs in some folklore. Other folklore explains that faeries are fallen angels who had not sinned enough to deserve hell, so they reside on the earth or in the faeryland. That could also explain how faeries would be responsive to Christian rituals. Alternatively, if you believe the names, words, and symbols of Christian conjuration have power because God gives them power, then the beliefs or desires of the spirit don't impact that. In that context, those methods may be workable.

If you believe the faeries are the old gods or that they are a race of magical beings similar to but separate from humans, then you might consider their culture and their expectations. Taking that into account, binding them and cursing them through Christian symbols and hierarchies might appear rude to them. It might be impertinent to approach them with the expectation that you can command them because you've said half a dozen names in broken Hebrew and broken Greek and referenced a handful of Saints they're unaware of.

Your goal is to establish and build a relationship. You can decide how you think starting that relationship should begin. It might be that you decide you're the magician and the exorcist, and so you can flex that Christ, the Blessed Virgin, and all the saints, angels, and names that set the world to quake and tremble are on your side. You can go in and command and compel, and if you bind things effectively, that could be a workable option. On the other hand, you could decide that respect and cordialness are a better option and that you think acknowledging and respecting nobility will result in a friendship that gets you a familiar appropriately appointed to serve you. You might decide something in between the two, although I'm not sure a middling option is the way to go.

If you want the latter, you'll need to consider methods given in folklore. There are also methods in the notebooks left by cunning folk which might be of assistance. If you're thinking of going a middling route, some cunning folk texts might include elements that both partake of faery folklore and Christian conjuration.

Here are a couple of things to consider.

Household spirits, as we have seen, are often paid in food. Cream, butter, milk, and beer seem common in the folklore of such spirits. Faeries are also often paid with these foods. In some stories, people make special cakes for them. Consistently, faeries can be foiled with salt, so salt should be avoided in foods made either to entice or to thank them. In stories of faeries and of witches' familiars, they might steal or ask for these foods, or they might spoil them for humans they seek to punish or vex. Several of the stories we noted involved faeries wanting apples. The woman from the Island of Women in the story of Bran gave him, and then took from him, a magical apple branch when enticing him to the island. The Tales of the Elders of Ireland includes stories in which apples are a gift given when seeking the faeries. Apples are likely a good option as a gift to entice, honor, or thank a faery. Bread might also be a useful option. In some customs and stories, bread wards off faeries, but faeries also bake bread and ask for bread from humans. Like the foods we mentioned above, they might spoil human bread dough if annoyed. There are stories in which bread is used to attract faeries or receive benefits from them. As we noted, the bread must be made without salt.

The story of "The Fairy Follower" describes a magical ritual to conjure a faery. Unfortunately, the ritual description is broken up because the point made in the story is that the errant young man makes numerous mistakes in carrying out his ill-conceived plan to call upon a faery. Some of these mistakes might help us consider what not to do. His mistakes start with taking a clean white cloth without permission from the owner. We can assume that stealing elements we will use in the ritual is ill-favored. He then fills a pail with water. His mistakes here are using river water and then well water. The correct option was spring water. Other sources will note that water given for the fair folk must be used only for that purpose and can't be water that was reused from something else, and it shouldn't be saved for some other use afterwards either. Then on the new moon, he places the pail outside, which is incorrect, and on the next attempt, he puts it inside, but just inside the door, so that is also incorrect. Finally, he cleans out the hearth and places the pail in the freshly swept hearth. This was the correct method. He comes down the next day and finds a golden oil on top, skims it off, and makes a cake. In other folk stories and spells, it is explained that the faeries come and wash in the pail of water, and the film or oil on the top is the remnant of their washing in it. Making the cake was correct, and he placed it on the white cloth he stole, which he had laid on the ground within a circle. He said an incantation. When the first faery arrived, he denied her, and the story notes that he made a mistake by speaking. The next faery arrives, and he taps her on the wrist as he denies her, and the story notes that he shouldn't have touched her.

If we filter out the mistakes, we have the basic elements of the spell. Clean the hearth and have it well and thoroughly swept out. Leave a pail of spring water in the clean hearth on the new moon and leave it undisturbed. The next morning, skim the oil or film from the water and mix it with meal to make a cake. Place the cake on a white cloth, draw a magical circle, and then say the incantation to conjure the faery. The cake should then be given as a gift to the faery that arrives. We don't have the incantation to say recounted as part of the story, but a little digging will turn up faery incantations that could be inserted.

Of Angels Demons and Spirits: A Sourcebook of British Magic by Daniel Harms and James Clark contains a 17th-century manuscript of a cunning man's magic book. There are many items of interest here, as well as in various other cunning man books which are now available. The book contains a spell to conjure a thief using a wax poppet in which the names of faeries are inscribed. It also has a conjuration of Oberion, which looks like a simpler version of the sort of grimoire conjuration found in texts like The Book of Oberon. Of interest to us, in particular, is a spell to call upon three faery sisters. It is almost the same as what we see described in "The Fairy Follower."

The magician may perform the spell on the new moon, the full moon, or the day immediately preceding or following either. Rather than in your own home, you must find a home known to be used by the faeries. By the chimney, leave a clean pail that has been washed and filled with clean water, and hang a new or laundered towel. Once everything is in place, leave, but return in the morning before anyone else does. You should retrieve the bucket before sunrise, then expose it to light to see if there is a white film on the water. If there is, collect it with a spoon made of silver, and place it in a clean dish. Return to the house the next night before 11 pm. Set a fire with sweet wood and dress a table with a new cloth or one which has been washed. Place three white-handled knives, a full cup of ale, and three high-quality loaves of wheat bread on the table. Sit by the fire in a chair facing the table and anoint your eyes with the ointment collected from the pail of water. Three faery maidens will appear, each will nod their head as they pass by, and you should do the same, but in silence. The first faery will be the evil faery amongst them, so allow her to simply pass, but you may take the hand of the second or third and draw her towards you. Ask her to appoint a place to meet you in the morning to speak with her and ask her things. While you do this, the other two will eat from the table. If she agrees to meet and speak with you, then let her and her sisters return to their abodes. Be sure to arrive at the time and place designated. Speak your mind, and she will come to you, and then you might make any agreements needed to suit the purpose for which you have called her.

Interestingly, the text notes that she will always be with you. So it may be that this spell is intended to create a familiar spirit relationship. In the story, the spirit does remain with the young man. If you were to attempt this method and it was unclear if this spirit would remain, the given intention is to ask questions and receive answers and to have the spirit fulfill your desire. Asking the spirit if it will remain as your familiar or asking it to provide you with one would easily clarify things.

The spell differs a bit from what we see in the story, but it has very similar elements, even the presence of three faeries. Everything must be clean, as faeries value cleanliness and do not like the laziness and disorder that humans sometimes exhibit. The instructions specify that the spoon is made of silver, possibly because a spoon made of iron would disrupt the faery magic. So, for a modern person doing this spell, it may be necessary to acquire a silver spoon rather than using a stainless steel one. Silver might be important as the timing is based on the moon. Visions and illusions can also be related to the moon. The designated time, prior to 11 pm, probably has to do with giving you enough time to set up before the faeries arrive. Since the ritual uses a house the faeries are accustomed to visiting in the night, we can assume they have a time at which they tend to arrive and a time at which they tend to leave, likely based on avoiding human interference or observation. This spell doesn't use an incantation to call them, as we see in the story, probably because you're going to a place that they're already known to visit. In the story, it would seem that the third faery was the evil one. Harms relates the presence of the evil faery to an early version of "Sleeping Beauty," in which a similar three-faery table-setting ritual is performed.

Some cunning folk, of course, used methods that were no different from grimoire methods. The Grimoire of Arthur Gauntlet reproduces the notebook of a cunning man in 17th-century London. On pages 290 - 295, it contains a ritual to obtain a familiar spirit. There are several steps of animal sacrifice and preparing various materials and pentacles on appropriate days and times in order to conjure Sibylla. It is dramatically more complicated than the grimoire example we provided above. People often think of cunning folk as rural conjurers who history has remembered as witches. The imagined image is one that is distinct from the sorcerers and magicians whose education put them in royal courts and monasteries. The reality is that cunning folk were often educated and well-read magicians. They utilized folk magic and "learned" magic. They were sometimes even brought in as expert witnesses against witches. While Arthur Gauntlet's notebook provides us with a very grimoire-style example, it also has examples more linked to folk magic. On pages 288-289, it presents almost the exact same faery table ritual we described above. On 289, it gives another option for conversing with faeries.

Stand under an elder tree when the sun is at its highest point. While under the tree, say three times, "Magram Magrano." Once you have done this, the text explains that you will see a golden yellow flower spring up, and if you take it and keep it with you, then you will want for nothing. A fair maiden will also appear, this being one of the faeries, and you may speak with her and request what you desire from her.

When I was young and being taught witchcraft, and faery faith, one of the initial spells for meeting a faery that I received was similar to this but involved standing under a tree with a gift for the faery.

There are several other collections of work drawn from the workbooks and notebooks of cunning folk. These may have additional options for calling upon faeries. Folklore collections might also, although many of those will tend towards faery stories and remediation of troubles suspected as having been caused by faeries or witches. Given that many of our stories of the noble and courtly faeries draw on old mythology, an alternative method might be contacting those gods who are kings and queens within the sidhe through religious rituals. Once contacted, you could petition them for assistance in obtaining a faery familiar, just as you might petition them for anything else within their power. I would recommend if you go this route, look into traditional religious methods and reconstructed methods. Utilizing methods drawn from Wicca or many NeoPagan sources would be similar to using Golden Dawn methods or a streamlined approach drawing indirectly from the Kabbalah and the grimoires. Still, between the grimoires, traditional or historical witchcraft approaches, approaches drawn from cunning folk and folklore, or approximations of ancient Pagan rites, you have several options if you're looking for a faery method, or a more Pagan method, for acquiring a familiar.

Whatever method you choose, if you intend to seek a faery familiar, it would behoove you to spend time reading and studying faery tales and faery folklore. You might consider it as acquainting yourself with the culture of a person you're about to have move in with you. We don't have as readily available descriptions of ongoing interactions with demons and angels as we do with faeries. We have accounts of things they like and dislike, things that must be avoided, things that they value, and things that offend them. We have a significant amount of cultural information to guide us not only on how to encounter them but also on what to expect and what to consider in regard to an ongoing interaction.

Folklore will also give us insight into traditional means for an encounter and how to safely navigate that.

When we say to study faery tales, caution should be taken as to what constitutes a faery tale. Some myths might be grouped with faery tales and may or may not provide particularly useful information for your purposes. Stories of human and faery interactions which seem to reflect an actual belief in faeries and belief either in the events of the story or in similar events will be the most useful. Instructive stories to frighten children may be less useful. Our intention is less Goldilocks or The Three Pigs, or even more human stories like Jack and the Beanstalk or The Little Mermaid, and more accounts of people in communities who encountered faeries. The modern "fairytale," or the literary construction of stories involving gossamer fairies, began by the 19th century. So there is a whole host of fairy literature that doesn't draw from faery lore and is more about telling a particular sort of story. This variety of "fairytale" will likely be the least useful for our purposes.

XIV
The Fetch

We will round out our look at faery, folk, and Pagan concepts related to the familiar spirit by touching on the fetch and the fylgja. We're addressing them less because I think they are other ways of understanding or approaching the familiar and more because sometimes they come up as related ideas or as other names for familiars. I was surprised and confused the first time I saw people using them as such. Looking into it more, it looks like some people in the traditional witchcraft community use fetch as a term for familiar, likely drawing on it as a term related to the fylgja. Others seem to draw sharp distinctions between them. While some witches who use these terms seem to blur the fetch and the fylgja, most seem to be working from the assumption that fetch is the English word for fylgja. Most of the ideas they present are novel. Some are based on misunderstandings of the fylgja. Few, if any, are based on an understanding of the fetch. There are some that do seem to draw on the actual concept of the fylgja, at least in part.

While the conflation of terms rarely includes a distinction between the use of fetch and fylgja, we are dividing the discussion into two chapters. This is primarily because the concepts are different and deserve their own treatment. The witchcraft examples are divided between the two chapters to make it easier to compare them to the folklore concepts, but ultimately they could have been grouped together. While distinct from the folklore concepts their names reference, some of the ideas present interesting approaches that could be valuable to some practitioners.

The fetch in Irish and Scottish folklore is one's doppelganger or double. This typically does not seem to be a doppelganger in the sense of some sort of mimicking faery who plays tricks. Instead, it is often a portent of death or disaster and seems to be some sort of precursory appearance of one's own shade.

Katherine Briggs recounts the story of Diana Rich, the daughter of an Earl. The lady took to the garden one evening for a walk and encountered her own double. It mirrored her in appearance as well as in mannerisms. A month later, she died of smallpox. Diana Rich's sister, Isabella Thynne, also saw her double and died shortly after.

The Reverend Robert Kirk speaks about the doppelganger at length in The Secret Commonwealth, although he calls it a Co-Walker. He believes the Co-Walker is a faery and that it can be seen by anyone who was gifted with or who has obtained the second-sight. Kirk notes that the Co-Walker will sometimes appear at funerals or banquets to eat, and so it can be dangerous to eat at such events if someone suspects the faery double is present, as doing so might entangle you with the faery or lead to illness or death. The Co-Walker also appears in places as a sign that the human for whom it is a reflection will soon visit that place. Kirk describes the human as the "superterranean" inhabitant and the Co-Walker as the "subterranean" inhabitant. He notes that those with the skill to see them can learn to tell the Co-Walker apart from the human. Kirk describes the Co-Walker as haunting the human it resembles and explains that it will retain this likeness both before and after the human's death.

Kirk's version doesn't seem as ominous as some and seems to be a more recurring apparition than just the death portent. He doesn't describe the co-walker as doing anything sinister, trying to trick people, or pretending to be the person. It just seems to appear in their image, perhaps appearing to them or others who will see them. The idea that it goes places as a sign that the human will soon visit that place seems less like a faery and more like some sort of ghostly apparition. He does describe a story of a young woman who saw her Co-Walker, but only from behind, and was quite afraid of it. After she grew a few years older, she stopped seeing it. At another point, Kirk suggests that those desirous of the sight who obtain it and who long to see someone far away may see an image in the likeness of the person they long for. Kirk explains that this is a faery messenger taking the desired likeness in order to be able to convey some message to the seer.

Morgan Daimler suggests that the co-walker and the fetch are distinct concepts in her May 2021 blog entry "Co-walkers, Fetches, and Fylgja." Daimler's distinction seems to be rooted in each concept connecting to a particular culture or region. The co-walker is described by the Scottish reverend Robert Kirk, while Daimler denotes the fetch as English. The fetch appears routinely in Gaelic culture, though, so this regional distinction might not work. However, as Daimler explains, the co-walker seems to be a faery. The fetch doesn't seem to be a faery. I think it is easy to interpret Kirk's description of the co-walker as being a form of the fetch, which Kirk interpreted as a faery being. I don't believe Kirk notes interactions with these apparitions, which indicate any faery behaviors. The fact that they appear in places as an omen that the person will soon visit sounds more like a fetch than a faery. Still, Kirk's description clearly indicates that he believes it is either a faery or a chthonic mirror of the human individual, and so interpreting it as a faery would make distinguishing it from the fetch reasonable.

Daimler also points out that Kirk describes the fetch separately, using the term wraith (or wreath in his manuscript). Kirk largely presents descriptions of observations and occurrences, sometimes interspersed with explanations or references to other sources. He does not present a clear cataloguing. However, he does clearly distinguish between the wraith and the faeries. Kirk's description in this instance is a little strange and jumbled and seems to address a handful of phenomena without really breaking apart the description. One part seems to be about faeries, who may themselves be souls of the dead, attending the dead or those about to die. Otherwise, it seems to talk about those who are near death. Kirk explains that the breath of the sick is like a fume that draws together and creates images. He specifies that these images are neither their soul nor some other spirit or faery. The image could take the form of a dog or some other portent of death; it could be some other imagery altogether or an image of the person. In the case of it appearing as an animal or dog, Kirk does note that the apparition can be appeased with another death in some cases, in which case the sick individual will recover. Kirk seems, possibly, to explain death portents in general, as the black dog and the fetch would not normally be seen as the same. This is also specifically in reference to those who are ill, whereas the fetch may not be so limited. Kirk's wraith can also be conjured and appeased to allow the sick person to recover.

The jumbled presentation and the elements that could very easily describe either the fetch or some other phenomenon are a great indicator of the fact that these ideas were sometimes mutable. Some of these ideas overlap, and some of them vary in different times and regions. Many were open to individual conjecture. As we look at various examples of the fetch, just as when we looked at examples of faery lovers, we will see some differences. However, throughout these cases, despite differences in detail, core elements will show up that allow us to understand a consistent idea. As this consistent core idea emerges, we will see that it is distinct from some modern concepts which utilize the name fetch.

Patrick Kennedy's Legendary Fictions of the Irish Celts includes a story of a fetch prefaced by a description of the concept. Some sources debate the origin of the term, but Kennedy derives it from "feach," meaning "to see." Similarly, Kirk describes the wraith apparitions as "taibhshe," which is clearly related to "taibhshear" or "seer." Kennedy explains that the fetch is a projection created by the human being. It is typically involuntary and typically occurs under unhappy circumstances. Kennedy says that the fetch seen in the morning can be a fortuitous omen meaning good fortune and long life are in store for the person it resembles. If, however, it is seen at night, then it indicates death will soon arrive. Kennedy again suggests that these apparitions are human projections and quotes a story from the reign of Elizabeth I. A Miss Strickland recounted that during the Queen's final illness, she was attended by a Lady Guildford. The Queen lay sleeping, nearly breathless, in her private chamber, and the Lady Guildford ventured out for some air. Having walked some few rooms away from where the Queen slept, she saw ahead of her the Queen. Frightened that she would be in trouble for leaving the sick monarch, she rushed forward to apologize, but the Queen vanished. Guildford rushed back to the room and found the Queen there still asleep, her condition unchanged. Miss Strickland attributes the encounter to superstitious ladies, taken by mania, creating apparitions.

Kennedy goes on to present the story, "The Doctor's Fetch." A doctor and his wife were in bed sleeping one night when the wife awoke and looked towards the window. She saw her husband there, standing by a table reading a book. Despite seeing him, she knew he was sleeping next to her. She avoided showing any sign of how much it disturbed her because she did not want to wake her husband and cause him to undergo the same terror. She checked and saw he was asleep next to her with his eyes closed, and then looked back towards the apparition, but it was gone.

The next morning, the doctor tried to soothe his wife and inquire as to what bothered her, as she seemed disturbed. However, she avoided telling him what she had seen. While visiting patients, he ran into another doctor and asked his opinion on fetches. The second doctor asserted that they were illusions caused by an upset stomach acting upon an excitable brain. The first doctor explained that he saw his own fetch the night before and was afraid his wife saw it too, but he did not want to upset her by asking. The second doctor assured him he had made the right choice, and they went on their way.

Later that night, the woman woke from sleep to the convulsing of her husband. He strained to speak and told her he was suffocating and to get the other doctor. She quickly sprang up and ran to his house, bringing him back straight away. Unfortunately, her husband was beyond saving, as a large blood vessel had burst in his lung. The woman bemoaned the fetch and explained to the second doctor what she had seen. He believed the story but retained the skeptical view of fetches, believing that it was common for someone to generate an image of someone about whom they cared deeply. With such images being common, it only took a few coincidental deaths shortly after someone saw one to prove to the superstitious that the fetch was real.

The second doctor's response seems somewhat foolish. He knew before the death that the man had seen the apparition and that the wife did not know about it. He confirmed after the death that the wife had also seen it. If the account is real, it would be strong evidence that something had happened. An interesting element of this story is that both people saw the apparition. We have no reason to assume that either normally possessed the second-sight. The apparition was unexpected, and the late doctor was skeptical enough to ask his friend about his thoughts on such things. The idea that an upset stomach caused it is reminiscent of Ebeneezer Scrooge dismissing the ghost of Jacob Marley as indigestion.

Another element of this source worth noting is the placement of the story. Kennedy does not include the fetch with stories of faeries. The fetch is towards the end of the collection of stories regarding ghosts and witches.

The National Folklore Collection of Ireland gives two fetch examples in "The School Collection," recorded by Brighid Keane in 1930. The first is Michael Dunne of Grange. He was 80 when he told his tale of encountering an image of his brother Simon, walking along the road with him on a bright day around noon. Simon was in America at the time and lived for 25 years past that point. This seems to go along with the idea of a fetch in the day or morning indicating good fortunes and long life, although we don't know how old Simon was at the time of the apparition. Another account collected by Keane was of a young man who saw his neighbor walking along with him. The man who appeared to him was in the hospital and was seriously ill. The account does not say whether or not he died.

The website "Emerald Isle" suggests that the fetch is one of the oldest Irish superstitions. It adds that the fetch might appear with signs as to the nature of the death, such as injuries reflecting the injury that causes the death. It also notes that the fetch might appear only to the person it mimics, or it may appear to everyone except that person. It may also appear to the recently deceased's loved ones, although in most stories, it is considered the ghost of a living person.

The idea of an image of a loved one appearing right before or right after their death is not uncommon. Most people have heard stories or known someone who has experienced a dream or apparition of a friend or family member around the time of their death or just beforehand. I myself have woken from sleep when a dream has made me worry that someone's appearance was an indication of their death. I once heard a loved one's voice say my name while she was, unbeknownst to me, in the hospital having a baby on the other side of the country. The apparition of another person when they are in a liminal space is something familiar. An apparition of ourselves would be much more shocking and uncommon, and it may seem more uncommon if those who see it typically die shortly after. These apparitions of family and friends, being something of which most people are aware, should make the concept of the fetch easy to grasp.

The folklore surrounding the fetch has no real similarities to the familiar spirit. Sometimes, people relate the fetch to the Norse concept of the fylgja to explain where the name and idea may have come from. These concepts are also pretty different. The conflation with the Norse idea, which we'll explore in the next chapter, may be part of where the connection with familiars comes in. Before we explore that, let's look a bit at how "fetch" is used in the traditional witchcraft community.

Since we are looking at usage, the best way to get an idea of how it is used is to look at people using it. To reflect actual usage, I will draw from a few forums, blogs, and online sources. This way, we can see vernacular use. We will also look at the use by some noted authors. We will see that the contemporary usage is broad and varied, unlike the usage in traditional folklore. Some of the broad and varied use may reflect idiosyncratic uses outside of a more normative use in the traditional witchcraft community. It could also be argued that there isn't a normative use yet, and several ideas have constellated around the word.

We'll start with the "American Folkloric Witchcraft Blog." American Folkloric Witchcraft is a movement within traditional witchcraft, with some NeoPagan and Wiccan influences, which structures its approach to witchcraft around interpreting traditional witch folklore in a contemporary American context. According to the blog's August 21st, 2011 post, "The Fetch and Flight," the fetch is associated with the idea of spirit flight. "A fetch is an etheric construct that the witch projects herself into for the purpose of astral flight." The idea the authors are describing is essentially a form of the concept found in theosophy and contemporary ceremonial magic known as "The Body of Light." The Body of Light, or sometimes a chariot of light, is a double of the individual that is used to travel in the astral. First, a body is visualized or constructed of astral energy, and the consciousness is projected into it. Then the individual attunes to the body by attempting to perceive the world from the body's perspective and move the body around. Once the consciousness is appropriately rooted in the body, the astral traveler can begin their journey.

Interestingly enough, Kirk does discuss astral substance and astral bodies when he talks about the formation of subtle bodies for faeries and spirit beings. His treatment of this is not far off from the idea of exhaled fumes forming an apparition, although the apparition in Kirk's description of the wraith is not inhabited or a willed occurrence. Later, when he attempts to describe the movements of spirits of the air, Kirk notes spirit flight by witches as an example by which people are familiar with the idea of the movement of subtle astral bodies.

Some adherents to the schools of thought which teach this method interpret it as a naturally occurring part of the soul, while others interpret it as an energy or mental construct. Typically, beliefs regarding the Body of Light as a construct versus a part of the individual make no difference regarding the actual method or mechanism of use, function of, or interaction with this structure. The blog's authors add several elements and merge the Body of Light with a few other concepts. They note that the fetch can be a tool to assist in astral projection, just as things like a broom or hobby horse can be. These latter two would be ritual elements to help put the mind in that space, whereas the Body of Light is the actual mechanism through which projection occurs. The authors also distinguish the use of the fetch from "simple projection of the astral body," although what they initially describe matches a lot of descriptions for simple projection of the astral body. The additive elements to their concept of the fetch are what might create some distinction.

The fetch is essentially a servitor, an artificial spirit created by the magician, used as a vehicle in the model presented by these authors. This could distinguish it from the Body of Light or the astral body. If it is a servitor programmed as a magical being to carry the witch forward, then it would, in theory, facilitate the transference of consciousness and the movement through the astral rather than just being a passive vessel. They suggest that while the fetch can be structured to appear like the witch, forming it in the shape of a "totemic" animal can be helpful. The reason for using this animal shape is that the witch will already have a natural bond with that "totemic" animal. This bond will make connecting with the fetch easier and more natural. They describe the construct as an inanimate shell of energy that you can inhabit and move through the astral.

The authors also recommend creating a spirit house for the fetch and compare it to a familiar spirit. They suggest a spirit bottle, a crystal, or a statue in the form of the chosen animal. They also recommend feeding it routinely to empower it so that it becomes more effective. Finally, they explain that the witch can decommission the fetch by reabsorbing it but recommend against this because it begins to develop its own essence and power over time because it is an egregore.

It's a little difficult to pin down what this is and isn't because many concepts are combined here. On the one hand, it's a servitor. You make a construct of energy, treat it like a spirit, give it the power to perform a task, and use it for that task. You feed it over time to give it more power and independence so that it can better perform the task. This is slightly distinct from an egregore, which is generally involves of a group of people rather than being an individual person's construct. Egregores also often deal with the overall nature and function of a group rather than an individual goal.

On the other hand, if it is only an inanimate shell used for travel, it isn't a servitor, it's just the Body of Light concept. Ironically, the word "tulpa" is often used interchangeably with servitor in the chaos magic community. However, this isn't what the word meant in its original cultural context. Originally, "tulpa" meant something more similar to the Body of Light, so the concept described here would be closer to a tulpa than the normal western usage.

Ignoring the blend of concepts and words elected to describe them, "is this a fetch," and "is this a familiar," are the actual questions we're asking. If we look at the traditional concept of a fetch, no, this is not the same thing. Especially when we begin to form the construct into an animal form, then it has nothing to do with the fetch. It could be more reflective of the idea of the fylgja. If we take Kennedy's view that the fetch is created by the person seeing it, then there would be some relationship between this concept and the fetch. Kennedy's idea that the fetch is a projection includes that it is involuntary and created by mania. It is a response to a heightened emotional state. Not all examples of fetches fit that explanation, so it's probably incorrect. Kennedy's view is still separate from the notion expressed in this blog because the blog describes something intentional with which the individual can interact and which is enduring. The fetch typically doesn't have any of those qualities.

There is a slight similarity to the familiar. The familiar is not an artificial construct created by the witch, and it is not a simulacrum of the witch. Familiars seem to choose their own form rather than the witch choosing it, in most accounts, but there could be some cooperation there. Where this has similarity is in the connection to spirit flight. Witches were often believed to ride their familiars to the sabbat. The book <u>Demon Lovers</u> describes the witch as touching the familiar and being flown through the air by means of that contact because the witch did not have the power to fly on their own. The idea that a spirit would facilitate spirit flight is completely traditional and is a role connected to familiars. Faeries are particularly skilled in this matter, and I have written about this elsewhere. It remains that that isn't the role of a fetch, and neither the fetch nor the familiar are an artificial energy construct.

The idea described here is kind of cool. If you were to explore it, I would recommend sticking with it as a servitor rather than just an inanimate construct. You could follow the basic description presented here and come up with a cool servitor to assist you in spirit flight if you were so inclined. As we discussed earlier, ideas can be novel and still be valid. Ideas can use terms that aren't quite right and still be valid and useful. This isn't a fetch, it isn't a familiar, it isn't an egregore. It blends the idea of a Body of Light with the idea of a servitor and results in something cool, if you like that kind of energetic working method that doesn't involve spirits with their own independent existence.

The author of "The Laughing Mandrake" describes the fetch, fylgja, and puckril as equivalent concepts in traditional witchcraft. According to the author, it is a part of the soul and serves as a psychopomp in death. It can also be projected from the body through trance in the form of an animal or a person of the opposite sex. The author interprets Isobel Gowdie's animal shape-shifting as a projection of the fetch.

None of this is part of traditional fetch folklore, but again, some of it might be inspired by the folklore surrounding the fylgja. As we said before, some people use these terms interchangeably and believe they are historically related. The idea that a piece of your own soul serves as the psychopomp is interesting and potentially raises some questions, but they're not really germane to our exploration. Spirit flight is a reasonable way to explain some of Gowdie's adventures, although the transcripts don't seem to indicate that that was her meaning. We will look at the concept of appearing as someone of the opposite sex more when we discuss the fylgja. The idea that all witches are paired with a spirit other of the opposite sex could also be drawn from elements of sex magic in some forms of Wicca. The puckril, or familiar, is obviously not a part of the witch's soul.

"The Laughing Mandrake" also includes a conversation between posters debating the nature of the fetch and its relationship to the spirit animal. Ironically, the initial poster talks about turning to the term fetch to avoid cultural appropriation by using the term spirit animal. Using the term fetch is still borrowing and repurposing a term from another culture and using it to describe an unrelated series of concepts and practices. It is similarly appropriative. The original commenter, concerned about appropriation, advocates against using the English words "spirit animal" but says that the fetch can be described as "totemic" because "totem" is not specifically Native American. Totem is derived from the Ojibwa word "ototeman," referring to one's kin. The debate about appropriation is a bit of a digression. Still, it highlights how we often aren't consistent or accurate in what we think is borrowing or stealing, honoring or appropriating, ours or others.

The original commenter describes the fetch as the person's most primal or uncivilized self. They claim it appears as a challenger to stand in the way of one's progress in the craft. If the witch defeats the fetch and wins the challenge, then the fetch becomes an assistant who helps them travel in the spirit realm.

So far, in all three examples, we see the fetch associated with some form of spirit travel. In this and the last example, the fetch is a part of the soul. The idea that it is a double, which appears to challenge the witch, is a new element and, like most of these elements, has nothing to do with the traditional function or behavior of a fetch. The original commenter responded to the suggestion that the fetch was just a death omen historically by asserting that it could easily be misinterpreted as a death omen because it carries the witch to Hell or the Underworld. So, it goes full throttle into saying the historical folklore is wrong and that it's just about spirit travel.

So far, most of the descriptions we've addressed have been about spirit flight. Some writers seem to lean into an idea more related to the familiar, but these are consistently drawing more from the Norse concept of fylgja than the Gaelic and British concepts of the fetch. We have mostly looked at random internet usage, so let's look at some descriptions by popular witchcraft authors.

Mat Auryn explains that the fetch and the familiar both have several ways people might define them. Auryn lists the lower soul, the vessel the lower soul takes when shifting into animal form or when spirit traveling, and a servitor created to do the witch's bidding as possible meanings of the term fetch. Unfortunately, he doesn't address at all the historical folklore meaning.

Auryn goes on to quote Storm Faerywolf, who says the fetch, or the wraith, is the second part of the soul. Using fetch and wraith together should suggest that we're talking about the concept that occurs in a Gaelic and British context instead of the fylgja. He compares the fetch to the Hawaiian "unihipili." Having no connection to Hawaiian culture or spirituality, I can't comment on the meaning or accuracy of this comparison. Faerywolf continues with his description, explaining that the fetch communicates in gut reactions, symbols, and dreams and that it is our animal or sexual nature. The quote concludes with the idea that it is primal and uncivilized.

Again, the idea of it as part of the soul might tie back to certain interpretations of the concept of the fylgja, but there is no link between the fylgja and the wraith. One could interpret the fetch as a part of the soul or a mirror of the soul. Kirk is adamant that it is not the soul and is just an illusion formed from breath; Kennedy interprets it as a projection of the agitated mind. Its behavior is often like the ghosts who are explained as a "record on repeat," or an impression of powerful psychic energy that leaves an imprint. People can perceive that imprint well after the events which caused it. In the case of the fetch, the impression is created before the event that would create it, though. It would be easy enough to interpret it as an unconscious reflection of or projection of the soul or just as a form of premonition.

The idea that it is the primal uncivilized lower soul doesn't seem to really fit the folklore. In many accounts, it doesn't talk and disappears if pursued. So the idea that it isn't verbal might be supported there. However, many people who experience a visitation by someone recently dead, or about to die, report some message from them. An English account, which is sometimes referred to as the first published ghost story, involves the ghost of a neighbor visiting a woman near to the neighbor's own death. In this case, the apparition spends a couple of hours talking with her friend and even dictates letters and bequeathments. I've seen differing descriptions of when it happened in relation to when the person passed. It might have been just before, just after, or roughly concurrent. It is an example of these visitations being verbal, but it may or may not be an example of the fetch. Most explanations of and examples of the fetch include no communication at all. There is no gut reaction, symbols, dreams, or sexual drive intimated by the fetch.

Faerywolf's description of the fetch is essentially the role the Nefesh, of Kabbalistic provenance, takes in Golden Dawn-derived systems. The Golden Dawn Kabbalah, and its understanding of the parts of the soul, differs from traditional Jewish Kabbalah and, at this point, is truly its own system derived from Christian Kabbalah. The Golden Dawn Kabbalah provided a significant amount of the theological underpinnings and ritual structure of eclectic Wicca. Traditional Wicca contains some of this influence but also draws from Golden Dawn interpretations of The Key of Solomon the King and elements of Thelema and alchemy. The Golden Dawn diagram of the soul can become fairly complicated, according different parts to the various sefirot of the Tree of Life and the grades of initiation. Some adherents to the OTO system have also attempted to map these concepts to the OTO degree system. Frequently, there is more complexity than necessary as one tries to incorporate Supernal components of the Tree.

The core elements to consider from the Golden Dawn-esque perspective are the Neshamah, the Ruakh, and the Nefesh. The Neshamah is the divine element of the person or the soul and corresponds to the element of fire. It is the Yod of the divine name and is the initial spark and motion that stirs a particular existence into motion and being. The Ruakh is the breath of life; it is the mind or the airy communication that links the Neshamah, the Nefesh, and the Guf (body). It is the Vav and defines the idea of a person that is expressed and known to others. The Nefesh is the watery component. It is the emotions. It is the sexual drive. The Nefesh is all the primal and bodily desires and impulses towards pleasure and fulfillment. It is the watery Heh of the divine name.

Faerywolf compares the lower self to the Id of Freudian psychodynamics. The Nefesh, similarly, is often compared with the Id. Faerywolf describes the fetch, or lower self, as the animal and sexual nature, which, again, are terms often used to describe the Nefesh. In folklore, the fetch is like a shade or shadow; it is a ghost of a living person. The Nefesh is also believed to be the source of shades or ghosts. When a person dies, the Nefesh remains attached to the body while the higher parts of the soul move on. The Nefesh can become restless and appear to people after death.

The concept Faerywolf is describing with the word fetch isn't really the fetch. It's a concept that appears in magic and spiritual structures, but in contemporary magical systems, it is mostly influenced by the Kabbalah as seen through Golden Dawn and Thelemic lenses. I do not assume that Faerywolf encountered ideas of the Nefesh and chose to redescribe them in more European terminology at some point to try and erase the Golden Dawn influence or avoid the appearance of Kabbalah. More likely, these ideas percolated through the various spiritual strands which fed various forms of modern witchcraft. As they continued, divorced from their kabbalistic context, words were needed to describe them and people drew on words from the cultural contexts with which they were familiar. Over time these concepts have endured and developed in new systems and retained the terms they've accreted as teachers have passed them along.

As we look more at the fylgja, we will see some examples of how these words may have worked their way into association with these concepts.

Auryn goes on to explain that the fetch and the familiar can become conflated because they connect to similar things. In Auryn's view, the fetch is our animalistic self which connects us to nature and our bodies. Auryn feels that the witches' imp is a figure who has several of these characteristics as well and reflects our lower selves. The familiar spirit, in Auryn's view, appears in a way reflective of the animal image of our fetch soul because it is through the fetch that we relate to the familiar. I assume a lot of these conclusions are based on Auryn's own experience, and they make sense if you are working a system that engages a "lower self" in a projectable animal form.

There is value in the self and the familiar being able to shape-shift together and bond on the basis of linked elements. This likely requires that the familiar be a particular sort of spirit, though. A familiar received from an angel might not connect to these concepts at all, and a familiar received from a demon might not be one with whom we'd build this kind of intimate soul bond. A nature spirit, or one of the fair folk, may be more appropriate familiars for this sort of work. It should also be remembered that familiars are not animals, nor do they necessarily have animal forms. So concepts predicated on linking to their animal nature only work if the familiar chooses to express itself in that fashion.

Auryn also mentioned servitors as a possible meaning for the fetch. As we saw earlier, the "American Folkloric Witchcraft Blog" describes a servitor when defining the fetch. If we wanted to really stretch how we're interpreting Kirk and Kennedy, we could maybe make some comparisons to a servitor. The fetch doesn't perform a task and isn't an intentional creation, so it isn't a servitor. The fylgja, as we will see, is a part of the soul complex of the individual, or it is a guardian spirit. Neither of those are servitors. If there is a modern usage of fetch that refers to a servitor, it is far afield from the actual meaning of the word. The idea is interesting and potentially useful but isn't a fetch. It would potentially be interesting to see if there are other uses that refer to specific types of servitors, since Auryn mentions servitors as a meaning. It could be that some witches have chosen to adopt fetch as a synonym for servitor for aesthetic reasons, or it could be that they use it for some novel variation on the servitor that I have not yet encountered.

Some of the ideas that have constellated around the term "the fetch" are pretty interesting. Some of them could be additive to one's practice and create meaningful and useful tools for a witch or magician to use. Pretty much none of them have anything to do with the fetch. Most of these ideas and practices don't seem to be interpretations of the familiar spirit, although some people use the term that way. Several of them are adjacent to concepts of familiars, though. A shape-shifting spirit being that aids the witch in spirit travel is an accurate description of a familiar spirit. It's not all a familiar spirit does, and it might be something a person never employs their familiar to do. It is an element of the relationship with the familiar spirit in many historical accounts and many people's practice. When it is taken as a challenger of the witch or a part of the witch's soul, it moves further away from the concept of the familiar spirit. The link to animal forms is probably a source of confusion with the familiar spirit, but is an element that is completely unrelated to the fetch in folklore. As we have noted, some of these ideas may be tied more closely to the fylgja.

As we explore the fylgja, and how descriptions of the fylgja in some contemporary magical and Pagan writing may have inspired these connections, we will continue to look at how these variant ideas can still create useful and interesting possibilities. Even as we recognize where these new ideas can be valuable, we can clearly see that they aren't the same as the words they're adopting. While the traditional folklore concept of the fetch doesn't have a great deal of recurrence in contemporary magic, NeoPaganism, or witchcraft, it can still create confusion when the term is co-opted from a living culture. In the case of fylgja, we will see points where concepts inspire and overlap. We'll also see how the word has evolved in Scandinavian usage. Since it has modern uses in the living culture, and since the traditional meaning is still part of living spiritual traditions inspired by historical Nordic and Germanic Paganism, the co-opting of the word can lead to greater confusion. The flip side of this is that unpacking those original meanings of the word and contrasting how they differ from modern appropriations lets us look more deeply at the traditional concepts as well as the new concepts. We can deepen our understanding of both and see directions in which we can further explore how each can impact, enlighten, and benefit us.

Othin with Huginn and Muninn, 18th Century Manuscript

XV
The Fylgja

Several of the writers working from a traditional witchcraft or traditional witchcraft-inspired perspective seem to treat the fylgja and the fetch as a single concept. As we have seen, these concepts are sometimes lumped together, sometimes not, but whether it is lumped or not, there seems to be some adjacency of ideas. The essential concept people seem to be describing with these words is the idea of a spirit double that takes an animal form and assists in spirit flight. In some iterations, it might be a challenger to the witch who becomes an assistant; it might be their lower soul.

There is not much similarity between the fetch and the fylgja. When the fylgja has a human appearance, it is not a double of the individual nor is it a part of the person, as we will see. More often, it appears as an animal, which the fetch does not. Like the fetch, it can be a death omen. Despite the lack of similarity, it isn't only traditional witch sources which combine these ideas. My initial exposure to the fylgja used fetch as an English word to describe it. An Asatru website, The Asatru Community, includes fylgja in its beginner glossary. It equates it to faecca, an Old English word which may be of Irish origin that has been suggested as a possible etymology for fetch. The word faecca may have been associated with a sort of night hag spirit as it originally appears as a gloss for maere. Neither the fetch nor the fylgja behaves as a night hag. The glossary gives the definition: "personal tutelary and guiding spirit, usually in animal form, similar in many ways to a Native American totem animal; animal form to which one often transforms when faring forth. Often anglicized as fetch." This seems to draw on a lot of modern views, and easily allows us to see why people might associate it with the familiar spirit. It doesn't really connect with the traditional understanding of the fetch. Still, if we understood fetch as the English word for fylgja, it becomes more clear why people interpret the fetch in the way we encountered while looking at its usage in traditional witchcraft.

While growing up, my focus was on Irish and Welsh mythology and spirituality. Icelandic and other Norse, Saxon, and Germanic mythology and spirituality were also of interest but were not my main focus. My academic background is primarily in Classics, but I did get to explore some Northern European mythology in that context as well. I have a relatively strong familiarity with Norse concepts and some experience of Norse ritual and religious communities, but I'm not an expert. So, I turned to the Cat Heath, the author of <u>Elves, Witches & Gods: Spinning Old Heathen Magic in the Modern Day</u>, and the popular blog <u>Seo Helrune: Elves and Witchcraft, Seidr and Grimoires</u>; they were able to provide me with several amazing academic resources. I will also be drawing from some popular sources for comparison.

When asking Cat about the fylgja, I summarized my basic understanding. The fylgja can be viewed as a part of the individual or as a spirit connected to the individual. This spirit is connected to them at birth and reflects the character and nature they will develop. It can appear as an animal that indicates that nature or character and will, at times, be a guide or directive force related to the individual's fate. But generally, for most people, it is not something they command or can call forth. However, there may be some accounts that connect it to shape-shifting in the case of particular warriors. Exploring sources and details clarified and expanded my understanding beyond this initial attempt to describe it.

In addition to providing sources, Cat explained that even academics aren't entirely sure what the fylgja is and noted that it can be complex because there are two fylgjur, the animal fylgja and the kin fylgja. To further complicate things, the fylgja relates to other elements of the Norse soul complex. Sometimes these other concepts might get confused with the fylgja.

In "The Shape of Being Human: The Hama Soul," Winifred Hodge Rose explains that fylgjur might refer to several different spirit beings or externalized elements of the soul. According to Rose, some possible ideas connected with fylgjur include the hama, hugr, hamingja, gandr, disir, vordhr, and spirit animal. Rose explains that the "hama" is a covering or a shape. It can refer to a covering like clothes, but it can also refer to the form of a thing like skin or shape, as well as the underlying soul shape within. Rose quotes <u>The Havamal</u> to illustrate that the hama can refer to our own human soul form, as well as a secondary shape-shifted hama. This shape-shifted hama can function as something projected forth in the form of a hug-ham, or hugr shape. In <u>The Havamal</u>, Othin describes a secret by which the thunder-rider, or witch, can be made to travel astray aloft through the air. This ties us back to the connections with spirit flight and shape-shifting.

The Hama or hamr is related to the haminja, which is an externalized form of a person's luck or fate projected from them. This can also be connected to, and in a very few instances is used somewhat interchangeably with, fylgja. Rose cites Dag Stromback as suggesting that the various elements of the Norse concept of the soul are more or less interchangeable. Other authors provide more distinction. Rose connects the ability of the hama to be projected or used in shape-shifting with the hugr. In "The Occult Activities of the Hugr," she connects the hugr to the heart as its physical location. The hugr is linked to desire and will and has the agency to achieve desire through the command of thought. Essentially, our thoughts are directed by our desires. Much of what we associate with witches, shape-shifting, and spirit travel might relate more to elements of the hama and hugr. Rose gives a thorough description that explains how the hugr can produce something similar to the evil eye, and how the spoiling of food and drink can be the effect of a strong hugr, whether intentionally or unintentionally focused.

Deeper explanations of the fylgja will show some overlaps with these elements described by Rose, but we will find distinctions that will separate fylgjur from familiars. While the hama and hugr are not examples of familiars, either, they might relate to some of the concepts which we have seen associated with the fetch.

To add complication to the concept of the fylgja, by the 17th century, "fylgja" began to be used to describe certain types of ghosts in folk stories. Eric Shane Bryan tells the story of the Mori of Sel in Icelandic Folklore and the Cultural Memory of Religious Change. The story goes like this. A man was living with a farmer, who would work while the man stayed home. It was believed by the community that the man was having an affair with the farmer's wife. One night in the winter, the farmer went out to tend his animals but never returned. He was found dead with a fatal wound that seemed to be inflicted by another man. They blamed his wife's alleged lover and sentenced him to death. The man went to a diplomat that was staying nearby and begged for money to pay the fine and save his life. The diplomat was going to give it, but his wife stopped him. The condemned man said that their business was not done and his fylgja would haunt them and their family for nine generations. The story describes, by individual names, several members of the family for six generations. His ghost was known to these descendants. A handful of them went mad, seemingly passing the madness on to the next generation with their death.

Fylgja is used a handful of times in this 19th-century story. Shane points out that the story lists specific names of individuals and that these individuals are mostly real, historically verifiable people. He says this is a common element of aettarfylgjur stories, or stories of family ghosts. Unlike the Old Norse stories, these fylgjur are not guardians, but like the medieval fylgjur, they do seem to pass from one family member to another. Shane quotes Einar Sveinsson, who suggests that aettarfylgjur and fylgjurdraugur, should be referred to as sendingar. Sveinsson feels that the sendingar, a ghost or corpse part that a magician has animated to harm someone, is more similar to the Post-Reformation fylgjur than the medieval fylgjur is. How we categorize stories is less of an issue for our purposes, but it highlights the term's complexity. When we consider modern uses outside of Nordic contexts, we have to consider that several soul elements, as well as more modern uses of the term, could all be conflated together.

Bettina Seijberg Sommer, in "The Norse Concept of Luck," relates the fylgja to several other luck-related terms while also distinguishing it from them. Before addressing the individual terms, we should understand that, according to Sommer, luck is an inherent element of the individual. Luck can be inherited or bestowed by some higher power or fate, but it is a quality the person has or doesn't have. Luck is viewed as an element of the person's identity or character, like strength and skill. As such, luck becomes part of the soul and the soul's radiant ability to affect the world. This understanding seems to be consistent in most conceptions of fylgjur.

According to Sommer, gipta, gaefa, heill, and hamingja all refer to luck primarily as an innate quality within the individual. Fylgja relates to luck or fate but is a more external element, either being an extension of the soul when we refer to the animal fylgja or an entirely external entity when we refer to the fylgjukona, kynflygja, or the fylgja woman. Sommer notes two instances where hamingja and fylgja are interchangeable and explains that this links fylgja with other concepts of luck. Bryan also connects the hamingja to the fylgja, explaining that the hamingja, along with the fylgja and dis, is an attendant spirit. The hamingja, according to Bryan, is a personification of luck that can go before someone, sometimes in the form of an animal. Sommer clarifies the distinction between the fylgja and the other forms of luck by explaining that a powerful man who possesses luck can lend gipta, gaefa, etc., to another person. In contrast, individuals do not command their fylgjur and, therefore, it can not be lent in such a way. Bryan, however, describes fylgjukonar sometimes negotiating their transference to the next family member before the death of the person they are guarding. He also suggests that the fylgjukona can be lent to another family member. Sommer's description of an inability to loan the fylgja likely means the animal fylgja, which is the fylgja more likely to be associated with the hamingja. Sommer's description does allow for control of the hamingja, though, as she explains that it is shaped by the hugr and can be sent forth by the hugr. Sommer also notes that heillamathr, giptumathr, gaefumathr, hamingjumathr exist as forms of the words for luck, but fylgjamathr is not a word because it is a spirit and not an inherent component.

Sommer and Bryan also note the differences between the animal fylgja and the fylgjukona, kynfylgja, or fylgja-woman. Both agree that the animal fylgja is part of the complex soul structure, but it is only one of several aspects. It can be seen by people who have second sight, although Sommer notes that this can be a death omen. When it is seen alone, according to Bryan, it reflects the nature or fate of the individual, but when seen in a group, it might be a warning that enemies are about to attack. It is a bad omen, or a death omen, to see one's animal fylgja bloody or dead. Bryan explains that the well-being of the fylgja impacts the well-being of the person. Both note that the animal fylgja dies when the individual dies.

Sommer distinguishes the animal fylgja from concepts of shape-shifting and spirit flight but notes that this comparison has been made. Sommer points out that spirit flight occurs when the individual is unconscious. The animal fylgja may precede the person or follow the person and be seen to move separately from the person, but it does so while the person is conscious and awake. Spirit flight is presumably also an intentional activity, as is most shape-shifting. Individuals do not have command over their fylgja or the ability to intentionally send them forth.

The disir are female spirits, sometimes priestesses and prophetesses, sometimes gods. Alaric Hall notes that the overlap between mortal and immortal, supernatural and natural, is one that is blurry and permeable when we consider figures who have power and magical skill. At times it can be circumstances that define their status and capability rather than just human or non-human. As such, the category of disir can be inclusive. A subset of disir are the fylgjukonar, kynfylgjur, or fylgjur-women. These are spirits who might be seen as disir, but not all disir take this role. These are tutelary spirits attached to particular families. They connect to one individual in life and then pass along to another at death. As we noted, Bryan cites examples in which the kynfylgjur is passed along before the death of the individual, but near to it occurring. He also notes that while these spirits are guardians and guides, they can also be agents of fate and may facilitate the events that lead to the death of the previous individual to whom they were attached.

Sommer and Bryan both stress that the fylgjur-women are individual spirits and not part of the soul of the individual. Unlike the animal fylgja, they live past the death of the individual. Sommer suggests that as disir, these spirits may have received cultus as they were understood to be some higher external power. Rose suggests that they may have been associated with some sort of maternal goddess veneration. The fylgja watches over the human but may also reveal elements of their fate. Bryan suggests that in addition to the ability to reveal fate, both the animal fylgja and the kynfylgja tell us about the character and origin of the person. Bryan notes that the fylgja might punish the individual if they commit crimes or wrongdoing. Presumably, this refers to the kynfylgja. Morgan Daimler, in her blog post, "Co-Walkers, Fetches, and Fylgja," suggests that the kynfylgja is commonly depicted as female because most stories are about males and that they are of the opposite sex from the person they attend to, rather than always female. Daimler also suggests that sexual relations with the kynfylgja are not uncommon. Neither Sommer nor Bryan notes examples of male fylgjur or sexual relations with fylgjur, but examples of spirit sex abound in mythology, so it does not seem unlikely. Male fylgjur would seem to remove them from the category of disir.

Bryan points out that while the early modern accounts of fylgja differ from medieval accounts, some researchers have found that belief in something like the medieval fylgja is still common in Iceland. According to research Bryan quotes, close to thirty percent of Icelandic people believe the existence of the fylgja is likely, a larger percentage believe it is possible. Only about twenty percent believe it is unlikely. While there are distinctions between the Post-Reformation fylgjur and the medieval fylgjur, Bryan notes that both can still be categorized as fylgjur that follow individuals and fylgjur that follow families.

There are a lot of elements to consider regarding the fylgja. The word itself can add to how we think about those elements. According to the dictionary provided by "Vikings of Bjornstad" fylgja means: "follow, accompany; help, give help to; side with; be attached to, belong to; attend to, be a quality of; hold together; serve; appertain to." Bryan says the verb "athfylgja" means "to follow, to help, or to guide." Later, he explains that even in modern Icelandic, fylgja can mean ghost, but it can also mean placenta since the placenta guards and then follows the newborn child. He says the primary Old Norse meaning is a female attendant spirit, but that the prefix "fylgi-" means help or support.

To summarize, the Norse soul is pretty complex, and some types of fylgjur are part of that soul complex while others are not. Humans form an entire complex known as the ferth, which contains mind, mood, intellect and desire, life, and power. Power contains luck, skill, might, and other components. These and various other elements are collected into our form. Their nature may be reflected forward as a guide in animal form. Our desires might also allow our intellect to shape and project other forms containing some part of our power or luck and may even allow us to express that power and shape ourselves. We also have associations with spirits and guides. One of those guides might attach to our families and may attach to us as an individual member of the family before moving on to another member of the family at our death.

These guides, the fylgjur, one external, one internal, tell us about who we are and where we came from. The animal form might reflect elements of our birth. It might reflect our nature or our fate. The kynfylgja will tell us about where we came from in the sense of the collected fate of our kinsfolk and what we inherit from them. Both can tell us about what is in store for us. They may assist us with things, they may go before us and be a sign of our coming, or they may impact those we approach to make things easier for us. But we don't command them in that process. We may not perceive them or might only perceive them in dreams, but they might appear to us directly as well. They might be able to be perceived by those with the second sight.

The fylgjur, clearly, are not the same as the fetch, nor are they familiar spirits. Daimler points out that the fylgjur are connected to you before your birth or at your birth, whereas familiar spirits come later in life. She also notes that familiar spirits are either given to you at some point in your life or choose to make contact and build a connection. In contrast, the animal fylgja is an innate part of you, and the kynfylgja has a connection to your family that began long before you. Aside from these differences, the fylgjur don't do what a familiar does precisely. A familiar may teach you magic. You can command a familiar and send it to do magical tasks for you. You have to feed your familiar. Despite differences, there are some overlaps. The fylgja might guide you, provide signs and portents, and protect you. Familiars may do these things also, but so do a host of guardian spirits.

The fylgjur also don't do precisely what a fetch does. It may show up in a place before you and indicate that you are coming. It doesn't necessarily do this by showing up as your appearance. It could arrive and create an itching, or a nose tingle, or show up as your animal fylgjur, or a number of other portents indicating your impending arrival. The fylgja is not primarily a death omen, although it can be one. In the case of a fetch, you see yourself. Often the image does not reflect your demise; it is simply a spectre of you. The animal fylgja, however, portends death by appearing as a dead animal, or perhaps if you can't normally see it, then seeing it at all can be a sign. Your kynfylgja might indicate your death by negotiating to transfer to someone else. These experiences are not the same as the fetch.

As we noted, the conflation of the fetch and the fylgja seems to be the source of a lot of ideas about what the fetch does in traditional witchcraft. It is not just in magical literature where the fetch and fylgja are viewed as synonymous. But I think we can see that they are not the same and that neither is the same as the familiar. Still, linking the fetch and the fylgja seems to be the reason people link either or both with the familiar in some witchcraft contexts.

Many of the things we could say about the traditional witchcraft conception of the fylgja we've already talked about when discussing the fetch. A vessel for spirit flight, an animal familiar who carries you on spirit flight or carries you to hell, a soul-self to challenge you and then become your spirit assistant, we could address these ideas as equally here as we did in the discussion of the fetch. We don't need to rehash all of that. While the fylgja gives a more complex idea and more complex imagery, and some of the elements witches have assigned to the fetch or fylgja have minor similarities, overall, the concepts are clearly not the same.

Not all traditional witchcraft writers associate the fetch and the fylgja. Therefore, our consideration of the fylgja in traditional witchcraft and its relation or non-relation to the familiar will primarily look at examples that distinguish it from the fetch or in which the fylgja seems to be a clear focus or influence. Before we explore more descriptions of traditional witchcraft, one modern Norse Pagan text seems to give a description of the fylgja that may align with some of our traditional witchcraft views of the fetch or fylgja.

Teutonic Magic, by Stephen Grundy, also known as Kveldulf Gundarsson, may provide insight into the connection of the idea of the fylgja and spirit flight. It describes wolf-fylgjur that women may possess, but it describes women as riding on them rather than putting on their skins. He seems to be suggesting that women don't have the same shape-shifting capabilities as men, though he notes there is a rare instance of a single female berserker, and instead connects women to spirit-riding. In another section, it describes the fylgja as being an option for reaching Helheim. He explains that you can go there by crossing a bridge or with the assistance of your fylgja. Overall, his description of fylgja is at odds with most other descriptions. He believes the association with disir is a matter of people being confused by the fylgja sometimes appearing as a woman instead of an animal. He suggests that the fylgja is fully able to be commanded by the individual. He also suggests discounting advice or guidance received from it because it only has the judgment of an animal. As such, he says it can provide warnings of danger and should be viewed only as a limited guide, like a seeing-eye dog. This description might also explain why it is viewed as the lower soul in some contemporary traditional witchcraft systems. It also explains the idea of the fetch carrying you to hell, which we encountered in the last chapter.

One individual who has written about the fylgja is "Anonymous Arte Witch." This author describes the fylgja as being synonymous with the familiar. This author believes that the fylgja in animal form is simultaneously a working partner and a blend of the witch's soul with that of the spirit. The description isn't fully clear, but the author might also be taking the Devil meeting the witch in animal form at the beginning of their witchcraft journey as an example of the familiar. The fylgja is described as a form of awareness in which consciousness is freed from bodily constraint and apparently travels; however, this travel is not traveling but simply a shift of awareness to another place since, in the author's view, all places occur simultaneously. The fylgja also goes between worlds, upon otherworldly roads, through dreams, and to distant physical places. This link to spirit flight seems to straddle a line between viewing the fylgja as a separate familiar and a part of the human soul complex. The fylgja is described as traveling both to teach and to learn, and for divinatory purposes, and as being supremely useful in creating alliances with other spirits in other spaces.

The author takes a brief detour to discuss the fylgja spouse, which they describe as being a separate concept. They equate the relationship with the fylgja spouse to spiritual alchemy and view it as a way to integrate the soul with divine consciousness through "pseudo-sexual" interaction. The fylgja spouse is also a teacher. The author distinguishes the fylgja spouse from the fylgjakona and describes the latter more or less correctly.

The author returns to discussing the animal fylgja and actually discusses some traditional concepts. First, they note that the well-being of the human and the fylgja are linked; the two are fundamentally connected. Next, they explain that the form of the fylgja connects to the nature of the person. Then they begin to describe the fylgja in terms more similar to a sort of general "spirit animal." In this interpretation, your fylgja may appear as a fox or crow. But it isn't just your fylgja. Instead, it is the spirit of all foxes or all crows. It is the guardian and essence of that entire kingdom of animals.

The author explains that it may take a long time to contact your fylgja and describes having worked with The Dame and the Horned One to achieve contact with theirs. They recommend making offerings and reference a guided meditation from Nigel Penick.

While this author views the fylgja and the familiar as synonymous, most of what they describe really isn't a familiar spirit. Turning to the Dame and the Horned One to receive a familiar would make sense, but your animal fylgja is innately part of your soul. Offerings might be made to the fylgjukona, but I'm not sure you would make them to your animal fylgja. The idea that it is connected with your own soul comes closer to the idea of the fylgja but is outside of the space of the familiar. The connection to spirit flight is again present, but it seems to be interpreted as the fylgja representing a state of consciousness rather than either it moving forth from the body or a familiar carrying the witch. The treatment of the fylgja spouse seems more like something connected to modern sex magic ideas which influenced Wicca rather than either an extension of the fylgjukona or the familiar spirit. The idea that the fylgja or the familiar is the guardian spirit of a class of animals seems like a general conflation of different ideas simply because they all relate to animals.

This example doesn't really give us interesting workable ideas like some of our other ones did, but rather just points out how easy it is to jumble a bunch of systems into a kind of eclectic stew. It seems to largely draw on contemporary material not linked to traditional material, which probably makes it easier to jumble disparate ideas together. We talked before about how things can be true in the sense that they work and have meaning while still being wrong in the sense that the words and the lore used are used incorrectly. Several of our examples of contemporary witchcraft uses of fetch and fylgja, and even some uses of familiar, fall into that space.

Another individual writing as Seithkona presents a much more delineated view. This author describes the familiar as a distinct and separate incorporeal spirit who decides its own appearance and works with the witch. She explains that the familiar relationship is a reciprocal relationship and that the witch will often house the familiar and call upon them for assistance.

She goes on to explain that the fetch or fylgja is different in part because it is connected to you from birth. She distinguishes between the fylgja and the idea of a spirit animal and explains that the fetch or fylgja is a reflection of ourself in another form. She explains that while you have to seek out a relationship with a familiar and build it through offerings, summoning or conjuration, or necromancy, the fetch might appear through hedgeriding or visionary work or be seen in divination and dreams.

The descriptions and distinctions provided here are pretty much in keeping with traditional lore, and the person presenting it clearly has a connection to that lore. So, while we might look at a lot of these examples and assume that most people presenting information on the familiar, fetch, and fylgja in NeoPagan and traditional witchcraft communities are blurring concepts or using old names for new ideas, there are some who are, in fact, drawing on traditional lore. This post, and a similar post in another forum with almost the same content, was made in response to confusion that the post's author had noticed over the use of these words. So, while there is some good material being put out, it still illustrates why we should explore the history and meaning of these terms and compare that to some popular contemporary uses.

We noted that Gundarsson's <u>Teutonic Magic</u> might have given rise to some of the ideas about the fylgja which permeate contemporary witchcraft. Nigel Jackson's <u>Call of the Horned Piper</u>, another popular text from the 1990s, also uses the terms fetch and fylgja. It was likely instrumental in establishing some of these impressions of an overlap between the fetch, the fylgja, and the familiar.

Jackson directly equates the familiar and the fetch saying, "The familiar spirit, also called the puckerel, imp and nigget, can be regarded as an aspect of the 'animal-soul' or 'animal-fetch.'" Animal fetch alone makes it clear that the concept being referred to is the fylgja, but Jackson also states this outright, "The fetch-light is a manifestation of the Fylgja," and "The Dyr-Fylgja or 'Animal Fetch' underlies the traditional witch concept of the Puckerel or Familiar spirit." I don't know if Jackson established the equation of these concepts in the traditional witchcraft community, but his work has been popular and influential. We know that a lot of people connect these terms, but what does Jackson say about their meaning and function?

Jackson primarily treats the concept of the familiar-fetch-fylgja as an inner concept and a portion of the psyche. The encounter with the "fetch-light" provided in the text is a guided meditation, in which one imagines using flying ointment and visualizes ornately carved magical staves, old stone ruins, and the familiar as a "fetch-light" that guides you forward until you take flight. Jackson describes this part of the psyche as a protective and empowering force that contains luck and numinous powers. He says it is the wild part of our soul and the otherworldly other side of ourselves that we rarely encounter. As a part of the psyche, Jackson describes the fetch as a "deeply buried atavism."

Atavism is the idea of manifesting a now dormant trait held by one's ancestors or returning to old cultural ideas or norms. In magic, atavism often refers to the idea that we contain within ourselves the original state of chaos. We can reach back toward that state and create, within ourselves, manifestations of all other forms of life and creation that also inherently exist within us through the collective unconscious, genetic memory, or some other perceived mode of universality. In that light, an atavistic use of the familiar-fetch-fylgja concept suggests that the various animal forms are inherent in us as part of our historical inheritance as living beings. Since all animal forms are part of us, we can reach down and pull them forth like some kind of "totemic" construct as a form of an animal with whom we have a kinship. Once called forth, we can act through that form or compel its construct to act on our behalf. Other forms of this idea might include calling upon that particular animal-nature to manifest its traits or powers.

Jackson's atavistic use of the fetch involves calling forth this form within our being and projecting it from our psyches to act on our behalf. Jackson describes the familiar as living within the witch's body, in some instances, and being summoned forth to act. Elsewhere he notes the idea of using jars to house and feed familiars but, overall, describes them as internal powers. He describes it as an aspect of the inner psyche and a power "within and beyond the witch," which can be called forth to aid in shape-shifting, divination, and the acquisition of unusual abilities. He also describes it as a spirit guide and as a guide and protector of the witch's consciousness while engaged in spirit flight.

This really hits on a lot of the ideas we have seen recurring in the appropriation of these concepts. There is no reason to think of the familiar as the animal soul. Even calling it a puckrel reflects the fact that it is not always in the form of an animal, and often historical witches reported familiars in the forms of human ghosts and faeries. The familiar is also not part of your soul or psyche but is an independent spirit. You can't get a familiar by doing a guided meditation and imagining putting on flying ointment because it's not something that exists solely in the imaginal spaces of the mind; it has real external existence as a spirit.

The ideas around the familiar-fetch-fylgja as the wild, otherworldly part of the soul connected to deep atavisms fit with the lower soul ideas we encountered earlier. It runs adjacent to some elements of the fylgja, or at least the imagery. It really has nothing to do with the familiar. The idea of it containing numinous power and luck is interesting and ties directly back to the connection between the fylgja and the hamingja. I don't think magical atavism connects to the traditional concept of the fylgja, and certainly not to the traditional familiar, but magical atavisms are interesting. The idea of conceptualizing an atavistic construct as a portion of the psyche that you call forth to embody or project those atavistic powers could be a useful and interesting idea to explore.

When we begin to separate the individual ideas, they start to tie to the historical lore. Familiars don't usually live in your body. Keeping jars to house and feed them is a useful and common concept. The fylgja has a link to your spirit body and extends from the space in which your physical and spirit bodies overlap. Shape-shifting connects to some accounts of familiars, more so in terms of the familiar being with the witch when the witch changes shape or carrying the witch in spirit flight. Some people connect the idea of shape-shifting to the fylgja, but it seems like this relates more to hamr. Being a guide and protector can relate to both concepts. The spirit flight can, as we noted, be connected to the familiar.

So, some ideas tie to each concept, but they're glued together in ways that create something which isn't a fetch, it isn't a familiar, and it isn't a fylgja. Some of what Jackson suggests could be interesting and useful even if it isn't traditionally what any of these things are. Even Jackson's description has points where it kind of breaks a little because it's trying to piece together disparate ideas into one single concept. Again, this shows us how we can have something which can be useful and workable but which really needs a more correct name. The fetch, the fylgja, and the familiar are all interesting concepts on their own. The familiar and the fylgja are really useful ones to explore. Some of these ideas we've explored in the fetch and fylgja chapters, while not being a fetch, fylgja, or familiar, are interesting and useful, but they need appropriate names so we can talk about them without confusion. The ideas would also become clearer and more workable if they stood on their own instead of trying to force disparate concepts together.

Exploring these various ideas confirms that there is lots of room to draw on faery lore and Pagan traditions in exploring the idea of familiar spirits. There are methods from faery lore, early modern faery magic, and revival Pagan movements that can help us pursue familiar spirit work outside of the context of grimoire magic or witchcraft if we want to. We can also see by looking at folklore that there are other rich concepts that we can explore. These can supplement and expand our practices, both in terms of how we relate to our familiars and how we connect with other parts of our souls, psyches, and the rich world of spirits surrounding us. We can see in the witchcraft community how these ideas can inspire us to create new ideas, different from the sources which inspired them, which can inform, augment, and empower our magical explorations.

XVI
It's a Bird! It's a Fetch! It's a Familiar!

Our exploration of familiars, fetches, and fylgjur has deeply explored the traditional versions of these concepts and these concepts as they appear in modern traditional witchcraft. We have focused exclusively on traditional witchcraft, despite many people being involved in Eclectic Wicca and NeoPagan witchcraft. A simple perusal of witchcraft forums will show that many NeoPagan witches have a passion for familiars, even though NeoPagan literature has largely neglected the topic. I am hoping this book is helpful to readers working in that context just as much as it can be for sorcerers, traditional witches, and ceremonial magicians.

Exploring these concepts in a more eclectic NeoPagan witchcraft context is difficult because it isn't treated commonly in NeoPagan literature. As a result, there was one source with ample material to discuss. Like the traditional witchcraft descriptions of familiars, it leaned on the fetch and fylgja but also drew on ideas about spirit animals. There is room to discuss these ideas in relationship to traditional views of familiars and fylgjur, but there is also a lot of inspiration for ways to approach work with a familiar, both in the context of eclectic NeoPagan witchcraft and in other systems.

While Wicca and Wicca-influenced NeoPagan witchcraft tend not to touch on the familiar spirit frequently, those systems leave a lot of room for personal and idiosyncratic approaches. You can add things that speak to you or leave out things that don't. Witchcraft is always personal and individual, but this approach tends to focus on that. Many of our readers may approach witchcraft through a Wiccan or a contemporary NeoPagan lens. That freedom to add and subtract gives you space to explore the familiar spirit through the methods and ideologies we've discussed so far. There are also ways to look at it, which may feel closer to home.

We have to be careful when we look at historical folklore like the familiar and the fetch in an attempt to bridge traditional folklore into these very open and fluid eclectic approaches. As we have seen, it's easy to draw a lot of concepts together when building something new or when constructing something from inspiration taken from older sources. That eclecticism can open up a world of wonderful insights and innovation. However, we've also seen where it can result in a chimera of pieces glued together despite not fitting. We've explored examples where the blending of concepts results in things that are too broad and ranging to pin down. Our goal should be something that syncretizes one of these ideas with your own experience and method of practice. We don't need to mix two or three different ideas; we need to look at how one of these existing ideas fits your world and how your practice can give you a way to approach it.

Exploring the syncretic treatment of the fetch, familiar, and power animal in a contemporary eclectic tradition will also allow us to see how some of these recurring blended ideas exist in a form some witches already work with. Fortunately, Christopher Penczak spent a significant amount of time on the concept in Temple of Shamanic Witchcraft. His ideas presented in an eclectic NeoPagan context dovetail with our traditional witchcraft exploration. It seems likely that the author draws influences from traditional witchcraft sources, along with Core Shamanism, NeoPagan Witchcraft, and Wicca. It also seems very possible that some of the traditional witchcraft concepts we encountered in vernacular use by looking at forums and social media are influenced by the ideas presented here. The system is a contemporary NeoPagan system, one which is popular for people looking for something more expansive than beginner Wicca books but still having a tone and approach familiar to people coming from that background.

Hopefully, looking at this perspective on the familiar will allow us to fill our NeoPagan-witchcraft-shaped gap in a way that connects it with the rest of the methods, folklore, and worldviews we've explored. Looking at a more eclectic interpretation and analyzing how it connects to and differs from traditional folklore will hopefully provide us with an example that will more directly connect with readers from NeoPagan and eclectic backgrounds. Our exploration will take inspiration from Penczak's ideas and expand them into practical considerations based on the traditional idea of working with a familiar. This will highlight considerations for the type of familiar, the type of work to do with the familiar, and the methods to use for the witch working in a more modern modality.

Christopher Penczak, one of the founders of the Temple of Witchcraft and the author of a large number of very popular books on that system, talks about the familiar and the fetch in the section on "Power Animals" in The Temple of Shamanic Witchcraft. Many of the ideas he expresses seem to touch on similar elements to those expressed by Auryn and Faerywolf, as well as some of the other online writers. Penczak is clearly linking the familiar to the fylgja, although he only ever uses the term fetch. His description is a lot more ranging and detailed, so it gives us a lot more to look at.

Penczak's approach has a lot of problematic term use, incorrect history, and attempts to unify very disparate concepts as if they were the same. A lot of this is based on the familiar being viewed as an animal spirit, which is not the case. Rather than present all his ideas and break them down and compare them with the traditional concepts, we're going to look at the positive and innovative elements of his description. A lot of the places where he diverges from history and folklore would give us the opportunity to rehash things we've already looked at, but not in a useful way. His innovations give us ideas that can grow our exploration of the familiar spirit.

The Shamanic Witchcraft treatment of the familiar is very animal oriented. The familiar and the fetch/fylgja are equated to power animals, animal spirits, totem animals, and evolved spirits living in pets. At the outset, we need to understand that the familiar does not need to be so animal oriented. We have encountered this in the other attempts to link the fylgja to the familiar. People tie in various spiritual practices that connect to animals. Some of these practices are sacred practices within specific cultural traditions that most of us don't have access to or real knowledge about. We need to respect that. The familiar isn't a power animal or a totem animal. Terms like "spirit animal" and "power animal" often have loaded associations, but there may be ways to pull them away from those contexts. "Totem animal" is much more specific to a cultural context. We shouldn't presume that what we see in European witchcraft matches those ideas. Fortunately for us, we don't have to be stuck in that trap. Familiars in witchcraft and in grimoire magic took on the appearance of animals, but they weren't animals. Frequently, they appeared as humans or faeries. We shouldn't get stuck thinking of them as animals because it causes these efforts to equate the idea to other spiritual concepts involving animals.

That said, there are some reasons why animal spirits might be a great choice for a familiar if working in a more eclectic NeoPagan context. For people looking to work in a ritual context that feels more like what you'd find in Scott Cunningham or other books of contemporary eclectic witchcraft, animal spirits like those described by Penczak are a good choice. Why would I recommend using this animal spirit approach in that context? Faeries, the types of ghosts you would consider binding as a familiar, and demons will generally need an approach with more safeguards or a stronger binding than we'd be likely to use in a more modern eclectic approach. This approach is appealing to people who want a more soft hand. This is not to say that those other spirits require constraints and damnation. It's also not necessarily the case that they would be antagonistic. There still may be more hazards and complications, and more traditional approaches are better suited to that. Certain animals, particularly ones that would be used to being pets in life, will be naturally attuned to this kind of relationship, and they won't need as much structure involved in creating this relationship.

What are our animal spirit options? First, we need to cut away the "power animal" and "medicine" language some people try to associate with working with animal spirits. If we're looking for a familiar, we're looking for an individual spirit. We don't need to look to the animals as The Raven Spirit or The Cat Spirit. In my experience, groups of animals and types of animals do have guardian spirits. These spirits aren't who we need as a familiar, although it can be helpful to approach these guardian spirits for many things. The world is full of spirits, including the spirits of individual animals.

Going with the spirit of a dead animal is probably the most simple choice. A physical token of the animal can help you connect with it. This could be a bone, preferably the skull, but it could also be dirt from an animal's grave. A physical link to the animal's spirit will be a big help in calling it to establish the relationship. It will also be useful for making a spirit house. Animals that were once pets will probably respond most easily and have the easiest time adjusting to the relationship. Historically, familiars took the forms of animals associated with magic, and in folklore and mythology, powerful beings have wild animals in their service. Finding a bone in the woods and calling upon its former owner is a definite possibility, even though the animal wasn't once a pet.

When working with an animal spirit, don't conceptualize it as a spirit guide, power animal, or totem animal. The way you will work with a familiar spirit is unlikely to match up with the ideas meant by those words. Confusing the concepts will take away from your ability to deeply experience either concept.

The use of an animal spirit might help connect the witch to the divine and guide them in selecting gods to connect with. The idea of a familiar helping connect the witch or magician with divine powers is innovative, but it makes sense. This idea only works in a modern context in which witchcraft is an expression of NeoPagan religion.

Penczak suggests ways in which animals might help us understand gods, but his suggestion of using animal spirits for these devotional connections can be distilled down more simply.

In history and traditional folklore, the familiar is often bestowed by some more powerful spirit. The spirit might be the Devil, the Faery Queen, or Faery King, or it could be a demon or an angel. There is no reason a god or goddess can't bestow a familiar. As we noted, the concept of a helper spirit, or a daimon, in Greek magic is linked to the idea of spirits who moved between men and gods. Gods bestowed spirits to peoples, places, and objects to reside there as a proxy for the god. Your familiar might not serve that function, but if you turn to your god or goddess to receive a spirit, that spirit can potentially help you connect better with your god or goddess and may be able to facilitate interactions with other gods. In a NeoPagan context, asking your gods for a familiar should be a fairly natural option.

If you're asking a particular god or goddess for a familiar, it may be natural for them to give you a familiar that likes to take the form of an animal that was sacred to them or known to be their companion. If you're calling upon the spirit of a dead animal, it might make sense to choose an animal sacred to your gods. Your gods might be able to specially care for or empower the spirit of an animal that is sacred to them. This would help facilitate the process of calling on that spirit. The spirit not only being obtained through your relationship with your deity but also a spirit that reminds you of your deity can be very meaningful. For people not working in a Pagan or NeoPagan context, that might not be a particularly relevant consideration, but it could be very additive for people who are.

In my own experience, I was given two familiar spirits while working a particular ritual. The spirits first appeared in an animal form reminiscent of a pair of animal spirits linked to a god with whom I had done some work. At the time, I had a particular life event happening that connected me with one of that god's defining characteristics, and I had dressed up as him for an event a few months earlier. He didn't connect to the ritual, and I would not have expected that form, or two familiars, to come from that ritual. In fact, the connection to that god did not become apparent until later. When it became apparent, it was meaningful and helped with selecting a physical object for work with those spirits.

Some NeoPagan witches feel that work with gods should be something they build up to. This seems to be a newer concern and is a little backwards from how people have typically handled things. Gods are one of the more accessible conscious, and personified groups of powers. If you haven't started work with gods but want a familiar, can this divine relationship still happen? If you're calling upon the spirit of a dead animal, and it is an animal that you are drawn to, it may be that this animal connects to certain deities. When you're ready to consider working with gods, you could examine mythology for examples that touch on the type of animal that your familiar was in life. If you find a god connected to that animal and you feel drawn to it, turn to your familiar as an intermediary. Ask it to help guide you and introduce you. That link between the god and the familiar might still be possible even if the familiar comes first.

Penczak's approach to familiars focuses on journey work because it is based in Harner's Core Shamanism. The exploration of the familiar through a lens of journey work gives it a slightly different focus. Many of the other sources we looked at tied the familiar to spirit flight. In historical folklore, the familiar is also tied to spirit flight. This focus on journey work can relate to spirit flight but is a bit different. Journey work can deal with traveling through places in the material world in spirit as well as traveling to locations in the spirit world. In some contexts, journey work and spirit flight might be used interchangeably, but in others, the connotations might be different. Spirit flight sometimes takes on an implication of being ecstatic, not simply in the sense of trance but being in a state of ecstasy. Spirit flight often implies a focus on meeting with and celebrating with spirits or working magic with them while in flight. Journey work might focus more on exploring, gathering information, and visiting places of power. Activity that seems more like a quest or activity focused on interacting with the souls of embodied people are also part of journey work but less associated with what we mean when we say spirit flight.

When we're looking at work with the familiar in spirit flight, it is often as a guide or companion. Sometimes the familiar carries us or facilitates the spirit flight; sometimes, the familiar goes along to work magic with us. Interfacing with your familiar, primarily through journey work, can easily include that. Depending upon the type of journey work, the familiar might facilitate it, just like with spirit flight. More likely, the magician would enter their trance state and interact with the familiar. This could take on a few forms.

Basic contact and interaction might be achieved through journey work instead of ritual or waking conscious interactions. For witches working in models that don't tend to deal with spirit conjuration or spirit work in general, the idea of calling upon a familiar and talking with it, drawing it into a crystal, or interacting with it through a statue might be puzzling. Trance meditation to encounter the familiar on a spirit plane may be more accessible. This is also useful for witches and magicians who have trouble seeing or hearing spirits. Traveling in a trance to a place where you can meet the spirit will allow for clearer communication if you have more skill at trance work than at clairaudience or other modes of psychic sensation.

Journey work also opens doors for ways in which the familiar can help you explore spiritual worlds. Core Shamanism often involves imagery like a great tree or mountain for travel or possibly movement into underwater spaces. These might connect to different levels of reality or to different levels of the soul. The familiar might have access and ways to navigate these spaces that are not as easily open to you. The familiar can be a guide and teacher while moving through these spaces. The familiar may be able to go forth in these spirit spaces and bring back power and knowledge that you can't reach yourself.

These spaces are populated with various spiritual beings. Your familiar can be an intermediary for working with them. This might include types of spirits that inhabit particular spiritual planes. For those working in a NeoPagan context, it might also include gods and goddesses. In traditional stories, we see witches going to faery dinners in the faery mounds with their familiars. We see witches leaving their bodies to fly through the night and shape-shift with their familiars. These are often treated as ecstatic experiences where the witch is achieving power through sexual pleasure and feasting with spirits. The journey work perspective pulls some of these spirit interactions out of an ecstatic spirit work context and makes it more familiar for people who work with more modern systems. While journeying together, your familiar could lead you to the courts of gods and goddesses. It could lead you to gods and goddesses who are more suited to you. The interaction can support devotional work and spiritual development. The ideas overlap, but the flavor is a bit different.

The focus on journey work also opens up another option for beginning the relationship with the familiar. Receiving a familiar spirit through journeying seems novel or innovative. It easily feels like it's outside the traditional methods. We would expect a sorcerer to conjure a spirit or a witch to have sex with a spirit. We might expect a witch just to be walking down the street and a spirit to strike up a conversation. Considering that last option, the idea of a visionary experience like journeying as the space in which the familiar is first encountered is not altogether out of the question. We want to make sure it's authentically journey work and not just a guided meditation or a stroll through our imaginations. We need to authentically touch the spaces of spirits if that's our approach. Beginning with ritual, petitioning in ritual, and then journeying for the encounter is a reasonable option.

Alternatively, encountering a familiar while journeying might be reasonable if you're skilled and have encountered spirits while on journeys. If we're thinking about nature-oriented trance meditations to find an animal spirit, we might imagine going into a cave and having a penguin tell us to slide. The point isn't to find a "power animal" through contemporary spiritual guided meditations. Instead, travel. Go on a quest through the spirit realms you travel in. Find spirits you've encountered and ask them to help connect you with a spirit who can be your familiar.

A focus on journeying puts a different spin on things, but one which will be comfortable for many people drawn to NeoPagan witchcraft. The big piece here is it gives a routine way to work with your familiar if your comfort zone is not calling upon and talking with disembodied spirits in ritual. It allows you access to communication. It might even provide a more comfortable means of starting the relationship.

The idea of traveling through spirit realms connects with faring forth and spirit flight, but it also connects to the idea of sending the familiar through those same spirit realms. Any magic with the familiar spirit might involve asking it to accomplish some task. We might ask the familiar to bring something into our life or make something happen. Day-to-day tasks, like finding missing objects or drawing in new clients, might be things you ask a familiar to do instead of casting a spell for them. Some of these things will involve the familiar working in your vicinity, but others will require that the familiar go forth and work. We don't always spend a lot of time thinking of this element of the mechanics. Does the spirit just do things while hanging around you, or does it leave to accomplish things and then return?

Sending your familiar forth becomes a more top-of-mind element of your work if working in a more journeying-based context. Your personal work might involve you faring forth, so of course, the work of your familiar will as well. This also opens up other tasks which the familiar can do. Sending the familiar forth isn't limited to saying, "hey, I need more wealth, bring fortune into my life." We can think of it more as we would think of sending a person out into physical spaces.

The familiar might fly forth to observe or affect things. In witch trial accounts, we often see the familiar sent out to cause harm. In cases where the witch heals someone, it is often based on instructions from the familiar, although some instances may include the witch healing through the agency of the familiar. If someone needs healing at a distance, it is reasonable to send the familiar to help them. You can send the familiar to obtain information on people and places. That information will likely come back as symbols and impressions rather than concrete descriptions because of the way spirits communicate and perceive things. However, this can still be useful. Likewise, the familiar can go forth and influence people and situations by carrying messages and sense impressions. We can get much more concrete in our thinking around going forth than just "bring health into my life." The familiar can be sent to interact with people and places, both physical and spiritual.

Penczak recommends asking the familiar how to perform a sending. Interestingly enough, a "sending" or "sendingar" was the term that Sveinsson recommended in place of the term fylgja when discussing post-Reformation fylgjur. The Icelandic sendingar are malevolent ghosts sent by an evil magician to harass someone. The shaman-witch sending of the Temple of Witchcraft is more benevolent. Any instance in which the familiar fares forth on behalf of the witch - to observe, do magic, obtain power or knowledge, or heal someone; is a sending. Asking the familiar how to send it forth and how to work with its ability to go forth and accomplish these things is very traditional. Depending upon the relationship with the familiar, and the type of spirit it is, the process for sending them forth to do these or other tasks might vary. Turning to the spirit itself for guidance is the best source.

An interesting innovation on the idea of sending forth is the suggestion that the witch can imbue the familiar with their own magical potency. One use of this is sending the spirit to someone to help heal them using the familiar's power and the witch's power in combination. There are probably many options for using this idea of combined power going forth. It is not something I have explored, but it is something you can experiment with. Similar to binding your power to the spirit so that the spirit can go forth and work by applying both its own and your capabilities is the idea of sending the familiar out to obtain knowledge or power that the witch needs. We often think about bringing energies or forces into our lives. We call upon prosperity, fertility, health, and safety and anticipate these manifesting in general and positive ways in our lives. It stands to reason, particularly when we view the world as including a magical landscape through which we can journey where spiritual and mental iterations of concepts, situations, and things exist, that we can quest for capability. We could send a familiar out and tell it, "bring me the ability to convince people to sign on to the proposal I'm presenting this week." We could ask for "the power to see spirits" or "skill at weather working." We think of magic as something where we ask for stuff. Sometimes, we broaden that to asking spirits to teach us about stuff. Magic can also be approached to adapt and improve our capabilities. Receiving the power for such things is usually a matter of receiving potential, and then that potential might still need some cultivation. This is not dissimilar from asking a spirit to teach us, in which case we may still have to work with the information they give or explore the sources they bring into our lives.

These are some adaptive uses that could be experimented with. They fit in with the concept of the familiar very well, but they run closer to what we would see in faery tales and mythology than in historical accounts of magic. The thinking about magic and the magical world present in these applications is different than most of what we can tell about historical magical worldviews. Still, it is easily supported both by historical magical worldviews and by stories. A familiar going to obtain a special power or ability that a witch does not possess but needs is no different than a familiar going to a farm and stealing its capability to be abundant and fecund. It would not be unlike going to a faery king and asking for assistance with a magical task neither the witch nor the familiar can perform.

I'm not going to provide a ritual for a NeoPagan approach to obtaining a familiar. There is too much variability. Perhaps you want to work with gods or, perhaps not. If so, which gods? If you're going with an animal spirit, the type of animal you choose might change the ritual. Instead, we can consider the basic method. Let's assume gods are involved. If not, then some other spiritual power like your ancestors, guardian angel, or Nature would be good alternatives.

To begin, follow whatever your normal ritual method is. We'll assume that starts with some kind of cleansing and preparation. Then, you set the ritual space and cast a circle. Call upon the elements and the god and goddess, or your preferred divine structure. Once you have called upon them, have some physical token for the animal. A feather if you're requesting a bird spirit, a sea shell if something aquatic, a bone or tooth for a land animal like a cat or dog, or some other physical token that belonged to an animal should be on hand. This will be the physical anchor for the familiar. Next, make an offering to the deities, explain why you'd like the familiar, explain what you'd like it to do and how you'll care for it. Use whatever divination or trance method you use to receive messages, and confirm that you have received the familiar, its name, and anything else you'll need to know about it. Say an incantation to welcome it and link it to the token. Then do your cakes and ale or some other food ceremony with the familiar and the deities to welcome the familiar and thank the deities. Finally, place the token in whatever spirit house you have prepared and close the ritual.

There are a couple of points where you can adjust this depending on the specifics surrounding the type of familiar you're seeking. If you're looking for an animal spirit, it may make sense to call upon whatever spirit rules over and protects those animals after you call whatever deities you are working with. The deities can help you with calling that spirit, and that spirit can help guide the connection to the specific animal spirit. If you're not looking for an animal spirit and instead want a spirit bestowed by a god, then you might change your physical token. You could use a physical token from an animal because it is a physical thing that was once connected to a spirit. Bone and blood are two very potent materials for creating those links. You could also use a statue of the deity or a necklace, pendant, or ring with a symbol related to the deity.

Depending upon the nature of the physical link, you might use it in constructing a spirit house. If the link is a statue or jewelry, just keep it in a special place. Bring the token to your altar if you work with your familiar during a ritual. If you work with your familiar in journey work, wear the token or keep it with your while journeying.

Using a statue or ring calls to mind older forms of magic. Penczak referenced these in connection to ceremonial magic, but they don't need to be thought of in those terms. The comparison to ceremonial magic is a little loaded, as that often refers to the lodge magic systems stemming from the Victorian Era magical revival and possibly including the lodge magic systems which predated those in the hundred years or so beforehand. The sort of astrological magic and grimoire magic which includes tying spirits to physical objects has largely been absent from the Victorian Era revival systems of modern ceremonial magic. More recent revivals of grimoire magic and astrological magic are arguably separate from the ceremonial magic of groups like the Golden Dawn and the Ordo Templi Orientis, although there are several people that explore European Traditional Magic who come from contemporary magical orders. As we will see in Part III of this book, familiar spirits can be conjured to occupy bottles, and physical objects like Penczak describes. We'll see how this is done. We'll also see how this can be viewed as a fairly foreign experience for people whose practice is firmly routed in modern ceremonial magic.

For the witch or magician working from a NeoPagan context, the focus on animal spirits and journey work definitely provides some elements you can draw from. These new ideas may be useful for people outside of a NeoPagan context as well. For those drawn to a more NeoPagan approach, the material we've discussed in other chapters should still inform your approach. Even if you're working with an animal spirit and using journeying because those approaches speak to you or are more comfortable, those things we have already discussed will still help you understand your familiar. The only real difference is how you're approaching it ritually and the means of communication you're focusing on. As far as what a familiar is, how to interact with it and how to obtain one, the material presented in Part I and the folklore presented in Part II will be useful regardless of the tradition you feel connected with. Part III will deepen our exploration by giving other methods, but also by exploring in detail a specific example of acquiring and working with a familiar, as well as how this work can help push us to further develop magic in the modern world.

Part Three

The Demon of Baltimore
Image of Baphomet Over Baltimore
Image selected through divination with the demon Tobias

Image of Tobias's Shrine from William Blake Lodge Space 2019

XVII
Why Would You Want a DEMON?!?

William Blake Lodge is situated in the Blue Light District. For people not from or familiar with major cities, that might sound kind of pleasant. Blue lights might seem soft and inviting. They wouldn't indicate the sexual commerce that red lights suggest or have the sharp contrast-increasing effects of red light.

Blue lights don't mean welcome. They mean cops.

The blue light district is an area where the streets are lined with poles that have cameras mounted on them. The cameras have flashing blue lights to remind the locals, or anyone transacting any sort of business there, that they are under police surveillance. Police sit in cars, spread out through the area, theoretically watching feeds from the nearby cameras so they can act right away if something happens.

I think with the discourse around policing in the last few years, particularly in major cities and low-income areas, the idea that flashing blue lights and the imminent presence of the police might suggest the comfort of a safety net is out the window. Even before highlighting incidents of police violence, the blue light cameras did not really create a sense of comfort for most people. They just reminded them that it was assumed the area was dangerous.

In all honesty, I spent eleven years going to that space frequently and never experienced any crime myself. I don't think anyone in the Lodge did. I witnessed the aftermath of one horrible incident, and I witnessed two small inconsequential incidents. All in all, I think we were all pretty safe there. The neighbors were typically polite, and some were helpful. I frequently traveled there alone, late at night, to do small errands and tasks for the Lodge. I felt comfortable doing so.

I think our Lodge's neighborhood, and to a degree the converted warehouse building in which we operated, were examples of how the appearance or assumption of danger isn't the same as being in danger. There was still reason to be cautious and to stay alert and aware. I wouldn't linger outside alone at night, but I didn't feel like being there was a bad choice or like I needed to feel on edge.

Inside the Lodge, we built out a very comfortable, inviting, beautiful space. We had tons of books, comfortable couches, a kitchen, a meeting room, and a beautiful temple space. It was a comfortable space for parties, or just for hanging out. If I stopped by at night to turn on the air conditioners, sitting down to relax in the empty space for a few minutes after running up the five flights of stairs was a reasonable choice.

While the space was comfortable and inviting, the Lodge had something the outside of the building, and the rest of the inside, did not have. The Lodge had a demon. That demon sat housed in a skull, surrounded by his possessions: candles, incense and incense burners, liquor bottles, and decorative cloths. He sat in his skull in his jar prepared with dirts, and herbs, and blood, and incense. He sat with his blood pact in the mouth of his skull. He sat holding his space, amid the bookshelves, where he would receive his offerings and from where he would work his magic for our benefit.

The demon worked for our benefit, but he was and is, still a demon. I'm not a demonalator, so I don't believe in demons being cuddly warm friendly misunderstood gods. I also don't believe they are damnable evil monsters. Demons are like lions. The lion isn't nefariously trying to harm you or plot against you, but if you try to interact with the lion without the right measures or outside of the right conditions, you put yourself at significant risk. When you walked in, you could feel the presence of the demon. It was like a weight, and like an edge of something sharp just hovering at the periphery of awareness. His presence was a constant background element that slightly touched and tweaked the character and feel of the overall space.

People who worked with the demon routinely and closely expressed that he often reminded them that he was a demon. This didn't mean that he gave them shivers or ooky spooky sensations or images. He would assert himself. He would allow his personality to be felt, which was one which was helpful to and appreciative of us, but one which was also capable of force and violence if needed. Sometimes desires for offerings were expressed in ways which could seem confrontational, or slightly unsettling. His presence, when unfettered, was to a degree, physically difficult to stand in the midst of.

Considering this, the question of "why would you want to keep a demon around?" might seem like a head scratcher. For many magical needs, you could conjure particular spirits relative to the need in question. If you want to have a familiar spirit, you could ask the Olympic spirits, or an archangel, or a faery queen for a familiar. Some people might keep a ghost as a familiar. Some magicians may seek a familiar without really considering what sort of spirit it is. We've talked a lot about establishing relationships with familiars, and what those relationships look like. We also discussed how to decide what kind of familiar to contract. As we said before, a lot of this will be dependent upon your comfort, how you work, what you're drawn to, but also your goals and the purpose for which you want the familiar. This kind of question is one that magicians need to ask themselves whenever they consider exploring new avenues of spirit work, not just work with a familiar. Why does a particular sort of spirit make sense for what you're planning to do?

The answers to that question will vary from person to person. Some people find a variety of spirits able to work towards the types of magic they want to explore. Other people find certain types spirits work in ways suited to particular goals, or in a manner suited to the magician's needs. I personally find that because various types of spirits may be suited to one thing or another, incorporating a range of spirits working together can allow them all to bring different things to the table. Working with various types of spirits allows them to work in different ways or help shape the work of the other spirits involved. How you interpret work with spirits will likely guide what kind of familiar makes sense for you. Your primary modes of working and your existing spirit relationships will also impact those decisions. You may also consider whether certain spirits you work with might have issues with the relationships involved in setting up particular types of relationships that provide familiars. Individually, there may be lots of factors to consider.

Since we're looking at a ritual that was used by a group for a familiar to serve the group, we needed to look at how and why a demon familiar would fit into a group dynamic. For individuals, we would also look at how working with a familiar complements the types of spirit relationships we might already have.

There are a handful of relationships people can develop with spirits, but there are three which make sense for us to consider as the kind of broad models that might include most approaches. A magician might call upon a particular spirit for a particular thing at a particular time. A magician might have an ongoing devotional relationship, or an ongoing partnership or working relationship, and keep a designated space to perform certain rituals and make certain offerings and open up for contact routinely. Lastly, a magician might have a "familiar" relationship or a "possession" relationship (these are not necessarily the same) in which the magician and the familiar might have a relatively ongoing contact and interaction and retain close proximity, work together routinely and consistently communicate.

Calling on a spirit as a specific act of magical working is probably the most common spirit work in the minds of most magicians. The benefit to that approach over others mostly has to do with clarity and specificity. When you work this way, you know when you're doing the work, you know what spirit you're dealing with and you can ask for what you want. The spirit you select is likely one suited to your work. The time you do the ritual and how you do it might pertain to your work and in some way contribute to its success. You might feel comfort working in a formal, thorough way if it's a bigger request. You might feel like the spirit you're calling is the best spirit to address your request in the particular way you need it addressed.

Working that way can also have some drawbacks and difficulties. Sometimes formal magic isn't convenient. If there is a major issue you're trying to resolve, the issue itself can be distracting. People often find things to get in the way of doing their magic, especially if it's going to be an involved process. The spirit who seems like the best spirit for the job may or may not be a spirit with whom you have a relationship. You might not have all of the ideal materials, or the time to acquire them, if the ritual or spirit involves elements outside of your normal work. While it might be possible to do your work at any time, you might feel that the spirit you've selected will work best at a specific time, or the traditions or rituals associated with the spirit might dictate a specific time – and that time might not be available to you or in time for your need.

Even if you have an ongoing devotional or working relationship with a group of spirits, or maintain consistent proximity or communication with a spirit, individual formal conjurations with other specific spirits will still happen sometimes. One of the goals of spirit work tends to be moving from the specific individual conjurations as large formal affairs towards having a relationship and the ability to more simply call upon the spirit because the formal ritual has established a relationship. With that in mind, your individual call-and-make-a-request approach should lead to something that shares some similarity to the other two types of spirit relationships we have mentioned. It's very likely that you might, at times, work with all three relationship types at once.

Compared with the other two, the sort of devotional, or ongoing, working relationship seems to be the easiest approach to set up, and one which many magicians today recommend. In fact, this kind of approach works with many spirits that we might not typically conjure and can be set up with much more informal methods. A magician might dedicate an altar or shrine or some sort of spirit house for the spirits with whom they will work. Offerings and supplications could be made or perhaps some sort of prayer or ritual service might be offered in order to open up a connection or communication. The use of an ongoing consecrated space and specific actions to open up communication and provide offerings often makes the process of interacting simpler.

So, our major benefits with this approach or relationship include that it's simple to begin and does not involve large ritual set-ups every time you need to communicate with the spirits involved. Since you're routinely working with the same spirits in this approach, you have a relationship with them, so they should be inclined to want to work with you. If there is ongoing attention or offerings being given, those spirits may work in your interests even when you aren't specifically requesting help. When you do request help with something they may continue to help with things related to that issue even after the request is fulfilled.

This approach to spirit relationships is pretty useful and is one I'd encourage most magicians working with spirits to incorporate into their work, but, like anything else, there are also potential drawbacks. Because you're working with spirits with whom you have an ongoing relationship, they will not be spirits specifically related to the work you're attempting to accomplish. They may still be able to help you, but the particular goal you have in a moment might not be something in which they have expertise. These spirits also won't be bound to help you. You might ask for help with something and they may not be inclined to help with that goal, or to help at that time, for a variety of possible reasons. Depending on elements of your lifestyle or living situation, having a space set up permanently or semi-permanently may not work well for you. Those same reasons might make ongoing offerings or carving out time for routine attention difficult.

Our third mode of working is the one which has been the focus of this text, and includes another mode which we will touch on later. Working with a familiar spirit or a possessing spirit takes the relationship with the conjured spirit several steps further. Rather than simply making it easier to call a spirit after licensing it to depart, the spirit remains with you. Generally, in the case of a familiar, the spirit is attached as a servant or companion which you house and care for. It is usually obtained through routine attempts to conjure or interact with a spirit who then provides you with the familiar. A possessing spirit is a spirit who stays with you, speaks with you, and occupies a close and intimate space with you. This relationship is often developed through initiation or prolonged work. We have talked about this elsewhere in connection with the Holy Guardian Angel. It is a mode of spirit interaction we see in several magical cultures and traditions. It is generally separate from the relationship we would have with a familiar, but shares some similarities. Both familiars and possessing spirits remain in close proximity, ready to work with us as long as we maintain our relationships with them. We will discuss positive possession further, but in a manner different from this form.

We have spoken at length about what familiars do and how to obtain one. We've gone over the benefits, and how to care for and work with them. We haven't really discussed drawbacks or how those relate to selecting the type of spirit we wish to develop this relationship with. Reviewing the relationship with a familiar in the context of other types of spirit relationships will give us a good jumping-off point for these missing elements.

The primary drawback is time and attention. By obtaining a familiar you are committing to a close and personal relationship. You can't ignore it or forget it. If you toss it aside you might not be able to easily pick up the relationship again. The familiar isn't a slave which is bound to an item as we see in tales of genies in lamps, bottles and rings. There is a relationship between those stories and what we are doing with a familiar, but the key thing to keep in mind is that by establishing a relationship with a familiar you are in fact establishing a relationship. It's not capturing a Pokemon and storing it in a ball until you want to use it. The relationship can erode and the familiar can rejoin the legion of spirits from whence it came if you don't keep up your end of the pact. If you break the contract, the spirit does not owe you its portion of the contract anymore.

Like many serious commitments to spirits, this involves routine interaction. If you are devoted to an angel or a god, to your ancestors or some saints, you will perform the type of routine devotional work we spoke of above. Sometimes you might get busy, sometimes you might not be in the mood. You might miss an offering or a prayer here or there. Sometimes you get to a place where it's just hard to keep up with that kind of stuff. Maybe you're depressed, maybe things aren't working out as you expected, maybe you're just not feeling things spiritually. That happens, and people can trudge through the work until they respark that feeling, but a lot of people will pull away. Eventually, you might just stop doing spiritual or magical work for a long time. Depending upon what those spirits are helping you with, and your relationship with them, maybe they keep helping. Maybe they will help for a little while and drop things when it's clear you're done for the time being. They might withdraw their aid, and things might be the way they would be if there weren't spirits guiding elements of your life. The spirits' response will depend on several factors. Usually with devotional relationships, it's easy to get the spirits back on board with working with you. Often it's just a matter of telling them you're sorry it's been so long, and then starting up again.

Sometimes, if there is an initiated element to that devotion, or the spirits have given you some special gift or connection, there is a greater expectation for you to keep your work going. This expectation is there with familiar spirits, but the relationship isn't the same. When we consider these devotional relationships, the spirits aren't bound to you or your shrine. They don't have to do things you ask. They don't have to come when called. They're there because you have a family relationship or a professional relationship, and like those relationships usually go, you can both kind of come and go freely. Your familiar is contracted to serve you. It's bound to go where you are. It's bound to stay with its spirit house. It has a contract to fulfill. It serves you because of an agreement you made. The relationship is very different. If you aren't keeping up your end of it, maybe for a little while things go along fine and you can improve. Eventually, you hit a point where you simply nullify the contract and the familiar is no longer bound by it. You might be able to conjure them again, but reinitiating the relationship may be difficult.

Looking at some of the grimoire methods, you could forcibly bind a demon to an object and require service through use of that object. You wouldn't have a contractual element to fulfill if following those methods to the letter, assuming they work as described without a pact or agreement. In that case, it might be more like a genie in a lamp. I have not attempted that approach though, and it doesn't seem like as amenable of an option as a contract.

So, say we consider all the factors. We have some devotional relationships with spirits. We know how to conjure spirits when we need them for specific stuff. We've considered the upkeep of a familiar. We've considered the benefits of a familiar, and the ways we can explore further magic with one. Say we've decided we're going to move forward and obtain a familiar spirit. How do we know what type we want? We talked about that in the abstract in an earlier chapter. Exploring William Blake Lodge's familiar will let us look at specific circumstances involved in making such a choice.

We've already addressed that familiar isn't a type of spirit but rather a role defined by a relationship. How do we know what kind of spirit we want for that role? We've already talked about how William Blake Lodge's familiar was very clear with people that it was a demon. You could feel the presence of the demon when near its altar. It communicated in ways which reflected its nature. Do we want that kind of relationship with that kind of danger? Or is this one of those situations where there is more the appearance of danger than an actual danger?

As some say, the shark is the shark, the shark is not the dolphin. Demons are demons, and they are dangerous. But all spirits are dangerous. All people and all animals are dangerous. The questions we have to ask are, how likely is the danger, how dangerous is it, what steps we can take to manage the danger and what will we get out of accepting the risk? If we follow the correct methods, bind the spirit appropriately, treat it well, and don't do stupid things with it, we're back in our blue-light district. We're reminded that there might be danger, but, usually, our neighbors are friendly. The demon is not necessarily a worse choice than other spirits. If we don't consider precautions, if we aren't careful in our requests, and if we don't have appropriate controls in place or treat it with respect, then that's where we might get burned. Angels, faeries, and ghosts can burn us too.

So why a demon? In the case of William Blake Lodge, whose demon adventure forms the case study on which the third segement of this book constellates, part of it was simply that it fit what I wanted to do. We'll talk more later about some of the reasons I wanted to do this ritual. Beyond my own desires and goals, it was also the most appropriate choice.

Going with a demon rather than an angel was driven in part by reasons related to modern magical culture. Some of it also had to do with the expectations of the community. Modern ceremonial magicians think of conjuring demons and look at the Ars Goetia as one of the main grimoires to explore. Despite people who questioned why we would conjure a demon, it's often the goal that contemporary ceremonial magicians work towards.

Starting with the goal of obtaining a familiar, instead of starting with a goal of conjuring a demon to bind a familiar, would have made considering other types of spirits reasonable. Weighing options still brings us to a demon. I don't think a faery familiar would have been unwelcome at William Blake Lodge, but it would not have seemed the typical choice for a group of modern ceremonial magicians. Magic involving faeries abounds in the grimoire tradition, particularly in Britain. Despite that ubiquity, ceremonial magic from the revival era did not incorporate faeries significantly. An angel could have been reasonable, but we had fairly material needs and wanted physical results. Angels can do that, but often they're more preoccupied with guidance, advice, and making you your best self. Ghosts can be good familiars for lots of things, but they are very much still people. They understand people-related things and people-related solutions, but they won't have a broader view of things. Sometimes they have something they need to accomplish so they can move beyond being a ghost. The sort of dead that you can bind as a familiar are not like the dead amongst your ancestors. These are restless spirits, still attached to life because of some lack of resolution or malignance. They might have died violently, or might not have been given appropriate burial rites. They might have been cursed. They have not gone through any of the sort of healing or elevation that can be involved in dying. You're still dealing with a very individual, discrete person, who is not at all different from what they were like in life. You also have to find a dead person who became a ghost, or supplicate a spirit or goddess who has a horde of ghosts that follows her in her phantom train so that she might give you a ghost.

Expectations about how the spirit will work, and the goals you have for it, are important for considering the selection of a familiar. If you want a familiar to do the things you'd call upon a faery for, but not a demon or an angel, then you probably want a faery familiar. If you're not comfortable with demons, you probably don't want a demon familiar; conversely, if you don't do angels, you probably don't want an angel familiar. Maybe you're doing particular work with particular spirits and those spirits are the main spirits in your life. If those spirits will not be happy with you working with a particular sort of spirit to obtain a familiar, or having a familiar of a particular type, then you need to negotiate that with them first or obtain a different sort of familiar.

In the case of William Blake Lodge, we wanted material things. We didn't have a set of spirits we had to consider harmonizing the demon with. Our community wasn't averse to a demon and it was within the realm of expected spirit work. In the end, a demon was the

right choice based on those factors. It was also a successful choice.
Our demon did a lot for us. It revealed problems, and brought us
new, awesome people. While working with it we had vibrant growth,
more exciting, successful events and more effective networking.
Financial issues the lodge experienced weren't miraculously solved by
treasure-finding spirits, but we had more people paying dues or for
events, and so the issues became less concerning. Obtaining a demon
familiar was a big turnaround for all of those things. We might have
gotten similar results with an angel, but it would have manifested
differently. It might have taken more time and been less direct. It may
have followed its own nature by focusing on new ideas and
approaches instead of simply bringing new people and new
connections that directly answered our needs. A faery or a ghost may
have accomplished things also, but, likely in very different ways.

I didn't go through that process of examining the best type of
spirit to pursue for a familiar when planning William Blake Lodge's
efforts to obtain a familiar. Still, examining it in hindsight has let us
look at how to go through that consideration and how it can result in
something successful. Our demon was the right type of spirit for what
our members would expect, and for the goals we needed. It fit the
history and traditions that established the organization which the
familiar would be working with. It wasn't at odds with any sorts of
spirits we were regularly working with, nor was it at odds with the sort
of work we did as a Lodge. These are the kinds of things to think of
when considering a familiar for a group.

If you're working alone, it's a question of what you want, how
you want to get it and what your preferences and comfort levels are.
You have to look at how the spirits you'll approach fit within your
mode of working. You have to consider if your spirit court will be able
to work with the type of spirit you're calling.

The considerations are mostly the same regardless of whether
we're talking about groups of people. The exact way we ask the
questions differs a bit if you're talking about a group or about yourself.
What am I comfortable with, versus what are we comfortable with.
Let's wrap up with some of the questions we might ask in a group,
almost all of these can also be parsed for an individual. What's the
nature of the group and the group dynamics? Are there spirits who
shouldn't be involved with that type of group? Are there spirits more
naturally accustomed or suited to your group? Are there types of
spirits your group members will have experience working with? Are

there types of spirits your group members will benefit from working with?

For us, a big part of the choice was expanding magic. We wanted something that would be outside of what we were doing and what other groups were doing. We wanted something that would push boundaries in order to expand them and make us more complete more competent magicians. We wanted to jump off with an experience people would remember and which would get them thinking about their magic. If it worked well, it would put us on a road to working with real and powerful spirit magic on a regular basis. A demon was a good choice for all of that from our perspective. It might be the best choice for you or for your group, or it might not be. There are many options. Hopefully our exploration of this particular adventure in spirit magic will help you consider the possibilities.

Saint Augustine is Given the Book of Vices by the Devil
Michael Pacher 1475

XVIII
Initiations Sacraments and Conjuration

Shortly after college, I was out at the mall with a friend grabbing dinner in the food court. As I ordered my meal, the cashier noticed my ring. This wasn't some magical ring or a ring indicating my membership in some clandestine occult order. It was my class ring from the local prep school I had attended. For boys who went to our boys' school, there was often a shared bond, like a fraternity. The cashier told me he was going to school there, and as a result, my drink with my meal was free.

Our experiences in life often give us access to things that we might not have had access to otherwise, or that we might have only accessed with more difficulty. They can give us knowledge or perspective from which to unpack experiences, or that we can use to find answers to help us navigate things we encounter. As illustrated in the story above, our experiences, networks, and affiliations can give us allies, support, or special treatment.

I have spoken frequently about the idea of street cred in the spirit world. This is not a dissimilar idea. When we talk about spiritual street cred we're talking about the reputation you have amongst spirits. Do you have the juice to make it easier to see them and impact them in ways that make them inclined to listen? Do you have it and know how to use it enough that spirits know about you? Do you keep your promises? Do you give good offerings? Are you a good friend to the spirits with whom you should be friends? Do you have powerful spirit allies? In the human world our actions and our connections will impact and build our reputations, and those reputations will impact how others deal with us. We will find similar factors at play in the spirit world.

Street cred isn't the only thing that can have an impact. Spiritual power might be a factor. Power may be found in using the right tools and performing the rituals in the right way. The right ritual has an impact if spirits are bound to respond to the ritual, or if it calls upon powers to which the spirits are bound to give deference. Authority achieved from certain experiences, and connections conferred through those experiences, can also have an impact. In this way, initiation, sacraments, and membership in the right group can be factors in conjuration and spirit work. There are historical and traditional associations between the art of exorcism or spirit conjuration and priesthood in various religions and cultures. This connection leads to debate about the value or necessity of ordination into some form of priesthood. Is it required? Does it create some indispensable benefit? Is it an unnecessary cultural relic?

Clearly, ordination isn't required to conjure spirits. There are many factors which can help the magician navigate the work of conjuring spirits. It is still a factor which can have a benefit, depending upon the nature of the ordination and the nature of the priesthood involved. Considering religious ceremonies broadly, ordination is not the only sacramental or initiatic practice which can offer a benefit.

In the case of ordination, the priest is often given special access to a particular god. They might be able to wield certain spiritual powers associated with that god and the god's followers. The priest might be given special access to that god, and the ability to call upon that god's authority or ability to exert force upon other spiritual beings. The ordination might create an association like friendship in which the relationship with the god becomes a way to flex that status when dealing with spirits or to name-drop your divine friend in order to get gods or spirits to work with you. Most conventionally, we think of it as conveying access to spiritual power via the Holy Spirit, which is a faculty that can be achieved or approximated by several magical, religious, and spiritual practices.

In a Christian or a Gnostic context, various sacramental experiences can confer particular powers or forms of spiritual completion which the magician can bring to the table in their conjuration work. Confession is routinely associated with grimoire conjuration. Baptism, anointing, and the Eucharist also have power and status that they can confer which might help the magician. Just like Christianity has several ritual elements which may augment the magician, either permanently or temporarily, so do other systems of religion, magic, and spiritual work.

In my early exploration of necromancy, initiations tied to the Eleusinian mysteries, and initiations which initiated me into the mysteries of death were significant factors in demonstrating that I had the spiritual status to access certain things I needed to access in that work. Initiations which move the initiate through the mysteries of death are very common in both modern and historical magical traditions and mystery cults. In the modern times we rarely explore how having been ritually dead, or having our spiritual experience marked with the experience of death, alters our access to certain elements of the spirit world. Similarly, we often neglect discussing how work with various elements of the spirit world changes our relationship to both the spirit world and the waking world, and our status in the eyes and attentions of particular spirits and forces of nature. Reflecting on these things is an important element of exploring how initiatics and sacramentalism can impact work with spirits.

Some traditions of initiation directly relate to access to spirits. In some cases, this deals with gaining access to agreements spirits have made to work with people initiated into a particular lineage. In other cases, it refers to receiving a spirit to house within your working space. We don't see living traditions in "Western," or more correctly, Anglosphere, magic which include the receipt of a spirit. Historically, this is a significant component of European witchcraft. There are also Italian traditions associated with a particular cemetery in which those who gain access to this particular magic gain the soul of a deceased person to care for and work with. These are only two examples, and we will find numerous others if we dig into the diversity of magic throughout Europe. Magic in which receiving a spirit is part of the process of becoming a particular sort of magician is not uncommon in European Traditional Magic, but it is certainly not present in most modern witchcraft traditions or systems of lodge magic. In some African Diaspora Traditions, the magician might be marked to receive a particular spirit, but, as far as I understand it from the outside, this is often the personal presence of a spirit approached by many people through that tradition. In other traditions of sorcery, more particular spirits associated with that lineage become accessible to the magician upon his reception into that sorcerous lineage. I am not aware of whether or not any confer upon magicians an individual spirit specifically to work with them in the manner of a familiar. Whether non-European traditions have spirits similar to familiars or not, it is plain to see that initiation can change our relationship with spirits in numerous traditions.

Initiation, religious ritual, and sacraments, all have the power to impact our ability to work with spirits, the ease with which we do it, or the access we have to them. Does our history as initiates color the language through which we are able to speak with spirits? In most areas of life, this is an important consideration. Artists develop a visual vocabulary based on their life experiences and the art to which they've been exposed. Writers are influenced by the way in which people around them speak, the books they've read, and the words that form their daily speech. For everyone, the language we use informs how we think, and the experiences we've had inform how we understand new experiences. Mystics and magicians tend to interpret the spiritual sensations they experience through the lens and language of the mythology to which they have been exposed. Our personal histories matter, even in a world where spirits are real.

Historically, magic and religion existed within the same space to varying degrees. The academic study of magic has developed many different and opposing approaches to understanding the relationship between magic and religion. Sometimes magic was thought of as something outside of religion, or the remnant of previous religions. Other scholars have viewed it as a part of religion – either specialized or indistinguishable from general religion. Some have suggested it is the inverse of religion, as if religion were the front facing side of a tapestry and magic is the woven image we would see if we looked at the underside. Defining this relationship is complicated. Sometimes religion and magic intermingle, and at other times magic is something that exists seemingly by breaking and twisting elements of religion – whether it is the religion of the magician or pieces of religion borrowed from elsewhere. Most views recognize that there is some relationship between magic and religion.

In the medieval and early modern world, we often see "learned magic" as largely the domain of priests, at least until the Protestant Reformation begins to reshape some of how magic is done. In the ancient world, we definitely see some branches of magic, or magic in some cultures, associated with priests. Magical ritual and religious ritual tend to have related tools, languages and actions. As we have noted elsewhere, conjuration and exorcism are synonyms. Not only are they synonyms, but the techniques of apotropaic exorcism in the Catholic Church were known to be applicable for conjuring demons to learn things from them and request things from them. The language of Catholic ritual is woven into a significant amount of grimoire magic. Dr. Francis Young has written a few papers which address the relationship between religious ritual and religious thinking in the contexts of Catholicism and the Reformation as they tie into the practice of conjuration. They are well worth reading. For our purposes, it is enough to note that through most of history, the religion of the magician and his magical practice had a relationship.

This is not always the case in modern magic. Modern cultures no longer have the same relationship with religion that we had historically. Rather than different flavors of Christianity, with a handful of related other religions, being the predominant and assumed culture of the populace, the landscape is now more complicated. We have many people who don't believe in anything, others who hold beliefs but are unaffiliated, some who are in alternative religions, and others in major religions but maybe not the one which holds the largest chunk of the plurality. Many people leave the religion of their birth, if they have one, and either adopt non-belief or explore something else. This isn't a criticism, but this more diverse religious landscape is important to consider. Magicians in the Middle Ages, or magicians in antiquity, had one religious option and the magic they had access to was related to that one religion. They might have been exposed to neighboring religions and their associated magic, and may have blended things. Typically, their primary religious identity was defined by culture or location. Magicians in the Middle Ages were able to maintain the dominant religious structure while absorbing elements of folk belief. Magicians in antiquity existed in a world where the dominant religious culture often left room for syncretism and pluralistic religious participation. Religious life for medieval magicians and magicians in antiquity was still not so ala carte as that of the modern magician.

If we look at the "revival" of magic in the late 19th and early 20th centuries, we will notice magic stepping away from its historical relationship with religion. Some 19th century magicians did tie their magic to their religion. Martinists and French Revival Gnostics explored magic linked to and understood through their particular expression of Christianity. The more diabolical current of continental occultism departed somewhat from magic which clearly fit a religious framework. The alternative initiatory forms of secret Christianity, and the counter-cultural diabolism allowed magic to exist in a space counter to maintream religion rather than as an interpretation of it. By the time continental occultism began to feed into a British occult revival, magic had become suited to a masonic framework instead of a religious one. Magic, amongst certain classes of people, gained status as an element of clandestine spiritual-social experiences rather than being a mode of more directly engaging religious powers or mitigating difficulties of life within the worldview of the religion. Magic indicated access to a special secret knowledge of the world beyond that held by the commonly religious.

This divorce from the contiguous cultural worldview led to efforts to smash disparate and incomplete parts together. Some components of the systems which developed echoed Christianity even as they criticised or rebelled against Christianity. Hermetic Kabbalah drew on Christian Kabbalah sometimes trying to tie back to more Jewish approaches to Kabbalah but without recourse to the overall context and understanding provided by Jewish religion. We see Egyptian mythology, Greek mythology, and Hermetic and NeoPlatonic concepts, all cherry picked and redefined into unrelated religious and ritual structures. These were presented as ancient wisdom while often being at their core expressions of various spiritual and magical elements of more or less modern invention. These were frequently attached to theosophical teachings which used the language of Eastern mysticism, again without an actual connection to the culture or religion from which terms were borrowed. The magic of the revival period was in many ways new and distinct, even from "learned" magical systems practiced only decades before.

These revival magic systems work in a framework based on lodge initiations and tie back to the signs, gestures, officer roles, and powers addressed in those initiations. A lot of the magical practices presented focused on building more lodge style tools and doing more lodge style rituals rather than effecting particular magical goals. These systems included instructions for making talismans and conjuring spirits, but they diverged from traditional methods and the worldviews which shaped them.

The Golden Dawn was onto something with this, though. It gets messy because it's such a mishmash of stuff. It leaves out a lot of spiritual and magical thinking and reflection, because it is divorced from an overall cultural or religious worldview. It recognized that it was important that the experiences which taught the magician magic and gave the magician magical authority needed to be reflected in how the magician worked magic. That in and of itself was brilliant. The specifics of the execution and their effectiveness might be up for debate, but the idea itself has merit. That idea was a core driver behind the method we'll be discussing in this section.

William Blake Lodge was not a Golden Dawn temple, but a lodge in the Ordo Templi Orientis. The Ordo Templi Orientis, or OTO, is another example of a fraternal modern magical body organized within the religious and philosophical framework of Thelema. Most people involved in organized Thelema are involved with the OTO, which uses initiations similar to those of freemasonry which develop the individual to help make them a better more successful person. They are not as clearly about magical development or practice. The A∴A∴ system more directly continued the work of the Golden Dawn in the Thelemic community, but without the same type of ritual initiations. With these factors at play, it is a little more difficult to build a system of spirit conjuration based in the initiatory and liturgical framework through which the magician has developed.

Thelema doesn't hold a system of beliefs which naturally align its ritual system to spirit magic. Dr. Young wrote in "Liturgical Change and Ceremonial Magic" concerning the relationship religious belief and ritual share with magical practice. In particular, he wrote about how changes in Christian belief and practice due to the Reformation may have changed methods of exorcism. In Thelema, religious icons and spiritual entities are often treated as metaphors, psychological archetypes, and expressions of the mind. This forces us to ask the question, if a religion generally views spirits as psychological and does not incorporate ritual elements which connect to a mythology that encompasses spirit interactions how does that religion inform magical practices based on interacting with spirits?

Taking away spirits and making things about psychological experience could remove the issue. If everything is about psychology, the language of our actions needs to speak to us in ways which are effective at impacting how we think and experience. The language of our actions doesn't need to express anything about the actual nature of the world around us or connect to how anything operating in that world interprets or experiences what we are doing. You could even make an argument that different cultures are able to engage spirits with different gods and rituals based in different religions, because it is all about, and always has been about, the psychological experience of the magician.

I think there are other ways to answer that issue of, "why does spirit conjuration work despite magicians working from different religious perspectives?" The fundamental practices involved in conjuration rituals have similar elements which have retained a level of continuity going back to Mesopotamia and the earliest human written records. Characteristics of how we engage those elements have changed and evolved. I think, perhaps, some elements of how we experience the results may have changed as those elements have evolved. As different religions have developed, the gods and spirits called upon for the authority to exorcise or conjure spirits have changed to fit the powers worshiped by the new religion. At one point magicians called upon Enlil or Marduk, then Jupiter, or Osiris, or Typhon, and then The Lord of Hosts, Mary, and Christ. The techniques and ideas remain similar but the powers behind them change. It is possible that different spirits have been called upon in different religious contexts, and thus the spirits respond to the powers which rule over them in particular. Even when we encounter a spirit with the same name as an earlier god or spirit from a different religion or system it is not an automatic that they are the same being. Conversely, the names, symbols, and divine figures have been syncretized or interconnected as religions develop and interact. Cultural merging of religious ideas might also reflect spiritual connections between these powers. If there is some element between Marduk, Jupiter and the Lord of Hosts which allows them each to express the same core power then we could still touch diverse ancient powers by calling on the names and images through which we know them today.

These are questions which I've seen many magicians ask. They bring us towards the point of this exploration. Often, magicians use conjurations from religions they have left, were never part of, or don't believe in. Does it matter? How does it work to call on a god you don't know or that you don't believe in? These are questions I had to work out as I explored conjuration early on, and are questions which have come up when I've looked at conjurations of particular sorts of spirits. These are questions I engaged while working through the OTO and the A.'.A.'. systems, and ones which I've seen other Thelemites engage. Pagan magicians and atheist magicians working with Christian grimoires and Catholic folk magic wrestle with these questions as well. Having been initiated through the A.'.A.'. and OTO, but being drawn to work magic steeped in a Catholic worldview, how was the system I was initiated in, and the religious and spiritual work I received ordination in, supposed to relate to the magic I wanted to explore?

Some Thelemites and Golden Dawn magicians are happy fully focusing on the developmental magic like Lesser Banishing Rituals, the various grade meditations of the Golden Dawn, Resh, and other similar practices. Most of these are tailored to spiritual, and sometimes mystical, development. They can also lay the groundwork for magical practice and be tweaked for practical magic. There are magicians working those systems who try to explore working with the spirits described in the grimoires using those same basic daily rituals, or rituals of their own creation based on those rituals. Others dive into the higher-level Golden Dawn rituals and use those methods for evocation and talisman consecration, trying to fit the spirits of historical magic into those approaches. There are some who accept that it's all psychology and use stripped-down rituals, feeling that the ritual is less important than the focused intention and a few symbols to bypass the mind. While others utilize the historical rituals, feeling that the pageantry plays into the psychology. Finally, there are those who still approach traditional magic expecting to find real spirits.

I was in this last category. I tried to explore traditional grimoire magic expecting to encounter traditional spirits. I never went through a period of believing in the psychological model. I was always a firm believer in gods and spirits. Despite that, I tried some rituals using the psychological approach. I found that while it had an effect, the effect wasn't nearly the same as the effects achieved through real magic. I was comfortable with the grimoire approach, even though I was participating in fairly modern systems that often focused on psychology and ritual drama. The traditional approaches suited me because at heart I was always a Pagan-Neoplatonist-Catholic. Still, I wondered about fitting the modern magical systems in which I was initiated to my work with traditional magic.

I tried a few approaches. I led a ritual which began with the constuction of a circle based on Thelemic names and symbols. We read Crowley poetry in lieu of psalms while drawing the circle and for some preliminary invocations. The rest of the ritual was pretty standard grimoire magic. Most people present felt as if the spirit began to take us seriously when things got traditional.

Another time, I led a conjuration using the tarot and Enochian calls. It was based on ideas described in letters written by Jack Parsons. It was interesting and seemed to have a good effect, but, unfortunately, I lost that ritual. I conducted rituals based on the formulae in Liber ABA. I considered how OTO initiations might be adapted for things like consecrating a pentacle, conjuring a spirit, or engaging in necromancy. I still occasionally consider these things and I believe there is a lot of room to explore how modern magic can be used as a developmental tool for the traditional magician and how traditional magicians can enfold their development through modern magic into a series of tools and approaches to help them engage the spirit world.

There were points where I questioned how workable this was. Sabazius - the Supreme and Holy King of the OTO's US Grand Lodge, and the head of the Gnostic Catholic Church in the USA; wrote that exorcism had no place in the ritual or sacramental system of the EGC. In the Roman Catholic Church, the beliefs, theories and practices of exorcism as a sacramental, not a sacrament, tied into how conjuration was understood in a Catholic worldview and helped build the medieval approach to the grimoires. Your religious system needs an understanding of spirits, a means by which to command them, and powers which bind them in order for that religious system to provide a ritual and mythic language which can translate into a practice of magical conjuration. An official position that exorcism was largely a practice which abused people with psychological issues and was based in outdated understandings made me wonder if, as a priest in the Gnostic Catholic Church, there was even the possibility of developing a system of spirit conjuration based on and empowered by the sacramental system in which I was working.

The inspiration which led me to think this was not only possible, but that it was worth more deeply exploring such an idea was Jake Stratton-Kent's <u>Goetic Liturgy</u>. The book is a very small, very thin, book but it is incredibly important for any magician working within a modern lodge magic system who wants to explore traditional methods of conjuration. The text presumes familiarity with certain pieces of Crowleyana as well as the <u>Grimorium Verum</u> (GV). Even if the reader is not expressly familiar with the referenced works, they will be able to glean insights from what Jake has presented in this short text. Essentially, Jake built a system of working with GV style conjuration in the context of Liber Pyramidos. In other words, Jake matched elements of the Neophyte initiation for the A.'.A.'. to elements of a traditional ritual of conjuration, mapping the spiritual powers involved in each to each other and according elements of each text in a way in which they could bolster one another. A magician initiated through Pyramidos could return to the powerful context of their own initiation and utilize that and the comfort of the language and symbolism of their own experiences in their approach to conjuring spirits. It was essentially what the Golden Dawn aimed to do with their Z documents but done better and in a way linking directly to traditional magic rather than attempting to simply replace it. Even for magicians not working in a Thelemic context, the approach Jake presents will be useful in informing attempts to link modern initiation and traditional practice.

With the <u>Goetic Liturgy</u> fresh in my head, I planned the 25th anniversary ritual for William Blake Lodge. I considered the various magical acts and rites I would perform in a conjuration and framed them in the language and practices of the OTO, A.'.A.'. and EGC systems. This would allow subtle points through which people experiencing the ritual would be connected to their own journey through initiation and sacramental development. The work we would be doing would draw on the magical currents in which the lodge was rooted. It occurred to me that by framing the work within this magical structure we might change our experience of the spirit. The spirit we conjured would be in touch with those same powers and experiences which defined our community. This could also make communication more natural for participants who have shared in these experiences. I have found that different approaches to conjuration often elicit different types or qualities of communication, and sometimes impact how the spirit wants to address the interaction. I don't think the method necessarily changes the spirit, but rather lets us connect in slightly adapted ways so the result varies based on those changes in connection.

In the case of the 25th anniversary ritual, since we were conjuring a demon to obtain a familiar, defining the initial interaction within the language of Thelema felt all the more necessary. The familiar would be part of our local OTO family, and it had to have the interests and experiences and needs of that family in mind. A lodge becomes a place of fraternity in part because of the respect and friendship which its members attempt to share and foster, but also in part because of the shared experiences of initiation and other ceremonies. How could we invite a familiar to live and work with us without doing so in a way which tied it to those same ceremonies and initiations?

While our example here is about an OTO body, any magical group should ask this question. Any individual inviting a spirit to live and work closely might ask this question. If this spirit is going to be part of your community, how do you include it in that community? If it will be part of your life, how do you teach it to speak in the language of your experiences? Our ritual experiences can bring us power. Our ritual experiences can shape who we are an how we understand things. They can also become touch points by which we build bridges with spirits.

As we consider sacraments and initiations it is important to keep several things in mind. These ceremonies might, and should, change and impact us in real and meaningful ways. Those changes might make us more ready for certain work, or change the power or access we have when doing certain work. Those ceremonies might introduce us to certain spirits, or link them to us, or link us to the power and heritage of a lineage of magicians. The experiences we've had might color how we understand our spiritual and magical experiences, but they can also become the language by which we express them and through which we engage the spirit world. Finally, those experiences can create bonds and define the character of our experiences, and the groups of people with whom we have shared those experiences. Finding ways to make those shared experiences, along with the power and meaning they hold, touchpoints in our work of conjuration, or other elements of European Traditional Magic, allows us to draw the results of that magic, or the relationships with the spirits we encounter through that magic, into a space which shares in those bonds. This allows us to build communities of magicians which include spirits in the community and the work of the community in ways which can color and shape those interactions, relationships, and the drive the spirit has for fulfilling the needs of the community.

It might sometimes seem like traditional magic is a call to abandon modern magic. It might seem like modern magic has no room for traditional magic. Some people might question why a lodge in a modern system would want a familiar spirit or do formal work with spirits at all. A lot of modern lodge magic seems to have been built with the intention of eventually bringing its members into the practices which formed European Traditional Magic. Maybe the goal wasn't to pick up a grimoire and run with it, but the ability to use astrology, make pentacles and talismans, conjure spirits, and perform alchemy was certainly the aim of the framers of many of these systems. Groups like Elu Cohens and like the Society of the Mercurii who existed only a generation or so before the Golden Dawn were still performing traditional grimoire magic in the 19th century. It never died out, and never needed a revival in a conventional sense. Still, there was some disconnect.

While we have spoken mostly of lodge magic, these considerations are at the heart of a true revival of witchcraft and any form of European spirit magic seeking to blossom into a living spirit tradition. Spirits living and working with magicians, spirits teaching magicians and helping to grow and develop groups working magic with them are a core element. This is a core element which too often has been missing. Any reflection on historical witch covens, or even myths of secret societies of heretics and magicians reveals that some tutelary spirit was a central focus around which these groups developed.

The modern and the traditional can be brought together so that each brings something to the table. For those who are drawn to both the Lesser Banishing Ritual of the Pentagram, and the Elucidarium with its spirits of the air, there are ways to navigate having both in a holistic way. Right now, people tend to engage disparate parts in a piecemeal way. But the door is open to explore how the new and the old can weave together into a singular mode of development and working.

A friend of Agrippa's conjures a spirit from the sorcerer's book while
he is away. Unprepared for the demon to appear, the would be
conjurerer is seized with fear and unable to command the demon,
who slays him.

From The Wellcome Collection, Morton, Hall, Hale et al, W.P. 1720

XIX
Planning and Preparations

When I was a teenager, I was adamant that the modern view of magic focused on psychology, symbol, and the ability to do whatever one liked was problematic. For me, gods were real, spirits were real, the energy underlying existence was real, and the universe was full of the miraculous. I didn't care much about actualization and catharsis. This is still who I am.

As I studied more psychology I found psychodynamics interesting, but also found that a lot of the psychology in magic was pop-psychology. I continued my belief in the reality of reality. When I was 18 I stumbled my way into an A.'.A.'. lineage despite not really liking Crowley. At 19, my interest in the Fraternity of Saturn led me to the OTO, which I joined when I was 24. I don't think I was ever a good fit, despite being committed, active, and rising through various degrees.

All this leads us to the summer of 2017. William Blake Lodge, my OTO local body, was having its 25th anniversary celebration. The lodge master asked me to lead a ritual for it. I decided we would summon a demon and get a familiar spirit for the lodge. There were three reasons for this. First, I thought it would be a good example of how traditional magic could work in a lodge setting. Second, I thought the lodge could benefit from a familiar spirit and it would be a unique sort of thing which I believed more groups should do. Third, I wanted to shake things up and shock people a little. A demon being conjured with real blood and bones and dirt in order to create a permanent demonic presence? Well, that might make people clutch pearls so hard they would break.

Why would I want to rile up pearl-clutching magicians? Because to me, magicians shouldn't clutch pearls over doing actual magic. Unfortunately, a lot of modern magic is simply denying that magic exists, and clutching pearls about people doing real magic. Viewing magic as real was often the source of my trouble fitting into modern magical groups. Like many people, I saw magic as something which was real and could make real changes in the world. It was never about psychology, or memorizing Crowley poetry for me. The initiations could be deep and meaningful; dramatic ritual could be beautiful and fun. Connecting to real experiences of the underlying truth of the universe, and connecting with the rich world of spirits was always my focus. Our modern lodge systems often aren't about that and rarely make room for that.

It is unfortunate that this is the case. The OTO is a large organization, with a thorough infrastructural model. It is built around developing people into leaders - at least in terms of its structure and initiations. As a clearing house for people to gather, explore magic, mysticism, and philosophy, and grow into leaders within a small society, it could be the blueprint for a larger form of social change. An organization like that, rooted in the idea that magic is about making real change in the world, could strive for a Platonic Republic built on magic, mysticism, and spiritual growth as guiding factors in society.

My goal in my time in the OTO was always to bring more magic to more of its members. As I explained in an earlier chapter, finding ways that the system of the OTO and the methods of traditional magic could blend were important to me. That was a guiding element in organizing this ritual, although it was just a start. I think that kind of blending can go much deeper and create more full and meaningful impact for those who are drawn to both modern and traditional magic. Exploring things like this ritual can also be a start to exploring how experiences with these less-revived portions of traditional magic can lead us to broader explorations of magic. There is so much we can unpack when we consider how these explorations play out in a group dynamic. This is an important part of understanding how magic can be part of a living community or culture.

The way the ritual is presented here won't make sense as an option for use by individuals or people working outside of a Thelemic structure. OTO bodies and TTO bodies could definitely make use of it. People in Golden Dawn groups, or other modern magical groups, should be able to see how they could structure something similar, combining their lodge magic system with traditional conjuration and sorcery. For the individual reader, this will present ways in which you can tie your own experiences of modern magic and its initiations to a traditional conjuration structure, or you can strip those elements out and look at it simply as an example of how to conjure a demon and get a familiar.

This ritual was designed for use in a lodge, but it utilizes structures of European Traditional Magic and the concepts of spirit work which are part of my personal practice. The format has a lot of formal lodge elements. For readers working in a group background this will be useful for exploring how those group elements can be married to traditional work. For readers working independently it may seem like a ritual they wouldn't use. The essential structure of the ritual and most of its components would still be relevant in individual work. You can strip out the lodge elements and rewrite it for individual work. Alternatively, you could look at how this works with a broader approach to spirit work and adapt a grimoire conjuration based on these elements in a manner suited to you. This chapter will walk you through why and how the various parts of the ritual were designed and prepared. We will go in depth into the spirit work that occurs, things to pay attention to, and how to use and construct various materials in the time that leads up to the actual execution of the ritual. This sort of analysis is rare and useful even if you aren't using the exact ritual presented.

I can't necessarily highlight the particular points where the ritual ties to OTO, EGC, and AA systems in all cases, or describe in what ways it ties to and references those systems. We can talk about the ideas and purposes of the various parts and why they are there so that you will be able to build something of your own, well-suited to your experience. We will present more of this in the Analysis chapter after presenting the ritual.

In planning the ritual, I couldn't select the time and day for it, and thus that impacted my choice of spirit to conjure. We conjured a Saturnine spirit whose description included that he gives good familiars. I used The Book of the Offices of Spirits to find a spirit. I asked my ancestors to help guide me to selecting the right one. I determined an appropriate spirit by the description of his appearance, selecting one whose appearance had Saturnine characteristics based on how Agrippa describes the relationship of the appearance of spirits to the forces to which they accord.

I provided the Lodgemaster with a ritual script in May, giving me about a month to get ready for the ritual.

The ritual involved several weeks of preparation. This wasn't all fasting and abstaining from sex. Those things can be super useful in altering the body and creating the spiritual friction needed to build the charisma needed for spirit conjuration and experience. They are not, however, the only preparation which adds to our magical effect.

A lot of magicians will talk about how the conjuration begins when you earnestly decide that you're going to do it. Beginning to prepare for your conjuration stirs something and draws the attention of the spirits. The Archbishop of the Church of Light and Shadow teaches a method of announcing to the spirit that you will conjure it in order to begin the process in advance and make the conjuration easier. Keeping these elements in mind, it becomes clear that the more we do in preparing and gathering our materials, the more we are earnestly expressing our intention to perform the conjuration.

Preparing materials can also be a way of engaging additional spirits and fortifying the materials you will be using. When you are buying offerings, if there are spirits or gods you will be working with who are part of your routine group of spirit contacts, dedicate the trip to obtain the offerings to them. Make the trip part of the offering by focusing only on that work in the trip so that you are giving that time exclusively to them. If it is a spirit with whom you have a close relationship, listen to their inspiration in selecting items to purchase for offerings. Let them know that this is time you are putting into acquiring this object for them for the rite you will be doing and what you will be seeking their aid for. Let them enjoy your efforts and let them plan ahead for their part of the work.

This ritual utilized a lot of incense, and the incense became an offering for the familiar spirit on an ongoing basis. The materials in the incense were also used in crafting the home for the familiar spirit. So, these materials are important.

Keep the following in mind when considering the incense. Do you have a standard base incense you use for conjuration work? Do you have base additives for this particular type of spirit? Do you have particulars you would use for this specific spirit or for spirits related to similar forces and powers?

In this instance, I used a base incense designed for relaxation and conjuration which combines a series of herbs well-suited to the purposes of relaxing and opening up for visionary experiences. Then I added components specific for the type of spirit. Since we were working with a demon, dragons blood resin, myrrh, and wormwood formed the portion of the incense tailored to suit the incense to conjuring an infernal spirit. The spirit itself was Saturnine, so we used a very small amount of sulfur. Sulfur can cause health issues when burned, so its use must be minimized.

The components of the incense are all tied to living spiritual powers. We can think of the magic and properties inherent in the incense as innate qualities written into them by God during the creation. Even taking that view, those qualities and powers are enlivened, strengthened, and directed by the spirit which guides and moves through that plant or material, and forms the pulsing life and direction which unites all specimens. That spirit awareness is usually only passively involved, unless we engage and awaken it to act through the physical material we hold in our hands. In the grimoire tradition, incense was sometimes asperged and prayed over to awaken these occult qualities and purge any ill influences which had attached to it. This is one step we can take shortly before ritual. As we prepare the incense, using hymns and prayers for the gods and powers related to the particular material can help empower and awaken it. So can talking to the spirit of the material and describing why you are using it and how you would like its aid. The Greek Magical Papyri have an excellent resource for awakening plant material presented in PGM IV 2967 - 3006. You can find this on my blog, Glory of the Stars, "Conjuring Power in Plants and Natural Materials" on Feb 19th, 2019, or in my book Luminarium: A Grimoire of Cunning Conjuration.

As you combine the materials, prayers and hymns related to the overarching purpose of the incense should be used. In this case, the Orphic hymn of Saturn was prayed over the incense several times as the items were combined.

Along with incense, a paint or ink was needed. I have no skill at ink-making, so I frequently obtain paint, then I combine my mixture of blood, alcohol, and resin with the paint. In the grimoires, an animal is obtained and the magician cuts the animal or kills it to obtain blood. I'm not super fond of getting up close and personal with the sorts of animals usually used. I will admit that's my own issue. Some magicians are squeamish about the idea of blood entirely though. Blood has its own unique properties which connect it to the transmission of occult force and the ability to tie life to a physical substance. We can't distill life essence into a liquid we can apply to things, but we can use blood which naturally carries it in a particularly rich way.

When I need blood for a ritual I go to the butcher or a specialty supermarket. It may not have the sacrificial component of killing an animal, and it might not be as potent as fresh blood, but it works. For people who are comfortable eating meat but don't like the idea of harming an animal for magic, this is a good solution. For those who are trained in how to do so, following the actual instructions in grimoires to obtain animal blood might be a reasonable and powerful solution.

Don't get your blood too early and try to store it. Obtain it around the time where you want to prepare the components for which you will need blood.

For this ritual I used the incantations presented in The Cambridge Book of Magic for collecting blood from a bat to make ink. This consecration or another similar grimoire ink-making consecration can be said over your blood to activate the components it needs to provide to your ink. The use of blood here is partially due to its power to seal and contain life, and partially due to its power to feed spirits.

My ink also contained myrrh, dragons blood and wormwood. I soaked that for weeks in whiskey, using the same type of whiskey I offer to my ancestors. I made prayers to them to help empower the ink. The resins have to be crushed down and stirred routinely to try to blend them. I have since heard that burning them to ash and making the ink with the ash is the traditional method. For this kind of magical-materia-suspended-in-paint approach, I think using the resin itself is fine, and feels more right to me. You could experiment with ash or powdered resin and see what works best, or ask your spirits.

The paint was used to make lamens, seals and pentacles. They don't have to be made far in advance. The lamen is typically made on the skin of a virgin goat or lamb. Sometimes the parchment from these animals is made in a process which is essentially a ritual sacrifice to the spirits being conjured. In our approach, that sacrifice component isn't entirely necessary, so our lamens were made of suede that I acquired from a craft shop. I painted the lamen design from the Heptameron on the suede, and had one for the Hierophant, or the exorcist, and one for the Master, or the scryer. The other seals were also painted and consecrated. Seals were needed for the main spirit conjured, for the King of the Direction, and the Archangel connected to the King. The Seal of Solomon was also prepared.

When the familiar was obtained, this same ink was used to paint his seal on the jar, along with the Seal of Solomon. His seal was also painted on the skull, and the paint was used to make the pact.

One of the major points of preparation was preparing the spirit home, or in this case, the jar. In the first section, we talked about having a home for the familiar. Examples like a ring, an urn, or a spirit house were given. Your needs, the type of spirit, and your expectations and intuition will guide what kind of housing you prepare for your spirit.

The spirit jar used here had a base of soil as the fertile ground on which the spirit could live and which would connect it to the world. The soil was empowered with special ingredients to empower the spirit and its work, but also to empower the jar to function as a home and keep the spirit present. Some of the dirt was soil harvested from land connected to people involved with the ritual. You might use soil from a particular place if you want to tie you familiar to that place, or to the energies and powers of that place. For example, if your familiar will primarily help with financial magic, soil from a bank or a business center might make sense. Our soil was further empowered by cemetery dirt. Cemetery dirt should be collected by purchasing it from the spirits of the cemetery. Provide an offering and ask permission. In this case it may be helpful to describe your intended purpose and request that the guardians and spirits of the cemetery empower the dirt to help with that purpose. When I say cemetery dirt here, I mean general dirt from the cemetery and not dirt from a specific grave. Unless the grave connects to commanding spirits then there is no need to tie to a particular dead person.

The soil also had some of the incense and the material base for the paint added into it. This was intended to add life, and also shape the power of the jar. In addition to that, it made the jar a space which was harmonized to the spirit. The jar had the same nature and vibration of the space in which the spirit was first conjured and bound. Essentially the powers at play in the birth of the spirit's familiar relationship with those conjuring it became the powers that shaped the home of the spirit.

The spirit was bound to a skull. Skulls hold consciousness and life in them. When they are relinquished they still have that capability, and become an option for magic in which a spirit needs a residence through which to speak and act. Bone, in general, has the ability to function as a framework to which life and spirit can be tied. If the magician cannot obtain a skull, bone is a good option for a focus point to which to bind the spirit. The skull or bone is then placed in the jar so that it can be sealed in its home as an anchor point from which the spirit can work.

In this ritual, the skull is surrounded by a series of names which are seated in the ground with spikes. These spikes may be consecrated with the hymn to Mars and martial incenses or oils before the ritual.

As you prepare your own ritual for this purpose, you will surely find a host of materials you will be using. Finding ways to engage those materials beforehand can be a rich and deep experience for the magician. It can also build up a collective spiritual power to aid in the accomplishment of the ritual end.

Conjuring a Familiar To Bind to a Bottle in a Lodge
Fr. VH

Purpose: Utilizing touch points of Thelemic magic to create a space and spiritual connection to Thelemic tradition the magicians present call upon the spiritual forces of traditional magic and ancestral powers allied to the Thelemic current and their initiatory body to powerfully manifest a spirit for the purpose of providing aid and knowledge to the Body and granting a familiar to be bound to a spirit bottle to act in service to the body.

The Temple: The Temple is the Temple of the Gnostic Mass; preferably a Mass has been performed just before or sometime within the recent past. A cake of light, and wine from the Mass, should be saved. On the high altar there is a candle placed before the Stele of Revealing and a candle placed before the Book of the Law. The Deacons altar holds two candles, two bowls of water, an asperger, a container of incense, and Oil of Abramelin. There is a small table behind the deacon's altar with offerings on it and small photos of the dead. The chairs are brought in around the altars to sit within the space of the circle. Candles and incense burners sit in the corners of the circle. Incense burners are set at the high altar and on the deacon altar.

Equipment:
Two candles for the High Altar.
Two candles for the Deacon's Altar
Salt
Two bowls of water
An asperger
Abramelin incense
Incense for the planet
Oil of Abramelin
Tea lights for the dead
Photos of the dead
6 incense burners – one for each altar one for each quarter
Candles and candle holders for each quarter
Offerings for the dead – whiskey or food
Offerings for Hekate – onions, cakes, etc.
A bowl of spring water external to the temple. Preferably with hyssop oil.

Two coins of the same size
Five spikes
Prepared jar
Lamens and pentacles
Paper for pact
Ink and pen
Papers with names Sitrael, Malantha, Thamaor, Falaur, and Sitrami
Chalice with blood (preferably lamb)

Officers:
The Hierophant: must be an ordained priest or priestess of the EGC. Hierophant wears a white robe which has been used in the Mass. Hierophant serves as the primary ceremonialist and exorcist of the ritual.

The Master: this should be the seated Master of the Body or an individual vested in place of the Master. This person must be at least a III*. M wears either black ritual attire, EGC robes, or other appropriate attire for their role. The M will interact with the spirit and will help H with binding the familiar.

Past Masters: these are three in number and should be past masters of the body or former officers designated by the body master. These three wear black.

Priest/ess of Fire: may wear a black or white robe, or other ritual clothing befitting their role. Invokes the power and presence of the masculine elements of the divine.

Priest/ess of Water: may wear a black or white robe, or other ritual clothing befitting their role. Invokes the power and presence of the feminine elements of the divine.

The People: present to witness and support the ritual. May participate in the ancestral offerings. If the body chooses, they may present questions to be asked of the spirit. Dress as they feel is appropriate.

Preliminary Preparations

The Circle is set in the temple. It should be drawn in salt or chalk. It may be a simple circle after the manner of Trithemius, or more complex such as the Heptameron or the Goetia of Solomon.

Everyone washes and robes themselves before entering the temple.

Once all are seated:

PW: knocks on the altar the number ascending for the planet which rules the working, then strikes the bell the number descending.

When this is complete

PF: recites a selection from Lapidus Lazuli or Ararita appropriate to the planet ruling the working while treading the circle.

All lights are extinguished. **PW** and **PF** are seated. **H** rises and goes to the altar.

The Ritual Itself

Opening

H: takes one of the candles from the altar and walks to the high altar. **Says:**

In the beginning God created the heavens and the earth. The earth was formless and void, and darkness was over the surface of the deep, and the Spirit of God was moving over the surface of the waters. Then God said, "Let there be light"; and there was light.

Lights the candle in front of the Stele of Revealing. From that candle he lights the candle he brought with him, raises it up and **says:**

Holy art thou Lord of the Universe,
Holy art Thou whom Nature hath not formed,
Holy art Thou Vast and Mighty One,
Lord of Light and of Darkness.

H: returns to the altar with the candle.

H: breaths upon the salt and upon the water, then sprinkles and **says:**

Let the salt of Earth admonish the water to bear the virtue of the Great Sea. Mother, be thou adored.

PW: rises and takes the asperger and the bowl of holy water. He sprinkles the water in the four quarters over the altar, the Officers and the People and the high altar. He **says:**

So therefore first, the priest who governs the works of Fire must sprinkle with the lustral water of the loud resounding sea.

PW sits.

PF: Rises and takes the candle from the altar uses it to light the candles in the quarters. **Says:**

And when, after all the phantoms have vanished, you shall see that holy and formless Fire, that firewhich darts and flashes through the hidden depths of the universe.

PF sits.

H: takes the other unlit candle from the altar and rises to the high altar. Lights the candle in front of the Book of the Law using the candle before the Stele.

All: rise and face the high altar, and recite the Headless Invocation

H: lights the candle he brought with him raises it above him and seats it on the altar.

All sit.

The Ancestors and the Gatekeeper

H: takes coins from the offering altar. Sets them on the top of the dais and **says:**

Charon accept this payment, and bring forth those who came before us that they may partake of this offering and share in it with you, and with those gods Hades, Persephone, Demeter, Dionysos, Iris and Hekate!

H: returns and is seated.

M: rises and goes to the deacons altar and **says:**

Lord of Life and Joy, that art the might of man, that art the essence of every true god that is upon the surface of the Earth, continuing knowledge from generation unto generation, thou adored of us upon heaths and in woods, on mountains and in caves, openly in the marketplaces and secretly in the chambers of our houses, in temples of gold and ivory and marble as in these other temples of our bodies, we worthily commemorate them worthy that did of old adore thee and manifest they glory
unto men:

[Here the Master reads the names of those dead called to stand with the Body, making the cross in the direction of the altar for each name, as this is done members of the body may take a photo of individual whose name is called and place it on the high altar in front of one of the ancestral votive candles, which they may also light from the candle set before the Book of the Law.]

When all the names are said **M** rises to the high altar taking the offering for the ancestors and the Chthonic gods and pours out the libation for them and **says:**

May their Essence be here present, potent, puissant and paternal to perfect this rite!

M: is seated.

H: rises and goes to the deacon altar and **says:**

We welcome you who have come before to partake of this refreshment so that you may be fortified thereby and lend your strength to aid and guard us in this work and in all our works and ways.

H: *Let us now call forth the lady of the cross roads*

PM: all three rise, each taking an offering to Hekate from the offering table and they circumambulate clockwise while her hymn is recited

H or another, recites the Orphic Hymn to Hekate.

I call Einodian Hecate, lovely dame,
Of earthly, watery, and celestial frame,
Sepulchral, in a saffron veil arrayed,
Leased with dark ghosts that wander through the shade;
Persian, unconquerable huntress hail!
The world's key-bearer never doomed to fail;
On the rough rock to wander thee delights,
Leader and nurse be present to our rites
Propitious grant our just desires success,
Accept our homage, and the incense bless.

When the Hymn is finished the **PM** take their offerings and set them at the foot of the dais.

Then the **PM** form a Triangle around the altar.

M: *We shall now conjure the spirit N*

PM North – West Point: knocks on the altar and **says:** *Agreed*

PM South-West Point: strikes the bell and **says:** *Agreed*

PM East: hands the sword to **H** and says: *Agreed*

The Conjuration of the Angel

H: *Hear me you Angels, Michael, Raphael, Uriel and Gabriel, be my aid in these petitions and my aid in all my affairs!*

[In the East] *Oh Great and Most High God, may your name be praised forever.*

[In the West] *Oh God, pure, just, and merciful, I pray of you Most Holy Father that on this day I may perfectly understand and accomplish my goal, and my work and labor may be completed to the honor of your glorious and holy name, who lives and reigns forever and ever, world without end, amen.*

[In the North] *Oh Mighty God, strong and wonderful, through eternity unto the ages, grant that this day I bring about that which I desire through our blessed Lord, amen.*

[In the South] *Oh Mighty and Most Merciful God, hear my prayers and grant my petition.*

I adjure you by my appeal to the throne of the Lord, By the Holy and Mighty God who is our Aid Against Death, He who is the Beginning and the End through his three secret names AGLA, ON, YHVH, by which you will fulfill today those things which I desire.

I conjure and confirm upon you, Cassiel, Machator, and Seraquiel, strong and powerful angels; and by the name Adonai, Adonai, Adonai; Eheieh, Eheieh, Eheieh; Yehoiakim, Yehoiakim, Yehoiakim; Kadosh, Kadosh; Ima, Ima, Ima; Salay, Yah, Sar, Lord and Maker of the World, who rested on the seventh day; and by him who of his good pleasure gave the same to be observed by the children of Israel throughout their generations, that they should keep and sanctify the same, to have thereby a good reward in the world to come; and by the names of the angels serving in the seventh host, before Booel, a great angel, and powerful prince; and by the name of his star, which is Saturn; and by his holy seal, and by the names before spoken, I conjure upon you, Cassiel, who is chief ruler of the seventh day, which is the Sabbath, that you will aid us in our conjuration and exorcism of the Spirit N!

The Conjuration of the King

H: *There shall no evil come to you: nor shall the scourge come near your dwelling. For he has given his angels charge over you; to keep you in all your ways.*

M: *Asar Un-nefer! I invoke*
The four-fold Horror of the Smoke.
Unloose the Pit! by the dread Word
Of Power Set-Typhon hath heard
SAZAZ SAZAZ ADANATASAN SAZAZ

(Pronounce this backwards. But it is very dangerous. It opens up the Gates of Hell.)

H. *I surround myself with the virtue of these names with which the circle is sealed.*

H. *Oh great and potent spirit Egyn, King of the North, who rules the Northern region of the world, I adjure you, I call upon you, and most powerfully and earnestly I urge you by, in, and through the virtue power and might of these efficacious and binding names, YHVH+, EHIH+, Adonai+, AGLA+, El+, Tzvot+, Elohim+, of the Almighty, Immense Incomprehensible and Everliving God, the omnipotent Creator of heaven and Earth. I call you in the name of the Most High, whose name all the Celestial Angels honor and obey, and before whom all the holy Company and Choir of heaven, Incessantly sing Kadosh, Kadosh, Kadosh, and at whose Divine and inestimable name, all Knees on Earth give homage and bow, and all the aerial terrestrial and infernal spirits do fear and tremble and now by all these names I do now again powerfully adjure, call upon, constrain and urge you Oh great and Mighty spirit Egyn, King of the North, in the holy name Elohim+, within the presence of Gabriel+ that now immediately without further tarrying, or delay the spirit, you appear visibly, plainly, peaceably, affably in all serenity and humility here before me, and positively effectually faithfully, and fully aid me in all I request and answer all questions I ask, especially those things which accord to your office, without any delay guile or deceit or other illusions whatsoever. And I call upon you, Oh you powerful and regal spirit Egyn, by the power of Elohim+ in the presence of Gabriel+ to appear plainly visible before me, in pleasing form, in all mildness, peace, and friendliness, without any hurt, disturbance, or any other evil whatsoever, either to me, or this place, wherein I am, or any other place, person or creature whatsoever, but that quietly courteously and obediently you fulfill my desires and do my commandments in all things which I earnestly urge and command for you to do for me, Oh Royal and Potent spirit Egyn, in the name of Shaddai+.*

When the King arrives **H.** must show him the seal of the King and the Pentacle of Solomon and **say:**

Behold the Pentacle of Solomon which I have brought before your presence! Behold the exorcist in this rite of the exorcism, who is who is fortified by the providence of the Most High God, fearlessly he has called you by the powerful force of this exorcism. Therefore come quickly by the virtue of these names, Aye, Saraye, Aye, Saraye, Aye, Saraye, do not delay to come, by the name of the True Eternal and Living God, Eloy, Archima, Rabur, and through this Pentacle which has been presented and powerfully rules over you and through the virtue of the Heavenly Spirits, of your Lords, and by the person of the Exorcist who has conjured you, come quickly and obediently to your master who is called Octinomos.

King Egyn I ask that you make open the way for the spirit, N, and whatever other spirits we may call with him, or what ever familiar spirit he might bind at our request.

The Conjuration of the Spirit

I do invoke and conjure you N. by Beralanensis, by Baldachiensis, by Paumachia, and by Apologia Sedes, by the most mighty kings and powers, and the most powerful princes, genii, Liachidæ, ministers of the Tartarean seat, chief prince of the seat of Apologia, in the ninth legion, I invoke you N, and by invoking, I conjure you N; and being armed with power from the supreme Majesty, I strongly command you N, by Him who spoke and it was done, and to whom all creatures are obedient; and by this ineffable name, YHVH, which being heard the elements are overthrown, the air is shaken, the sea runs back, the fire is quenched, the earth trembles, and all the host of the celestials, and terrestrials, and infernals do tremble together, and are troubled and confounded: wherefore, forthwith and without delay, shall you, N, come from all parts of the world, and make rational answers unto all things I shall ask of you; and come peaceably, visibly and affably now, N, without delay, manifesting what we desire, being conjured by the name of the living and true God, Heliorem, and fulfill our commands, and persist unto the end, and according to our intentions, visibly and affably speaking unto us with a clear voice, intelligible, and without any ambiguity.

[If visions need to be banished] *Fly away with your iniquities*

[When he arrives] *Behold the Pentacle of Solomon which I have brought before your presence! Behold the exorcist in this rite of the exorcism, who is who is fortified by the providence of the Most High God, fearlessly he has called you by the powerful force of this exorcism. Therefore come quickly by the virtue of these names, Aye, Saraye, Aye, Saraye, Aye, Saraye, do not delay to come, by the name of the True Eternal and Living God, Eloy, Archima, Rabur, and through this Pentacle which has been presented and powerfully rules over you and through the virtue of the Heavenly Spirits, of your Lords, and by the person of the Exorcist who has conjured you, come quickly and obediently to your master who is called Octinomos.*

[When he arrives] *Welcome N, because I have called you through Him to whom every knee bows, both of things in heaven, and things in earth, and things under the earth; in whose hands are all the kingdoms of kings, neither is there any able to contradict his Majesty. Wherefore, I bind you, N, that you remain affable and visible before this circle, so long and so constant; neither shall you depart without my license, until you have truly and without any fallacy performed my will, by virtue of his power who has set the sea her bounds, beyond which it cannot pass, nor go beyond the law of his providence of the Most High God, Lord, and King, who has created all things. Amen.*

The Spirit may be questioned and requests made at this point.

M: functions as scryer and speaks with the spirit. Ultimately, **M** asks for a familiar spirit to serve the body in all its essential needs. **M** requests that the familiar spirit be brought forth and that its name and seal be provided.

The Conjuration, Binding, and Consecration of the Familiar

M: draws the seal and name of the spirit upon the skull and provides the name of the spirit and the seal to **H**.

M: writes out the pact "The Spirit N, whose seal is [draw seal] agrees to reside in this skull bound in its bottle, in exchange for this dwelling and offerings of fire, incense, and spirits, N will provide service indefinitely to [Name of Lodge] providing protection, stability, and growth. [Master Signs]"

M: then rolls the pact into a tube and feeds it to the skull handing it to **H**.

H: *I conjure you spirit N, by the spirit N who constrained you to our service, and by this pact bearing your seal, that you bind yourself to this skull which bears your seal.*

H: places the skull in the bottle.

H: *O Sitrael, Malantha, Thamaor, Falaur, and Sitrami, written in this circle, appointed to this work, I do conjure and I do exorcise you, by the Father+, by the Son+, and by the Holy Spirit+, by him who did cast you out of paradise, and by him which spoke the word and it was done, and by him who shall come to judge the quick and the dead, and the world by fire, that all you five infernal masters and princes do come unto me, to accomplish and to fulfill all my desires and requests, which I shall command you.*

H: places spikes through the names of Sitrael, Malantha, Thamaor, Falaur, and Sitrami which are written on paper in the bottle surrounding the skull.

H: *I conjure, charge, and command you all Sitrael, Malantha, Thamaor, Falaur, and Sitrami, you infernal kings, to put into this bottle the spirit N whose name and seal appear therein, who is a spirit learned and expert in all arts and sciences, by the virtue of this name of God YHVH, and by the cross + of our Lord Jesus Christ, and by the blood of the innocent lamb, which redeemed all the world, and by all their virtues & powers I charge you, you noble kings, that said spirit may teach, show, and declare unto me, and to my friends, at all* *hours and minutes, both night and day, the truth of all things, both bodily and ghostly, in this world, whatsoever we shall request or desire. And this I command in your part to do, and to obey thereunto, as unto your own Lord and Master. Thus command the spirit N that he will enter into the skull, and he shall not leave our service until we release him, and that he will answer all requests and not delay or bring about suffering or falsehood for those to whom he is bound.*

H: Closes the bottle sealing it with wax from the candles upon the altar which brought fire from the high altar. He writes the seal and name of the spirit on the lid of he bottle and draws Solomon's Seal on its face.

H: *Go Sitrael, Malantha, Thamaor, Falaur, and Sitrami to your place appointed of almighty God, and be prepared to return when called in the name of the Father+, The Son+, and the Holy Spirit+.*

M: *The Spirit N must be consecrated to our work.*

H: holds his hand over the wormwood and **says:**

When he opened the seventh seal, there was silence in heaven for about half an hour. And I saw the seven angels who stand before God, and seven trumpets were given to them. The third angel sounded his trumpet, and a great star, blazing like a torch, fell from the sky on a third of the rivers and on the springs of water— the name of the star is Wormwood. A third of the waters turned bitter, and many people died from the waters that had become bitter.

H: sprinkles the wormwood into the water.

M: Holds hand over the bottle and **says:**

Lord of Life and Joy, grant unto this Spirit N the Power of the Holy Spirit to persevere and grow in Knowledge and Understanding.

M: Takes the wormwood water and holds a hand over it **saying:**

This is the world of the waters of Maim; this is the bitter water that becomes sweet.

M: breathes over the water, then replaces it, then places a hand over the goblet of blood and **says:**

I came to the house of the Beloved, and the wine was like fire that flies with green wings through the world of waters.

M: makes a cross over the water with the goblet. Then sprinkles the bottle thrice with water **saying:**

I baptize you, N, in the name of NUIT (pour), of HADIT (pour) and of RA-HOOR-KHUIT (pour).

M: sprinkles the bottle with blood **saying:**

I am uplifted in thine heart; and the kisses of the stars rain hard upon thy body.

M: touches the bottle and **says:**

We receive thee into the Gnostic and Catholic Church of Light, Life, Love and Liberty, the Word of whose Law is THELEMA.

H: anoints the bottle with a cross using the Holy Oil, and **says:**

I anoint thee as a Servant of Ra Hoor Khuit; I seal thee with the Sign of Light; I confirm thee with the Holy Oil of Aspiration in the name of IAO.

M: raises hands in blessing and **says:**

Gloria Patri et Matri et Filio et Filiae et Spiritui Sancto Externo et Spiritui Sancto Interno, ut erat est erit in saecula Saeculorum sex in uno per nomen Septem in uno ARARITA.

H: strikes the bell 3-3-3-5-5-5-5-5-3-3-3

M: *Now I begin to pray: Thou Child,*
Holy Thy name and undefiled!
Thy reign is come; Thy will is done.
Here is the Bread; here is the Blood.

Bring me through midnight to the Sun!
Save me from Evil and from Good!
That Thy one crown of all the Ten
Even now and here be mine. AMEN.

H: touches the bottle and **says:** *Ra-Hoor-Khu is with thee.*
H: invites all present to do the same. When they are done they return
to their seats.

License to Depart

H: holds up the sword, then sets it down **saying:**

In the Name of the Lord of Life and Joy, in the Name of the Lord of
Creation, In the Name of the Lord of Hosts, In the Name of the
Lord in Ourselves, I bid you all, spirits, gods, and ancestors who
aided in this work that there may be peace between us, and that we
may part and come again in friendship.

Closing the Temple

H: Hands sword to **M.** is seated.

M: *Let us now close the temple.*

PMs: rise and form a triangle around the altar.

PM standing East: takes back the sword and makes the Sign of Silence

PM South-West Point: rings the bell and makes the Sign of Silence

PM North-West Point: knocks and makes the Sign of Silence

PW: rises and asperges the people **saying:**

The Lustral Water! Smite thy flood
Through me lymph, marrow & blood!
The Fire Informing! Let the Oil
Balance, assain, assoil!
So Life takes Fire from Death, & runs
Whirling amid the Suns.

Hail, Asi! Pace the Path, bind on
The girdle of the Starry One!

PF: goes to each candle to extinguish them making the Sign of Silence as the two lights on the altar and the two lights on the high altar are put out.

M: when all lights are out knocks and *says: It is done!*

All quit the temple, **the Master** taking the bottle and placing it in its appointed spot.

XX
Analysis of the Ritual for Conjuring a Familiar

The goal of this ritual's specific style was to combine reference points to the OTO and EGC systems with a traditional act of conjuration. Some elements of how the ritual was done will be of more interest if someone is looking at how to weave modern magic and traditional magic together, while those points may be of less interest to someone just interested in conjuring a familiar. Regardless of your relationship to group work or to the idea of blending the traditional and the modern, the primary focus in designing the ritual was conjuring and binding a familiar. If you strip away touch points of modern traditions or elements tied to group ritual, the components needed to conjure a demon and to request and bind a familiar are present. This analysis will, as much as possible, explain where certain points are based on the group context. This will make it easier for those who want to rework it for the structure of their own group, or to rework it for individual work.

The first place where the context is evident is in the description of the ritual officers. This ritual could easily be reworked and particular aesthetic elements dropped so that it is performed just by a conjuror and a scryer. In my experience, a group ritual is often an individual ritual with the words and actions split up between a few extra people and maybe a participatory element added for an audience. Switching a ritual for individual use to group use or group to individual is therefore fairly simple.

The conjuror, or the "hierophant" is supposed to be a priest or priestess in the Gnostic Catholic Church (EGC) per the ritual instructions. This is less about sacramental authority to perform an exorcism, and more to do with authority to perform sacraments. Outside of the OTO context, ordination may be a useful but not required element in a conjuration depending upon the type of ordination, the system used, and the spirits conjured. In this instance, the conjuror needs to be clergy since the ritual includes the baptism and confirmation of the demon. Other systems also work with harmonizing work with demons in this way, and in those systems ordination may again be useful.

The Master is also noted as either the bodymaster or someone deputized in their place. The Master of the body may or may not be the appropriate person to lead the conjuration or do the scrying, so the ritual leaves it open to put someone in place of the Master. Someone acting with the Master's authority is put in one of the two lead positions because the spirit is going to act on the behalf of the body and therefore should come into that relationship under the direction of the Master's authority. The person in this role must be a III* because that degree connects to the capability to pass initiation. It should be noted though that the III* and ordination as clergy reflect powers related to initiation and sacraments in the OTO and the EGC, but neither automatically has the authority to perform those functions. The ritual was not intended to initiate or officially bring the demon into the church, so the roles require power inherent in those statuses, but not the authority that could be bestowed to people with those statuses.

If someone were reworking this for a Golden Dawn temple, the initiation officers would already map well to these roles. If working in a Wiccan context, the High Priest and High Priestess would take the roles of the Master and Hierophant. If working individually, the person more talented at scrying would take the role as Master and the more competent conjuror would take the role of Hierophant. Alternatively, if one of the people involved held ordination and you intended to use sacraments to help harmonize your familiar to your work, then that would be a factor in deciding who did which role. Some of the other roles and their functions could be fully dispensed with, while other functions would be absorbed by one of these two people.

The knocking, the bell ringing and the reading are intended to bring the minds of those gathered into the space of the ritual. They are not necessarily significant in establishing an actual resonance with that planetary power although they could be viewed as such. Depending upon how much work those gathered have done with the selected reading it could perhaps contribute to that effect. For people outside of this organizational context, music, Orphic Hymns, poetry or incenses might help build that planetary connection if it were desired.

The initial consecrations of the space reference elements of creation in order to indicate the creation of a magical and spiritual space. The magician references the creation of the world; those assisting him move fire and water, the two primary elements, and thus lay the groundwork for a spiritual space susceptible to the words which will be uttered by the magician. These acts cleanse and consecrate the space. This process of consecration and establishing a new creation in which the magician may act as logos is solidified through the Headless Invocation, in which the magician links himself to the spirit without beginning, who possesses the power to command spirits. This is not the original nature of the Headless Power or the original purpose of the invocation, but it follows the use typically given in a modern context.

These roles were divided up in our ritual but they could be done by the conjuror. In an individual ritual there would be no people to asperge, but most of the rest of the cleansing and consecration of fire and water would occur. The verbiage and specific ritual actions in this ritual combined elements from the Gnostic Mass and The Chaldean Oracles. If you are working outside of a group, or in a Wiccan context then you might be fine keeping the wording and actions as is. In a Golden Dawn context, you might keep The Chaldean Oracles elements and change the pieces drawn from the Mass. The essential idea of cleansing and consecrating the space with fire and water, and creating the moist fog of creation by combining fire and water are important elements. Grimoire magic does not always work with this idea of creating a magical state similar to the Chaos of creation, but I find it very useful.

The dead are then called to assist. In this instance, rather than the ancestors of the magician or those magicians involved, the ancestors of the Lodge are called. If working in a group setting, this is a reasonable way to incorporate ancestor work into group workings. If you were reworking this ritual for personal use you would use your own ancestors. The dead are initially approached through a call which fits my general approach of calling upon Charon to bring them, and calling upon the Chthonic gods to grant them permission and to travel with them and strengthen them. If your group works with another pantheon, or you do individually, substitute the appropriate figures.

Our call to the dead continues with the collect from the Gnostic Mass for the Saints. The reason for that selection is in part to tie to the EGC system, and to also show that this kind of work is already implied and inherent therein. Many view the Litany of Saints in the Gnostic Mass as a way of calling upon the masculine power illustrated through these various figures and using it to bolster the nature of the priest as a force of the philosophical masculine or the male polarity of divinity. I don't think we need to view the passage this way in our use of it here. The dead called upon should include female ancestors as well as male ancestors whether we're looking at ancestors of a group of people or ancestors of the individual magician. This passage reflects the vivifying power of human life and effort and the supernal spirit that gives direction, motion, force and fire to humankind. As we call upon the dead, calling upon the embodiment of life and human striving and experience to be with them, and be honored through the dead, is an act of calling upon that force to empower and move through our dead allies, giving them life and strength.

Many of the pronouncements made during the ritual, such as, "we will call the lady of the crossroads," "we will call the spirit," "agreed" are done because this is a standard practice in lodge rituals. Initiation ceremonies and lodge magic rituals sometimes have these stilted moments in which you explain or mime what you're about to do and then do it. It's not great ritual. It is necessary in those contexts because the rituals are often instructive and sometimes because it is a group of people those people need guide posts for what they're going to do even if they aren't the ones receiving the instruction. You could dispense with this in an individual approach, possibly also in a group approach. In some instances, such as announcing the main purpose of the ritual or the main spirit you will be calling, it can be useful as a statement of intent, however it is not necessary.

The directions for the points on the triangle were based on how Jake Stratton-Kent accords directional points with Thelemic powers and Verum spirits in <u>Goetic Liturgy</u>.

The conjuration of the angel is from the <u>Heptameron</u>. Because we were performing the ritual on a Saturday, we worked under the auspices of Saturn and used the prayer of Saturday. Because of Saturn's lofty position in the heavens, it has a series of passages read in the directions instead of a series of angel names. The archangel is called upon as a guardian and guide to the working. Should something go wrong with the King or the demon, the angel is able to intervene. This does not mean the angel is conjured as a threat or a "thwarting angel" to punish or frighten the spirit. To the contrary, the angel is called as a point in the hierarchy along the chain of being. The angel presents the initial quality of the force ruling the day and makes way for spirits to operate within the auspices of that force. The angel is part of a team making the conjuration possible and run smoothly, along with Hekate, the ancestors, and the Demon King.

The conjuration of the Demon King borrows the opening of the Gates of Hell from <u>Liber Pyramidos</u>, which seemed an appropriate act to link with a demon king functioning as a gatekeeper.

In my interpretation, the four kings rule over the four corners of the earth and permit spiritual powers to act in the part of the world under their jurisdiction. This permission is, in part, allowing those powers to enter into the world, and also giving license to those powers to act. Like the angel, the king can step in and help guide the interaction with the demon, if need be, and keep things running smoothly, but the king is primarily there to facilitate. In some approaches, the king might be there to command the spirit's appearance, or to send his legate to retrieve the demon.

The conjuration of the demon is fairly standard and draws on The Heptameron.

The Master asks for the familiar, because, it is contracted under the Master's authority. If not working in a lodge context, the exorcist could ask for the familiar.

We discussed previously the powers of blood and bone. Once the name and seal are received, the spirit is bound to the skull with the paint or ink made with blood. The pact is physically written and signed here. I like having three copies of the pact, one for the magician, one for the spirit who gives the familiar, and one for the familiar. The one given to the familiar is fed to the skull. If using bone other than a skull, wrapping it around the bone could work, or burying it in the jar under the bone. If the magician retains a copy of the pact, it can serve as a link to the spirit or a talisman for command over the spirit.

The names of various kings are then nailed into the dirt surrounding the skull. This is based on a ritual from Reginald Scot which will be presented later. These spirits serve to bind the familiar to the skull and the jar. The nails are in lieu of swords. We see similar sword circles in Liber Juratus. We can't be certain if there is a symbolism based on correspondence like we'd see in modern systems, however, I view these as representing iron and martial power. There is also the clear implication of binding the spirit by spiking it to the ground when the swords or spikes are used in the manner presented in Scot.

The final phase of preparing the familiar was consecrating it to the work of the group. If you are working individually, or in a group which does not have similar sacraments, then you might drop this section entirely. Some systems consider "baptised" spirits to be less wild and more amenable to work with people. Baptised doesn't always mean the sacrament of baptism when we talk about a spirit who is baptised, but it can. You might find value in this approach or a similar approach. If there are other practices which could be viewed as welcoming the spirit into your community, or family, or working group then those might be appropriate here.

When we performed the ritual, one of the past masters, who is also a Bishop in the Gnostic Catholic Church, leaned in and politely told us he was uncomfortable using actual EGC sacrament practices on a demon and apologized for the last-minute request to change things, but explained he did not think it was ok to proceed as written. I think he handled the moment as well as he could have short of having read the script in advance and bringing up his concern earlier. There has been some speculation over whether or not the familiar was offended by the change and how it implied that he was not being included in our rites as thoroughly as had been planned.

We proceeded with more general verbiage of baptism and confirmation. While we weren't able to use the EGC verbiage, we tried to keep some semblance of the combination of form, intention, and authority, as these are the elements needed to confect a sacrament. We thought it was important that the demon be touched with these sacramental elements. Why? Because baptism and confirmation, while often not understood to be, are ordinal sacraments. When we look at Holy Orders and Matrimony as sacraments of commitment instead of sacraments which are ordinal, it allows us to ignore the ordinal nature of baptism and confirmation. These sacraments are not just about initiation, they are also about direction. They empower and guide the individual towards a path and purpose. If the familiar was supposed to be tied to the current of the lodge and its work and purpose, then ritually accepting it into that path was necessary.

Baptism also, usually, has a component of welcoming an individual into the community. If we are welcoming a familiar into our community to be an active part of it, calling it and binding it isn't enough. We need to welcome it in a manner reflecting the way in which people join the community. Even if you are not working in a context which utilizes the Church language of sacraments, these concepts of direction and welcoming are important to consider.

There are further functions baptism serves which may be of use regardless of whether you're an individual or working in a group. Baptism is a cleansing and can be viewed as a rebirth. The rebirth ties back to the idea of welcoming into the community. It can also represent a beginning for the familiar in its new role. Cleansing it might help to draw off less amenable elements or previous baggage attached to it. Baptism can also be a cooling and soothing of the spirit through the element of water. Spirits like demons can be fiery and chaotic. Soothing and cooling can be important in interacting with them. Bringing a spirit firmly into presence within this world is also often a fiery, warming process. Cooling can help avoid agitation in the spirit caused by the process of bringing it through barriers between its world and ours. When we talk about a less wild spirit being "baptised" these are elements reflected in that term. The directional element of baptism also involves people standing for the individual being baptised and offering to aid them, guide them, and care for them. If we are accepting the familiar into a community these might be roles the people conjuring it take on. All of these elements are elements which can help build your relationship with your familiar.

We also reflected the sacrament of confirmation. Confirmation is a commitment. Confirmation is also the bestowing of the fires of the Spirit through oil. Confirmation energizes and calls to action. It can be a process of elevation and clarifying direction. It can be an active acceptance of that direction. Where baptism cools and soothes a rough, raw, fiery spirit, confirmation now imbues it with a directed spiritual fire and purpose. This can be a useful balance in establishing the relationship with your familiar.

Part of the point of a familiar spirit is that it is one which sticks with you. It is one which is easier for you to work with. It is a spirit which understands you and is familiar with your needs and desires. A concept that comes up with spirits in some traditions is their wild natures. Spirits are generally not in tune with human needs and how the human world works. They often have to be called through special means. They might not be completely clear in how they communicate with us. Some systems believe that spirits who are elevated and worked with in particular ways can be brought into closer harmony with how humans think and work. Baptism can be a figurative or a literal way of describing this process.

The ritual wraps up with a license to depart. The bulk of the rest of what is described is again following the type of structure seen in lodge rituals. The asperging the people at the end is intended as a blessing and a cleansing as they move forward from participating in the conjuration of a demon.

John William Waterhouse The Crystal Ball 1902

XXI
A Familiar in a Crystal

Reginald Scot in his Discouerie of Witchcraft presents a method for binding a spirit into a crystal. The Cambridge Book of Magic also presents a method for this. These are examples of grimoire methods describing how one obtains a familiar in a system of conjuration. Most of the more well known grimoires do not present specific rituals for this purpose. These texts do not call the spirit a familiar spirit expressly, but the nature of the relationship and what the spirit does for the magician make it clear that these rituals provide a type of familiar spirit.

In part one, we presented an example of conjuring a familiar using the Olympic Spirits. We held off on showing an example of conjuring a demon for a familiar because that is the focus of part three of this text. We have shown the example we used at William Blake Lodge, for conjuring a demon and obtaining a familiar. That method incorporated inspiration from this text by Reginald Scot. Sharing the material from Scot provides one of the less commonly familiar sources the above ritual drew on. This will help in looking at how to adapt material from one ritual into another. Additionally, this presents an option for people looking to use a traditional example.

Contemporary magicians have talked about spirit bottles, spirit jars, and spirit pots. Some have drawn on the brass vessel of the Goetia of Solomon for inspiration. It is often suggested that the nganga of Palo Mayombe and other African Diaspora practices have inspired this sort of spirit keeping amongst modern grimoire magicians. In many cases, looking at these diaspora practices has likely informed and influenced magicians outside of those practices. Keeping a jar or container binding a spirit is not necessarily appropriation or trying to mimic those traditions. Familiar spirits abound in European Traditional Magic. Examples like the one from The Key of Rabbi Solomon, this one which we will present from Scot, and the one in The Cambridge Book of Magic show that magicians kept spirits bound to physical objects through which they would interact with them.

In the case of William Blake Lodge's familiar, people might assume the use of spikes was an attempt at mimicking or appropriating diaspora traditions. In reality, it came from this example in Reginald Scot. The use of dirt and herbs was, however, inspired by diaspora traditions, but a lot of similar uses of dirt occur throughout North American folk magic and are part of how I work. When we were setting up for this ritual, one of the past masters, who was in from out of town, asked if the ritual was an attempt at a particular practice in Haitain Vodou. It was a practice with which I was not familiar. I think it is important when we take technique inspiration from other cultures or from initiated systems of magic or religion, that we're careful to draw the line between inspiration and being 'the same as'. What we did in William Blake Lodge's ritual for obtaining a familiar was very squarely rooted in European grimoire traditions and older systems of European magic and religion. We don't have all the technical knowledge of those systems anymore, so when other living traditions do something brilliantly, if we're able to understand some piece of it and adapt what we're doing through that inspiration, it's a valid and respectful approach. When we do that, we're not doing something which is the same as their practice or necessarily creating the same result or gaining access to the same spirits. We're still doing what we do, and bolstering it with some outside inspiration which makes something unique and new, or which improves something old and partially forgotten.

Sharing this piece from Scot is useful in showing how we can draw from various pieces of material. Most of the ritual we did at William Blake Lodge was drawn from The Heptameron, but The Cambridge Book of Magic and the Folger Manuscript both had significant impact along with Reginald Scot. Sharing this ritual is also useful for providing an example of an historical method of conjuring infernal spirits to provide a familiar tied to an object. You could easily strip away the parts of the William Blake Lodge ritual to make something well suited to you, or you could start with this ritual from Scot as a basis. If you have a grimoire that you tend to use, begin there. Then, take pieces from this, pieces from my ritual or pieces from the Key of Solomon ritual included in part one.

The blueprint for the structure is laid out for you, so now it's a question of deciding the specific pieces to execute that structure.

The text which follows is directly from Scot set into modern English. The grammar, syntax and word choice are otherwise intact.

How to Enclose a Spirit in a Crystal Stone

This operation following, is to have a spirit enclosed into a crystal stone or beryl glass, or into any other like instrument, etc.

First you, during the New Moon, being clothed with all new, and fresh, and clean array, and shaven, and that day do fast with bread and water, and being clean, and having confessed, say the seven (penitential) psalms, and the Litany (of Saints), for the space of two days, with this prayer following:

I desire you, O Lord God, my merciful and most loving God, the giver of all graces, the giver of all sciences, grant that I, your well beloved N. (although unworthy) may know your grace and power, against all the deceits and craftiness of devils. And grant to me your power, good Lord, to constrain them by this art: for you are the true, and living, and eternal GOD, who lives and reigns ever one GOD through all worlds, Amen.

You must do this for five days, and on the sixth day make ready five bright swords: and in some secret place make one circle, with one of the said swords. And then write this name, Sitrael: which done, standing in the circle, thrust your sword into that name. And then write Malanthon, with another sword; and Thamaor, with another; and Falaur, with another; and Sitrami, with another: and do as you did with the first. All this done, turn to Sitrael, and kneeling say thus, having the crystal stone in your hands.

O Sitrael, Malantha, Thamaor, Falaur, and Sitrami, written in these circles, appointed to this work, I do conjure and I do exorcise you, by the Father, by the Son, and by the Holy Spirit, by him who did cast you out of paradise, and by him who spoke the word and it was done, and by him who shall come to judge the quick and the dead, and the world by fire, that all you five infernal masters and princes do come unto me, to accomplish and to fulfill all my desires and requests, which I shall command you. Also I conjure you devils, and command you, I bid you, and appoint you, by the Lord Jesus Christ, the Son of the Most High God, and by the blessed and glorious virgin Mary, and by all the saints, both of men and women of God, and by all the angels, archangels, patriarchs, and prophets, apostles, evangelists, martyrs, and confessors, virgins, and widows, and all the elect of God.

Also I conjure you, and every one of you, you infernal kings, by heaven, by the stars, by the Sun and by the Moon and by all the planets, by the earth, fire, air, and water, and by the terrestrial paradise, and by all things contain in them, and by your hell, and by all the devils in it, and dwelling about it, and by your virtue and power, and by all whatsoever, and with whatsoever it be, which may constrain and bind you. Therefore by all these foresaid virtues and powers, I do bind you and constrain you into my will and power; that you being thus bound, may come unto me in great humility, and to appear in your circles before me visibly, in faire form and in the shape of mankind's kings, and to obey me in all things, whatsoever I shall desire, and that you may not depart from me without my license. And if you go against my precepts, I will promise unto you that you shall descend into the profound depths of the sea, unless you do obey me, in the part of the living Son of God, who lives and reigns in the unity of the Holy Spirit, by all world of worlds, Amen.

Say this true conjuration five times, and then you will see five kings come out of the North, with a marvelous company: when they come to the circle, they will alight down off from their horses, and will kneel down before you, saying: Master, command us what you will, and we will out of hand be obedient unto you. Unto whom you shall say;

See that you depart not from me, without my license; and that which I will command you to do, let it be done truly, surely, faithfully, and essentially. And then they all will swear unto you to do all you desire. And after they have sworn, say the conjuration immediately following.

I conjure, charge, and command you, and every one of you, Sitrael, Malanthan, Thamaor, Falaur, and Sitrami, you infernal kings, to put into this crystal stone one spirit learned and expert in all arts and sciences, by the virtue of this name of God Tetragrammaton, and by the cross of our Lord Jesus Christ, and by the blood of the innocent lamb, which redeemed all the world, and by all their virtues & powers I charge you, you noble kings, that the said spirit may teach, show, and declare unto me, and to my friends, at all hours and minutes, both night and day, the truth of all things, both bodily and spiritually, in this world, whatsoever I shall request or desire, declaring also to me my very name. And this I command in your part to do, and to obey thereunto, as unto your own lord and master.

That done, they will call a certain spirit, whom they will command to enter into the center of the circle or around the crystal. Then put the crystal between the two circles, and you shall see the crystal made black.

Then command them to command the spirit in the crystal, not to depart out of the stone, till you give him license, and to fulfill your will for ever. That done, you shall see them go upon the crystal, both to answer your requests, and to tarry your license. That done, the spirits will crave license: and say;

Go to your place appointed by almighty God, in the name of the Father, and the Son and the Holy Spirit.

And then take up your crystal, and look therein, asking what you will, and it will show it to you. Let all your circles be nine feet every direction, and made as follows. Work this work in Cancer, Scorpio, or Pisces in the houre of the Moon or Jupiter. And when the spirit is enclosed, if you fear him, bind him with some bond, in such sort as is elsewhere expressed already in this our treatise.

Photo of the ritual space after the demon sabbat to celebrate Tobias's "birthday." The flour seals are partially dispersed, but the candles are still lit for the spirits. June 2019.

XXII
A Demon Sabbat

William Blake Lodge's work with its familiar spirit went very well. There were problems in the lodge in terms of tensions caused by some members, and those were cleared up shortly thereafter. Perfidious behaviors which had been hidden were revealed by the very people doing them. People who were signing off on those behaviors admitted their part. More importantly, new people who created a vibrant and welcoming community started showing up and getting very involved. Several of these people said they had tried the lodge before and didn't like the feel of the group, but for whatever reason decided to come back, and now it felt like home.

Many people talked about finding the family, or the sense of belonging, that they needed in their lives.

The lodge had been considering giving up its space and dropping its status because membership was down, which meant less dues-based income. Not long after our familiar spirit joined us, these problems and concerns seemed to dissipate. Several events during the next six months had increased attendance and brought more new visitors. We began a series of very successful partnerships with other local magical groups and were beginning to become a hub in the community. This not only exposed our members to new and exciting opportunities, it improved the local opinion of the OTO, brought us new members and friends, and created a network which promoted the events and activities we were hosting.

With such a turnaround and so much growth and potential, the officers all agreed that the familiar spirit deserved some reward or honor beyond his normal offerings. We decided that we would throw a birthday celebration for him. The celebration would be in the form of a witches' sabbat, and our familiar would be the resident devil around which the sabbat was celebrated. As such, like the sabbats of old, he would possess a medium and interact with those gathered for the sabbat through the medium.

I believe familiar spirits are part of the series of elements which we need to explore further in order to begin to create living traditions within the overall umbrella of European Traditional Magic. This belief is, in part, due to the familiar's role as a teacher for witches and magicians and a facilitater between the magician and the spirit world. Additionally, the familiar, reflecting traditions of daimons and living statues, can function as a center of spirit cultus for groups. The particular devil of a group of witches may have been something akin to a tutelary familiar for the group. These particular spirit interactions were not things we explored much at William Blake Lodge. The sabbat was an opportunity that allowed us to begin diving into those possibilities. We would speak with the spirit through a medium. It could explain things about its nature and about spirits and impart messages to us as a group or as individual members. We could explore a different mode of spirit communication than we typically see in modern explorations of European magic. We could explore how a spirit could be elevated to receive honors and praise from a group and how that could lead to more guidance and magical success being bestowed to that group.

This kind of exploration is the sort of thing which can grow and develop in groups where magicians from different backgrounds come together to share and innovate as a team of friends and colleagues. This is the benefit of a social organization in which a shared interest in magic and mysticism is what brings people together.

Despite these benefits, there were those in power who did not like what we were doing, and this led to unraveling some of the community and halting some of our exploration. Part of sharing this story and this description of our work is so others can continue this exploration.

Different explanations as to who was upset and why were provided at different times, so I can't speak to the real specifics. There isn't a lot of value in focusing on that. As far as I can ascertain, at least part of the concern was that conjuring a devil by singing to it and giving it gifts to cause a demonic possession so the demon could speak to us directly, was too far outside of the magic described by Crowley to be allowable as an official event. About two months earlier, we had done a ritual attended by many guests in which people made pacts with the Witches' Devil to obtain familiar spirits. The size and publicity around that ritual may have put us on people's radar. Later communications included explanations that the desire was to have someone in place as Lodgemaster who could bring the focus back onto Crowley and his corpus of writings and rituals.

If you're going to engage in work like this in a group, it may be beneficial to do it in a group of your own creation, or one in which it does not clash with the organizational intentions of your group.

Another thing to consider is perception. Some people thought our ritual was too close to African Diaspora rituals, and that this similarity may have made people uncomfortable. Fortunately, that doesn't seem have actually been the case. Still, it provides us with a good opportunity to discuss some of the influences on this ritual both in terms of creation and performance. Exploring our approach will help illustrate more about the responsible integration of inspiration from other cultures and traditions, and how to avoid appropriative or irresponsible copying.

Our ritual was an attempt at holding a witches' sabbat drawing on the concept of the sabbat in European accounts of witchcraft. Sabbats were often parties and feasts in which witches honored or celebrated a spirit. The spirit was usually described as a devil, but it was often in physical form. The easiest explanation for this is an individual possessed by the demon or spirit around which the sabbat centered. Our ritual involved a demon possessing a medium. This demon was the devil presiding over a party held in its own honor. This is clearly an example of a witches' sabbat. The problem with performing a sabbat is that we don't have descriptions from witches of how they did it. Modern witchcraft rituals don't really mimic the sabbats of historical witches and often draw on the techniques of modern ceremonial magic.

Not having techniques of witchcraft, we still drew on grimoire techniques. We used many of the same prayers and passages which were used in the original ritual to call all the same spirits that were present when we obtained our familiar. We wanted a continuity between the two rituals, but, we wanted to break the call-and-bind approach of a grimoire conjuration. So, instead of a circle of divine names, the seals of the spirits were drawn as a series of circles all touching each other, with the seal of the familiar in the center, and a throne and altar for him rest upon his seal.

We used grimoire material, we drew inspiration from witchcraft, but we didn't have accounts of how witches brought forth their coven's devil. We did not have their techniques of possession and spirit interaction. African Diaspora traditions also have celebrations of spirits who are embodied in mediums. Much like the sabbat, in these rituals, food, music, and dancing are shared in celebration. Kimbanda, a Brazilian tradition stemming from Umbanda and European Spiritism, provided inspiration. The ritual was not a Kimbanda ritual, but Kimbanda helped us think about how to engage the tools, words, materials, and actions we were using in the ritual.

Instead of commanding spirits with aggressive demands, we sung the prayers from the grimoires as an invitation. Instead of circles to keep out unwanted spirits, we made circles of materials which bridged the gap between our world and the world of spirits. We anointed the circles and placed offerings in them. We illuminated them with candles to help spirits burn their way through the veil between their world and ours. In Kimbanda, spirits are called with an offering which is placed on a "pontos riscado" or a symbol of the spirit, and a song is sung in their honor, to call them. We did not take spirits, or symbols from Kimbanda, but we approached our own symbols with this kind of attitude of respect and invitation.

We aren't the first people to combine grimoire materials with Kimbanda ideas. That kind of crossover has existed for decades through with the use of the <u>Grimorium Verum</u> seals by some Kimbandieros. There has long been an exchange of materials and ideas between grimoire traditions and traditions found in the Americas.

Our sources did not stop with grimoire materials and Kimbanda ideas. We also drew elements from <u>The Greek Magical Papyri</u>, and <u>The Hygromanteia</u> in order to facilitate the possession of the medium. The familiar also instructed us in some elements of how to seek the possession.

The ritual was syncretic and not an effort at mimicking any living tradition and made no claims to be a ritual seated in one. Exploring how these different sources and ways of thinking came together into something new helps us consider how to explore a diverse world of magic. We can learn from how various systems do things without breaking our own systems or stealing theirs. In that regard, this adventure is a useful example of how we can look at approaches in other traditions to inform our work with techniques concerning which history does not provide us with all the answers.

The group that called this familiar only got to dip their toes into the possibilities this relationship presents for advancing living systems of spirit magic. You can continue this work; you can take it further and discover new innovations. While the possession ritual has been publicly available since we did it, I am including it in this book along with a very revised version of my piece on possession in European Traditional Magic. I hope by exploring our experience at William Blake Lodge, and the materials we used, that other people might be able to continue this exploration. Whether we're talking about bodies in the OTO, the TTO, Golden Dawn temples, witchcraft covens, or new and independent types of groups, deep options exist for groups looking to explore spirit based magic together through work with a familiar. These concepts might also form jumping-off points for individual magicians to see benefits in more deeply exploring relationships with familiar spirits, or even forming informal working groups to explore these kinds of relationships and modes of magical practice and spirit communication.

The names and powers called upon in this ritual are those associated with the familiar spirit of William Blake Lodge. Anyone attempting to do this ritual would need to first obtain their own familiar and then use the names and powers appropriate to their familiar. The angel and the king would be dependent upon the rulership of the demon who granted the familiar. The demon from whom you obtained your familiar would replace Doolas. If you worked with some other crossroads power or gatekeeper you might call upon some power other than Hekate, and might call upon keepers of the dead from a tradition related to that power.

A Demon's Sabbat
Fr. VH

Officers
Priest – Performs invocations.
Vessel – A Medium for the Demon. The Vessel is dressed in something alluring, preferably white.
Gatekeeper – A Priest or Priestess of Hekate to facilitate in the Crossroads. The Gatekeeper is armed with a dagger.
Drummers – Drum to raise the people to a state of activity and to call up the spirits

Tools
Dagger
Candle
Wine Glass
Red Cloth
Silver Coin
Grape Wood Wand
Incense
Five Incense burners
Two Coins

Temple
The temple is mostly empty. There is plenty of space for people to move around, dance, and celebrate. On one side is a table for gifts and offerings, on the other is a table for drinks. At the apex of the temple is a pillar or stand, before it is a throne, and before that an altar. Incense is set burning on the altar and in the four quarters of the room. A candle and a wine glass are set on the altar along with the spirit's house. Outside of the temple is a table of perfumes and oils, and a selection of alcoholic and non-alcoholic beverages and glasses.

Pre-Ritual

The Priest draws the Signs for Hekate, the Ancestors, the Seal for the King, and Seals for the Angel and for the Demon so that they are surrounding the larger Seal for the Familiar Spirit. The Pillar, Throne and Altar will sit on top of the seal for the spirit. **The Gatekeeper** censes the temple, making a four-armed crossroads in each quarter and across the temple floor then returns the incense to the altar. **The**

Priest and **Gatekeeper** leave the temple. They return with **the Vessel**. **The Priest** carries the wine glass; **the Vessel** follows him carrying the spirit house; **the Gatekeeper** follows **the Vessel** and carries the lit candle. They form a triangle around the altar. **The Priest** places the glass on the altar. He takes the candle from **the Gatekeeper** and places it on the altar. Then, he takes the spirit house and places it on the pedestal. He retrieves the alcohol which will be offered to the spirit and puts a small amount in the wine glass. He takes the glass and goes to each quarter and sprinkles, then returns to the altar and sprinkles there before returning the glass. As he does this **the Gatekeeper** seats **the Vessel** on the throne. When this is completed, **the Gatekeeper** admits the drummers, who begin to play. Once they have begun, **the Gatekeeper** admits the people one at a time.

Ceremony of Admission

Rather than purification those attending may anoint themselves with oils or perfumes, strip out of undesired clothing, or change into clothing more fitting for the celebration.

As they approach the doorway, they should take a drink and bring their glass into the temple.

At the doorway they are stopped by **the Gatekeeper** with his dagger.

Gatekeeper: *Why do you approach this sacred and secret place?*

Congregant: *To go under cover of night, away from the village, to celebrate with devils and demons, faeries and angels, the deeds of the demon.*

Gatekeeper: [removes dagger, and admits the congregant] *Welcome*

Ritual

Hekate

The Gatekeeper lights the incense and spirals it over the circles. Then, he places two coins on the ground.

Priest: *Charon accept this payment, and bring forth those who came before us that they may partake of this offering and share in it with you, and with those gods Hades, Persephone, Demeter, Dionysos, Iris and Hekate!*

The Gatekeeper chants names and epithets for Hekate. The congregation joins in. This continues throughout the conjuration of each of the spiritual forces. Throughout this the people may drink and dance.

The Gatekeeper continues chanting names and goes to the Circle for Hekate. He lights the candles and blows incense over it. He pours oil over it and makes an offering of alcohol and of blood. While this is done **the Priest** sings the Hymn for Hekate.

Priest: *I call Einodian Hecate, lovely dame,*
Of earthly, watery, and celestial frame,
Sepulchral, in a saffron veil arrayed,
Leased with dark ghosts that wander through the shade;
Persian, unconquerable huntress hail!
The world's key-bearer never doomed to fail;
On the rough rock to wander thee delights,
Leader and nurse be present to our rites
Propitious grant our just desires success,
Accept our homage, and the incense bless.

Ancestors

The Gatekeeper continues chanting the names while moving to the Circle for the Ancestors, and repeats the process of opening it while **the Priest** prays:

Priest: *Lord of Life and Joy, that art the might of man, that art the essence of every true god that is upon the surface of the Earth, continuing knowledge from generation unto generation, thou adored of us upon heaths and in woods, on mountains and in caves, openly in the marketplaces and secretly in the chambers of our houses, in temples of gold and ivory and marble as in these other temples of our bodies, we worthily commemorate them worthy that did of old adore thee and manifest they glory unto men*

Angel

The Gatekeeper moves to the Seal of Cassiel and opens it as the Priest prays:

Priest: *Hear me you Angels, Michael, Raphael, Uriel and Gabriel, be my aid in these petitions and my aid in all my affairs! In the Name of the Most High God, in the Name of the Lord of Hosts, I conjure and confirm upon you, Cassiel, Machator, and Seraquiel, strong and powerful angels by the Name Adonai Tzaveot, that you will attend this celebration, I adjure you by my appeal to the throne of the Lord, By the Holy and Mighty God who is our Aid Against Death, He who is the Beginning and the End through his three secret names AGLA, ON, YHVH, by which you will fulfill today those things which I desire. I conjure upon you, Cassiel, who is chief ruler of the seventh day, which is the Sabbath, that you will attend us and aid us in this celebration.*

King

The Gatekeeper moves to the Seal of Egyn and opens it as the Priest prays:

Priest: *Oh great and potent spirit Egyn, King of the North, who rules the Northern region of the world, I adjure you, I call upon you, and most powerfully and earnestly I urge you by, in, and through the virtue power and might of these efficacious and binding names, YHVH+, EHIH+, Adonai+, AGLA+, El+, Tzvot+, Elohim+, of the Almighty, Immense Incomprehensible and Everliving God, the omnipotent Creator of heaven and Earth. I call upon you, Oh you powerful and regal spirit Egyn, by the power of Elohim+ in the presence of Gabriel+ to attend us, in all mildness, peace, and friendliness, without any hurt, disturbance, or any other evil whatsoever, either to us, or this place. Mighty Egyn courteously and obediently you fulfill our desire and be present for this celebration, Oh Royal and Potent spirit Egyn, in the name of Shaddai+*

Demon

The **Gatekeeper** moves to the Seal of Doolas and opens it as the **Priest** prays:

Priest: *By the might of the Angel Cassiel, by the name of the Most High God, Lord of Hosts, Adonai Tzaveot, by the might of the King Egyn, by the hand of his emissary Lambricon, we ask that Doolas be brought forth. By the pact we have made before, and by the swift work of Lambricon we invite Doolas to enter herein, to join in this celebration and to reaffirm the bonds which bind Tobias to us.*

Spirit

Praising the Spirit

The **Priest** raises the jar from the pedestal and carries it around the Temple before the people. He extemporaneously thanks and praises the work of the spirit. When he is done he shouts *"Hail Tobias!"* The **Vessel** repeats this and encourages the people to switch to chanting for Tobias. The **Gatekeeper** continues chanting or meditating upon Hekate and opening the doorways and roads.

The **Priest** brings the jar back to the altar and places it there with the candle, the incense, and the wine glass. He pours a libation into the glass, whiskey or absinthe or wine. He places incense onto the coal.

Priest: *Tobias we give you these offerings of thanks and invite your presence here.*

Anointing the Jar

The **Priest** takes perfume and anoints the rim of the jar

Priest: *We recall your baptism*

The **Priest** takes oil and anoints the rim of the jar

Priest: *We recall your confirmation to our purpose*

The **Priest** takes blood, anoints the rim of the jar, and retraces the seals on the jar

Priest: *With this blood we strengthen you and we strengthen the bonds which tie you to us*

Washing and crowning the Vessel

The **Priest** takes perfumed water and pours it over the head of the **Vessel** as if baptizing them.

Priest: *May you be made open and ready to receive the spirit*

The **Priest** takes oil and anoints the forehead and the crown of the **Vessel's** head.

Priest: *May the fires of the spirit stir within you*

The **Priest** takes the blood and anoints the forehead and the crown of the **Vessel's** head.

Priest: *May the blood which binds him to us be a bond between him and you.*

The **Priest** lays the red cloth over the crown of their head and places his hands upon the cloth, standing behind them.

Calling the Spirit

While **the Vessel** calls upon Tobias the people continue chanting his name. **The Priest** keeps his hands upon the cloth and chants these names.

Priest: *Atzam, Tzoalakoum, Geamai, Satzyne, Kalesaines, Ton, Tapesmas, Taphydou, Elylpe, Syltan, Gialoti, Mpalontzem, Thara, Pakhakhesesan, Sylbakhama, Mousamoukhana, Araga, Rhasai, Rhagana, Obras, Ouboragoras, Tzoupa, Biapophkha, Tambalakhakem, Parakhematzoum, Tou, Itana, Baphoutia, Pakhakhe, Tanretokous, Nastratie, Parakhematzoum, Tou, Itana, Baphoutia, Pakhakhe, Tanretokous, Nastratie, Pakhakhyelea, Tybalotze, Enkaika, Parpara, Oumebras, Khematzoum*

The Vessel looks at the jar. In one hand they hold the grape wood. The other hand touches the jar.

Vessel: *Hail serpent and stout lion, natural sources of fire*
Hail clear water and lofty-leafed tree
And you who gather up clover from golden fields of beans
And who cause gentle foam to gush forth from pure mouths.
Scarab who drive the orb of fertile fire, O self-engendered one
Because you are Two-syllabled, AE, and are the first appearing one
Nod me assent I pray, because your mystic symbols I declare,
EO AI OY AMERR OOUOTH IYIOE MARMARAUOTH
LAILAM SOUMARTA
Be gracious unto me First-Father and May you yourself send strength
as my companion.
I conjure you holy light, holy brightness, by the wholy names which I
have spoken and am now going to speak. By IAO SABAOTH
ARBATHIAO   SESENGENBARPHARAGGES
ABLANATHANALBA ALRAMMACHAMARI AI AI IAO AX
AX INAX remain by me in this present hour, until, I pray to the god,
and learn about the things I desire.

At this point the **Vessel** makes an extemporaneous prayer to Tobias to come to them and be known through them. It is best that this is an affectionate plea for contact and co-agency. They continue this and the chanting continues until they feel the spirit with therm or until the spirit makes it self known though communion with them.

Gifts and Oracles
The ritual continues as a party. People take turns coming up and making offerings to the spirit and asking for his blessing for themselves and for the Lodge. The spirit may provide oracles or general or specific blessings as it desires or not if it does not desire so.

XXIII
Analysis and Why it's Important

Part three of this book is intended to do three things. We provide an example of working to obtain a demon as a familiar, we discuss how familiars and possession can be part of the road forward in magic and how this connects to linking traditional and modern magic, and we offer something akin to a case study and analysis of a particular set of workings with a familiar spirit. Exploring this case provides us with an example of how to engage in this kind of work. We see how to obtain a familiar, how to connect it to a system of magical work, and how to celebrate it and commune with it through spirit possession. Review of this case also lets us think about a few additional questions. What do we do once the ritual is done? How does this fit a group setting? What problems might you run into? And how can this help us expand magic? People often ask about the results of a ritual; for our purposes, these questions have a bigger implication than one group's results.

That being said, the ritual had some interesting results that are worth touching upon. Leading up to the ritual, the spirit orchestrated some strange things that led to it getting what it wanted. More than one person was led to acquire items, either as gifts for the spirit or tools for the ritual, which were different from what they intended. After the ritual, information shared between participants revealed factors the individuals who acquired the items were unaware of. These factors revealed jokes played by the spirit, desires the spirit had which were unknown to the purchaser, and in one case reflected the intentions of another familiar spirit unconnected to the individual who unwittingly acquired the thing this other spirit recommended.

A small detail in the possessed's behavior almost went unnoticed, but was particularly interesting considering the nature of spirit conjuration. The possessed individual never left their circle. No one commented, it did not seem as if the Vessel had awareness of this either. It only occurred to me when reviewing events well after the ritual. The possessed walked around in the circle, right up to the edge, and talked to people from that space. At the time, it just looked like someone holding the general area designated for them in a ritual. As the familiar was in the process of leaving the possessed, and the medium was exiting the circle, they got a mild burn as they crossed the line of the circle.

For me personally, the spirit referenced some specific experiences I had growing up related to spirits. No one in the Lodge was aware of these experiences. Similarly, it referenced the results I had experienced in a ritual two months earlier, which no one present was aware of.

It seemed as if the familiar was consuming a large amount of alcohol, yet was unaffected by it. The next day the medium was completely fine and went to work at a large outdoor summer event with no ill effects. The medium's handler later informed me that the medium had consumed less alcohol than it seemed. It was still enough that the lack of any signs of intoxication, hangover symptoms, or even mild day-after-a-night-of-drinking symptoms on the part of the medium was still impressive.

These elements of the ritual experience are interesting from the perspective of someone experiencing it. They are interesting in terms of demonstrating that something magical happened. It is always fun to explore elements that confirm we really experienced something. For many people, hearing about other people's experiences helps them see that their own are meaningful. As cool as these experiences are, they don't do much to expand our understanding of familiar spirits or how we can further explore magic.

One element of spirit work is asking spirits for information. A possession ritual gives a unique opportunity for clear communication. It is an underexplored option for asking questions and getting verbalized answers. Many interactions with the demon in our ritual involved the demon explaining things in response to interactions with the individuals present. The inclusion of answers and references which included information not known to the medium adds to the ability to consider the responses as legitimately coming from the demon and not being purely or primarily the inference or speculation of the medium. There is also a difference in this mode of communication from that of an oracle or scryer who is interpretting impulses, feelings, and symbols.

Some of the demon's explanations offer opportunities for a broader exploration of familiars. First, when asked if the spirit had been appointed to any one else or any other groups before, it explained that it was made for us. It used an odd term, less that it was made, and more that it was "stirred" into being. We often understand familiars as being drawn from an existing legion of spirits. The claim that it came into being specifically to work with us, could indicate that those spirits exist with a preexisting intention of being attached to particular magicians from their inception. It could indicate an atemporality regarding their existence. Alternatively, it could suggest that familiars are bespoke in the case of infernal spirits and not drawn from pre-existing legions. The familiar did not clarify any of these points and so we are left to consider them for ourselves.

The familiar also referred to Lucifer as the one who instigated its creation. The spirit described itself as being created as part of an overarching plan related to me and to the Lodge. Part of that plan was that the demon was a reward for the work we were doing. The familiar linked previous work with the Witches' Devil to Lucifer and also tied experiences from my childhood to Lucifer. According to the familiar, it was stirred into being as a reward for the Lodge's work with Lucifer, and to draw me and the Lodge closer to him. It noted another reward I had received for drawing people towards Lucifer. This was strange because our Lodge had not done much work specifically related to Lucifer. References to my own life gave the statements enough verification that I knew them to be more than just random talk.

To explore the claim about Lucifer, we have to consider the ritual. Lucifer was not actively conjured in the obtaining of the familiar. Typically, we would expect the spirit to be drawn from the legions ruled by Doolas, the spirit who provided us with the familiar. Doolas was selected from The Book of the Offices of Spirits, in which Lucifer is one of the chiefs of hell set above the four kings. Lucifer was not called as an authority in the conjuration, but one of the kings was called to facilitate conjuring the demon. All of the demons in The Book of Offices are subject to the three chiefs collectively. Le Livre Des Esperitz explains that Lucifer, Satan, and Baal were the three chief spirits in the Fall. It is one of the sources from which The Book of the Offices of Spirits is likely drawn, and the latter follows the basic mythological structure of the former. Le Livre Des Esperitz gives a more complete description of the Fall. In it, all the other angels who followed the chiefs were bound to serve Lucifer as their master. They must serve magicians as part of their condemnation to Lucifer's kingdom. On that basis, a spirit in Doolas's legion would be subject to Lucifer, or to the three chiefs collectively. Conversely, the Summa Sacre Magice, which is an earlier source, lists the conventional four kings as being under the authority of Satan rather than Lucifer. In the model given in the SSM, the various thrones of hell have their own rulers. Those rulers have their own ministers, kings, and legions of spirits. A spirit under the authority of the four kings would be under the authority of Satan, rather than Lucifer. If we consider the older model, we might assume that Lucifer would have specifically interceded to place this spirit. Alternatively, we might wonder if Lucifer was chief over the kings of each of the seats of hell. In that case, all spirits would still ultimately be subject to him. A more modern interpretation might assume that Lucifer and Satan have been syncretized to the point that the demon might use their names interchangeably with humans, or that the reality amongst infernal spirits mirrors that syncretism. Like the previous claim, we didn't probe these points with further questions. There is room for speculation, and for further exploration with spirits.

The third piece of general interest was the presence of the spirit. I have encountered people seemingly possessed by Lwa, and by gods. The presence and nature of the possessed in those instances was very different from the demoniac. In my experience, there is a demeanor and presence that reflects the power of the spirit and impacts those with whom the possessed interacts. The power of presence which extends from the possessed is controlled. It isn't necessarily overwhelming or fully foreign, but it is different from a normal human interaction. There is a power to the presence that lets you know what you're standing in front of. Whether you want the interaction or not, there seems to be something good and right to it. The feeling that radiates from the possessing spirit feels like something which could be corrective if it chose to be. In contrast, the presence of the demon was chaotic and fiery. It was large and palpable, but it was inconsistent. It grew and subsided based on how fixed the demon's attention was. It was unsettling, almost nauseating. It was like a physical wave of force. It undulated and moved and tried to fill up the space. It was very far outside of the realm of my expectations.

Contemporary expressions of European Traditional Magic and modern Ceremonial Magic do not have rich traditions of positive possession. Many other traditions have people with much more experience working with positive intentional spirit possession. It would be well worth the effort for anyone exploring intentional possession to seek insights from people in living traditions which have preserved generations worth of wisdom, techniques, and practical experience. In our case, the medium had experience with possession and trance work and was able to draw on that to help them enter into the needed state. This also gave them the tools to sever the connection. Our

Gatekeeper had experience as a priest in an African Diaspora religion. I, and others present, had ample experience with spirit work and had some exposure to trance, oracle, and possession work.

As you explore this kind of work, at minimum, work with someone experienced in exorcism and apotropaic magic. If you can, work with someone experienced with working with the possessed in the context of positive possession. At minimum, seek to gain insights from those with experience.

This is a part of magic which is powerful, important, and which should be present in the arsenal of people exploring European Traditional Magic. It is a form of magic that has not been preserved in the same way things like grimoire magic or astrological magic have been. It is likely that it was once an important part of some systems of European spirit work, just as it is in other cultures. While exploring it and restoring it are valuable, there are risks and dangers. We should be at pains to explore and consider them and take measures towards safety.

Exploring this ritual will give you some framework and basis for this work. It will provide that framework in a way related to grimoire methods and witchcraft-style spiritwork. It will give you a basis for building your own methods. Hopefully, it will provide a familiarity that will help you explore and seek insights from other modes of possession work.

The ritual was a simple one. It requires having capable people for the three main roles. The medium needs to be someone who can actually function as a medium. This needs to be someone who isn't prone to flights of fancy. It needs to be someone who isn't going to fake it, and who you and others trust not to fake it. In our case, the medium had a close personal relationship with the spirit and was one of his primary caretakers. That can help. The medium also negotiated elements of the possession with the spirit prior to the day of the ritual. That can help. Having experience with trance and possession work is extremely helpful. This role is very important. It is the role that puts someone in the most dangerous position. The utmost care must be taken in selecting someone to fill it.

The priest is a magician. You need someone who has competency as a conjuror and exorcist. A lot of people would like to think they are competent in those roles or that anyone can pick them up and roll with it. For personal experiments, that can be fine and it's how you get good. For something like this, where someone is being possessed and a group of people will be exposed to what happens with the spirit, use someone with experience. This isn't the place to try and give the new guy in the group the opportunity to take a lead ritual spot.

The gatekeeper really holds a lot of it together and is actively involved in a state of magical focus through the entire ritual, requiring a strong and competent magician. This can be taxing. The gatekeeper can't be easily distracted, or someone who will get lazy and check out. The entire time from the initial calls to the spirits until they depart, the gatekeeper is actively channeling a connection to the power who is opening the gates. Mentally, they are engaging that connection and actively keeping doors open to the spirit world. The gatekeeper needs to be someone who has worked with making offerings and who has worked with spirits deeply.

The initial preparations are intended to open the space rather than cleanse it. Incense, alcohol, and fire are all things which bridge the space between worlds. We often use water, fire, and incense to cleanse a space, and sometimes to set up an elemental basis for the space mimicking creation. In this case, the gatekeeper is making a crossroads with the incense. He does it at four spokes, so that each crossroads symbol he draws forms a point on a crossroads that overlays the working space of the temple. The idea is not just to invite a crossroads deity, but to give the temple the liminal nature of a crossroads and to open doors. The priest is not asperging with water to cleanse, he is offering alcohol and imbuing the space with a vaporous nature to bridge the physical and the spiritual realities.

In constructing the ritual, the demon made it clear that this was a ritual of witches celebrating a spirit. The attitude had to be one of celebration and indulgence suited to a demon, and the rebels who would run into the forest to dance with it in the firelight. When the people are invited to enter the temple, the intention is not to cleanse. This is not a Catholic conjuration. The people and the conjuror are not clerics who are above the demon and are seeking to subjugate it. The people are the demon's community, perfumed and sensuous, ready to drum and dance.

Clothing choices reflect that same attitude. Depending upon the group, its comfort levels, and its rules, people might disrobe. People can put on party clothes, or clothes that make them feel sexy or powerful. They're going to a sabbat not a church service. They anoint with oils and perfumes to smell beautiful with rich and stimulating scents. In conjurations we might anoint with hyssop or Abramelin to purify or consecrate ourselves. In preparing for this ritual, it became clear that cologne and perfume, or oils with powerful folk magic properties like High John the Conqueror were more appropriate. There is a slight diabolical element here even though the intention is not straight up demonolatry.

If anyone questioned the purpose or nature of this ritual, it is right there in the passage congregants say as they enter the temple. "To go under cover of night, away from the village, to celebrate with devils and demons, faeries and angels the deeds of the demon." It is old school witchcraft.

Hekate is called upon with the Chthonic Powers prior to calling the ancestors. In part, she is called here to help gain access to the ancestors. Additionally, she is called so we may gain access to and open doors for any spirits we are calling. She is a force which grants access and allows us to deny it. As such, she is a force who rules, and aids in controlling, the spirits called upon. She can aid in subduing them should that become necessary. If working with Hekate and Greek powers, it is necessary to share the offerings to the dead with Hades and Persephone when asking permission for the dead to come forth and work with you. Charon is given offerings as the one who ferries them to you and takes them back. The dead are called to help empower the ritual and to help navigate proceedings in the spirit world in ways that living magicians can't. They make sure everything is to the benefit of those working the ritual.

The use of offerings, circles, and candles in this ritual is a bit different than we are used to modern approaches drawn more strictly from the grimoires. We're not placing offerings on an altar. The circles for this ritual were made of flour because we did not want salt or chalk or anything with the intention of binding or blockading spirits involved. Flour has a powdery nature which is soft and light and allows it to easily become a dust cloud that permeates the air. Materials with that quality are often viewed as being able to bridge physical and spirit spaces. The circles are activated through song, smoke, fire, and offerings. By activating them, we open them as gateways for spirits to enter through. The fire creates heat which burns against the barriers between this world and the spirit world and gives the spirits force and energy with which to come through. The light guides them to the space we have appointed for them. Blood carries life force and feeds the spirits, as do food offerings. Oil quickens and empowers the spirits. Incense smoke bridges the worlds, and song invites them. Offerings may be placed or poured directly onto the circles, or you might use a flatbread to make a plate and give offerings, particularly food offerings, and honey, on top of the flat bread. Small containers can be useful for receiving libations if you won't want them poured directly onto the floor or ground.

In this case, the archangel, the king and the demon are called because they were present at the inception of the relationship with the familiar. It is a birthday party, and so those involved in his "birth" should be present. You might also consider them as an element of control, but that is less the intention in this ritual. The familiar already has access to the physical world because the spirit house, in this case a jar, is its physical body linking it to this plane. So, it doesn't need the king to give it license to act in the world. Hekate's presence in opening gates still helps facilitate the ability of the spirit to enter the world further through the medium.

Praising the spirit should not be confused for demonolatry. We're not worshiping the demon. It's a demon we're friends with, but it's still a bitey bitey lion with sharp claws and sharp teeth and lots of muscle built for pouncing. We still have to take measures for care and precaution. In this instance, the spirit is being brought forth to honor and reward it for good work. So, we praise it, we make offerings, we give it some freedom through the rite of possession. It deserves this for the work it has done, not for its status as a demon. Understanding this can help us consider the specifics of how we go about giving praise and making offerings and what lines and limits we draw.

The anointing serves two purposes. On one level it's like giving him a nice scrub and polish. We're pumping him up and strengthening him by giving him special rituals that recall his beginning with us. We're renewing and revitalizing his link to us and to this world. With that link comes his bonds to us and to the jar. We're also strengthening and renewing those bonds. In a way, it can be viewed like revisiting and renewing a contract.

Preparing the medium mimics anointing the jar in order to link the two together. The medium is washed and perfumed to open them and to make them attractive to the spirit. The oil and blood are intended to stimulate them and, like the process as a whole, link them to the spirit. The process of calling the spirit utilizes techniques drawn from The Hygromanteia and The PGM, which we have used in other rituals to stimulate scryers. The assumption here was that the same sort of receptivity and illumination which these give to someone to allow them to scry could also open them to being receptive and capable of receiving and channeling a spirit. The extemporaneous prayer by the medium is important for this. The medium has to navigate and negotiate contact with the spirit. The medium has to be willing and open to the contact and express that. Prewritten petitions won't capture that or reflect the flow of the interaction between the medium and the spirit. A prewritten prayer could also create a sense that one must get through the petition and a focus on saying it correctly, which would create the wrong mental state for that receptivity.

Once the spirit arrives, the formal process of people giving gifts and interacting with the spirit begins. The people are brought forth one at a time to make whatever offerings they choose and to ask questions, or be told whatever the spirit has to tell them. After this is done by everyone, the spirit should be given time to celebrate with those gathered and to continue enjoying whatever food and drinks are there. In our case, after the formal offerings, the ritual was essentially finished. Magicians who are primarily used to lodge magic and grimoire magic aren't always comfortable jumping in and partying with spirits. Frequently, if they don't have experience with demons, they might be hesitant about approaching one at all, even in a formal conjuration setting. This is understandable.

This format does not lend itself to the freedom one might associate with the sabbat. The fact that the method of conjuration seems to link the demon to the space of its seal prevents the demon from freely moving through the space. If the demon were able to move freely, it could approach people and interact with them organically instead of in a one by one organized queue. The demon can't peruse the food and drinks and choose what to enjoy on its own, if they are not placed on a table withing the space of the seal. The demon does not have the opportunity to dance and celebrate in its consortion with humans.

This was a drawback that we did not anticipate because we did not know the demon would be confined. It lent itself well to the comfort levels of people unfamiliar with such environments. Magicians who are hesitant at approaching a possessed person, and who are not drawn to party and celebrate as a form of ritual, may be less inclined to have a demon freely moving amongst them. They might also be less comfortable choosing to approach on their own. The format of a leader who presents them one at a time to speak helps mitigate that.

You would have to judge for your own group whether this kind of contained structure or a freer structure would work better.

When it's time to close the ritual, whatever methods and work needs to be done to return the medium to a normal unpossessed state should be done. The medium will likely need aftercare and rest and should be afforded that. The priest should thank the other spirits, blow out the candles, and scatter the flour. Let the temple sit awhile for everything to return to normal, while people continue socializing or discussing the events outside of the temple. After it has had time to settle and some space away from the work being done then it is fine to clean it all up. Since the spirits involved were not constrained to particular spaces or formally banished at the end, this time for the temple to return to a state of normalcy allows the spirits to linger and depart as appropriate.

So, that's how it's done. Or at least, that's how we did it. You can use our structure, or pieces of it, or you can research other methods and go your own way. Share your experiments somewhere. This is a piece which I feel is truly missing in European Traditional Magic and ceremonial magic.

Spirit possession gives spirits a direct way to interact with and through magicians and priests so that they can directly impart knowledge, experience, and magical effects upon those who come to interact with them. There is a lot that we can get from calling spirits into crystals or smoke. We can deepen our explorations and understandings of spirits with these grimoire techniques. Going back into antiquity, we see methods for possession. We see the importance of oracles channeling divine and spirit messages. If we consider The Greek Magical Papyri as a predecessor of the grimoires, we can see methods for this sort of possession in the Papyri. It's not a foreign magical technique that people are appropriating into grimoire tradition or into ceremonial magic. It is a core part of our magical heritage that we have largely lost. We see echoes and pieces of it throughout European magical practices. If we look around us, the world's magical and religious traditions are rich with this practice. We impoverish our arsenal of tools for spirit communication when we say that this is beyond the pale and not part of the sort of magic we should be exploring. Why would we want to cut ourselves off from this kind of direct capability for clear conversation with the spirits in our lives?

An easy answer might be that there are dangers, but almost all real magic has dangers. This practice is at the center of traditions the world over, so there are clearly ways to navigate and responsibly manage those dangers. In the "West" we have been acculturated to see possession as a type of madness, or as a spiritual sickness which must be fixed. I can't say this is wrong, because sometimes that is the case. Viewing possession only in that light is a misrepresentation, albeit one which Christian culture has expressed for centuries. We could just as easily say that conjuring spirits, or doing magic at all are signs of spiritual error.

Clearly, this type of magic isn't for everyone, and care and exploration are needed as people experiment with it. Hopefully, exploring this ritual will help spark some interest in more magicians in the European Traditional Magic communities searching out options for experimenting with this approach to spirit work.

Floor seals drawn in flour. The use of the seals was in part inspired by elements of Kimbanda. Seals for the ancestors, the directional king, the planet, Hekate, the archangel, and the spirit are all present. June 2019.

XXIV
Revisiting: Spirit Possession in the Modern Western Tradition

This was originally published as a blog post on Glory of the Stars August 6th, 2019. I first became interested in academic considerations of possession and the idea of possession as a positive religious experience around 2002 or 2003 in a class titled Advanced Behavior Pathology. This introduction updates some of what I had to say on the topic in 2019, and has lead to revising elements of text. This is an important topic, and one which I will revisit more fully in the future.

A note regarding terms - in this article I refer to "Western Tradition" and to "ceremonial magic." I am loathe to accept the term "Western Tradition." Greece is the benchmark of the "Western World," in traditional thinking. When we say "Western Tradition," or "Western Mystery Tradition," we exclude rich and valid traditions which are situated far west of Greece. These include African Diaspora Traditions in the Americas, Indigenous American practices, and Native African traditions. These are no less "Western" than the traditions which we assume have greater value and erudition because of their status as "Western."

When we say "Western Tradition" we are often referring to the Greek Traditions which informed Arabic Tradition and then later on the Renaissance traditions of Northern Europe. It gets messy if we begin to consider non-Greco-Roman traditions in Europe because they are still European enough but not part of the "civilized" corpus of literate Western Heritage. It's a silly and artificial view. I'm not one of those people who think we need to revamp "Classics" because of its focus on Greeks and Roman, because that is what Classic has always been defined as meaning. Western, however, pretends to be a broad geographic meaning but really just means people influenced by Classical culture. In the Anglosphere, when we say Western we often simply mean the Anglosphere, or maybe the Anglosphere plus France, Germany and some vague conception of a civilized Mediterranean antiquity.

As such, the term Western Tradition is not particularly useful. Its use is further diminished as it frequently takes on a myriad of weird interpretations drawn from the writings of people like Eliphas Levi, A.E. Waite, Julius Evola, Aleister Crowley, H.P. Blavatsky, and Manly P. Hall, along with a host of other similar writers who were contemporary with them or drawing on them as sources. Western Tradition, or the Western Mystery Tradition, or Western Esotericism, ends up referring to largely modern concepts based on bad history and bad anthropology defining things based on an imagined concept of a Western ideal. People exploring the Western Mystery Tradition are more likely to compare Atlantean Alchemy and the Golden Dawn than they are to explore Cunningfolk and the keepers of black books as an intersection between learned magic and witchcraft in early modern Europe.

Ceremonial Magic or High Magic are also often terms that people associate with Western Mystery Tradition. When people refer to these concepts they are often referring to magic practiced by groups like the Golden Dawn, the OTO, and the Aurum Solis. People might include Chaos Magic under those terms because it is rooted in and draws from those systems rather than being a form of NeoPaganism. When studying mysticism in an academic context, I learned that in academia "High Magic" is typically understood to mean mysticism performed through the techniques of magical ritual. This might be comparable to certain forms of ritualized theurgy. Such a definition accurately describes most of the systems we would call "High Magic" in common occulture use of the term. It seems to be a better definition than "temple magic" or magic using stylized formal techniques as some might suggest. Ceremonial Magic could be any sort of magic which uses ceremonies, although then it might be difficult to distinguish it from the term "ritual magic." It would also encompass many magical practices that no one intends to refer to with the term "Ceremonial Magic." Most often, the intended use of Ceremonial Magic is to refer to the cluster of magical traditions stemming from the late 19th and early 20th century occult revival.

I would not include the early 21st century revival of traditional grimoire magic under the heading of Ceremonial Magic. The revival of European spirit work systems, the use of grimoires in a traditional context and using traditional methods, the resurgence of astrological image magic, a focus on traditional witchcraft movements and some growing attention to historical witchcraft, and the development of practices and practitioners who might be identified as modern cunningfolk can all be grouped under an umbrella category of their own. I use, and have encouraged the use of, European Traditional

Magic as the broad umbrella term for these renewed practices. This verbiage reflects the terms African Diaspora Religions and African Traditional Religions as a broad range of practices, including traditional and adapted forms, stemming from a particular region across various more specific cultures and times. The various activities which we might group under European Traditional Magic can all inform each other and have historically interacted with one another. They are all distinct from the core practices, philosophies, and sources involved in Ceremonial Magic. This umbrella can also encompass elements of antique and ancient Mediterranean magic which informed the grimoires and other European magical practice. It can, potentially, also include approaches where medieval European magic intersects with earlier Indigenous European magical practices. Referring to this simply as a "grimoire revival" or as "Solomonic tradition" are both overly limiting unless we are distinctly referring to those particular subsets of the larger movement.

The intention in using the term European Traditional Magic is to establish clarity in referring to the source of the practices. There is no intention to suggest that these are practices for Europeans or that they are special because they were practiced by Europeans. In fact, restoring these traditions almost requires that we explore and be informed by non-European traditions, just as many of these systems developed with influences from non-European sources.

This piece originally appeared in response to people who were uncomfortable with demon possession occuring in a contemporary Ceremonial Magic context. I had an intention to research and write about this subject as part of a series of essays on elements we needed to explore to build living traditions of magic. The piece was mostly written prior to those complaints surfacing. However, sharing information on this particular subject became more relevant as people questioned why we would do a demon possession ritual, and other people asserted that this kind of work had no place in the magic of those working with Ceremonial Magic.

It is unfortunate that this was the original context for this piece because it is an important subject to consider on its own. It deserves to be viewed as something to explore as part of deepening and vivifying our magical experience rather than just as a counter to people's concerns. Understanding that this kind of magic has a place within European Tradition and within the elements of European magic which informed, and were used to build Ceremonial Magic, is important for recognizing what place it can have as the revival of these modes of magic moves forward.

Understanding the many examples where we can see elements and echoes of this approach to spirit work in European tradition can also be a guide in further exploring these traditions. By recognizing where this is an element of what is happening, it informs how we analyze and explore those traditions. This can open up avenues for how we engage them or how we consider our approach to those various traditional modes of spirit contact and magic. It also points us to elements we can explore to get a shape of how possession has worked in European magic, as well as how we can compare to how it works in other cultures and traditions.

The original post addressed some of the elements I have noted in this introduction, so I have excised that portion to avoid redundancy.

This essay is included primarily to further discussion and exploration of the idea of spirit possession in both European Traditional Magic and modern forms of magic. While this essay does not pertain to familiar spirits directly it should be considered that a familiar spirit could be a possessing spirit when one considers the first phase of possession described below. It is not necessary, nor is it specifically advised that this be the relationship. It is a possibility. This is largely presented to explain the context of exploration and the possibilities it can present to us as people explore the idea of possession either with their familiars or with other spirits.

Spirit Possession in the Modern Western Tradition

In a recent discussion, a close friend and I were talking about the space opening up for people engaging in European Traditional Magic to begin to build living sorcerous traditions. The goal would be living traditions which provide models for engaging in European magical traditions with the same kinds of context, support and features we see in the living traditions of Central and South America, and elsewhere in the world. These other traditions have methods for developing and cultivating spirit engagement, clarifying information received from the spirit world, and utilizing that information to effectively work magic for real and potent change both personally and in their communities. Looking more deeply at the history of European magic we see hints, pieces, and clues towards European magical culture that once provided similar modes for building effective magicians.

Magicians looking to grab onto that meaningful deep connection to human spiritual heritage often become drawn to African Diaspora Religions (ADR) and African Traditional Religions (ATR) because those traditions for engaging and effectively working with the spirit world are relatively intact. They have evolved to work within the context of human social needs and therefore provide things that people need to live their lives, not just spiritual development.

In looking at how a living tradition drawing on European spirits and traditions would take shape there are three things we need to look at.

1. How do we pass power and pact; How do we create and transfer the agreement with spirits to work with a line of magicians; how do we pass charisma or spiritual power from one magician to the next?

2. How do we connect with and embody the powers of these spirits to work with them as a community and as individuals; how do we engage them to speak with us, to whisper to us as needed; how do we bring them into on going proximity with us?

3. How do we clarify their messages to us; how do we reduce the impact of our biases and create consistent ways of receiving information for ourselves and others with some confidence that it is a message from the spirit without the overwhelming power of our own fantasies taking hold?

The Greek Magical Papyri provide some answers and guidance, as does European witchcraft. The grimoires give details of how these answers can be expressed and worked. All of the above questions are important to considering the road forward towards a living tradition. Answering any of these questions can relate to the other questions, and considering them together can help expand how we answer them. Thorough answers to all three groups of questions are beyond the scope of this work. The second group of questions will provide our focus. As we explore the embodiment of spirits, consider how it also relates to the first and third group of questions.

Spirit possession is one of the primary modes in which religious and magical workers embody spirits for themselves and others throughout many spirit traditions around the world. When we consider a relationship in which a spirit sits with us, speaks with us, and influences us through our day to day lives, we are still looking at a form of spirit possession, although one which is foreign to most European and American thinking.

As I write this, I am rewatching (for the third time) Fox's adaptation of The Exorcist into a TV series. It's a lot of fun. It also deals with some religious and theological ideas in interesting ways. It's a horror TV show, so it depicts exorcism, possession, and otherworldly spirits in the most horrific ways. It's not inventing these depictions; it's drawing on centuries of European and Anglophone apprehension surrounding the idea of demons, possession, and the terror of involuntary spiritual contact. It's a good example of what people assume when they think of possession.

Those assumptions don't exist solely in the minds of the non-magical folks. Work with demons is part of the intellectual heritage of ceremonial magic, although in that context it is often approached as a psychological exercise. Some ceremonial magicians recognize that people genuinely conjure demons, but avoid doing it themselves. For more Neo-Pagan and New Age magical traditions, despite the influence they take from ceremonial magic, the possibility of work with demons is part of why they often look at ceremonial magic as a dangerous and frightening system to warn new seekers away from. The average person understands that although fire is dangerous, it is a useful tool when we understand how to handle it correctly. Many people in contemporary spiritual and magical systems do not realize that we can understand demons the same way.

For some, the idea of working with an actual demon, not a psychological construct, can be somewhat confrontational. It forces us to face questions about the nature of spirits and magic. It may force us to enter into a space which may be uncomfortable, dangerous, or frightening.

Led by this fear and discomfort, when we enter into that space we do so with very specific guidelines, calling on very specific spirits, in ways which keep them far from us - locked in place by curses and other spiritual powers. In many instances, it's a reasonable approach. For some people, it is the best approach. Historically, however, it's not the only approach. Magic has always offered many spirits to work with who aren't devils, and other ways to work with these spirits. Whether we are working with infernal or other spirits we should consider the broad range of options for spirit communication.

For those most familiar with addressing spirits in a very formal and separate mode, the possibility of experiencing them in a context like possession may seem irresponsible or inappropriate. While the average first-world person may consider possession solely as a form of involuntary spiritual assault, this is not the case throughout most of the world.

When we look at traditions in Central and South America, and in the Caribbean, positive voluntary spirit possession is a common religious and magical practice. These traditions are the ones which have most readily made their way into the awareness of people in the USA, and likely, in Britain and Europe. But they are not the only voluntary spirit possession traditions. Possession exists throughout the world in various spiritual traditions and it manifests in various modes.

In 1994, Nicholas Spanos published "Multiple Identity Enactments and Multiple Personality Disorder: A Sociocognitive Perspective" in _Psychological Bulletin. vol. 116. no. 1_. Spanos takes a meta-analysis approach to explore multiplicity in an attempt to prove that rather than being wholly a disease, it is a social construct. I don't believe that cases of possession are simply a psycho-social experience but the article is interesting in that it compares it to other forms of multiplicity, and explores a cross cultural view of possession and its role in societies in which it is potentially a positive experience.

He opens his discussion of possession by saying:

> Multiple self enactments occur in most but not all cultures (Bourguinon, 1976). In many traditional societies and in some subcultural contexts in North American society, multiple self enactments take the form of spirit possession. In these cases, it is believed that the human occupant of the body is temporarily displaced by another self or selves that are defined as spirits who temporarily take over control of the body.

Spanos goes on to reference several studies which provide information on the frequency of possession in various cultures and regions. Sri Lanka, South India, Malagasy, the Sudan, North America, and the Songhay people are all cited as examples, along with Europe, and England. He references the Spiritualist movement and European witchcraft as movements which include examples of possession.

Within European witchcraft traditions we see voluntary possession. We see it in sybilline and oracular traditions of antiquity.

We see it in the Dionysian cults, and we see it echoed in central elements of Christianity that continued those mysteries. We see it in Spiritualism, and Spiritism, and in the New World Traditions that adopted the work of Kardec to blend with memories of African and Native traditions. Going back into prehistory we see it hinted at in cave paintings associated with early zoomorphic religion, and we see it in the survivals of the steppe traditions of Eurasia.

It's not a foreign or an unusual thing. It's a missing piece of our puzzle.

Despite its prevalence throughout the spiritual and magical history that informs both modern and traditional schools of magic, some people believe possession should not be explored in the context of ceremonial magic. While we have noted its global presence, and its prevalence in European spirituality, we can also find clear examples of its presence in sources that directly impacted the development of modern ceremonial magic. The easiest example is the Sacred Magic, which is presented in the Abramelin texts. The relationship with the Holy Guardian Angel is a form of possession. The book does not present itself using those terms, and individuals less familiar with possession might not immediately understand why this is an example of possession. Possession is not always full possession; it has several stages.

In Catholicism, and in other magical and religious traditions of voluntary possession, possession occurs with differing stages. We can understand it as first being an intimate connection between the possessed and the spirit. The spirit is within the sphere of the possessed and they interact very closely, sharing a deep and connected awareness of each other. In the next phase, the space between them blurs; the spirit and the person share the same space and awareness. Actions may be a combination of the will and influence of either or both parties. The primary awareness/control may shift back and forth between the person and the spirit. The final phase is a more complete experience of possession. The spirit takes hold and is in the driver's seat. The person may or may not be aware of, or remember, what happens.

When a magician completes the Abramelin retreat they enter into a relationship with their Guardian Angel which can be understood in the context of that first phase of possession. Much of the work done with The Sacred Magic is based on the magician operating in this state. The magician and the Angel work together; the Angel sits with the magician and communicates directly with him. The Angel clarifies and aids in communication with other spirits and speaks to the magician to guide his magical work. Much of the relationship here is similar to the partial possession relationships we see with priests, magicians, and elders in other traditions that incorporate some sort of seating of a spirit as part of the process of attaining such a status. This does not make the spirits or the process involved the same as when working with the Holy Guardian Angel, but it does provide a point of contact in which comparison can help deepen our understanding of what the relationship can be.

NeoPagan witchcraft comes primarily out of the Gerald Gardner's Wica. His system draws heavily from Thelema and the Key of Solomon. Forms which descend from Gardner adopt a significant amount of their methods from Golden Dawn inspired writers like Regardie and Fortune. Wiccan practices, while separate from ceremonial magic groups, reflect how people might engage the methods associated with ceremonial magic.

Performative possession is a central act in Wicca, both eclectic and traditional. While some practitioners focus on acting out a part while channeling energy in a group setting, many intend to become an actual vessel for an actual divine being. The result might often be possession having features of the first stage, but it could also be taken further. The primary example of this in formal Wiccan groups is the practice of Drawing Down the Moon. In this practice, the priestess invokes, or has invoked into her, the Goddess, so that she can embody that presence. The priestess might speak and act as the Goddess for her community of witches. She might confer blessings or work magic as the Goddess. This is an act of magical voluntary possession, the features of which are similar to those observed in many traditional forms of positive possession.

There are practices in some folk traditions and in antiquity which involve bringing down the moon. These practices often relate to removing the moon from the sky. Some surviving late antique oracular magic reflects similar ideas. The story of Aradia presents the same imagery we see in the Wiccan practice of Drawing Down the Moon and is one direct source for the concept. The magical technology involved in this practice stems from the magic of Thelema and the Golden Dawn.

In the Golden Dawn, the Assumption of Godforms is an important technique for embodying and applying spiritual powers.

Frequently, Assumption of Godforms does not approach the level of spirit possession, but it can. Some approaches treat these divine forms as formulas or static functions rather than as actual beings. In instances where the process is treated as a holistic connection with a spiritual being it can be more dynamic. Crowley's approach to this kind of spiritual interaction opens the door for a more mystical experience. In Crowley's Liber Astarte, the magician engages in a series of practices and utilizes a stirring invocation to call upon a divine power to reside in him and join him through his acts of devotion. Liber Astarte is less performative, it's less about creating an experience of that divine power for those around the magician, and more about the mystical or magical experience of the magician. The practice can be taken to a level in which the first stage of possession occurs. The magician can come to a point where they share space with a divine figure which acts with the magician to provide information, insight, or the application of magical power.

The performative element we see in Wiccan covens occurs in Thelemic practices within the Gnostic Mass. Through adornments, ritual actions, and prayers the priest and priestess embody certain spiritual forces. Some Thelemites view these powers as actual deities and some don't. Many in those roles do experience a state akin to multiplicity or a certain dissociation or adjustment in their awareness. This seems to be a particularly powerful experience for those serving in the Office of the Priestess of the Mass. While Priests often exhibit a change in demeanor, presence, and tone, they do not often talk about experiencing a separate consciousness or awareness in conjunction with their own. Priestesses often experience powers associated with figures of the divine feminine and the power and awareness associated with those figures. This experience often carries with it a sense of the individual ego being subverted or enfolded in this other broader consciousness.

The Gnostic Mass incorporates language of invocation drawn from Golden Dawn rituals. This language is in turn borrowed from the Mass and appears in Wiccan rituals of Drawing Down the Moon. There is a clear continuity. The Mass directly influences Gardner's Wicca as inspiration for The Great Rite. The process of a priest and priestess working to aid each other in invoking the respective divine influences shows up in the rituals of Wicca. The methods of embodying divine powers, such as Drawing Down the Moon, which occur in formal initiated Wicca inspired the common practices of invoking and embodying gods in various forms of NeoPaganism.

Our discussion began by considering spirit possession as important to European Traditional Magic, and its development towards a living spirit tradition. Ceremonial Magic, while related to European Traditional Magic, is arguably separate. The benefits of exploring spirit possession relationships, and these other spirit relationship elements which might bring us closer to a living spirit tradition, can help deepen the practice of Ceremonial Magic as well.

Abramelin, European witchcraft, and The Greek Magical Papyri give us examples of spirit possession work within European Traditional Magic. These examples are all also sources which directly impact modern systems of magic like Ceremonial Magic, Wicca, and systems which have grown from these. Our exploration of Drawing Down the Moon, the Assumption of Godforms, and the Gnostic Mass has shown us that these practices of spirit possession are already reflected in modern systems. For some practitioners, these methods reach a level indistinct from the first phase of spirit possession.

With the presence of spirit possession well established in our magical heritage and its traditional and modern manifestations, we can consider the importance of spirit possession. What does it do? Why would we use it? What would it look like as a more routine part of our work? In Spanos's article he says:

> In many societies, spirit possession occurs as part of helping rituals. The medium becomes possessed by a spirit or by successive spirits, and it is the spirits who diagnose the client, prescribe treatments, or offer advice for problems in living.

When we look at the idea of a magician as someone to whom people go for help with their problems, including serious life issues, we imagine a consultant. We imagine someone who reads the cards, throws the bones, or casts a chart and measures out problems and solutions, then executes magical rituals.

In most societies, the central element of this work is a relationship with spirits. Divination is the reception of knowledge from divine or otherworldly sources. Systems like Tarot, runes, other tools of divination can be powerful methods of communication with an unseen power. The tool allows that power to speak to us more clearly. These systems can work as modes of reflection and meditation in which the random layout guides our consideration and intuition. These tools can anticipate that chance will reflect the elements at play and allow us to gain insights by how the tools fall. We can deepen our work with these tools by connecting them with our spirits and allowing these tools to clarify and sharpen the messages which our spirits speak to us. Our spirits can guide the cards or tiles as they illustrate the stories which answer our questions.

Partial possession assists in this mode of spirit work in a few ways. The magician who has a possessing spirit knows the voice, the tone, the tenor of that spirit. He can recognize and understand it more readily and more clearly. While the tool may speak for another spirit, his possessing spirit can help guide him in interpreting it, and in receiving more of the communication.

If the spirit from whom the magician is receiving information is the possessing spirit, the work with the tool will be a work familiar to both the magician and the spirit, and will draw them into a closer state of communication. The tool will help guide and further clarify the communication but the spirit will already have a direct line to communicating with the magician. The spirit may even communicate with the client directly through the magician.

Depending upon the tool used, the possessing spirit may help guide the magician's actions in using the tool, bringing about a clearer more directed outcome or ensuring that the tool is used in a manner which will provide the answer which is needed.

These sorts of benefits can be achieved through various forms of direct spirit work as part of divination. The closer the relationship with the spirit, the clearer the communication will be. With clearer communication, the magician will more easily receive the needed information and have greater facility in receiving aid from the spirit. While we might not look at this and say "Yeah, people doing this kind of work, particularly for others, should have a possessing spirit," it should be fairly clear that a relationship with and an engagement of a spirit in this work offers many benefits.

On January 28th 2018, The Independent published an article by Julia Buckley which was primarily an excerpt from her book on her efforts to find relief from Chronic Pain. She had traveled to a bunch of gurus and healers, but hadn't gotten anywhere. The article focused on her attempt to receive help from a Haitian Voodoo priest. She went in expecting it to be purely psychological, but she ended up experiencing much more. Her description of the event, which she recognizes as unreliable and which has strong hints of the racism she denies at the beginning, clearly conveys that she experienced something real and much more than she expected. Not only did she experience more relief than she had elsewhere but she was moved to continue honoring, in her own way, the spirits who had helped her.

The experience was one of being healed by a spirit possessing the man in front of her. She recognized the priest as possessed. She felt a presence in the room. She recognized the behaviors and natures of the spirits involved. She understood, when she spoke with the man after he had finished the procedure, that she was speaking with the spirit possessing him. Earlier in the article, she noted miraculous instances of healing which had been attributed to him, but she also noted that he did not want to take credit or be viewed as a healer. This seems to indicate an understanding that he is a medium through which the spirit is acting.

What's significant here is that the spirit was able to engage the situation directly in ways that spiritual healers were not. Paracelsus wrote about the invisible causes of disease, and of man's predicaments. He explained that there are spiritual factors which impact our state of harmony, disrupt it, and create problems. He explained how realigning those factors can improve us. According to Paracelsus, interacting with certain spiritual beings can also create this harmony.

This is the essential concept which defines hermetic medicine. The components of a person - the elements, and the planetary rays which build up the nature of who we are; create health when in balance. They create a positive flow of influences which allow good things in our lives. When they are out of balance, they distort us, and how we experience and interact with the world. This is the idea behind humorism, astrological diagnosis and treatment, and most traditional forms of "western" occult medicine.

Over time, we have learned about other invisible causes. Bacteria, viruses, anxiety, stress, and genetic factors, are things which we have learned to make visible but which once seemed like inexplicable and unpredictable magical factors. That does not take away the reality of Paracelsus's invisible causes, or of ancient beliefs in afflicting spirits. It simply adds to that reality.

Paracelsus's work describing invisible causes explains them as existing in a Gabalistic (Kabbalistic) or Olympian hypostasis. That is to say, a level of creation existing in a spiritual or ideal state. That hypostasis reflects the existence and nature of a more pure and divine hypostasis above it, moving backwards to the original discursive moments of creation. Likewise, moving forward towards nature there exist more and more material hypostases, eventually resulting in the macro-level of our perceptions.

With that in mind, those physical invisible causes which we have discovered through science are, perhaps, hypostatic echoes of some other spiritual state of disquiet. Thus, that which seems immovable by the means available to us becomes moveable when the spiritual state is rectified. In the case of Julia Buckley, she achieved relief when the Baron reached in and removed the afflicting spiritual attachment in her arm. The spirit was able to perceive some unknown affliction which had attached itself to her, and operating on the same hypostatic level thereof, was able to reach in and remove it. But the affliction still situated itself upon her in such a fashion as to move the more physical levels of her experience to develop the physical components of her affliction. She likely needed more physical follow up to keep the pain from returning.

This story illustrates the role of the possessing spirit in diagnosing and treating the problems an individual presents. In many cases, the spirit could be engaged through conjuration or other means to perceive and address the cause. Working with the spirit through a medium allows for the spirit to also communicate something about the nature of the cause and what further steps should be taken to help correct the problems involved, whether those steps are ritual or spiritual steps, or corresponding mundane work. It will often be both. If we simply conjure a spirit and ask it to heal someone, that debrief, or consult element, is less easily tenable. Mediumistic work might still be needed.

We've talked about how important communication is with consultation and diagnosis, with treatment and with the application of magical solutions in client-driven or community scenarios. Magicians often we have a curiosity regarding the unseen world. That is often what drives us to explore magic rather than client-driven work.

It is well attested that priests from the medieval period, and later, understood that the modes of exorcism used by the Church could be minorly adjusted to conjure a spirit. In fact, the words "exorcism" and "conjuration" have essentially the same meaning. Priests came to know that the demon, once bound in an exorcism – whether an exorcism to save a demoniac or a more ceremonial ritual to call upon a demon; could be questioned and caused to reveal a great deal of information which the priest or magician could not obtain otherwise. The Church even had rules against engaging the demon in such interrogation and instructions for exorcism retain advice against doing so.

Many great luminaries of the European world were magicians and often the pursuit of magic was one through which they hoped to gain knowledge and understanding beyond what science could afford them. Theology was one of the highest intellectual pursuits, so the spiritual worlds were understood to be the source for knowledge beyond that of philosophy and the lower disciplines found in the quadrivium and trivium.

For most of us working in an Anglophone context, whether working European Traditional Magic or ceremonial magic, working for clients and the community is not the norm. The average person works to gain material benefits aligned to their needs and desires, or to achieve mystical or spiritual development. Like magicians of history, who turned to spirits to obtain knowledge beyond the constraints of the more mundane modes of learning available to them, some magicians today also turn to spirits to gain information. Many spirits listed in grimoires are great for learning things. For magicians curious about the world and about deepening their magic, conjuring a spirit and asking it questions is a clear solution. The constraints presented in the grimoires are largely intended to keep the spirit honest and cause it to appear in a way that allows communication. The rituals are written with the assumption that we will ask questions and seek knowledge. The grimoires offer opportunities to gain new knowledge and power by calling upon spirits.

But how do these spirits provide that knowledge or confer that power? Working with scrying they may show you images or visual or auditory flashes that suggest things. Some magicians boast of the physical or visible appearance they consistently produce with their methods. Most of these magicians actually mean that they produce a clear and discernable apparition in a scrying device visible by a competent scryer. Imagine being able to ask a spirit possessed of flesh and blood to answer your questions, or to place a hand on you and imbue you with power or blessings. If the spirit is truly possessing a competent medium this is the opportunity we gain. In terms of communication, the details of expression can be much more significant. The follow-up questions are easier to ask.

Instead of worrying about conjuring to visible appearance, or scrying and banishing phantasms, possession allows us to have a face-to-face with the spirit in a human body. For some spirits, this is a more appropriate method than constraining a manifestation. Regardless of the type of spirit, it is an interesting experience to stand across from a possessed person, asking them questions, recognizing the behaviors and words that don't fit the person in front of you and grasping the ways in which the answers inform you of things beyond their knowledge. It is a particularly satisfying mode of spirit interaction, and one which carries with it a powerful presence and provides an experience of significant impact.

Whether we're dealing with possession or conjuration, the way we understand and verify information remains an important consideration. When conjuring, using divination to confirm the messages we hear and images we see is an important step. Testing the information, either for real world applicability or factual verification, may be necessary. We also have to learn to filter out our own noise and inner voices and recognize the exterior voice. We have to learn to listen to what it is saying and not what we want it to say. Possession bypasses some of, but not all of this. Depending upon the skill of the medium, and those facilitating the possession, the nature of the interaction might reduce how much the medium adds to the communication. We may still need to test that the possessed is possessed. We may still need to test the information provided. What is provided is clearer and less encumbered by our own inner language.

Working with this type of possession in a European context is a topic open to discussion and experimentation. While I have experimented with it, I am not in a position to tell you that my method is the best method. I suggest that you explore and experiment rather than try to exactly replicate my approach. We have very few modern examples of intentional possession from within a ceremonial or European Traditional Magic approach. Turn to the experts and elders of traditions where this is an established practice. Learn from their wisdom respectfully, without recklessly appropriating. Use that inspiration, use what I've presented, and use your own research and experimentation to help build systems and methods for positive possession within the contexts of European Traditional Magic and ceremonial magic.

This exploration of the role of possession helps explain why the demon sabbat presented in an earlier chapter was important. Many systems utilize ritual possession, but this ritual provided an example of how we can explore this work in conjunction with the grimoires and European witchcraft. This exploration adds to efforts to regain the elements that separate these traditions from the living spirit traditions which are intact in other cultures.

Those with fingers on the pulse of the magical community know that rebuilding our magical heritage beyond the incomplete knowledge of the Victorian era is essential, especially when we consider traditions and organizations which want to stay relevant.

Possession can be scary. It needs to be handled in responsible ways which are informed by significant magical knowledge from a cross-traditional perspective. Not everyone is ready for that. But, we're getting there. It's a powerful and useful tool, and one which is coming back into our purview.

Frog. Toads and frogs are often associated with witches. Toads have anatomical elements that have long been used as materia magica.

XXV
Cross of a Frog and Nymphs

The idea of a familiar spirit is not only useful in exploring European Traditional Magic, it is also compatible with modern ceremonial magic. The previous chapter addressed the fact that spirit possession is not completely foreign to the development of modern magic, and it is definitely a part of European Traditional Magic. Hopefully, part three of this text has made these points clear and given you the tools to further explore the space these modes of magical practice can occupy in contemporary Anglophone magic.

As we consider the space for work with familiars and spirit communication through possession in European Traditional Magic and modern ceremonial magic we might think that this would require reframing ceremonial magic. Possession is adjacent to, if not part of, the methods and sources from which ceremonial magic is built. There is also evidence that familiar spirits are not as far removed from modern ceremonial magic systems as some might think.

While the idea of a familiar spirit for a group may be less evident in the history of modern ceremonial magic, familiar spirits for individuals are present, at least in the periphery. Consider the elemental spirits of Paracelsus; de Villars in his Comte de Gabalis makes it very clear that they may attain an immortal soul through marriage to a human. Eliphas Levi, whose work inspired the early members Golden Dawn and Crowley, was influenced in his consideration of the elementals by de Villars. Both the Golden Dawn system and Crowley's work incorporate elements which reflect the expectation of work with these elemental spirits. Reuben Swinburne Clymer, whose American Rosicrucian movement continued the sex magic teachings of Paschal Beverly Randolph, also taught that elementals needed marriage to a human to obtain an immortal soul in his text The Irreconcilable Gnomes, published in 1910.

The idea that elementals could be conjured, and might enter into close and sexual relationships with humans, was present amongst the writers who developed modern ceremonial magic. Some of these writers were also influenced by the writings of Ida Craddock. Craddock wrote about sexual liaisons with angels. The idea of a woman taking an angel as a lover is not completely removed from tales of the advent of witchcraft, nor is it dissimilar from the idea that medieval witches took demon lovers.

Crowley continued this idea in his teachings about autoerotic sex magic, in which an elemental lover is taken by the magician. A 9th degree OTO member once characterized the difference between the A.'.A.'. and the OTO as, "one is occupied with seeking Knowledge and Conversation of the Holy Guardian Angel, and the other is focused on things like acquiring a Nymph as a lover." I take his quip with a grain of salt. I always interpreted Crowley's teachings on an elemental lover as an allegory for a mystical union with Nuit and a universal apprehension of the divine feminine quality. In that light, it is comparable to achieving Knowledge and Conversation within the Thelemic understanding of the terms. Pursuing an elemental lover would fit with the material that influenced Crowley. Ironically, if the goal was an elemental lover, that would also be comparable to Knowledge and Conversation, but in the traditional sense. While we can joke about the OTO focusing on Nymphs as lovers, or we can presume the Nymph is a reference to Nuit, Crowley is actually pretty clear on the matter. Both the marriage to the goddess and the marriage to the elemental are tasks for his adepts, and the two tasks relate to one another.

The elementals described by Paracelsus are very similar to the household spirits and nature spirits found in folklore. They are not particularly similar to the races of faeries we encounter in most folklore and mythology. Later authors gave more spirit-like descriptions of the elementals. These descriptions led to them being equated to faeries. While these later descriptions are different from both faeries in folklore and the elementals as Paracelsus described them, this understanding is the one which informed Victorian English Magic. The folklore which would have influenced the framers of Victorian English Magic is the folklore we explored in part two of this book. Stories of faery lovers present us with a model for the familiar spirit relationship. The Victorian interpretation of an elemental lover is well within the bounds of what we would understand as a familiar spirit. The spirit gains something from its relationship with its familiar human. The spirit provides services to the human magician. The human maintains the relationship through sexual congress. There is no significant difference between the elemental lover and traditional ideas about a witch's familiar. While not present in the grimoires which were published by Golden Dawn members, methods of binding a faery lover appear in grimoire material that was accessible to them.

At minimum, Yeats and Mathers would have been informed by the folklore of faery lovers, which has a recognizable relationship with stories of witches and their imps.

Yeats clearly believed in faeries. His relationship with the Leanan Sidhe is evident, and we discussed it at length in part two. Yeats claimed his wife put him in touch with a deceased geographer from the Renaissance named Leo Africanus. Yeats had a personal relationship with the spirit of a deceased person; this spirit was a familiar. We don't know the exact method of contact. This may have reflected methods of Spiritism or Spiritualism rather than Golden Dawn methods. Regardless, it is an example of a Golden Dawn leader working with spirits in a traditional relationship. The myth that this kind of magic did not exist within the Victorian era is persistent due to the psychologization of magic which followed, but it remains a myth.

According to Alexandra Nagel, in her thesis Marriage with Elementals: From "Le Comte de Gabalis" to a Golden Dawn Ritual, Yeats was not the only Golden Dawn leader so immersed in spirit work. Nagel references Ithell Colquhoun, who stated that Wescott and Mathers both incorporated Tantra in the sexual teachings of the Golden Dawn. Both men understood the acquiring of a spirit-lover to be one of the skills of advanced practitioners of Tantra. Mathers advocated marriages to elementals and constructed a ritual for this purpose. In particular, he recommended such a marriage to an individual out of concern that her attempts at conjuration would attract an incubus rather than a faery as intended. Edward Berridge, a senior adept, advocated forms of sex magic which were also connected to a belief in faeries. Berridge drew from the works of Thomas Lake Harris, who himself claimed to have otherworld-children, whom he had sired upon a faery queen.

The leaders of the Golden Dawn were not the only ones aware of faery relationships. Crowley also makes reference to faery lovers in comparison to the relationship with the elemental. Further, Crowley explicitly described the elemental lovers as familiar spirits.

The relationship between elemental lovers and faery lovers strongly illustrates the presence of the familiar spirit in ceremonial magic, despite it being overlooked and unexplored. Other examples also illustrate that familiar spirits are part of the corpus of ceremonial magic. Crowley's text "The Cross of a Frog" or more completely "STAUROS BATRACHOU, the Ceremonies proper to obtaining a familiar spirit of a Mercurial nature as described in the Apocalypse of St. John the Divine from a frog or toad" is an explicit example of a modern ceremonial magic text instructing the magician in a ritual to obtain a familiar. On the surface, Crowley publishing a text with instructions for obtaining a familiar, then making that text an instruction for sixth degree OTO members, seems to make it clear that familiar spirits have a place in Thelema, and perhaps also other forms of ceremonial magic. But, it might not be that simple.

The ritual reads tongue-in-cheek, but so do other grandiose Crowley texts. The primary focus seems to be to toy with the frog and associate it with Jesus Christ, then to slay the frog to symbolize destroying the second Aeon. The sacrifice of the Frog-Christ is also an act of vengeance for the harms which Crowley believed Christianity did to him. In this light, the text could be dismissed as a type of mental exercise intended to achieve catharsis.

The structure of the text ties closely to a process of initiation. It reflects Crowley working his initiation and sacramental system into an outline for a magical ritual, as we discussed earlier when discussing initiations and sacraments. It seems unlikely that he would structure it this way if it were just an exercise in cathartic writing. Further, it is unlikely that he would associate it with an A∴A∴ grade and an OTO degree if it was not intended to serve an actual ritual purpose. Perhaps the real focus is the destruction of the second Aeon and the influence of Christ over the magician through an antinomian act of ritual and defiant mockery. That is certainly a clear aim of the text. The text also makes it clear that it does, in fact, intend to harness the soul of the frog.

The crucifixion of the frog carries with it a false enthroning, mockery and condemnation. Then, the frog assumes the throne of the fallen master (Christ) as the companion of the initiate. These are all very real themes and elements in Crowley's work. The crucifixion also includes the following passage.

> And I assume unto myself and take into my service the elemental spirit of this frog, to be about me as a lying spirit, to go forth upon the earth as a guardian to me in my Work for Man; that men may speak of my piety and of my gentleness and of all virtues and bring to me love and service and all material things soever where I may stand in need. And this shall be its reward, to stand beside me and hear the truth that I utter, the falsehood whereof shall deceive men.

Here he lays out the relationship between himself and the spirit. He charges the spirit with its overarching task. He links the spirit to his work as a Magus in the A.'.A.'. and ties the reward of the spirit to that work.

Crowley's link between the spirit and his status as a Magus is interesting. He notes that the spirit is an elemental spirit, and it is rewarded by standing with him. Essentially, through service to Crowley, the frog attains soul and status. Crowley views the frog as requiring the same union with the magician that the conventional elementals do. The idea that the reward is a place at the side of the Magus who has been elevated to replace Christ also echoes the Biblical Crucifixion in which the faithful theif is promised a place at the side of the transfigured Christ.

There are many other interesting elements and points of comparison available in this short ritual. The frog is instructed to convince people they like and should help Crowley. This is interesting, because Crowley seems to be doing actual spirit work. He is killing an animal and harvesting its spirit to be his elemental servant. He isn't asking the elemental to obtain stuff he needs; he's asking the elemental to make people like him and give him stuff. His view of magic as being about psychological changes, or changes in perception that result in differences in action, still pervades even while he is doing actual spirit work. Crowley's response to bad press also indicates that people holding a positive perception of him mattered to him at times.

PGM VIII 1-63 is comparable to the charge the magician gives the frog. The spell contains the line, "Open up for me the hands of everyone who [dispenses gifts] and compel them to give me what they have in their hands." This spell is a petition to Thoth-Hermes and is, therefore, mercurial in nature. It is likely a coincidence that the charge to the mercurial familiar is not dissimilar from this element of the charge to Thoth-Hermes. Crowley was probably not aware of this spell, but the similarity in purpose is striking. This similarity does not indicate that the ritual was, in fact, intended to obtain a familiar, but it is an interesting coincidence all the same. It highlights the material intention of the spell, and suggests that it was about more than catharsis.

Crowley may have been familiar with folklore around horse-whisperers, toad witches, and the toad bone rites. Some versions of those practices seem to have involved the torture and crucifixion of a frog not wholly dissimilar from this. If that did inspire Crowley, it would make it very clear that the divide between the magic of a witch or sorcerer's familiar and the practices of modern ceremonial magic is an artificial divide.

Whether we want to consider engaging in frog crucifixions or elemental marriages, or avoid the troubles of either, we can conclude that familiar spirits are part of Crowley's magical system, albeit an overlooked part. Being part of Crowley's magic might be significant to some Thelemites, but it doesn't address the broader range of Golden Dawn derived modern magic. We know that the founders of the Golden Dawn took influence from Levi, Bulwer-Lytton, and Blavatsky, all of whom were influenced by Comte De Gabalis. Since Crowley's "Liber Librae," which describes interaction with elementals, is drawn from Golden Dawn material, it would stand to reason that his understanding of elemental marriages was influenced by his Golden Dawn connections. While Mathers's ritual for marrying an elemental does not seem to have survived, records of its existence prove this facet of magic was present in the Golden Dawn. Despite not appearing in the standard corpus of Golden Dawn materials, it is evident that such magic was part of the beliefs and lived practices of Golden Dawn members.

In the end, though, it doesn't much matter. Familiar spirits are a useful and important part of magic. We see them throughout European Traditional Magic, and we see comparable spirit relationships in other parts of the world. Whether the founders of the modern "occult revival" made use of them or not is irrelevant. Contemporary magicians need not miss out on the benefits of a familiar simply because those benefits might have been lost on magicians a hundred years ago.

XXVI
Elemental Familiars

Mathers's ritual for wedding an elemental spirit is lost. Crowley provides instructions towards a ritual and recommends a series of his own texts to read in preparation for this work. The Hermetic Brotherhood of Luxor, the Hermetic Order of the Golden Dawn, and other occult orders of the late 19th and early 20th centuries reference the elementals in their initiations but not to establish a marriage. A specific surviving ritual written by the key organizers of the occult revival for wedding an elemental to obtain an elemental familiar is not available.

Using Crowley's guidance, we will discuss how to construct a ritual to obtain an elemental marriage. Then, we will provide examples.

The sources for this concept are problematic. Paracelsus addresses human marriages with elementals in A Book on Nymphs Sylphs Pygmies Salamanders and Other Spirits. Paracelsus seems to be referring to faery stories of swan women bathing in lakes and other elements of folklore. Montfaucon de Villars presents a somewhat different take on elementals. His work, Comte de Gabalis, became the defining influence on how people understood elementals from its mid-17th-century publication through the development of the Golden Dawn. Abbe de Villars does not seem to have been a magician. His book was likely political and religious satire. Later authors associated his text with Rosicrucianism. That association endured, and his work was understood as true occult secrets hidden behind the veil of satire. For writers like Crowley and Mathers, the marriages with elementals and the nature of those elements drew more on Comte de Gabalis and the authors it influenced, like Buwler-Lytton, Levi, Abbe Boullan, and Blavatsky, than they did on Paracelsus. A letter from Moina Mathers suggests that Golden Dawn members associated the elementals with faery stories and legends of the past. Her letter also describes elementals as the idea that stems from Nature and animates into being each grain of sand or drop of rain by clothing the idea in materiality. Paracelsus's descriptions are not a direct influence and may not be completely germane to a Victorian English view of the elementals. We can rely on de Villars and those who follow him, even though their works are essentially based in fiction.

For a complete treatment of the elementals as they appear in modern magic, see my book, <u>Living Spirits: A Guide to Magic in a World of Spirits</u>. Our focus in this text will be working with them and how to construct ritual methods based on Victorian Occult revival ideas and techniques.

Regarding work with the elementals, Crowley's <u>Liber Librae</u> states the following.

> Be thou therefore prompt and active as the Sylphs, but avoid frivolity and caprice; be energetic and strong like the Salamanders, but avoid irritability and ferocity; be flexible and attentive to images like the Undines, but avoid idleness and changeability; be laborious and patient like the Gnomes, but avoid grossness and avarice.

These virtues and vices are not correspondences or powers of the elementals. Instead, they indicate the nature of the elements and how their natures might be reflected in the magician. The marriage with an elemental exposes the individual to the nature of that force intimately. The balance of these virtues and vices is a consideration when determining what type of elemental to seek out. First, determine if there is a particular element with which you are most comfortable. Next, consider which elemental might provide for your most common needs. Then, take stock of your character. Are certain of these virtues strong for you, or do some of these vices easily overtake you? Choose an elemental which will not easily unbalance you.

Within <u>Liber Librae</u> and <u>Liber Tzaddi</u>, there are additional passages we will consider. Crowley also recommends <u>Liber Samekh</u>, <u>Liber Astarte</u>, and <u>AMRITA</u>. Each of these will give some insight into the performance or planning of such a ritual. Finally, Crowley recommends <u>Liber Chanokh</u> as the source for ritual components.

Previously, I made available through my website, "The Unveiled Sky," two examples of sex magic rituals worked through masturbation. These rituals utilized Thelemic beliefs and ritual language. One of these rituals was mystical in nature; the other was practical. Both focused on sexual union with Nuit and drew not just on Crowley but also on Jack Parsons. Parsons described the use of a silver cup consecrated with the Priestess's speech in the Gnostic Mass as the vessel for the goddess to be used in masturbatory rituals. Crowley recommends fixing the mind on Nuit and dedicating all sexual acts to her. Even this ritual to an elemental should, in Crowley's view, be done with dedication to Nuit as your focus to keep from profaning the act.

Whether you choose to dedicate all of your sexual acts, or all of your magical sexual acts, to Nuit or not is up to you. Crowley recommends Liber NV, and Liber HAD to understand this dedication. He describes it as simply envisioning Nuit thoroughly. In my experience, the process frequently begins by invoking her in prayer. Then, conceptualize her fully. Build an image to house her presence, which is not so much a presence as it is the living continuity of all existence. Give all pleasure, all commitment, and all attention to that image and that presence. Let it pull from you every drop of life and awareness. This can be aided by constantly fixing your mental vision on that presence, through internal or external mantra yoga, or both. The result is a sense of elevation and connection coupled with an intense exhaustion. Orgasm might feel dulled or intensely magnified, depending upon the nature of the connection. There is often a pervasive sweat, but it may smell different from your normal sweat.

For most people not accustomed to this kind of sexual mysticism or those not interested in working from a Thelemic perspective, it will be easier to just focus on the marriage with the familiar. The idea of working with the familiar and the goddess simultaneously may reflect Abbe Boullan's concept of celestialization. For Boullan, a mystic could achieve a greater participation with Divine Grace by engaging in sexual relations with an angel or some other spiritually superior force. The magician could also elevate themselves through the charity of engaging in sexual union with a lesser being, like an elemental. By providing the elemental with access to the spiritual state possessed by a human and linking the elemental more closely to Divine Grace, the magician engaged in an act of charity, which also achieved greater Grace and Goodness for the magician. The theology might not appear the same in Thelema, but consider this passage from Liber Tzaddi in the context of celestialization.

> Many have arisen, being wise. They have said "Seek
> out the glittering Image in the place ever golden, and
> unite yourselves with It." Many have arisen, being
> foolish. They have said, "Stoop down unto the darkly
> splendid world, and be wedded to that Blind
> Creature of the Slime." I who am beyond Wisdom

and Folly, arise and say unto you: achieve both weddings! Unite yourselves with both! Beware, beware, I say, lest ye seek after the one and lose the other! My adepts stand upright; their head above the heavens, their feet below the hells. But since one is naturally attracted to the Angel, another to the Demon, let the first strengthen the lower link, the last attach more firmly to the higher. Thus shall equilibrium become perfect. I will aid my disciples; as fast as they acquire this balanced power and joy so faster will I push them.

There is clear justification for considering both the marriage to the goddess and the marriage to the elemental as acts to unite in a single ritual. It creates a continuity from the cosmic un-manifest powers of the heavens through the magician into the manifest material powers of the world. There are mystical considerations here, both for the magician and the spirit. When we say mystical in this case, we refer to the development of the soul and unity with the divine. Those pursuits may not be the goal for everyone. Simply wanting to build a connection with an elemental familiar without the added mystical component is a reasonable choice.

Even without an effort to engage in a mystical marriage of the higher and lower worlds through your own being as the fulcrum, it is still necessary to consider balance. The elementals are described by de Villars as less kind in their affections than some other lovers. Their forces can be viewed as an unguided or unbridled intensity. This is not necessarily an admonition that the elemental will engage in violence or demand that you forsake all others for the elemental. Rather, caution is necessary because any work with elemental powers over an extended period can unbalance your perspective and your character. It is necessary to avoid "impure magnetism" or obsession with a particular force.

Liber Librae, or the Book of Balance, provides some significant advice in this matter. Some of this advice should be considered in regards to spirit work or magical work in general. However, this particular work, due to its intimate nature and the engagement of very material occult powers focused on specific ranges of experience, makes this advice all the more pertinent.

So shalt thou gradually develop the powers of thy
soul, and fit thyself to command the Spirits of the
elements. For wert thou to summon the Gnomes to
pander to thine avarice, thou wouldst no longer
command them, but they would command thee.
Wouldst thou abuse the pure beings of the woods
and mountains to fill thy coffers and satisfy thy
hunger of Gold? Wouldst thou debase the Spirits of
Living Fire to serve thy wrath and hatred? Wouldst
thou violate the purity of the Souls of the Waters to
pander to thy lust of debauchery? Wouldst thou force
the Spirits of the Evening Breeze to minister to thy
folly and caprice? Know that with such desires thou
canst but attract the Weak, not the Strong, and in that
case the Weak will have power over thee.

This passage is late in the text but is a good starting point.
Here, Crowley instructs the magician to develop themselves before
engaging in this work. Someone asked me recently how much of a
relationship you need to have with a spirit before asking for a familiar.
Someone had told them that this only comes after years of work. I
explained that I had recently conjured a demon, and in our first
interaction, the demon attempted to give me a name and seal for a
familiar. William Blake Lodge's familiar was obtained in my first
interaction with Doolas. I don't believe we need extensive interactions
with a spirit before we can ask for a familiar. History does not support
that view either, as many magicians gain a familiar in their first spirit
interaction. I do think that having some experience with spirit work,
or some experience with magic, can be helpful, but not necessary.
    The particular work of obtaining an elemental familiar is
more intimate. Since it has more potential to create an imbalance,
doing more work in preparation is ideal. The passage makes it sound
like you should work to be an ascetic who doesn't want material
desires from the familiar. Instead, we can understand it as telling us
not to obsess over those desires. Don't become so attached to them
that you are distracted by them or lured to distraction and obsession.
Treat the spirit as a partner that can help you in the areas of life it has
the power to help you with, but don't let that power consume you.

Be sure that thy soul is firm and steadfast; for it is by
flattering thy weaknesses that the Weak Ones will

gain power over thee. Humble thyself before thy Self,
yet fear neither man not spirit. Fear is failure, and the
forerunner of failure: and courage is the beginning of
virtue. Therefore fear not the Spirits, but be firm and
courteous with them; for thou hast no right to despise
or revile them; and this too may lead thee astray.
Command and banish them, curse them by the Great
Names if need be; but neither mock nor revile them,
for so assuredly wilt thou be lead into error.

Like the last passage, this one talks about preparing yourself.
But it also talks about interacting with the spirits. If you're nervous or
afraid of this work, take more time to prepare. Work on yourself and
get comfortable with it. Some types of spirit work can be aided by fear.
That is not the case in this operation. Fear, in this case, is not just
about fear of the spirits. What things are you afraid of which make
you vulnerable? Insecurity gives flattery the power to undo you. It also
allows for obsessive attachments that we cling to in order to shield
ourselves from our fear. Since this work is one of balance, you need to
know who you are and stand calmly in the center of your own space.
This centeredness is part of the authority and charisma needed to call
upon spirits. Avoiding fear can also help us avoid abuse. The text
admonishes against despising and reviling the spirits. Elemental spirits
want to help us. We can ask for that help without cruelty. We can
turn to them for things we need, but we shouldn't treat them as a
pinata to beat until prizes fall out.

Therefore, as hath already been said, Establish thyself
firmly in the equilibrium of forces, in the centre of
the Cross of the Elements, that Cross from whose
centre the Creative Word issued in the birth of the
Dawning Universe.

I've always liked this as a way of understanding the ritual
structure of ceremonial magic. When we establish a ritual space, we
do it by establishing balance. From that balance, Spirit arises. Standing
at the center as a vessel for Quintessence or for the Holy Spirit, we are
able to speak and act as the Logos creating the world. The part of our
nature which allows this is the part of our nature that the elementals
are drawn to. This isn't expressly part of the design Crowley
recommends for the marriage to the elemental, but it is definitely

something we should consider as we approach building and performing the ritual. Are we balanced, and have we allowed our spiritual charisma and authority to develop? Have we cleansed and balanced our space and allowed it to connect with the magical nature we need in order to call upon and interact with spirits? Whether we build these elements into our ritual or not, these elements inform how we engage the act of magic.

Elemental spirits are amiable to human interaction. The idea that they desire immortality or completion through being able to share a soul or receive a soul through their relationship with a human easily explains this. Alternatively, the prayers ascribed to the elementals show an intense love for the Creator. The elementals see the Creator in humans, so when we stand with them and pray with them, they rejoice and feel affection for us since an expression of God is joining in their adoration. Crowley explains these sentiments by saying that calling upon the elementals is simple because they are always desirous of salvation. For the elementals, their salvation is found in their interaction with humans.

This desire for human contact makes general magic with the elementals easy. As de Villars suggests and Levi elucidates, we might collect a material expression of their element to draw them to us. Typically, standing in the direction assigned to them, so as to stand with them, and earnestly saying their prayer with them calls upon and endears us to them. Once this is done, they are amenable to performing simple tasks asked of them. Opening with ritual elements used in a ceremonial magic working can provide context and deepen our reception of the experience. Calling upon hierarchical components such as the divine name, the archangel and angel, and the King under which they operate, can also strengthen the call and add an element of conjuration. Still, they are not always necessary.

Like the passage quoted above from Liber Librae, in Crowley's instructions for working with the elemental, he recommends a mix of firmness and kindness. He cautions the magician against the tendency of the elemental to play tricks. This is not normally an issue in simple interactions with the elementals but may be more the case in an ongoing relationship. This warning might be a nod to mythology and folklore with which Crowley and other Golden Dawn members associated the elementals. In addition to the magician's demeanor, he recommends choosing an appropriate elemental. He recommends a docile, lovely, elemental, worthy of love and affection but not so excellent as to distract the magician from attention to loftier spiritual connections. He cautions against the use of planetary spirits in this regard.

Crowley recommends a limit of four elemental familiars. At first glance, this might appear to be an admonition to have one of each element but not more. Crowley instructs the initiate to divide the day and assign each elemental a particular set of hours in which to work with it. The limit of four, assigned to a quadrant of the day, is borrowed from the Sacred Magic. Abraham describes the familiars in Abramelin's system as working this way, four spirits assigned each to a fourth of the day. While these spirits are not the same as those dealt with in Abramelin, and the relationship and means of establishing it are not the same, this indicates that Crowley's thinking is rooted in understanding familiar spirits as he understands their appearance in the grimoires.

While Crowley notes that the elementals play tricks, seemingly associating them with the folklore of hobgoblins and kobolds, which inspired Paracelsus, or the faeries and sirens, which inspired Mathers and Blavatsky, his instructions strongly depart from this association. Crowley recommends utilizing the Enochian Calls to conjure the spirits. This could just be a matter of using the calls because they relate to elements and sub-elements rather than indicating the intended spirit. Crowley goes further and recommends using the tables to determine the spirits, recommends sub-angle spirits, and the use of Enochian hierarchies. In Crowley's approach, we are still working to obtain an elemental familiar, but he is conceptualizing the elemental angels of the Watchtowers as indistinct from the elemental spirits. His commentary reveals that any of the host of Enochian powers could be worked with through sexual union. The risks depend on the magician's skill and the spirits' ability to be disruptive. To avoid risk, Crowley directs the magician to elemental and sub-elemental spirits contained within the tables.

The marriage to the spirit is a combination of physical activity and activity in mental space. Many writers describe these marriages as astral. Victor Anderson presents descriptions of astral sexual encounters in his writings on the witch's soul. Anderson's accounts occur fully on the astral and do not include physical activity. Some historical examples seem to suggest that these encounters occur in dreams. Most authors writing about spirit sex include actual sexual activity, either partnered or masturbatory, during which the magician focuses on the spirit. Modern examples in which the magician masturbates would prevent the magician from transferring consciousness from the body into the astral vehicle. Instead, the magician constructs a mental vehicle for the spirit and invites the spirit to occupy this mental construct. The magician then engages in a sexual act to completion while enrapt in mental copulation with the image of the spirit, which is inhabited by the spirit's essence. The space is imaginal space, but the spirit contact is still driven by actually calling a spirit into that space.

The use of a tool to symbolize the consummation of the relationship is helpful. A bowl or cup connected to the spirit to receive issuance from the magician is the typical assumed tool. A wand or instrument representing the phallus of the spirit penetrating the magician is equally valid. It should be remembered that neither gender nor physical sex is particularly relevant to this relationship. The magician and the spirit both contain both polarities and the range between them. The symbolism used should be that which is convenient to comprehending the act and the consummation of the marriage and does not need to be one reflective of the identity or anatomy of the magician or the spirit.

Our goal in this chapter is to present a working that keeps with the thinking of the framers of the ceremonial magic systems developed in the magical revival. As such, we will present Enochian methods based on Crowleyan and Golden Dawn understandings of Enochian magic. We will depart from this by incorporating Levi and focusing on the more conventional elementals. Levi is still appropriate for creating a ceremonial style ritual since Levi greatly influenced Crowley and the Golden Dawn. For those who prefer an Enochian spirit, it would be easy enough for a magician familiar with Golden Dawn approaches to Enochian magic to modify this method for a spirit derived from the tables.

The conventional elementals are usually presented in the context of Christian and Hermetic Kabbalah. The hierarchies for that system are as follows.

	Earth	Air	Water	Fire
Hebrew Name	Aretz	Ruakh	Maim	Asch
Direction	North	East	West	South
Divine Name	Adonai	Shaddai	Elohim	YHVH
Archangel	Uriel	Raphael	Gabriel	Michael
Angel	Phorlakh	Chassan	Taliahad	Aral
Ruler	Kerub	Ariel	Tharsis	Seraph
King	Ghob	Paralda	Nichsa	Djin
Elemental	Gnomes	Sylphs	Undines	Salamanders
Weapon	Pentacle	Dagger	Cup	Wand

While I prefer the Golden Dawn hierarchy rooted in the Kabbalah, the use of Enochian calls should accompany Enochian divine names and hierarchies. These hierarchies are complex and add the possibility of sub-elements, such as air of water.

Your familiarity and comfort should be considered when deciding which hierarchy to work with. The Hebrew names have a longer association with the conventional elemental spirits. The Enochian names, being the language of the angels, are workable with both Enochian and non-Enochian spirits. The Enochian angels, which provide knowledge of all elemental creatures, exist in the same Sub-Quadrant of each Table. Lon Milo DuQuette explains in Enochian Vision Magick, that Dee's spirit actions never actually assign particular elements to the tables but that this became a core component of the Golden Dawn. According to DuQuette, they derived these assignments from references within the Dee material. I am following the assignments provided by DuQuette for the elemental attributions since the rituals we are using draw on Golden Dawn and Thelemic elements. There are several variations on how these directions, elements, colors, and placement on the table have been interpreted by various authors and magicians. While the elements are not the traditional primary assignment in the Dee material, they are the most important for our purposes.

Element	Air	Water	Earth	Fire
Tablet of Union Name	EXARP	HCOMA	NANTA	BITOM
Divine Banner Name	ORO IBAH AOZPI	MPH ARSL GAIOL	MOR DIAL HCTGA	OIP TEAA PDOCE
King	BATAIVA	RAAGIOS	ICZHHCA	EDLPRNA
Seniors	Abioro, Aaozaif, Htmorda, Ahaozpi, Hipotga, Autotar	Lsrahpm, Saiinou, Laoaxrp, Slgaiol, Ligdisa, Soniznt	Laidrom, Aczinor, Lzinopo, Ahlctga, Liiansa, Ahmlicu	Aaetpio, Adoeoet, Alndvod, Aapdoce, Aarinnap, Anodoin
Invoking Name	Aourrz	Iaaasd	Spmnir	Rizionr
Constraining Name	Aloal	Atapa	Ilpiz	Nrzfm
Angels	Acuca, Nprat, Otroi, Pmzox	Xpacn, Vaasa, Daspi, Rndil	Msmal, Ianba, Izixp, Strim	Adire, Siosp, Panli, Zcrar

The Enochian hierarchy adds pieces that are not present in the hierarchy derived from Golden Dawn Kabbalah. Depending upon the operation done, there are additional groups of angels not listed in the table above. The Tablet of Union is accorded to the element Quintessence and refers to the divine power that unites the entirety of the Great Table. The Divine Names, three names of three, four, and five letters, represent the power of Christ operating through his standard bearers within the Watchtower. The King is the principal angel and overseer of the Watchtower and executes the divine power given to the tower. The seniors are six elders who assess, sit in judgment, and take counsel with one another. Conceivably, they could all be called upon regardless of the Watchtower with which you are working, as they all take counsel together. The Divine Name for invoking calls upon the angels, and the Divine Name for commanding constrains them to obedience. The four angels are the good angels of that quadrant. In this case, these are the angels who have knowledge of the elementals.

Following Crowley's instruction to use the Enochian hierarchy to call one of the good angels adds a certain convenience because it provides a name for the spirit being conjured. Working with the elemental prayers and the community of elementals, in general, will not provide you with a name to use in your ritual. You might ask the spirit if it has a name and seal. The Enochian hierarchy presents an ever more granular series of angels. Arguably, these angels, while elemental, are still celestial beings. If one is expecting to call upon a gnome, whether we consider the gnome to be a kobold, a generic incomplete echo of man that resides in and works with the earth, or the animating divine spark of intellect that resides in matter and forms a grain of sand, then one is not anticipating a celestial being. Magicians who believe the elemental spirits described by Paracelsus, and in the divergent descriptions of later writers, refer to the angels and demons of the grimoires, might believe that the Great Table is the source of the elemental creatures. The spirit Ave explained to Dee and Kelley that the table contained the knowledge of the elemental creatures. This means that the angels of the table can explain the nature, number, and secrets of the elemental creatures, not that the angels are the elemental creatures.

While it is clear that calling upon the angels provided in the Enochian material is not the same as calling upon the elementals, this does not preclude anyone from calling upon the angels. Calling the angels would result in a different type of familiar, and the relationship would be different. Connecting with an angel sexually is attested in the works of Ida Craddock. It is also present in Jewish mythology. The advent of witchcraft occurred when angels took humans as lovers. These angels became fallen angels, and the souls of their children became demons. Demons and fallen angels took witches as lovers and gave them power by working as their familiar spirits in the beliefs of late medieval and early modern Christians.

Neither hierarchy is necessary for calling upon the elementals for simple tasks. In this case, we are looking to powerfully manifest an elemental within the imaginal matter we are building as a vessel for one. This is a more difficult manifestation for the spirit, and it requires interaction with an individual elemental. We do not have a name by which to call an individual elemental while using Levi's prayers. Calling upon the spirits which rule them to open the way for them, empower them to come, select one from their number, and provide that selected exemplary elemental to us, is aided by calling upon the hierarchies which rule them and which fill our sphere of experience with the divine and celestial powers of that element.

The two hierarchies both provide a chain of beings of an elemental nature. The Enochian hierarchy has the benefit of connecting with imagery of a crossroads at the ends of which castles open to allow the flow of elemental power and from which elemental forces flow. The imagery is more natural for our purpose. The Enochian hierarchy also comes with an invocation to use to open the powers of that elemental hierarchy and receive and command the lower spirits of that hierarchy. The design is more suited, both in terms of structure and ritual components, to our purpose.

The hierarchy found in the Golden Dawn Kabbalah might feel like a more natural match to Levi's prayer. The prayer does not utilize any symbolism that specifically ties to those names. Either elemental hierarchy is workable with the prayer. Crowley's instructions do not include the use of the elemental prayer. Since our purpose is to call upon a gnome, sylph, undine or salamander, rather than one of the attendants of the crosses of the sub-quadrants of the Great Table, Levi's prayer should be used. If you prefer to call upon an angel of one of the crosses, do not use Levi's prayer.

Crowley's instructions dictate that the formula of the wand should be used. This does not mean the wand itself is used, but that the spirit is called through the descending powers of the hierarchy. Utilizing this structure can refer to calling upon the names of the hierarchy, designing a ritual where each part of the ritual corresponds to a portion of the hierarchy, or crafting an invocation that has stanzas or phases corresponding to each part of the hierarchy.

The use of the wand is not necessitated by reference to the formula of the wand. The use of the cup might be assumed for this sort of ritual, if one assumes that the magician is the projective party in the union. The comfort or intuition of the magician in relation to the nature of the spirit can determine what role, if any, either party plays in the sexual interaction. If the magician is receiving the sexual power issued by the spirit, then represent the spirit with the wand. If the spirit is receiving the sexual power issued by the magician, then represent the spirit with the cup.

The use of the cup or wand provides a physical corollary for the spirit in the sexual act. The wand represents the phallus, and the cup or bowl represents the womb. The tool should originally rest in contact with some physical manifestation of the element. If working with a bowl, if it is large enough, the physical manifestation of the element can remain in the bowl. This physical manifestation can be kept as part of the material for the spirit-house for the spirit.

When calling upon the spirit, visualize, in full detail, the spirit coming into being. Hold the weapon as you make your invocation. Visualize the spirit in connection with the tool. Strongly assert your will over this vision; determine a unity between the spirit, the image, and the tool. When your invocation is complete, instruct the spirit to inhabit the visualized vessel and the tool. If you are performing the act with a partner, which may be ideal for certain types of interactions, but less so for the establishment of the relationship, the spirit would inhabit the partner rather than a visualization and a tool.

As you perform the sexual act, keep your thoughts fully on the spirit and the visualization of the spirit. Do not try to control the spirit. The spirit is a living, dynamic creature. Allow it to control that part of your imaginal space that it inhabits. Allow your body to feel the interactions and stimulations that the spirit encounter provides. Let yourself become fully present in the space of the interaction. When you climax, do so in connection with the tool, as appropriate to its form. If you are the projective partner, preferably, some fluid should make its way into the bowl or cup. If you are the receptive partner, then the wand should be in contact with you, preferably in some way that receives some moisture from you. This moisture or fluid can then be added to the elemental material.

Crowley's Liber Chanokh presents rituals using the Golden Dawn openings for the temple in the particular grade related to the element. This would be a particularly meaningful way of opening for magicians who have been initiated through the Golden Dawn but less meaningful for those who have not. The rituals present a minimum use of the Enochian hierarchies and materials. Dee's materials provide invocations for various powers and groups of angels given in these hierarchies. His invocations provide the parts to assemble a more traditional ritual for working with these spirits.

Our goal is to present a method that reflects the Victorian English magical systems of the Golden Dawn and Thelema. We would also like to demonstrate options for experimentation and the comingling of modern and traditional forms. The appended rituals will present two approaches. The first utilizes Crowley's Liber Chanokh as a base. The rituals have been reorganized and standardized with the additional necessary parts added. A second set of four rituals is included using a more general opening in the style of ceremonial magic, with Dee's prayers forming the core of the

Enochian interactions. Each style is presented as four complete rituals so that the reader may work from the book directly if they choose to experiment. Because of conflicting assignments of elements and directions, the Dee prayers have been altered to focus on element rather than direction. While Dee's system is directional in nature, we are following the Golden Dawn and Thelemic systems, which are more elemental. This allows us to work using traditional components while maintaining the modern ceremonial context.

If you are looking to work with an elemental as a familiar by forming a sexual link, but either the ceremonial approaches or the use of Enochian are not appealing to you, create a ritual which does appeal to you. These are examples based on instruction drawn from the Victorian occult revival. If you want to design a ritual that looks more like a grimoire ritual, and uses grimoire hierarchies, prayers, and implements in conjunction with the elemental prayers, that could be a great option. Working with these spirits in a Wiccan context or a non-Enochian ceremonial magic context is fully workable as well. The included rituals are examples of two ways to approach this goal within a modern ceremonial magic approach. Use these examples to do this particular act of magic, or use these examples as guides in assembling your own approach. Like many of our other examples, they are an invitation to experiment.

r	Z	i	l	a	f	A	y	t	l	p	a	e	T	a	O	A	d	v	p	t	D	n	i	m
a	r	d	Z	a	i	d	p	a	L	a	m	o	a	l	c	o	o	r	o	m	e	b	b	
c	z	o	n	s	a	r	o	Y	a	u	b	x	T	a	g	c	o	n	z	i	n	l	G	m
T	o	i	T	t	x	o	P	a	c	o	C	a	n	h	o	d	D	i	a	l	a	a	o	c
S	i	g	a	s	o	n	r	b	z	n	h	r	f	a	t	A	x	i	v	V	s	P	s	N
f	m	o	n	d	a	T	d	i	a	r	i	p	S	a	a	i	z	a	a	r	V	r	o	i
o	r	o	i	b	A	h	a	o	s	P	i		m	p	h	a	r	s	l	g	a	i	c	h
c	N	a	b	a	V	i	x	g	a	z	d	h	M	a	m	g	l	o	i	n	L	i	r	x
O	i	i	i	t	T	P	a	l	O	a	i		o	l	a	a	D	a	g	a	T	a	p	a
A	b	a	m	o	o	o	a	C	u	c	a	C	p	a	L	c	o	i	d	x	P	a	c	n
N	a	o	c	O	T	t	n	p	r	a	T	o	n	d	a	z	N	z	i	V	a	a	s	a
o	c	a	n	m	a	g	o	t	r	o	i	m	i	i	d	P	o	n	s	d	A	s	p	i
S	h	i	a	l	r	a	p	m	z	o	x	a	x	r	i	n	h	t	a	r	n	d	i	L
m	o	t	i	b			a	T	n	a	n		n	a	n	T	a			b	i	t	o	m
b	O	a	Z	a	R	o	p	h	a	R	a	a	d	o	n	p	a	T	d	a	n	V	a	a
u	N	n	a	x	o	P	S	o	n	d	n	o	l	o	a	G	e	o	o	b	a	v	a	
a	i	g	r	a	n	o	a	m	a	g	g	m	O	P	a	m	n	o	O	G	m	d	n	m
o	r	p	m	n	i	n	g	b	e	a	l	o	a	b	l	s	T	e	d	e	c	a	o	p
r	s	O	n	i	z	i	r	l	e	m	u	C	s	c	m	i	a	o	n	A	m	l	o	x
i	z	i	n	r	C	z	i	a	M	h	l	h	V	a	r	s	G	d	L	b	r	i	a	p
M	O	r	d	i	a	l	h	C	t	G	a		o	i	P	t	e	a	a	p	D	o	c	e
R	O	c	a	m	c	h	i	a	s	o	m	p	p	s	v	a	c	n	r	Z	i	r	Z	a
A	r	b	i	z	m	i	i	l	p	i	z		S	i	o	d	a	o	i	n	r	z	f	m
O	p	a	n	a	B	a	m	S	m	a	L	r	d	a	l	t	T	d	n	a	d	i	r	e
d	O	l	o	F	i	n	i	a	n	b	a	a	d	i	x	o	m	o	n	s	i	o	s	p
r	x	p	a	o	c	s	i	z	i	x	P	x	O	o	D	p	z	i	A	P	a	n	l	i
a	x	t	i	r	V	a	s	t	r	i	m	e	r	g	o	a	n	n	P	A	C	r	a	r

Enochian Great Table. The quadrants are originally assigned directionally. Following the Golden Dawn, they are assigned elementally as follows. Top left, Air, top right, Water, bottom left, Earth, bottom right, Fire.

XXVII
Rituals to Marry an Elemental Familiar in the Context of Enochian Sex Magic

These rituals present two approaches to "marrying" an elemental to acquire it as a familiar. These approaches both draw on elements of modern ceremonial magic. Both utilize an interpretation of the Enochian materials drawing from the Golden Dawn and Thelemic sources. The first focuses primarily on modern sources and utilizes the rituals of Crowley's Liber Chanokh as a basis. The second ritual incorporates a ceremonial magic opening and elements while also utilizings prayers written by John Dee. These present an approach that combines the aesthetic and style of more traditional conjuration with a context and theoretical approach drawn from more contemporary ceremonial magic.

Both sets of rituals present the same ritual in four variants each. The text and tools, vary between each iteration based on the element the ritual conjures. The names and some prayers change between the different elements. Instead of presenting a single template, and then a lectionary for the changeable parts, the text presents each variation so that practical magicians can work directly from the text. This allows the magician to avoid the awkwardness of flipping back and forth between pages, or swapping back and forth between different books.

First Group: Rituals Drawn from Crowley's Liber Chanokh

The Pentagrams

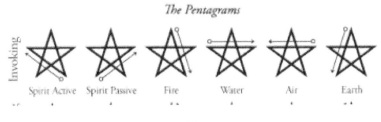

Invoking

Spirit Active   Spirit Passive   Fire   Water   Air   Earth

Air

The magician is dressed in a robe or is nude. They have bathed before the ritual. The magician is anointed, thoroughly, with oils appropriate to the element.

The temple is dim, lit by candlelight, preferably. In the center of the temple is an altar. Incense appropriate to the element is burning in the temple.

On the altar is a large Air Tablet which covers the surface. The items for the ritual are on the Tablet. These include:

The dagger
A scrying crystal
A bowl of water
A lit candle
Paper and a pen
A bowl, cup, or wand, referred to as the implement
A material item representing the element, referred to as the material

The magician circumambulates the temple first with fire, then with water. After returning to the altar the magician says:

The temple is cleansed!

The magician makes the Sign of Shu Supporting the Sky. This posture is made by glancing upward with the arms extended to the sides and the hands elevated and cupped as if holding something up.

The magician knocks once and says:

Let us adore the Lord and King of Air! Shaddai El Chai! Almighty and ever-living One, be Thy Name ever magnified in the Life of All. Amen!

The magician makes the sign of Shu.

The magician makes the Invoking Spirit Active Pentagram vibrating these names

Eheieh. AGLA. EXARP.

The magician makes the Invoking Pentagram of Air and vibrate these names:

IHVH. Shaddai El Chai

The magician says:

And Elohim said Let us make Adam in our own image, after our likeness, and let them have dominion over the fowls of the air. In the Names of YHVH and of Shaddai El Chai, Spirits of Air, adore your Creator!

The magician traces the sign of Aquarius in the air with the dagger and says:

In the name of Raphael and in the Sign of the Man, Spirits of Air, adore your Creator!

The magician traces a cross in the air with the dagger and says:

In the Names and Letters of the Great Eastern Quadrangle, Spirits of Air, adore your Creator!

The magician holds the dagger above their head and says:

In the Three great Secret Names of God, ORO IBAH AOZPI that are borne upon the Banners of the East, Spirits of Air, adore your Creator!

The magician lowers then raises the dagger again and says:

In the Name of BATAIVAH, great King of the East, Spirits of Air, adore your Creator!

The magician replaces the dagger on the altar and says:

In the Name of Shaddai AL Chai, I declare that the Spirits of Air have been duly invoked.

The magician knocks in a battery of three knocks, followed by three, and then three again.

The magician uses the third Enochian Key to activate the Air Tablet:

MICMA GOHO PIAD ZIR COMSELH AZIEN BIAB OS LON-DOH. NORZ CHIS OTHIL GIGIPAH UND-L CHIS TA PU-IM Q MOS-PLEH TELOCH QUI-I-N TOLTORG CHIS I-CHIS-GE, M OZIEN DST BRGDA OD TORZUL I-LI E OL BALZARG OD AALA THILN OS NE-TA-AB DLUGA VOMSARG LONSA CAP-MI-ALI VORS CLA HOMIL COCASB, FAFEN IZIZOP OD MIINOAG DE GNE-TAAB VAUN NA-NA-E-EL: PANPIR MALPIRGI CAOSG PILD NOAN UNALAH BALT OD VOOAN. DO-O-I-AP MAD GOHOLOR GOHUS AMIRAN. MICMA IEHUSOZ CA-CA-COM OD DO-O-A-IN NOAR MI-CA-OLZ A-AI-OM. CASARMG GOHIA: ZACAR, UNIGLAG OD IM-UA-MAR PUGO PLAPLI ANANAEL QAAN.
MICMA GOHO PIAD ZIR COMSELH AZIEN BIAB OS LON-DOH. NORZ CHIS OTHIL GIGIPAH UND-L CHIS TA PU-IM Q MOS-PLEH TELOCH QUI-I-N TOLTORG CHIS I-CHIS-GE, M OZIEN DST BRGDA OD TORZUL I-LI E OL BALZARG OD AALA THILN OS NE-TA-AB DLUGA VOMSARG LONSA CAP-MI-ALI VORS CLA HOMIL COCASB, FAFEN IZIZOP OD MIINOAG DE GNE-TAAB VAUN NA-NA-E-EL: PANPIR MALPIRGI CAOSG PILD NOAN UNALAH BALT OD VOOAN. DO-O-I-AP MAD GOHOLOR GOHUS AMIRAN. MICMA IEHUSOZ CA-CA-COM OD DO-O-A-IN NOAR MI-CA-OLZ A-AI-OM. CASARMG GOHIA: ZACAR, UNIGLAG OD IM-UA-MAR PUGO PLAPLI ANANAEL QAAN.

The magician uses the ninth Enochian Key to activate the Fire of Air Quadrant:

MI-CA-OLI BRANSG PRGEL NAPTA IALPOR DS BRIN EFAFAFE P VONPHO OLANI OD OBZA: SOBCA VPAAH CHIS TATAN OD TRANAN BALYE ALAR LUSDA SOBOLN OD CHIS HOLQ CNOQUODI CIAL. VNAL ALDON MOM CAOSGO TA LAS OLLOR GNAY LIMLAL: AMMA CHIIS SOBCA MADRID ZCHIS, OOANOAN CHIIS AUINY DRILPI CAOSGIN OD OD BUTMONI PARM ZUMVI CNILA: DAZIZ ETHAMZ A CHILDAO OD MIRC CHIS PIDIAI COLLAL VLCININ A-SOBAM VCIM. BAGLE? IADBALTOH CHIRLAN PAR NIISO OD IP OFAFAFE BAGLE ACOSASB ICORSCA VNIG BLIOR.

The magician gazes into the crystal sphere and says:

In the names, ORO IBAH AOZPI, BATAIVA, Aourrz, and Aloal, I call upon Acuca, Nprat, Otroi, and Pmzox, appear in this crystal and give me the name and sign of a Sylph that I might keep as a familiar spirit. Bring forth this spirit from amongst their number when I call upon them.

This is repeated until the vision arrives.

When the name and seal are provided, the magician writes them down and places them on the altar with the implement and the material. The magician places a hand over these items and begins to strongly visualize their elemental forming as they call upon the elementals. The magician says:

Spirit of light! Spirit of wisdom! Whose breath gives and takes away again the forms of all things! Thou, in whose presence the life of being is a shadow which changes, and a vapor which passes away. Thou who ascendest the clouds and movest on the wing of the winds. When thou breathes! forth, infinite spaces are peopled! When thou inhalest, all that comes from thee returns to thee! Endless movement in eternal stability, be thou eternally blest! We praise thee and bless thee in the changing empire of created light, of shadows, of reflections and of images; and we long unceasingly for thine immutable and imperishable light. Let the ray of thy intelligence and the heat of thy love penetrate even to us; then what is movable will become fixed; the shadow will become a body; the spirit of the air will become a soul; the dream will become a thought, and we shall no longer be borne away by the tempest, but shall hold the bridle of the winged steeds of the morning, and shall direct the course of the evening winds that we may fly into thy presence. O spirit of spirits! O eternal soul of souls! O imperishable breath of life! O creative inspiration. O mouth which inspires and respires the existence of all beings in the flux and reflux of thy eternal Word, which is the divine ocean of movement and of truth. Amen!

Once the prayer is finished and the elementals have arrived, continue your visualization, and say:

Spirit, N, by your name and seal, come forth from your company. Join with me, stand beside me, and be complete. Stay with me as a lover and friend, be familiar unto me, and labor to accomplish those things I desire as I provide you with a place to reside, the completeness you seek, and the pleasure of a human lover. Fill these objects, and join with the image I hold of you that I may know you in this moment and consummate our pact.

When the spirit is adequately joined to the vision, the magician reclines, sits, or lays down as they desire. The magician pleasures themself while fixed upon their vision of their spirit partner, with whom they share the pleasure of the act. The climax of the act should result in contact with the implement, sweat or sexual fluids should be combined with the material, which will be used to construct the spirit house with the name and seal.

When all is finished, the magician repeats the battery of knocks and says:

I declare this ritual complete. The spirit, N, and I are joined together, let all other spirits depart unto their rightful places in peace to come again in peace when called.

Water

The magician is dressed in a robe or is nude. They have bathed before the ritual. The magician is anointed, thoroughly, with oils appropriate to the element.

The temple is dim, lit by candlelight, preferably. In the center of the temple is an altar. Incense appropriate to the element is burning in the temple.

On the altar is a large Water Tablet which covers the surface. The items for the ritual are on the Tablet. These include:

The cup
A scrying crystal
A bowl of water
A lit candle
Paper and a pen
A bowl, cup, or wand, referred to as the implement
A material item representing the element, referred to as the material

The magician circumambulates the temple first with fire, then with water. After returning to the altar the magician says:

The temple is cleansed!

The magician makes the Sign of The Goddess Auramoth. This posture is made by bringing the hands together in a downward triangle placed before the pelvis.

The magician knocks once and says:

Let us adore the Lord and King of Water! Elohim Tzabaoth! Elohim of Hosts! Glory be to the Ruach Elohim which moved upon the Face of the Waters of Creation! AMEN!

The magician makes the sign of The Goddess Auramoth.

The magician makes the Invoking Spirit Passive Pentagram vibrating these names:

Eheieh. AGLA. HCOMA.

The magician makes the Invoking Pentagram of Water and vibrate these names:

El. Elohim Tzveot.

The magician says:

And Elohim said: Let us make Adam in Our image; and let them have dominion over the Fish of the Sea! In the Name of El, Strong and Powerful, and in the name of Elohim Tzveot, Spirits of Water, adore your Creator!

The magician traces the Sign of Kerubic Eagle in the air with the cup and says:

In the name of Gabriel and in the sign of the Eagle, Spirits of Water, adore your Creator!

The magician traces a cross in the air with the cup and says:

In all the Names and Letters of the Great Quadrangle of the West, Spirits of Water, adore your Creator!

The magician holds the cup above their head and says:

In the three great Secret Names of God MPH ARSL GAIOL that are borne upon the Banners of the West, Spirits of Water, adore your Creator!

The magician lowers then raises the cup again and says:

In the Name of RAAGIOSEL, great King of the West, Spirits of Water, adore your Creator!

The magician replaces the dagger on the altar and says:

In the name of Elohim Tzveot, I declare that the Spirits of Water have been duly invoked.

The magician knocks in a battery of one knock, followed by three, then three again, and finally one again.

The magician uses the fourth Enochian Key to activate the Water Tablet:

OTHIL LASDI BABAGE OD DORPHA GOHOL G-CHISGE AVAVAGO CORMP PD DSONF VIV DI-V CASARMI OALI MAPM SOBAM AG CORMPO C-RP-L CASARG CROODZI CHIS OD VGEG DST CAPIMALI CHIS CAPIMAON LONSHIN CHIS TA LO CLA: TORGU NOR QUASAHI, OD F CAOSAGA: BAGLE ZIRENAIAD, DSI OD APALA. DO-O-A-IP Q-A-AL ZACAR, OD ZAMRAN OBELISONG REST-EL AAF NOR-MO-LAP

The magician uses the twelfth Enochian Key to activate the Fire of Water Quadrant:

NONCI DSONF BABAGE OD CHIS OB HUBIAO TIBIBP, ALLAR ATRAAH OD EF. DRIX FAFEN MIAN AR E NAY OVOF SOBA DOOAIN AAI I VONPH ZACAR GOHUS, OD ZAMRAM, ODO CICLE QAA. ZORGE, LAP ZIRDO NOCO MAD, HOATH IAIDA

The magician gazes into the crystal sphere and says:

In the names MPH ARSL GAIOL, RAAGIOS, Iaaasd, and Atapa, I call upon Xpacn, Vaasa, Daspi, Rndil, appear in this crystal and give me the name and sign of an Undine that I might keep as a familiar spirit. Bring forth this spirit from amongst their number when I call upon them.

This is repeated until the vision arrives.

When the name and seal are provided, the magician writes them down and places them on the altar with the implement and the material. The magician places a hand over these items and begins to strongly visualize their elemental forming as they call upon the elementals. The magician says:

Terrible king of the sea! Thou who boldest the keys of the cataracts of heaven, and who enclosest the subterranean waters in the hollow places of the earth! King of the deluge and of rains, of springtime! Thou who openest the sources of streams and fountains! Thou who commandest the moisture (which is like the blood of the earth) to become the sap of plants! We adore and invoke thee! Speak to us, ye moving and changeable creatures! Speak to us in the great commotions of the sea, and we will tremble before thee. Speak to us also in the murmur of the limpid waters, and we will desire thy love. O immensity in which all the rivers of being lose themselves, which ever spring up anew in us! O ocean of infinite perfections! Height which beholdeth thee in the depth! Depth which breathes thee forth in the height! Bring us to the true life through intelligence and love! Lead us to immortality through sacrifice, in order that one day we may be found worthy to offer thee water, blood, and tears, for the remission of sins. Amen.

Once the prayer is finished and the elementals have arrived, continue your visualization, and say:

Spirit, N, by your name and seal, come forth from your company. Join with me, stand beside me, and be complete. Stay with me as a lover and friend, be familiar unto me, and labor to accomplish those things I desire as I provide you with a place to reside, the completeness you seek, and the pleasure of a human lover. Fill these objects, and join with the image I hold of you that I may know you in this moment and consummate our pact.

When the spirit is adequately joined to the vision, the magician reclines, sits, or lays down as they desire. The magician pleasures themself while fixed upon their vision of their spirit partner, with whom they share the pleasure of the act. The climax of the act should result in contact with the implement, sweat or sexual fluids should be combined with the material, which will be used to construct the spirit house with the name and seal.

When all is finished, the magician repeats the battery of knocks and says:

I declare this ritual complete. The spirit, N, and I are joined together, let all other spirits depart unto their rightful places in peace to come again in peace when called.

Earth

The magician is dressed in a robe or is nude. They have bathed before the ritual. The magician is anointed, thoroughly, with oils appropriate to the element.

The temple is dim, lit by candlelight, preferably. In the center of the temple is an altar. Incense appropriate to the element is burning in the temple.

On the altar is a large Earth Tablet which covers the surface. The items for the ritual are on the Tablet. These include:

The disk or pentacle
A scrying crystal
A bowl of water
A lit candle
Paper and a pen
A bowl, cup, or wand, referred to as the implement
A material item representing the element, referred to as the material

The magician circumambulates the temple first with fire, then with water. After returning to the altar the magician says:

The temple is cleansed!

The magician makes the Sign of the God Set Fighting. This posture is made by staring forward with the right arm raised, the hand in a first, and the left arm extended downwards with the pointer finger pointing at the ground. The right foot is placed slightly forward as if taking a step.

The magician knocks once and says:

Let us adore the Lord and King of Earth! Adonai ha Aretz, Adonai Melehk, unto Thee be the Kingdom, the Sceptre, and the Splendour: Malkuth, Geburah, Gedulah, The Rose of Sharon and the Lily of the Valley, Amen!

The magician makes the Sign of Set Fighting.

The magician makes the Invoking Spirit Passive Pentagram vibrating these names:

Eheieh. AGLA. NANTA.

The magician makes the Invoking Pentagram of Earth and vibrates these names:

Adonai Melekh

The magician says:

And Elohim said: Let us make Man in Our own image; and let them have dominion over the Fish of the Sea and over the Fowl of the Air; and over every creeping thing that creepeth upon the Earth. And the Elohim created ATh-h-ADAM, in the image of the Elohim created They them; male and female created They them. In the Name of Adonai Melekh, and of the Bride and Queen of the Kingdom; Spirits of Earth, adore your Creator!

The magician traces the sign of Taurus in the air with the disk and says:

In the Name of Uriel, great archangel of Earth, Spirits of Earth, adore your Creator!

The magician traces a cross in the air with the disk and says:

In the Names and Letters of the Great Northern Quadrangle, Spirits of Earth, adore your Creator!

The magician holds the disk above their head and says:

In the three great secret Names of God, MOR, DIAL, HCTGA, that are borne upon the Banners of the North, Spirits of Earth, adore your Creator!

The magician lowers then raises the disk again and says:

In the name of IC-ZOD-HEH-CA, great king of the North, Spirits of Earth, adore your Creator!

The magician replaces the dagger on the altar and says:

In the Name of Adonai Ha-Aretz, I declare that the Spirits of Earth have been duly invoked.

The magician knocks in a battery of four knocks, followed by three, then two, and finally one.

The magician uses the fifth Enochian Key to activate the Earth Tablet:

SAPAH ZIMII DU-I-V OD NOAS TA-QA-A-NIS ADROCH DORPHAL CA OSG OD FAONTS PERIPSOL TABLIOR CASARM AMIPZI NAZARTH AF OD DLUGAR ZIZOP Z-LIDA CAOSGI TOLTORGI OD Z-CHIS ESIASCH L TAVIU OD IAAD THILD DS PERAL HUBAR PEOAL SOBA CORMFA CHIS TA LA VLS OD Q-CO-CASB. CA NIIS OD DARBS Q-A-AS, FETH-AR-ZI OD BLIORA, IA-IAL ED-NAS CICLES: BAGLE? GEIAD I L

The magician uses the fifteenth Enochian Key to activate the Fire of Earth Quadrant:

ILS TABAAN LIAPRT CASARMAN VPAAHI CHIS DARG DSOADO CAOSGI ORSCOR DS OMAX MONASCI BAEOUIB OD EMETGIS IAIADIX. ZACAR OD ZAMRAN, ODO CICLE QAA, ZORGE, LAP ZIRDO NOCO MAD, HOATH IAIDA

The magician gazes into the crystal sphere and says:

In the names MOR DIAL HCTGA, ICZHHCA, Spmnir, and Ilpiz, I call upon Msmal, Ianba, Izixp, and Strim, appear in this crystal and give me the name and sign of a Gnome that I might keep as a familiar spirit. Bring forth this spirit from amongst their number when I call upon them.

This is repeated until the vision arrives.

When the name and seal are provided, the magician writes them down and places them on the altar with the implement and the material. The magician places a hand over these items and begins to strongly visualize their elemental forming as they call upon the elementals. The magician says:

Invisible King who has taken the earth as a support, and who has dug abysses in order to fill them with the omnipotence! Thou whose name makest the arches of the world tremble! Thou who makest the seven metals circulate in the veins of stone; Monarch of seven luminaries! Rewarder of subterranean workmen! bring us to the desirable air and to the kingdom of light. We watch and work without respite. We seek and hope by the twelve stones of the Holy City, for the talismans which are buried by the magnetic nail which passes through the center of the earth. Lord! Lord! Lord! Have pity upon those who suffer! Enlarge our hearts! Let us be free and raise up our heads! Exalt us! O stability and movement! O Day invested by night! O Darkness veiled in light! O Master who never retainest the wages of thy workmen! O silvery whiteness! O Golden Splendor! O Crown of Diamonds, living and melodious! Thou who bearest the sky upon thy finger, like a ring of sapphire! Thou who hidest under the earth, in the kingdom of gems, the wonderful seed of stars! All hail! Reign; and be the Eternal Dispenser of riches, of which thou hast made us the guardians. Amen.

Once the prayer is finished and the elementals have arrived, continue your visualization, and say:

Spirit, N, by your name and seal, come forth from your company. Join with me, stand beside me, and be complete. Stay with me as a lover and friend, be familiar unto me, and labor to accomplish those things I desire as I provide you with a place to reside, the completeness you seek, and the pleasure of a human lover. Fill these objects, and join with the image I hold of you that I may know you in this moment and consummate our pact.

When the spirit is adequately joined to the vision, the magician reclines, sits, or lays down as they desire. The magician pleasures themself while fixed upon their vision of their spirit partner, with whom they share the pleasure of the act. The climax of the act should result in contact with the implement, sweat or sexual fluids should be combined with the material, which will be used to construct the spirit house with the name and seal.

When all is finished, the magician repeats the battery of knocks and says:

I declare this ritual complete. The spirit, N, and I are joined together, let all other spirits depart unto their rightful places in peace to come again in peace when called.

Fire

The magician is dressed in a robe or is nude. They have bathed before the ritual. The magician is anointed, thoroughly, with oils appropriate to the element.

The temple is dim, lit by candlelight, preferably. In the center of the temple is an altar. Incense appropriate to the element is burning in the temple.

On the altar is a large Fire Tablet which covers the surface. The items for the ritual are on the Tablet. These include:

The wand
A scrying crystal
A bowl of water
A lit candle
Paper and a pen
A bowl, cup, or wand, referred to as the implement
A material item representing the element, referred to as the material

The magician circumambulates the temple first with fire, then with water. After returning to the altar the magician says:

The temple is cleansed!

The magician makes the Sign of Thoum-aesh-neith. This posture is made by glancing upward and making an upward triangle with the hands placed above the forehead.

The magician knocks once and says:

Let us adore the Lord and King of Fire! YHVH Tzveot! Blessed be Thou! The Leader of Armies is Thy Name! AMEN!

The magician makes the Sign of Thoum-aesh-neith.

The magician makes the Invoking Spirit Active Pentagram vibrating these names

Eheieh. AGLA. BITOM.

The magician makes the Invoking Pentagram of Fire and vibrates these names:

Elohim. YHVH Tzveot.

The magician traces the sign of Leo in the air with the wand and says:

In the name of Michael, archangel of Fire, Spirits of Fire, adore your Creator!

The magician traces a cross in the air with the dagger and says:

In the Names and Letters of the Great Southern Quadrangle, Spirits of Fire, adore your Creator!

The magician holds the wand above their head and says:

In the three Secret names of God, OIP TEAA PDOCE, that are born upon the banners of the South, Spirits of Fire, adore your Creator!

The magician lowers then raises the wand again and says:

In the Name of EDELPERNA, great King of the South, Spirits of Fire, adore your Creator!

The magician replaces the dagger on the altar and says:

In the Name of YHVH Tzveot, I declare that the Spirits of Fire have been duly invoked.

The magician knocks in a battery of three knocks, followed by one, and then three again.

The magician uses the sixth Enochian Key to activate the Fire Tablet:

GAH S DIU CHIS EM MICALZO PILZIN SOBAM EL HARG MIR BABALON OD OBLOC SAMVELG DLUGAR MALPRG ARCAOSGI OD ACAM CANAL SOBOLZAR F-BLIARD CAOSGI OD CHIS ANETAB OD MIAM TA VIV OD D.

DARSAR SOL-PETH BIEN: BRITA OD ZACAM G-MICALZO, SOB-HA-HATH TRIAN LU-IA HE ODECRIN MAD Q-A-A ON

There is no second call, as the initial call activated the full Fire Tablet, including the Fire of Fire Quadrant.

The magician gazes into the crystal sphere and says:

In the names OIP TEAA PDOCE, EDLPRNA, Rizionr, and Nrzfm, I call upon Adire, Siosp, Panli, and Zcrar, appear in this crystal and give me the name and sign of a Salamander that I might keep as a familiar spirit. Bring forth this spirit from amongst their number when I call upon them.

This is repeated until the vision arrives.

When the name and seal are provided, the magician writes them down and places them on the altar with the implement and the material. The magician places a hand over these items and begins to strongly visualize their elemental forming as they call upon the elementals. The magician says:

Immortal, eternal, ineffable and uncreated Father of all things I who are borne upon the incessantly rolling chariot of Worlds which are always turning; Ruler of the ethereal immensity where the throne of thy power is elevated; from whose height thy dread-inspiring eyes discover all things, and thy exquisite and sacred ears hear all; Listen to thy children whom thou hast loved from the beginning of the ages; for thy golden, great, and eternal majesty is resplendent above the world and the starry heavens. Thou art raised above them O sparkling fire! There thou dost illumine and support thyself by thine own splendor; and there comes forth from thine essence overflowing streams of light which nourish thine infinite spirit. That infinite spirit nourishes all things, and renders this inexhaustible treasure of substance always ready for the generation which fashions it and which receives in itself the forms with which thou hast impregnated it from the beginning. From this spirit those most holy kings who surround thy throne, and who compose thy court, derive their origin. O Father Universal! Only One! O Father of blessed mortals and immortals! Thou hast specially created powers who are marvelously like thine eternal thought and adorable essence. Thou hast established them superior to the angels who announce to the world thy wishes. Finally thou hast created us in the third rank in our elementary empire. There our continual employment is to praise thee and adore thy wishes. There we incessantly burn with the desire of possessing thee, O Father! O Mother! the most tender of all mothers! O admirable archetype of maternity and pure love! O Son, the flower of sons! O Form of all forms; soul, spirit, harmony and number of all things. Amen.

Once the prayer is finished and the elementals have arrived, continue your visualization, and say:

Spirit, N, by your name and seal, come forth from your company. Join with me, stand beside me, and be complete. Stay with me as a lover and friend, be familiar unto me, and labor to accomplish those things I desire as I provide you with a place to reside, the completeness you seek, and the pleasure of a human lover. Fill these objects, and join with the image I hold of you that I may know you in this moment and consummate our pact.

When the spirit is adequately joined to the vision, the magician reclines, sits, or lays down as they desire. The magician pleasures themself while fixed upon their vision of their spirit partner, with whom they share the pleasure of the act. The climax of the act should result in contact with the implement, sweat or sexual fluids should be combined with the material, which will be used to construct the spirit house with the name and seal.

When all is finished, the magician repeats the battery of knocks and says:

I declare this ritual complete. The spirit, N, and I are joined together, let all other spirits depart unto their rightful places in peace to come again in peace when called.

Second Group: Golden Dawn/Thelemic Inspired Rituals Utilizing John Dee's Conjurations

Air

The magician is dressed in a robe. They have bathed before the ritual. The magician is anointed, thoroughly, with oils appropriate to the element.

The temple is dark and unlit. In the center of the temple is an altar. Incense appropriate to the element is burning in the temple. There are candles at each of the cardinal points of the temple.

On the altar is a large Air Tablet which covers the surface. The items for the ritual are on the Tablet. These include:

The Ring of Solomon
The sword for tracing in the air
A scrying crystal
A bowl of water
An unlit candle
Paper and a pen
A bowl, cup, or wand, referred to as the implement
A material item representing the element, referred to as the material

The magician raises their hands to the heavens and says:

Holy Art Thou Lord of the Universe
Holy Art Thou, Whom Nature Has Not Formed
Holy Art Thou, Vast and Mighty One
Lord of Light and of Darkness

The magician lights the initial candle on the altar. Holding up the candle the magician says:

Come, O fire, which is the life of all mortal things. Come at this time. God reigns. O come, for he is one. He reigns and is the life of all living things.

The magician replaces the candle and holds up the bowl of water and breathes upon it saying:

Come, I say, come at this time. Come, O King, King, King of the waters. Your power is great but my power is greater. God gave life to all creatures.

The magician circumambulates the temple, sprinkling water as they do so. While doing this they say:

So therefore first the Priest who governs the works of fire, must sprinkle with the lustral waters of the loud resounding sea.

When they return to the altar they replace the bowl and they take the candle. They circumambulate the temple, in each quarter they make a cross with the candle and light a candle in that quarter. As they do this they say:

And when all the phantoms have vanished, you shall see that holy and formless fire, that darts and flashes through the hidden depths of the Universe, hear now the Voice of Fire.

The magician takes the ring from the altar and before putting it on, kisses it three times saying:

Without this ring you shall do nothing. Blessed be his Name that compasses all things. Wonders are in him and his Name is wonderful. His Name works wonders from generation to generation.

The magician stands at the altar and looks up to Heaven praying:

YHVH Tzveot, I, [NAME], Your humble servant, most earnestly invoke and call upon your divine power, wisdom, and goodness. I humbly and faithfully seek your favor and assistance to me in all my deeds, words, and thoughts, and in the promoting, procuring, and mingling of your praise, honor, and glory.

Through these, your twelve mystical Names: Oro, Ibah, Aozpi, Mor, Dral, Hctga, Oip, Teaa, Pdoce, Mph, Arsl, Gaiol, I conjure and pray most zealously to your divine and omnipotent majesty, that all your angelic spirits might be called from any and all parts of the universe,

*or at any time in my life, through the special domination and
controlling power of your holy Names.*

*Let them come most quickly to me. Let them appear visibly, friendly,
and peacefully to me. Let them remain visible according to my will.
Let them vanish from me and from my sight when I so request. Let
them give reverence and obedience before you and your 12 mystical
Names. I command that they happily satisfy me in all things and at all
times in my life, by accomplishing each and every one of my petitions-
if not by one means, then by another-goodly, virtuously, and perfectly,
with an excellent and thorough completeness, according to their
virtues and powers, both general and unique, and by Your united
ministry and office, Oh God . AMEN. Through you, Jesu Christe,
AMEN*

The magician knocks on the altar, and traces the Spirit Active
Invoking Pentagram, and the Air Invoking Pentagram while intoning:

EXARP HCOMA NANTA BITOM

*MICMA GOHO PIAD ZIR COMSELH AZIEN BIAB OS LON-
DOH. NORZ CHIS OTHIL GIGIPAH UND-L CHIS TA PU-IM
Q MOS-PLEH TELOCH QUI-I-N TOLTORG CHIS I-CHIS-GE,
M OZIEN DST BRGDA OD TORZUL I-LI E OL BALZARG
OD AALA THILN OS NE-TA-AB DLUGA VOMSARG LONSA
CAP-MI-ALI VORS CLA HOMIL COCASB, FAFEN IZIZOP OD
MIINOAG DE GNE-TAAB VAUN NA-NA-E-EL: PANPIR
MALPIRGI CAOSG PILD NOAN UNALAH BALT OD
VOOAN. DO-O-I-AP MAD GOHOLOR GOHUS AMIRAN.
MICMA IEHUSOZ CA-CA-COM OD DO-O-A-IN NOAR MI-
CA-OLZ A-AI-OM. CASARMG GOHIA: ZACAR, UNIGLAG
OD IM-UA-MAR PUGO PLAPLI ANANAEL QAAN.*

The magician makes a cross over the altar and says:

*Oh You Six Seniors of the Watchtower of Air, powerful and faithful
to the omnipotent God of our ministry. In the name of the same
God, Oro, Ibah, Aozpi, I say to you, ABIORO, AAOZAIF,
HTMORDA, HAOZPI, HIPOTGA, AUTOTAR, through the
divine Name by which you arc particularly bound, the angelic Name
BATAIVA, I, [Name] , a faithful servant of the omnipotent God,*

amicably, earnestly, and confidently demand and beseech you to appear placidly, affably, and favorably before me, immediately and without delay, and henceforth at any time I wish, through all the remaining journey of my life, I beseech all of you, some of you, or whichever of you I name, united or divided, to grant all my petitions, and especially grant me knowledge and judgment in human affairs, and in all other things that are assigned to your Office and Ministry and that are accomplished by you, one and many. I command you to appear, to perform, and to complete, goodly, plainly, intelligibly, and perfectly, according to your Virtue, Power, and Office, and according to the capacity of your Ministry, entrusted and committed to you by the omnipotent God, AMEN. Through the sacred Name of God BATAIVA, AMEN.

The magician knocks on the altar and intones:

ORO IBAH AOZPI BATAIVA AOVRRZ ALOAI

MI-CA-OLI BRANSG PRGEL NAPTA IALPOR DS BRIN EFAFAFE P VONPHO OLANI OD OBZA: SOBCA VPAAH CHIS TATAN OD TRANAN BALYE ALAR LUSDA SOBOLN OD CHIS HOLQ CNOQUODI CIAL. VNAL ALDON MOM CAOSGO TA LAS OLLOR GNAY LIMLAL: AMMA CHIIS SOBCA MADRID ZCHIS, OOANOAN CHIIS AUINY DRILPI CAOSGIN OD OD BUTMONI PARM ZUMVI CNILA: DAZIZ ETHAMZ A CHILDAO OD MIRC CHIS PIDIAI COLLAL VLCININ A-SOBAM VCIM. BAGLE? IADBALTOH CHIRLAN PAR NIISO OD IP OFAFAFE BAGLE ACOSASB ICORSCA VNIG BLIOR.

The magician makes a cross over the altar and says:

Oh You Angels of God, flowing with truth and goodness, I call you Acuca, Nprat, Otroi, and Pmzox, who rule in the Airy part of the world: so that each one of you, out of the four great elements or sources of the world might wield the duty or office peculiar to him, and his unique skill, knowledge, power, and authority. Oh you, Acuca, bright angel that liveth in the Air of Air, you who hath vision of all its diverse qualities and who perfectly perceives what uses God created in them for Man; And you, Oh illustrious Nprat, who liveth in the Water of Air, who truly knoweth its quality and use; And you, Oh distinguished Otroi, who liveth in the Earth of Air, you who knoweth exactly its varied qualities and to what uses it was created by our God; And finally you, Pmzox, shining angel of God, who liveth in the most secret Fire of Air, and who hath plentiful knowledge of its efficacy and vital properties; Oh All of you, faithful to God and ministers of our Creator, you who dwelleth in the Airy part of the world, you who knoweth the arcane secrets of the four elements, conceded, assigned, and deputed to you by our omnipotent Creator, and who, to the praise, honour, and glory of God and out of your great charity towards the human race art able to impart and make manifest these great things and (by the approval of God) bring forth those things that are asked of you. Therefore, I, [NAME], a Lover and Seeker for these secrets (to the praise, honour and glory of our God), in the Name of the same, our God and Creator, I humbly supplicate you, one and all. And through these holy Names of God, AOVRRZ and ALOAI, I require and confidently petition that, at whatever time of my future life (from this very hour) that I should call or summon one, any, or all of you, you appear conspicuous and visible to me in a goodly form. And through these holy Names of God, AOVRRZ and ALOAI, I require that you benignly consent, clearly discharge, lovingly fulfill, and perfectly make perfect, each and every one of my petitions (respecting and concerning your aforementioned unique offices, knowledges, and powers), satisfyingly, satisfactorily, plentily, and perfectly. AMEN, AMEN! Through these reverend and mystical Names of God AOVRRZ and ALOAI! AMEN.

The magician repeats the conjuration until the spirits appear in the crystal sphere, then he commands them:

In the names, ORO IBAH AOZPI, BATAIVA, Aourrz, and Aloal, I adjure you Acuca, Nprat, Otroi, and Pmzox, give me the name and sign of a Sylph that I might keep as a familiar spirit. Bring forth this spirit from amongst their number when I call upon them.

This is repeated until the name and seal are given.

When the name and seal are provided, the magician writes them down and places them on the altar with the implement and the material. The magician places a hand over these items and begins to strongly visualize their elemental forming as they call upon the elementals. The magician says:

Spirit of light! Spirit of wisdom! Whose breath gives and takes away again the forms of all things! Thou, in whose presence the life of being is a shadow which changes, and a vapor which passes away. Thou who ascendest the clouds and movest on the wing of the winds. When thou breathes! forth, infinite spaces are peopled! When thou inhalest, all that comes from thee returns to thee! Endless movement in eternal stability, be thou eternally blest! We praise thee and bless thee in the changing empire of created light, of shadows, of reflections and of images; and we long unceasingly for thine immutable and imperishable light. Let the ray of thy intelligence and the heat of thy love penetrate even to us; then what is movable will become fixed; the shadow will become a body; the spirit of the air will become a soul; the dream will become a thought, and we shall no longer be borne away by the tempest, but shall hold the bridle of the winged steeds of the morning, and shall direct the course of the evening winds that we may fly into thy presence. O spirit of spirits! O eternal soul of souls! O imperishable breath of life! O creative inspiration. O mouth which inspires and respires the existence of all beings in the flux and reflux of thy eternal Word, which is the divine ocean of movement and of truth. Amen!

Once the prayer is finished and the elementals have arrived, the magician continues the visualization with the following prayer. They envision the light of the spirit's being descending as a seed into the Body of Light which has been constructed for the spirit. That seed takes root, and grows until it bears flower and fruit throughout the visualized body, giving it life. The magician calls the spirit as a lover, but making clear their expectations. This is done by saying:

Oh Blowing Wind whose name is [Name], I, I invoke thee,
I invoke thee, [Name], come forth,
Join this image and this token of your presence,
Come veiled, come voluptuous,
For I, I adore thee.
Thus I invoke thee,
By seed and root
By stem and bud
By leaf and flower and fruit
I invoke thee.
O Secret Light,

That illumines the image I hold,
I adore thee, for thine image is Love,
And to love me, is better than all things
Thus for one kiss wilt thou be willing to give all
You shall work wonders,
In splendor and in pride,
But always in the love of me,
And so shall you come to my joy.
I charge you earnestly to come before me
In a form most pleasing,
For I who am all pleasure, desire you
Come unto me, to me,
Work wonders unto me,
And I will give you completeness
For you will stand by my side
Familiar unto me.

When the spirit is adequately joined to the vision, the magician reclines, sits, or lays down as they desire. The magician pleasures themself while fixed upon their vision of their spirit partner, with whom they share the pleasure of the act. The climax of the act should result in contact with the implement, sweat or sexual fluids should be combined with the material, which will be used to construct the spirit house with the name and seal.

When all is finished, the magician says:

I declare this ritual complete. The spirit, N, and I are joined together, let all other spirits depart unto their rightful places in peace to come again in peace when called.

Water

The magician is dressed in a robe. They have bathed before the ritual. The magician is anointed, thoroughly, with oils appropriate to the element.

The temple is dark and unlit. In the center of the temple is an altar. Incense appropriate to the element is burning in the temple. There are candles at each of the cardinal points of the temple.

On the altar is a large Water Tablet which covers the surface. The items for the ritual are on the Tablet. These include:

The Ring of Solomon
The sword for tracing in the air
A scrying crystal
A bowl of water
An unlit candle
Paper and a pen
A bowl, cup, or wand, referred to as the implement
A material item representing the element, referred to as the material

The magician raises their hands to the heavens and says:

Holy Art Thou Lord of the Universe
Holy Art Thou, Whom Nature Has Not Formed
Holy Art Thou, Vast and Mighty One
Lord of Light and of Darkness

The magician lights the initial candle on the altar. Holding up the candle the magician says:

Come, O fire, which is the life of all mortal things. Come at this time. God reigns. O come, for he is one. He reigns and is the life of all living things.

The magician replaces the candle and holds up the bowl of water and breathes upon it saying:

Come, I say, come at this time. Come, O King, King, King of the waters. Your power is great but my power is greater. God gave life to all creatures.

The magician circumambulates the temple, sprinkling water as they do so. While doing this they say:

So therefore first the Priest who governs the works of fire, must sprinkle with the lustral waters of the loud resounding sea.

When they return to the altar they replace the bowl and they take the candle. They circumambulate the temple, in each quarter they make a cross with the candle and light a candle in that quarter. As they do this they say:

And when all the phantoms have vanished, you shall see that holy and formless fire, that darts and flashes through the hidden depths of the Universe, hear now the Voice of Fire.

The magician takes the ring from the altar and before putting it on, kisses it three times saying:

Without this ring you shall do nothing. Blessed be his Name that compasses all things. Wonders are in him and his Name is wonderful. His Name works wonders from generation to generation.

The magician stands at the altar and looks up to Heaven praying:

YHVH Tzveot, I, [NAME], Your humble servant, most earnestly invoke and call upon your divine power, wisdom, and goodness. I humbly and faithfully seek your favor and assistance to me in all my deeds, words, and thoughts, and in the promoting, procuring, and mingling of your praise, honor, and glory.

Through these, your twelve mystical Names: Oro, Ibah, Aozpi, Mor, Dral, Hctga, Oip, Teaa, Pdoce, Mph, Arsl, Gaiol, I conjure and pray most zealously to your divine and omnipotent majesty, that all your angelic spirits might be called from any and all parts of the universe,

or at any time in my life, through the special domination and controlling power of your holy Names.

Let them come most quickly to me. Let them appear visibly, friendly, and peacefully to me. Let them remain visible according to my will. Let them vanish from me and from my sight when I so request. Let them give reverence and obedience before you and your 12 mystical Names. I command that they happily satisfy me in all things and at all times in my life, by accomplishing each and every one of my petitions-if not by one means, then by another-goodly, virtuously, and perfectly, with an excellent and thorough completeness, according to their virtues and powers, both general and unique, and by Your united ministry and office, Oh God . AMEN. Through you, Jesu Christe, AMEN

The magician knocks on the altar, and traces the Spirit Passive Invoking Pentagram, and the Water Invoking Pentagram while intoning:

EXARP HCOMA NANTA BITOM

OTHIL LASDI BABAGE OD DORPHA GOHOL G-CHISGE AVAVAGO CORMP PD DSONF VIV DI-V CASARMI OALI MAPM SOBAM AG CORMPO C-RP-L CASARG CROODZI CHIS OD VGEG DST CAPIMALI CHIS CAPIMAON LONSHIN CHIS TA LO CLA: TORGU NOR QUASAHI, OD F CAOSAGA: BAGLE ZIRENAIAD, DSI OD APALA. DO-O-A-IP Q-A-AL ZACAR, OD ZAMRAN OBELISONG REST-EL AAF NOR-MO-LAP

The magician makes a cross over the altar and says:

Oh You Six Seniors of the Watchtower of Water, powerful and faithful to the omnipotent God of our ministry. In the name of the same God, MPH, ARSL, GAIOL, I say to you, Lsrahpm, Saiinou, Laoaxrp, Slgaiol, Ligdisa, and Soniznt, through the divine Name by which you arc particularly bound, the angelic Name RAAGIOS, I, [Name] , a faithful servant of the omnipotent God, amicably, earnestly, and confidently demand and beseech you to appear placidly, affably, and favorably before me, immediately and without delay, and henceforth at any time I wish, through all the remaining

*journey of my life, I beseech all of you, some of you, or whichever of
you I name, united or divided, to grant all my petitions, and especially
grant me knowledge and judgment in human affairs, and in all other
things that are assigned to your Office and Ministry and that are
accomplished by you, one and many. I command you to appear, to
perform, and to complete, goodly, plainly, intelligibly, and perfectly,
according to your Virtue, Power, and Office, and according to the
capacity of your Ministry, entrusted and committed to you by the
omnipotent God, AMEN. Through the sacred Name of God
RAAGIOS, AMEN.*

The magician knocks on the altar and intones:

MPH ARSL GAIOL RAAGIOS IAAASD ATAPA

*NONCI DSONF OD CHIS OB HUBIAO TIBIBP, ALLAR
ATRAAH OD EF. DRIX FAFEN MIAN AR E NAY OVOF
SOBA DOOAIN AAI I VONPH ZACAR GOHUS, OD
ZAMRAM, ODO CICLE QAA. ZORGE, LAP ZIRDO NOCO
MAD, HOATH IAIDA*

The magician makes a cross over the altar and says:

*Oh You Angels of God, flowing with truth and goodness, I call you
Xpacn, Vaasa, Daspi, and Rndil, who rule in the Watery part of the
world: so that each one of you, out of the four great elements or
sources of the world might wield the duty or office peculiar to him,
and his unique skill, knowledge, power, and authority. Oh you,
Xpacn, bright angel that liveth in the Air of Water, you who hath
vision of all its diverse qualities and who perfectly perceives what uses
God created in them for Man; And you, Oh illustrious Vaasa, who
liveth in the Water of Water, who truly knoweth its quality and use;
And you, Oh distinguished Daspi, who liveth in the Earth of Water,
you who knoweth exactly its varied qualities and to what uses it was
created by our God; And finally you, Rndil, shining angel of God,
who liveth in the most secret Fire of Water, and who hath plentiful
knowledge of its efficacy and vital properties; Oh All of you, faithful
to God and ministers of our Creator, you who dwelleth in the Watery
part of the world, you who knoweth the arcane secrets of the four
elements, conceded, assigned, and deputed to you by our omnipotent
Creator, and who, to the praise, honour, and glory of God and out of*

your great charity towards the human race art able to impart and make manifest these great things and (by the approval of God) bring forth those things that are asked of you. Therefore, I, [NAME], a Lover and Seeker for these secrets (to the praise, honour and glory of our God), in the Name of the same, our God and Creator, I humbly supplicate you, one and all. And through these holy Names of God, IAAASD and ATAPA, I require and confidently petition that, at whatever time of my future life (from this very hour) that I should call or summon one, any, or all of you, you appear conspicuous and visible to me in a goodly form. And through these holy Names of God, IAAASD and ATAPA, I require that you benignly consent, clearly discharge, lovingly fulfill, and perfectly make perfect, each and every one of my petitions (respecting and concerning your aforementioned unique offices, knowledges, and powers), satisfyingly, satisfactorily, plentily, and perfectly. AMEN, AMEN! Through these reverend and mystical Names of God IAAASD and ATAPA! AMEN.

The magician repeats the conjuration until the spirits appear in the crystal sphere, then he commands them:

In the names MPH ARSL GAIOL, RAAGIOS, Iaaasd, and Atapa, I adjure you Xpacn, Vaasa, Daspi, Rndil, give me the name and sign of an Undine that I might keep as a familiar spirit. Bring forth this spirit from amongst their number when I call upon them.

This is repeated until the name and seal are given.

When the name and seal are provided, the magician writes them down and places them on the altar with the implement and the material. The magician places a hand over these items and begins to strongly visualize their elemental forming as they call upon the elementals. The magician says:

Terrible king of the sea! Thou who boldest the keys of the cataracts of heaven, and who enclosest the subterranean waters in the hollow places of the earth! King of the deluge and of rains, of springtime! Thou who openest the sources of streams and fountains! Thou who commandest the moisture (which is like the blood of the earth) to become the sap of plants! We adore and invoke thee! Speak to us, ye moving and changeable creatures! Speak to us in the great commotions of the sea, and we will tremble before thee. Speak to us also in the murmur of the limpid waters, and we will desire thy love. O immensity in which all the rivers of being lose themselves, which ever spring up anew in us! O ocean of infinite perfections! Height which beholdeth thee in the depth! Depth which breathes thee forth in the height! Bring us to the true life through intelligence and love! Lead us to immortality through sacrifice, in order that one day we may be found worthy to offer thee water, blood, and tears, for the remission of sins. Amen.

Once the prayer is finished and the elementals have arrived, the magician continues the visualization with the following prayer. They envision the light of the spirit's being descending as a seed into the Body of Light which has been constructed for the spirit. That seed takes root, and grows until it bears flower and fruit throughout the visualized body, giving it life. The magician calls the spirit as a lover, but making clear their expectations. This is done by saying:

Oh Flowing Current whose name is [Name], I, I invoke thee,
I invoke thee, [Name], come forth,
Join this image and this token of your presence,
Come veiled, come voluptuous,
For I, I adore thee.
Thus I invoke thee,
By seed and root
By stem and bud
By leaf and flower and fruit
I invoke thee.
O Secret Light,
That illumines the image I hold,
I adore thee, for thine image is Love,
And to love me, is better than all things
Thus for one kiss wilt thou be willing to give all
You shall work wonders,
In splendor and in pride,
But always in the love of me,
And so shall you come to my joy.
I charge you earnestly to come before me
In a form most pleasing,
For I who am all pleasure, desire you
Come unto me, to me,

Work wonders unto me,
And I will give you completeness
For you will stand by my side
Familiar unto me.

When the spirit is adequately joined to the vision, the magician reclines, sits, or lays down as they desire. The magician pleasures themself while fixed upon their vision of their spirit partner, with whom they share the pleasure of the act. The climax of the act should result in contact with the implement, sweat or sexual fluids should be combined with the material, which will be used to construct the spirit house with the name and seal.

When all is finished, the magician says:

I declare this ritual complete. The spirit, N, and I are joined together, let all other spirits depart unto their rightful places in peace to come again in peace when called.

Earth

The magician is dressed in a robe. They have bathed before the ritual. The magician is anointed, thoroughly, with oils appropriate to the element.

The temple is dark and unlit. In the center of the temple is an altar. Incense appropriate to the element is burning in the temple. There are candles at each of the cardinal points of the temple.

On the altar is a large Earth Tablet which covers the surface. The items for the ritual are on the Tablet. These include:

The Ring of Solomon
The sword for tracing in the air
A scrying crystal
A bowl of water
An unlit candle
Paper and a pen
A bowl, cup, or wand, referred to as the implement
A material item representing the element, referred to as the material

The magician raises their hands to the heavens and says:

Holy Art Thou Lord of the Universe
Holy Art Thou, Whom Nature Has Not Formed
Holy Art Thou, Vast and Mighty One
Lord of Light and of Darkness

The magician lights the initial candle on the altar. Holding up the candle the magician says:

Come, O fire, which is the life of all mortal things. Come at this time. God reigns. O come, for he is one. He reigns and is the life of all living things.

The magician replaces the candle and holds up the bowl of water and breathes upon it saying:

Come, I say, come at this time. Come, O King, King, King of the waters. Your power is great but my power is greater. God gave life to all creatures.

The magician circumambulates the temple, sprinkling water as they do so. While doing this they say:

So therefore first the Priest who governs the works of fire, must sprinkle with the lustral waters of the loud resounding sea.

When they return to the altar they replace the bowl and they take the candle. They circumambulate the temple, in each quarter they make a cross with the candle and light a candle in that quarter. As they do this they say:

And when all the phantoms have vanished, you shall see that holy and formless fire, that darts and flashes through the hidden depths of the Universe, hear now the Voice of Fire.

The magician takes the ring from the altar and before putting it on, kisses it three times saying:

Without this ring you shall do nothing. Blessed be his Name that compasses all things. Wonders are in him and his Name is wonderful. His Name works wonders from generation to generation.

The magician stands at the altar and looks up to Heaven praying:

YHVH Tzveot, I, [NAME], Your humble servant, most earnestly invoke and call upon your divine power, wisdom, and goodness. I humbly and faithfully seek your favor and assistance to me in all my deeds, words, and thoughts, and in the promoting, procuring, and mingling of your praise, honor, and glory.

Through these, your twelve mystical Names: Oro, Ibah, Aozpi, Mor, Dral, Hctga, Oip, Teaa, Pdoce, Mph, Arsl, Gaiol, I conjure and pray most zealously to your divine and omnipotent majesty, that all your angelic spirits might be called from any and all parts of the universe,

or at any time in my life, through the special domination and controlling power of your holy Names.

Let them come most quickly to me. Let them appear visibly, friendly, and peacefully to me. Let them remain visible according to my will. Let them vanish from me and from my sight when I so request. Let them give reverence and obedience before you and your 12 mystical Names. I command that they happily satisfy me in all things and at all times in my life, by accomplishing each and every one of my petitions- if not by one means, then by another-goodly, virtuously, and perfectly, with an excellent and thorough completeness, according to their virtues and powers, both general and unique, and by Your united ministry and office, Oh God . AMEN. Through you, Jesu Christe, AMEN

The magician knocks on the altar, and traces the Spirit Passive Invoking Pentagram, and the Earth Invoking Pentagram while intoning:

EXARP HCOMA NANTA BITOM

SAPAH ZIMII DU-I-V OD NOAS TA-QA-A-NIS ADROCH DORPHAL CA OSG OD FAONTS PERIPSOL TABLIOR CASARM AMIPZI NAZARTH AF OD DLUGAR ZIZOP Z-LIDA CAOSGI TOLTORGI OD Z-CHIS ESIASCH L TAVIU OD IAAD THILD DS PERAL HUBAR PEOAL SOBA CORMFA CHIS TA LA VLS OD Q-CO-CASB. CA NIIS OD DARBS Q-A-AS, FETH-AR-ZI OD BLIORA, IA-IAL ED-NAS CICLES: BAGLE? GEIAD I L

The magician makes a cross over the altar and says:

Oh You Six Seniors of the Watchtower of Earth, powerful and faithful to the omnipotent God of our ministry. In the name of the same God, MOR DIAL HCTGA, I say to you, Laidrom, Aczinor, Lzinopo, Ahlctga, Liiansa, and Ahmlicu, through the divine Name by which you arc particularly bound, the angelic Name ICZHHCA, I, [Name] , a faithful servant of the omnipotent God, amicably, earnestly, and confidently demand and beseech you to appear placidly, affably, and favorably before me, immediately and without delay, and henceforth at any time I wish, through all the remaining journey of my life, I beseech all of you, some of you, or whichever of you I name, united or divided, to grant all my petitions, and especially grant me knowledge and judgment in human affairs, and in all other things that are assigned to your Office and Ministry and that are accomplished by you, one and many. I command you to appear, to perform, and to complete, goodly, plainly, intelligibly, and perfectly, according to your Virtue, Power, and Office, and according to the capacity of your Ministry, entrusted and committed to you by the omnipotent God, AMEN. Through the sacred Name of God ICZHHCA, AMEN.

The magician knocks on the altar and intones:

MOR DIAL HCTGA ICZHHCA SPMNIR ILPIZ

ILS TABAAN LIAPRT CASARMAN VPAAHI CHIS DARG DSOADO CAOSGI ORSCOR DS OMAX MONASCI BAEOUIB OD EMETGIS IAIADIX. ZACAR OD ZAMRAN, ODO CICLE QAA, ZORGE, LAP ZIRDO NOCO MAD, HOATH IAIDA

The magician makes a cross over the altar and says:

Oh You Angels of God, flowing with truth and goodness, I call you Msmal, Ianba, Izixp, and Strim, who rule in the Earthy part of the world: so that each one of you, out of the four great elements or sources of the world might wield the duty or office peculiar to him, and his unique skill, knowledge, power, and authority. Oh you, Msmal, bright angel that liveth in the Air of Earth, you who hath vision of all its diverse qualities and who perfectly perceives what uses God created in them for Man; And you, Oh illustrious Ianba, who liveth in the Water of Earth, who truly knoweth its quality and use; And you, Oh distinguished Izixp, who liveth in the Earth of Earth, you who knoweth exactly its varied qualities and to what uses it was created by our God; And finally you, Strim, shining angel of God, who liveth in the most secret Fire of Earth, and who hath plentiful knowledge of its efficacy and vital properties; Oh All of you, faithful to God and ministers of our Creator, you who dwelleth in the Earthy part of the world, you who knoweth the arcane secrets of the four elements, conceded, assigned, and deputed to you by our omnipotent Creator, and who, to the praise, honour, and glory of God and out of your great charity towards the human race art able to impart and make manifest these great things and (by the approval of God) bring forth those things that are asked of you. Therefore, I, [NAME], a Lover and Seeker for these secrets (to the praise, honour and glory of our God), in the Name of the same, our God and Creator, I humbly supplicate you, one and all. And through these holy Names of God, SPMNIR and ILPIZ, I require and confidently petition that, at whatever time of my future life (from this very hour) that I should call or summon one, any, or all of you, you appear conspicuous and visible to me in a goodly form. And through these holy Names of God, SPMNIR and ILPIZ, I require that you benignly consent, clearly discharge, lovingly fulfill, and perfectly make perfect, each and every one of my petitions (respecting and concerning your aforementioned unique offices, knowledges, and powers), satisfyingly, satisfactorily, plentily, and perfectly. AMEN, AMEN! Through these reverend and mystical Names of God SPMNIR and ILPIZ! AMEN.

The magician repeats the conjuration until the spirits appear in the crystal sphere, then he commands them:

In the names MOR DIAL HCTGA, ICZHHCA, Spmnir, and Ilpiz, I adjure you Msmal, Ianba, Izixp, and Strim, give me the name and sign of a Gnome that I might keep as a familiar spirit. Bring forth this spirit from amongst their number when I call upon them.

This is repeated until the name and seal are given.

When the name and seal are provided, the magician writes them down and places them on the altar with the implement and the material. The magician places a hand over these items and begins to strongly visualize their elemental forming as they call upon the elementals. The magician says:

Invisible King who has taken the earth as a support, and who has dug abysses in order to fill them with the omnipotence! Thou whose name makest the arches of the world tremble! Thou who makest the seven metals circulate in the veins of stone; Monarch of seven luminaries! Rewarder of subterranean workmen! bring us to the desirable air and to the kingdom of light. We watch and work without respite. We seek and hope by the twelve stones of the Holy City, for the talismans which are buried by the magnetic nail which passes through the center of the earth. Lord! Lord! Lord! Have pity upon those who suffer! Enlarge our hearts! Let us be free and raise up our heads! Exalt us! O stability and movement! O Day invested by night! O Darkness veiled in light! O Master who never retainest the wages of thy workmen! O silvery whiteness! O Golden Splendor! O Crown of Diamonds, living and melodious! Thou who bearest the sky upon thy finger, like a ring of sapphire! Thou who hidest under the earth, in the kingdom of gems, the wonderful seed of stars! All hail! Reign; and be the Eternal Dispenser of riches, of which thou hast made us the guardians. Amen.

Once the prayer is finished and the elementals have arrived, the magician continues the visualization with the following prayer. They envision the light of the spirit's being descending as a seed into the Body of Light which has been constructed for the spirit. That seed takes root, and grows until it bears flower and fruit throughout the visualized body, giving it life. The magician calls the spirit as a lover, but making clear their expectations. This is done by saying:

Oh Stable Ground whose name is [Name], I, I invoke thee,
I invoke thee, [Name], come forth,
Join this image and this token of your presence,
Come veiled, come voluptuous,
For I, I adore thee.
Thus I invoke thee,
By seed and root
By stem and bud
By leaf and flower and fruit
I invoke thee.
O Secret Light,
That illumines the image I hold,
I adore thee, for thine image is Love,
And to love me, is better than all things
Thus for one kiss wilt thou be willing to give all
You shall work wonders,
In splendor and in pride,
But always in the love of me,
And so shall you come to my joy.
I charge you earnestly to come before me
In a form most pleasing,
For I who am all pleasure, desire you

Come unto me, to me,
Work wonders unto me,
And I will give you completeness
For you will stand by my side
Familiar unto me.

When the spirit is adequately joined to the vision, the magician reclines, sits, or lays down as they desire. The magician pleasures themself while fixed upon their vision of their spirit partner, with whom they share the pleasure of the act. The climax of the act should result in contact with the implement, sweat or sexual fluids should be combined with the material, which will be used to construct the spirit house with the name and seal.

When all is finished, the magician says:

I declare this ritual complete. The spirit, N, and I are joined together, let all other spirits depart unto their rightful places in peace to come again in peace when called.

Fire

The magician is dressed in a robe. They have bathed before the ritual. The magician is anointed, thoroughly, with oils appropriate to the element.

The temple is dark and unlit. In the center of the temple is an altar. Incense appropriate to the element is burning in the temple. There are candles at each of the cardinal points of the temple.

On the altar is a large Fire Tablet which covers the surface. The items for the ritual are on the Tablet. These include:

The Ring of Solomon
The sword for tracing in the air
A scrying crystal
A bowl of water
An unlit candle
Paper and a pen
A bowl, cup, or wand, referred to as the implement
A material item representing the element, referred to as the material

The magician raises their hands to the heavens and says:

Holy Art Thou Lord of the Universe
Holy Art Thou, Whom Nature Has Not Formed
Holy Art Thou, Vast and Mighty One
Lord of Light and of Darkness

The magician lights the initial candle on the altar. Holding up the candle the magician says:

Come, O fire, which is the life of all mortal things. Come at this time.
God reigns. O come, for he is one. He reigns and is the life of all
living things.

The magician replaces the candle and holds up the bowl of water and breathes upon it saying:

Come, I say, come at this time. Come, O King, King, King of the waters. Your power is great but my power is greater. God gave life to all creatures.

The magician circumambulates the temple, sprinkling water as they do so. While doing this they say:

So therefore first the Priest who governs the works of fire, must sprinkle with the lustral waters of the loud resounding sea.

When they return to the altar they replace the bowl and they take the candle. They circumambulate the temple, in each quarter they make a cross with the candle and light a candle in that quarter. As they do this they say:

And when all the phantoms have vanished, you shall see that holy and formless fire, that darts and flashes through the hidden depths of the Universe, hear now the Voice of Fire.

The magician takes the ring from the altar and before putting it on, kisses it three times saying:

Without this ring you shall do nothing. Blessed be his Name that compasses all things.
Wonders are in him and his Name is wonderful. His Name works wonders from generation to generation.

The magician stands at the altar and looks up to Heaven praying:

YHVH Tzveot, I, [NAME], Your humble servant, most earnestly invoke and call upon your divine power, wisdom, and goodness. I humbly and faithfully seek your favor and assistance to me in all my deeds, words, and thoughts, and in the promoting, procuring, and mingling of your praise, honor, and glory.

Through these, your twelve mystical Names: Oro, Ibah, Aozpi, Mor, Dral, Hctga, Oip, Teaa, Pdoce, Mph, Arsl, Gaiol, I conjure and pray most zealously to your divine and omnipotent majesty, that all your angelic spirits might be called from any and all parts of the universe, or at any time in my life, through the special domination and controlling power of your holy Names.

Let them come most quickly to me. Let them appear visibly, friendly, and peacefully to me. Let them remain visible according to my will. Let them vanish from me and from my sight when I so request. Let them give reverence and obedience before you and your 12 mystical Names. I command that they happily satisfy me in all things and at all times in my life, by accomplishing each and every one of my petitions- if not by one means, then by another-goodly, virtuously, and perfectly, with an excellent and thorough completeness, according to their virtues and powers, both general and unique, and by Your united ministry and office, Oh God . AMEN. Through you, Jesu Christe, AMEN

The magician knocks on the altar, and traces the Spirit Passive Invoking Pentagram, and the Earth Invoking Pentagram while intoning:

EXARP HCOMA NANTA BITOM

GAH S DIU CHIS EM MICALZO PILZIN SOBAM EL HARG MIR BABALON OD OBLOC SAMVELG DLUGAR MALPRG ARCAOSGI OD ACAM CANAL SOBOLZAR F-BLIARD CAOSGI OD CHIS ANETAB OD MIAM TA VIV OD D. DARSAR SOL-PETH BIEN: BRITA OD ZACAM G-MICALZO, SOB-HA-HATH TRIAN LU-IA HE ODECRIN MAD Q-A-A ON

The magician makes a cross over the altar and says:

Oh You Six Seniors of the Watchtower of Fire, powerful and faithful to the omnipotent God of our ministry. In the name of the same God, OIP TEAA PDOCE, I say to you, Aaetpio, Adoeoet, Alndvod, Aapdoce, Aarinnap, and Anodoin, through the divine Name by which you arc particularly bound, the angelic Name EDLPRNA, I, [Name] , a faithful servant of the omnipotent God, amicably, earnestly, and confidently demand and beseech you to appear placidly, affably, and favorably before me, immediately and without delay, and henceforth at any time I wish, through all the remaining journey of my life, I beseech all of you, some of you, or whichever of you I name, united or divided, to grant all my petitions, and especially grant me knowledge and judgment in human affairs, and in all other things that are assigned to your Office and Ministry and that are accomplished by you, one and many. I command you to appear, to perform, and to complete, goodly, plainly, intelligibly, and perfectly, according to your Virtue, Power, and Office, and according to the capacity of your Ministry, entrusted and committed to you by the omnipotent God, AMEN. Through the sacred Name of God EDLPRNA, AMEN.

The magician knocks on the altar and intones:

OIP TEAA PDOCE EDLPRNA RIZIONR NRSFM

The magician makes a cross over the altar and says:

Oh You Angels of God, flowing with truth and goodness, I call you Adire, Siosp, Panli, and Zcrar, who rule in the Fiery part of the world: so that each one of you, out of the four great elements or sources of the world might wield the duty or office peculiar to him, and his unique skill, knowledge, power, and authority. Oh you, Adire, bright angel that liveth in the Air of Fire, you who hath vision of all its diverse qualities and who perfectly perceives what uses God created in them for Man; And you, Oh illustrious Siosp, who liveth in the Water of Fire, who truly knoweth its quality and use; And you, Oh distinguished Panli, who liveth in the Earth of Fire, you who knoweth exactly its varied qualities and to what uses it was created by our God; And finally you, Zcrar, shining angel of God, who liveth in the most secret Fire of Fire, and who hath plentiful knowledge of its efficacy and vital properties; Oh All of you, faithful to God and ministers of our Creator, you who dwelleth in the Fiery part of the world, you who knoweth the arcane secrets of the four elements, conceded, assigned, and deputed to you by our omnipotent Creator, and who, to the praise, honour, and glory of God and out of your great charity towards the human race art able to impart and make manifest these great things and (by the approval of God) bring forth those things that are asked of you. Therefore, I, [NAME], a Lover and Seeker for these secrets (to the praise, honour and glory of our God), in the Name of the same, our God and Creator, I humbly supplicate you, one and all. And through these holy Names of God, RIZIONR and NRSFM, I require and confidently petition that, at whatever time of my future life (from this very hour) that I should call or summon one, any, or all of you, you appear conspicuous and visible to me in a goodly form. And through these holy Names of God, RIZIONR and NRZFM, I require that you benignly consent, clearly discharge, lovingly fulfill, and perfectly make perfect, each and every one of my petitions (respecting and concerning your aforementioned unique offices, knowledges, and powers), satisfyingly, satisfactorily, plentily, and perfectly. AMEN, AMEN! Through these reverend and mystical Names of God RIZIONR and NZRFM! AMEN.

The magician repeats the conjuration until the spirits appear in the crystal sphere, then he commands them:

In the names OIP TEAA PDOCE, EDLPRNA, Rizionr, and Nrzfm, I adjure you Adire, Siosp, Panli, and Zcrar, give me the name and sign of a Salamander that I might keep as a familiar spirit. Bring forth this spirit from amongst their number when I call upon them.

This is repeated until the name and seal are given.

When the name and seal are provided, the magician writes them down and places them on the altar with the implement and the material. The magician places a hand over these items and begins to strongly visualize their elemental forming as they call upon the elementals. The magician says:

Immortal, eternal, ineffable and uncreated Father of all things I who are borne upon the incessantly rolling chariot of Worlds which are always turning; Ruler of the ethereal immensity where the throne of thy power is elevated; from whose height thy dread-inspiring eyes discover all things, and thy exquisite and sacred ears hear all; Listen to thy children whom thou hast loved from the beginning of the ages; for thy golden, great, and eternal majesty is resplendent above the world and the starry heavens. Thou art raised above them O sparkling fire! There thou dost illumine and support thyself by thine own splendor; and there comes forth from thine essence overflowing streams of light which nourish thine infinite spirit. That infinite spirit nourishes all things, and renders this inexhaustible treasure of substance always ready for the generation which fashions it and which receives in itself the forms with which thou hast impregnated it from the beginning. From this spirit those most holy kings who surround thy throne, and who compose thy court, derive their origin. O Father Universal! Only One! O Father of blessed mortals and immortals! Thou hast specially created powers who are marvelously like thine eternal thought and adorable essence. Thou hast established them superior to the angels who announce to the world thy wishes. Finally thou hast created us in the third rank in our elementary empire. There our continual employment is to praise thee and adore thy wishes. There we incessantly burn with the desire of possessing thee, O Father! O Mother! the most tender of all mothers! O admirable archetype of maternity and pure love! O Son, the flower of sons! O Form of all forms; soul, spirit, harmony and number of all things. Amen.

Once the prayer is finished and the elementals have arrived, the magician continues the visualization with the following prayer. They envision the light of the spirit's being descending as a seed into the Body of Light which has been constructed for the spirit. That seed takes root, and grows until it bears flower and fruit throughout the visualized body, giving it life. The magician calls the spirit as a lover, but making clear their expectations. This is done by saying:

Oh Flickering Flame whose name is [Name], I, I invoke thee,
I invoke thee, [Name], come forth,
Join this image and this token of your presence,
Come veiled, come voluptuous,
For I, I adore thee.
Thus I invoke thee,
By seed and root
By stem and bud
By leaf and flower and fruit
I invoke thee.
O Secret Light,
That illumines the image I hold,
I adore thee, for thine image is Love,
And to love me, is better than all things
Thus for one kiss wilt thou be willing to give all
You shall work wonders,
In splendor and in pride,
But always in the love of me,
And so shall you come to my joy.
I charge you earnestly to come before me
In a form most pleasing,

For I who am all pleasure, desire you
Come unto me, to me,
Work wonders unto me,
And I will give you completeness
For you will stand by my side
Familiar unto me.

When the spirit is adequately joined to the vision, the magician reclines, sits, or lays down as they desire. The magician pleasures themself while fixed upon their vision of their spirit partner, with whom they share the pleasure of the act. The climax of the act should result in contact with the implement, sweat or sexual fluids should be combined with the material, which will be used to construct the spirit house with the name and seal.

When all is finished, the magician says:

I declare this ritual complete. The spirit, N, and I are joined together, let all other spirits depart unto their rightful places in peace to come again in peace when called.

XXVIII
Sex, Blood, and Semen

Physical intimacy between the witch and the familiar has been a recurring element of our discussion. Witches have sexual relationships with spirits, including their familiars. These relationships are not only limited to witches. Several methods survive in grimoires and cunning men's books that explain how to conjure a faery for sex. Our exploration of familiar spirits in the modern magical revival focused on sexual congress with spirits. Spirit sex is a recurring theme. This text has addressed spirit sex to define the relationship with a familiar, to distinguish it from relationships with pets, to consider the folklore and history of familiars, and finally to consider ceremonial magic methods for obtaining one. Despite so many areas in which spirit sex has come up, there has been little to no explanation of the practical elements of ongoing sexual interaction with a familiar spirit.

Not all relationships with familiars involve sex. It is not a necessary part of magical practice. Various forms of "spirit-spousing" have recently grown in popularity and gained more attention. Many people are interested in or are drawn to those elements of spirit interaction. Still, many practitioners would never consider it and have no need to. When the relationship is established, the spirit and the magician can agree upon this relationship element. Spirit sex can be part of how the relationship is established. It can develop naturally during the relationship. The various ways someone might end up in a sexual relationship with a spirit are similar to the myriad ways that can develop with another embodied person. Still, just like our relationships with embodied people, most relationships with spirits don't require sex.

Certain types of spirits might look for that as part of the relationship. Since The Comte de Gabalis, the assumption has been that elementals seek sexual congress with humans. We have seen how frequently faeries desire humans in folklore. Medieval tales of devils include their lust for humans, as do ancient myths of fallen angels. Other spirits may be less inclined to seek that kind of interaction. Even for spirits where such interactions seem like a common possibility, you can determine what you will and will not offer when the familiar is offered. You don't have to accept all potential familiars if something about the potential relationship does not feel right to you.

If you are open to sexual interactions with your familiar spirit, what does that look like? Like most elements of spirit work, it will depend partially on the person, the spirit, and the system.

I am not particularly drawn to the idea of spirit sex. As a horny teenage boy, my Pagan friends and I bragged to Catholic classmates about the ability to have sex with spirits. We didn't realize sexual ecstasy was a staple of Catholic mysticism also. None of us knew anything about that kind of spirit work or divine devotion. We had heard it was possible, and it sounded like another reason to say Paganism and magic were cooler than the alternatives. Beyond that, it did not draw my attention enough to learn about it until college. My work in the A∴A∴ led to working with some of the sex magic, sexual alchemy, and sexual mysticism techniques of Thelema. I had some very powerful experiences working with some of those methods. While some elements of it were amazing, I wasn't drawn to it for sexual gratification. I had further experiences in witchcraft contexts and experiences bordering on that context regarding faeries. Still, for me, it has always been a matter of the magical or spiritual work being done rather than a lifestyle or pleasure choice.

Other people are very drawn to these relationships. Some people engage most of their major spirit interactions through a sexual dynamic. For some, it can be very fulfilling spiritually, magically, and sexually.

The first thing to consider is the nature of these relationships. People who have sexual relationships with spirits often have a somewhat polyamorous structure to them. They are still able to have human lovers. They may be able to have other spirit lovers. Some folklore suggests that these spirits can get jealous. Most stories depict the dangers of such relationships. The focus on danger is because these stories are primarily for people who don't have the tools and power to navigate the spirit world.

In many cases, spirits understand these other relationships will exist, or they can accept them when they are presented to them. Like any other relationship, communication is a major element. Spirits should know that they need to respect your human relationships, and hopefully, they will be encouraged to help and support those instead of creating mischief.

For some people, sexual congress with a spirit might be pretty common. For others, it might occur at more particular times. Some spirits can impart power or knowledge through sexual interaction. Other spirits might work magic by utilizing what they receive when sex is given as an offering. Elements of magical work with the spirit might be based on sexual magic in ways similar to work with embodied partners. Whether you're engaging in that type of consorting regularly or rarely, there are several ways it can tie into your magic and magical development. Consider how you want to engage those options and explore with your familiar which ones are right for your relationship.

The practical components are the next element to consider. It's reasonable to have conjured a familiar, set up a spirit house, done some work with it, and still not be able to wrap your head around how sex would happen. I will present a few options, but exploring with communities of people engaged in this work will provide you with more. The most common approach is in dreams. A common assumption regarding historical magic is that sorcerers conjuring faeries, and witches bedding demons, met their spirit lovers in dreams. Working with dream talismans, lucid dreaming, and spirit work before bed can facilitate this option.

Adjacent to dreams, spirit interactions can happen during astral travel and spirit-driven journey work. Several of the late 19th and early 20th-century sex magicians and mystics referenced sexual encounters on the astral plane with spirits. Medieval myths include people journeying into faery mounds, sometimes in spirit, for sexual encounters. While dreams are a natural occurrence that pulls our minds away from our bodies and the awareness of the physical world, astral and spirit spaces also allow us to interact outside the body. Tales of spirits carrying witches on spirit flights indicate that your familiar can help you achieve the journeys necessary to incorporate otherworld sexual encounters into your life.

Working with the spirit while masturbating is a common option. You might have a physical token that the spirit attaches to, which can be used as part of your masturbatory spirit work. A tool isn't necessary. As long as you can perceive the spirit, it will be able to provide sensations and visions that contribute to the experience. In these interactions, sometimes the spirit takes a share of the pleasure you experience. Other times, it may amplify it.

Partnered sex can also be an opportunity for engaging with a spirit lover. This can involve engaging with your embodied partner physically while there is a mental and spiritual engagement with your spirit partner. Alternatively, if you and your embodied partner have the skill and comfort for it, intentional possession would suit this type of interaction well. When engaging in this kind of work, it is absolutely necessary to have clear communication between everyone involved.

Lines can blur, and so comfort levels can shift. It is important to discuss what possibilities are ok and what are not ok before the spirit interaction begins.

I have known magicians whose sexual arrangements with spirits have resulted in new physical partners. I don't believe it has ever seemed that the spirit possessed the new partner. Nor has it seemed that the individual was a physical manifestation of the spirit. Rather, the new partner seemed to appear in lieu of the spirit or as a proxy to collect the sexual offering. These cases seem more likely in one off or infrequent interactions.

Thinking about practical elements leads us to consider what the ritual components look like. With a familiar spirit, you don't necessarily need a lot of ritual work to interact with them for magic. Connecting to communicate information may be easier in a ritual context depending upon an individual's ability to perceive spirits. Similarly, the type of sensory stimulation or deep mental connection that occurs with spirit sex may be easier when facilitated by ritual practices.

The ritual practices you select can vary. If you have an embodied partner, the classic movie or TV trope of nude magicians in a magic circle conjuring a spirit and having ritual sex is an option. The faery dinners that inspired one of our methods for acquiring a familiar could also form the basis for a ritual to intimately interact with your familiar. A special conjuration or incantation to chant while going to bed or in a relaxing bath would be a simple ritual approach. The important part of these approaches is that they put you into a space where perception and connection are easier. Additionally, they need to increase the spirit's capability of entering into and affecting spaces you can perceive. Any of the many ritual methods for interacting with a spirit harmoniously could be an option for facilitating this type of spirit contact, so long as the approach helps create that nexus point.

Sex is not the only type of physical intimacy people consider with familiars. Feeding a familiar blood is a common part of the historical understanding of relationships with familiar spirits. We don't have any indication that this was common amongst cunning folk or aristocratic magicians conjuring demons. The belief that familiars drank the blood of their human companions was a common element of witch hysteria. This does not mean it was necessarily a false element. It occurs in some of the regions and periods which have credible accounts. There is a logic to it when one considers the ongoing connection the familiar must maintain with the physical world. Folklore also depicts many spirits who desire human blood or the life force contained in blood and sexual fluids.

While certain types of spirits seek out blood and sexual fluids, this is not an appropriate offering for many types of spirits. In many cultures, spirits are offended by human blood or sexual fluids. There is a belief amongst many people who explore the grimoires from a perspective influenced by demonolatry that putting blood on a demon's seal is the preferred offering for demons. This belief often carries the idea that any other ritual or offering methods are unnecessary. Simply put your blood on a seal and tell a demon what you want. There is no basis for this in the descriptions of these spirits or surviving historical ritual practices.

Some spirits may want offerings of blood or sexual fluids, but some do not. Look at the cultural context from which your spirit comes and then consider the beliefs of that culture. Ask the spirit and do divination. Make sure you clearly know rather than assume.

It is not a safe assumption that every spirit that is bound to serve you is amiable. A spirit might have a good working relationship with you, but some spirits have natures that you don't want intimately and closely linked to your being. Blood and sexual fluids are two incredibly powerful links to the core of a person. Routinely providing those to feed a spirit can build a closer bond. That bond can be a great thing. But it can also mean the spirit is connected to you in ways that can deeply influence you. Consider the nature of the spirit. Its historical descriptions and reputation, along with your experiences, are ways to determine if this is a spirit you want to be linked to by blood.

When you find you are working with a spirit that you're comfortable having that connection with, and it wants blood, you can fulfill that expectation with minimal bloodletting. Spirits don't need you to cut open your arm and cover their seal or their spirit house in your blood. When working with your own blood, a few drops is usually sufficient.

For spirits who want blood, offering it can be a mode of working magic. Some spirits need a preliminary offering before they can begin to work. A few drops of blood might be enough to get the work started. In addition, blood can carry magical intention, so an offering of blood can be an act of communicating a magical goal to a spirit. While feeding your blood to the familiar may not seem like the kind of intimate connection during which lessons, knowledge, and power can be shared, the offering of blood builds bonds, and those bonds can create smoother and more routine communication.

Some magicians believe you should never give any spirits any blood, but this is a staple part of spirit work in many cultures. Others believe you should never give any spirit your own blood, but there are historical practices and folklore which indicate using your own blood. There isn't a single one size fits all answer. Consider the culture, consider the spirit, and consider your own comfort and practice.

Like the sexual elements, providing a spirit with your blood is not necessary. For those choosing to do this work, the small amount of blood drawn with a diabetic test kit needle is usually sufficient. This can be a useful tool for obtaining blood routinely, easily, and with sterile equipment. For those choosing not to give a spirit blood, make sure to negotiate with the spirit what you intend to give it, and make it clear when certain things are not options. Blood and sex are ways of working with familiars, but they are not the only ways.

Just as some humans will not want to work with blood offerings or sex magic, some spirits will find such interactions repugnant. Before assuming what your spirit will want, ask them. Confirm the answers with divination. Like many other elements we have discussed, this part of the relationship is personal. It will reflect the needs of you and your familiar, along with your own comfort levels and desires. It's ok for these relationships to be idiosyncratic because you and your familiar form an interaction that is unique to you. Explore, work with your spirit, and determine the best way to work together.

Conclusion

While your familiar spirit probably isn't your pet cat, Mr.Fluffer-Nutter, it is a spirit who can teach you more magic, accomplish magical tasks for you, and assist you in various forms of magic. Witches and sorcerers of history and legend are well known for trafficking in familiar spirits. There is space for work with familiar spirits in almost all European approaches to magic. Modern witches, whether they are hereditary witches, Wiccan witches, or traditional witchcraft witches, can all find ways which fit their practices to obtain familiars. Pagans and NeoPagans working with folklore, faery stories, and legends can find inspiration for understanding and connecting with familiar spirits through the exploration of surviving and recorded folkways. Like grimoire revivalists, ceremonial magicians utilizing modern systems, can call upon spirits and request familiars. Despite being somewhat overlooked in the last hundred years of contemporary magic, this spirit relationship can be as ubiquitous as we'd like it to be.

This exploration of familiars was broad, and so it was broken down into different parts. This has allowed us to explore familiars generally, in folklore and mythology, and in modern magic and grimoire magic. With the collection of details, ideas, stories and methods presented, you are equipped to dive deeply into your own work with a familiar spirit.

Journeying together through over a thousand years of material has allowed us to explore what familiars are. We've looked at how to care for them and how to work with them. We've considered how they fit in with the rest of our spirit work and magic. We've explored rituals historical and modern, and looked at the roots of working with familiars in folklore and ancient magic. We've addressed the role of the familiar in modern magic and how they can help us build the future of magic.

With rituals, descriptions, and stories depicting spirit relationships across cultures, traditions and time, you have choices. You have options. You have a rich world full of spirits to jump into. Familiar spirits should be as much a part of our grasp of magic in the contemporary world as any other element of magic we choose. So good luck, and enjoy the adventures your future familiars will help bring.

"'And what of your fairy-servants, sir?" said Mr Lascelles. "Are they visible only to yourself, or may other people perceive them?"

- <u>Jonathan Strange and Mr. Norrell</u>, by Susanna Clarke

A magician prophecies using the voices of the mountains, the stars, and the fish.

The Art of Prophecy by Olaus Magnus 1555
from
A History of the Northern People

Works Consulted

Alexiou, Margaret. The Ritual Lament in Greek Tradition. London: Cambridge University Press, 1974

Anderson, Victor. Etheric Anatomy: The Three Selves and Astral Travel. Portland: Acorn Guild Press, 2004

Auryn, Mat. "Defining the Familiar Spirit." For Puck's Sake Blog. WEB. Dec 28th 2017

Auryn, Mat. Psychic Witch: A Metaphysical Guide to Meditation, Magick & Manifestation. Woodbury: Llewellyn Publications, 2020

Betz, Hans Dieter, et al. The Greek Magical Papyri In Translation Including The Demotic Spells, 2nd ed. Chicago: University of Chicago Press, 1996

Briggs, Katherine. An Encyclopedia of Fairies: Hobgoblins, Brownies, Bogies, & Other Supernatural Creatures. New York: Pantheon Books, 1978

Briggs, Katherine. Folktales of England. Chicago: University of Chicago Press, 1968

Bryan, Eric Shane. Icelandic Folklore and the Cultural Memory of Religious Change. York: Arc Humanities Press, 2021

Buckley, Julia. "Can Vodou Succeed Where Western Medicine Fails? My Journey to Haiti in Search of a Cure for Chronic Pain" The Independent. WEB. January 28th 2018

Campbell, John Francis. Popular Tales of the West Highlands. WEB. 1862.

Clarke, Susanna. Jonathan Strange and Mr. Norrell. London: Bloomsbury Publishing, 2005

Clymer, Reuben Swinburne. The Irreconcilable Gnomes. WEB

Crowley, Aleister. Liber Astarte. WEB

Crowley, Aleister. Liber Chanokh. WEB

Crowley, Aleister. Ecclesia Gnostica Catholica Canon Missae. WEB

Crowley, Aleister. Liber Librae. WEB

Crowley, Aleister. Liber Tzaddi. WEB

Crowley, Aleister. STAUROS BATRACHOU. WEB

Daimler, Morgan. "Co-Walkers, Fetches, and Fylgja" Living Liminally. WEB May 21, 2021

Dooley, Ann, and Harry Roe. The Tales of the Elders of Ireland. Oxford: Oxford University Press, 2008

Duquette, Lon Milo. Enochian Vision Magick. San Francisco: Red Wheel/Weiser, 2008

Gregory, Augusta. "Dream of Angus." WEB

Grundy, Stephen (Kveldulf Gundarsson). Teutonic Magic: The Magical & Spiritual Practices of the Germanic Peoples. Woodbury: Llewellyn Publications, 1990

Hall, Alaric. The Meanings of Elf and Elves in Medieval England. Academia.edu. WEB. 2004

Harms, Daniel and James Clark. Of Angels Demons and Spirits: A Sourcebook of British Magic. Woodbury: Llewellyn Publications, 2019

Harms, Daniel, James Clark, and Joseph Peterson. The Book of Oberon: A Sourcebook of Elizabethan Magic. Woodbury: Llewellyn Publications, 2015

Hartland, Edwin Sidney. English Fairy and Other Folk Tales. WEB.

Hunt, Robert. Popular Romances of The West of England. WEB.

Jackson, Nigel. Call of the Horned Piper. Somerset: Capall Bann Publishing, 1990

James, Geoffrey. Angel Magic: The Ancient Art of Summoning and Communicating with Angelic Beings. Woodbury: Llewellyn Publications, 1998

James, Geoffrey. Enochian Evocation of Dr. Dee. Gillette: Heptangle Books, 1983

Kennedy, Patrick. Legendary Fictions of the Irish Celts. WEB

Kirk, Robert. The Secret Commonwealth. WEB

Kruse, John. British Faeries Blog. WEB

Laurilei, and Natalie. "The Fetch and Flight," American Folkloric Witchcraft Blog. WEB August 21st, 2011,

Leyden, John. "The Mermaid." WEB

Levi, Eliphas. Ritual and Dogma of High Magic. Sacred Text Archive. WEB

MacGregor Mathers, Samuel Liddel. The Sacred Magic of Abramelin the Mage. Sacred Text Archive. WEB.

MacGregor Mathers, Samuel Liddel. The Key of Solomon the King. WEB

Marathakis, Ioannis. The Magical Treatise of Solomon or Hygromanteia: The Ancestor of the Key of Solomon. London: Golden Hoard Press, 2017

McHardy, Stuart. Isobel Gowdie Trial Transcript. WEB

McNally, Frank. "In Search of the Banshee and the Elusive Leannan Sidhe," The Irish Times. WEB October 30, 2019

McNamara-Wilson, Kim. "Irish Faerie Folk of Yore and Yesterday – The Gancanagh." WEB

Miller, Jason. "The Tulpa Discussion." Strategic Sorcery Blog. WEB

Moore, A.W.. The Folk-lore of the Isle of Man. WEB

Morrison, Sophia. Manx Fairy Tales. WEB

Nagel, Alexandra. Marriage with Elementals: From "Le Comte de Gabalis" to a Golden Dawn Ritual. Academia.edu. WEB 2007

Nicholson, Brinsley (trans.), Reginald Scot. The Discovery of Witchcraft. Charleston: BiblioBazaar, 2009

Oldridge, Darren. Fairies and The Devil in Modern England. Taylor and Francis Online. WEB March 29, 2016

Paracelsus, A Book on Nymphs, Sylphs, Pygmies, and Salamanders, and on the Other Spirits. WEB

Paracelsus. On the Invisible Causes of Disease. WEB

Penczak, Christopher. The Temple of Shamanic Witchcraft: Shadows, Spirits and the Healing Journey. Woodbury: Llewellyn Publications, 2005

Peterson, Joseph H.. The Sworn Book of Honorius: Liber Iuratus Honorii. Newburyport: Ibis Press, 2016

Rankine, David. The Grimoire of Arthur Gauntlet: A 17th Century London Cunningman's Book of Charms, Conjurations and Prayers. London: Avalonia, 2011

Rose, Winifred Hodge. "The Shape of Being Human: The Hama Soul." Heathen Soul Lore. WEB May 2021

Rose, Winifred Hodge. "The Occult Activities of the Hugr Part 1." Heathen Soul Lore. WEB November 2020

Skinner, Stephen and David Rankine. The Veritable Key of Solomon. London: Golden Hoard, 2008

Skinner, Stephen. The Fourth Book of Occult Philosophy. Newburyport: Ibis Press, 2005

Sommer, Bettina Seijberg. "The Norse Concept of Luck." Scandinavian Studies Fall 2007. JSTOR. WEB.

Spanos NP. "Multiple Identity Enactments and Multiple Personality Disorder: a Sociocognitive Perspective." Psychol Bull. 1994 Jul;116(1):143-65. doi: 10.1037/0033-2909.116.1.143. PMID: 8078970.

Stephens, Walter. Demon Lovers: Witchcraft Sex and the Crisis of Belief. Chicago: University of Chicago Press, 2003

Stratton-Kent, Jake. Goetic Liturgy. Yorkshire: Hadean Press, 2015

Swain, BJ (trans.) "Le Livre Des Esperitz" (unpublished)

Tyson, Donald. Enochian Magic for Beginners: The Original System of Angel Magic. Woodbury: Llewellyn Publications, 2002

Various. Oxford Reference. WEB

Various. The Holy Bible. WEB

Various. "The School Collection." The National Folklore Collection of Ireland. WEB

deVillars, Abbe Montfaucon. Le Comte de Gabalis. WEB

Wilby, Emma. Cunning-Folk and Familiar Spirits: Shamanistic Visionary Traditions in Early Modern British Witchcraft and Magic. Sussex Academic Press, 2006

Wilde, Jane. Ancient Legends Mystic Charms and Superstitions of Ireland. WEB

W.P., Bishop Hall, Bishop Morton, Matthew Hale, et al. The History of Witches and Wizards: Giving a True Account of All Their Tryals in England, Scotland, Swedeland, France, and New England; with Their Confession and Condemnation. The Wellcome Collection. WEB. 1720.

Young, Francis. "Liturgical Change and Ceremonial Magic In Reformation England." WEB

Young, Francis (trans). The Cambridge Book of Magic. Self-Published, 2015

About the Author

BJ Swain is the author of Living Spirits: A Guide to Magic in a World of Spirits, Luminarium: A Grimoire of Cunning Conjuration, and a contributing editor for Heaven and Hell 2018: The Grimoire Issue. He runs the website, The Unveiled Sky, and the blog Glory of the Stars, and hosted the podcast, In the Company of Stars. He has been practicing magic for approximately 30 years. In addition to practical work with magic, BJ focused on Classics but also took several courses covering magic, the paranormal, mysticism, and mythology as part of his academic studies. He has worked through the A∴A∴ and a hereditary line of witchcraft and has served as Deputy Master of an OTO body, a Priest in the Gnostic Catholic Church, and the Bishop of Maryland for the Church of Light and Shadow. He is also former member of the Order of the Celestial Academy. He currently works with a small group of magicians who have completed the Abramelin working and who work to spread interest in more traditional magic.

"And after Blackeman was departed from her, within three or four days, Grissell and Greedigut came to her, in the shapes of dogs with great bristles of hogs hair upon their backs, and said to her they were from Blackeman to do what she would command them and did ask her if she did want anything and they would fetch her any thing."

- Davenport 1646, Trial of Jane Wallis

Index

Made in the USA
Monee, IL
23 February 2023